The Cambridge Companion to Haydn

This Companion provides an accessible and up-to-date introduction to the musical work and cultural world of Joseph Haydn. Readers will gain an understanding of the changing social, cultural, and political spheres in which Haydn studied, worked, and nurtured his creative talent. Distinguished contributors provide chapters on Haydn and his contemporaries, his audiences and aesthetics, his working environments in Eisenstadt and Eszterháza, and humor and exoticism in Haydn's oeuvre. Chapters on the reception of his music explore keyboard performance practices, Haydn's posthumous reputation, sound recordings and images of his symphonies. The book also surveys the major genres in which Haydn wrote, including symphonies, string quartets, keyboard sonatas and trios, sacred music, miscellaneous vocal genres, and operas composed for Eszterháza and London.

The Cambridge Companion to

HAYDN

EDITED BY

Caryl Clark

CAMBRIDGE UNIVERSITY PRESS
Cambridge, New York, Melbourne, Madrid, Cape Town, Singapore,
São Paulo, Delhi, Dubai, Tokyo, Mexico City

Cambridge University Press
The Edinburgh Building, Cambridge CB2 8RU, UK

Published in the United States of America by Cambridge University Press, New York

www.cambridge.org
Information on this title: www.cambridge.org/9780521541077

First published 2005
Reprinted 2008

A catalogue record for this publication is available from the British Library

Library of Congress Cataloguing in Publication Data
The Cambridge Companion to Haydn / edited by Caryl Clark. – 1st ed.
p. cm.
Includes bibliographical references.
ISBN 0-521-83347-7 (hardcover) – ISBN 0-521-54107-7 (pbk.)
I. Haydn, Joseph, 1732–1809 – Criticism and interpretation. I. Clark, Caryl Leslie, 1953–
II. Title.

ISBN 978-0-521-83347-9 Hardback
ISBN 978-0-521-54107-7 Paperback

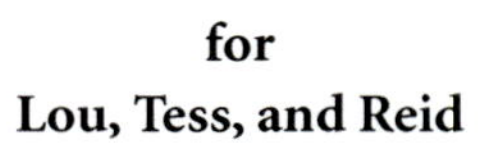

for
Lou, Tess, and Reid

Contents

Notes on contributors

Scott Burnham is Professor of Music and Chair of the Music Department at Princeton University. He is the author of *Beethoven Hero* (1995), translator of A. B. Marx, *Musical Form in the Age of Beethoven* (1997), and co-editor, with Michael P. Steinberg, of *Beethoven and His World* (2000).

Performer-scholar **Tom Beghin** is Associate Professor at the Faculty of Music, McGill University, Montreal. His discography, on the Eufoda, Claves, Klara, and Bridge labels, features music by Beethoven, Haydn, Moscheles, C. P. E. Bach, Zelter, and Mendelssohn, all performed on historical keyboards, and he is currently recording the complete Haydn works for solo keyboard. Essays on Moscheles and Haydn appear in *Haydn and His World* (Princeton, 1997) and *19th Century Music*.

Caryl Clark is Associate Professor at the Faculty of Music, University of Toronto, and is cross-appointed to the Department of Humanities, University of Toronto at Scarborough. Her publications on Haydn's operas appear in *The New Grove Dictionary of Opera*, *Studies in Music*, *Current Musicology*, *The Haydn Yearbook*, and *Early Music*. She is co-editor of three special opera issues of *The University of Toronto Quarterly*: *Voices of Opera* (1998); *Opera and Interdisciplinarity* (2003); and *Opera and Interdisciplinarity II* (2005).

James Dack is a Senior Lecturer in Music at Royal Holloway, University of London. He has been involved in the editing of Haydn's early masses in the *Joseph Haydn Werke*, issued by the Joseph Haydn-Institut, Cologne.

Michelle Fillion is Associate Professor in the School of Music, University of Victoria, in British Columbia. Her forthcoming book, *E. M. Forster from Beethoven to Britten: Musical Resonance in a Literary Life*, will be published by the University of Illinois Press.

James Garratt is Lecturer in Music and University Organist at the University of Manchester. His main research interests are in nineteenth-century German music, thought, and culture. His publications include *Palestrina and the German Romantic Imagination: Interpreting Historicism in Nineteenth-Century Music* (2002).

Rebecca Green is an independent scholar whose research interests include the operas of Joseph Haydn. She teaches at the University of Maine at Farmington.

Matthew Head is a Senior Lecturer in Music at the University of Southampton. His research explores music and culture in the German Enlightenment. His monograph, *Orientalism, Masquerade and Mozart's Turkish Music*, was published by the Royal Musical Society in 2000.

Mary Hunter is Professor of Music at Bowdoin College in Brunswick Maine. She is the author of *The Culture of Opera Buffa in Mozart's Vienna: the Poetics of Entertainment* (1999) and the co-editor of *Opera Buffa in Mozart's Vienna* (1997). She is currently working on ideas about performance at the turn of the nineteenth century.

David Wyn Jones is Reader in Music at Cardiff University. His published work has focused on Haydn, Beethoven, and aspects of music dissemination in the eighteenth century. He is the editor of the *Oxford Composer Companions: Haydn* (2002).

Katalin Komlós, musicologist and fortepiano recitalist, is Professor of Music Theory at the Liszt Academy of Music, Budapest. Since receiving her Ph.D. in musicology from Cornell University, she has written extensively on the history of eighteenth-century keyboard instruments and styles, including *Fortepianos and Their Music* (1995).

Lawrence Kramer is Professor of English and Music at Fordham University and co-editor of *19th Century Music*. His many books include *Classical Music and Postmodern Knowledge* (1995), *Franz Schubert: Sexuality, Subjectivity, Song* (1998), *Musical Meaning: Toward a Critical History* (2002), and *Opera and Modern Culture: Wagner and Strauss* (2004).

Melanie Lowe is Assistant Professor of Musicology at Vanderbilt University and holds a secondary appointment in Vanderbilt's program in American and Southern Studies. She has published articles on the music of Joseph Haydn, classical music in American media, and early adolescent girls and teen pop. She is currently completing a book on pleasure and meaning in the late eighteenth-century symphony.

David Schroeder is Professor of Music and Associate Dean of Arts and Social Sciences at Dalhousie University in Halifax. His books include *Haydn and the Enlightenment* (1990), *Mozart in Revolt: Strategies of Resistance, Mischief and Deception* (1999), and *Cinema's Illusions, Opera's Allure: The Operatic Impulse in Film* (2002). He has also written articles on Schubert, Enlightenment issues, and Alban Berg, and is a former advisory editor to *Eighteenth-Century Studies.*

Elaine Sisman is the Anne Parsons Bender Professor of Music and chair of the Music Department at Columbia University. The author of *Haydn and the Classical Variation* (1993), *Mozart: The "Jupiter" Symphony* (1993), and editor of *Haydn and His World* (1997), she has written numerous shorter studies of eighteenth- and nineteenth-century music, as well as the article on "Variations" in the revised *New Grove Dictionary of Music and Musicians.* She serves on the board of directors of the Joseph Haydn-Institut in Cologne, the Akademie für Mozartforschung in Salzburg, and the American Brahms Society, and is President of the American Musicological Society.

James Webster is the Goldwin Smith Professor of Music at Cornell University. He is the author of *Haydn's "Farewell" Symphony and the Idea of Classical Style: Through-Composition and Cyclic Integration in his Instrumental Music* (1991), and co-editor of *Haydn Studies* (1981) and *Opera Buffa in Mozart's Vienna* (1997). He has published widely on Haydn (including the Haydn article in the revised edition of the *New Grove Dictionary of Music and Musicians*), Mozart, Beethoven, Schubert, and Brahms, and on analysis, editorial and performance practice, and the historiography of music. His book in progress is *The Music of Mozart's Operas: Analysis in Context.*

Preface and acknowledgments

Joseph Haydn: accomplished composer, businessman, gentleman. That's the man we see on the front cover of this volume. No steely-eyed, brooding stare as with many a Beethoven image; no rambunctious, youthful or, alternatively, despondent Mozart; no dreamy-eyed Gluck gazing rapturously to heaven in the act of inspired composition. And definitely not "Papa Haydn"! For his gentrified English audience in 1792 Thomas Hardy painted a portrait of Haydn in the grand style. Seated in a plush upholstered chair surrounded by elegant drapery, a "classicized" and "anglicized" Haydn is depicted here, his humble agrarian roots long forgotten in the wake of his successes in a new and vibrant economy. Upwardly mobile London understood the trappings of success represented by the portrait and its symbols of the self-made man – the right (working) hand clasping a hardbound published score, the middle finger inserted between the pages of the volume as if to mark the site of success or to signal the imminence of music-making or its contemplative study. Hairline concealed by a prim wig, accentuating a wide brow, the revered and learned composer, having recently received an honorary doctorate from Oxford University, gazes out at his public – an audience versed in the rhetoric of self-determination and eagerly participating in aesthetic debates. There is no harsh judgment on the part of either subject or viewer here, and certainly no hint of the dismissal that history would soon deliver.

The triumphant moment recorded by Hardy's portrait did not repeat itself in Haydn's continental home. In the far-flung regions of eastern Austria, including Rohrau and Eisenstadt, and into western Hungary where Eszterháza was situated, the image of the successful composer and businessman was eclipsed by that of Papa Haydn, a moniker applied to the musical steward at the Esterházy court and ably transferred onto the aging master lauded throughout Europe who spent his last days in a small cottage in the Viennese suburb of Gumpendorf during the Napoleonic campaign. Use of the epithet peaked after the composer, and the *ancien régime* in whose shadow he had labored, passed away. Caricatured as a man of innocence from a long-ago time, Haydn was repackaged for nineteenth-century consumption. The composer's very gradual path towards compositional maturity and late fame grafted readily onto that patronizing image, which perpetuated a simplistic and deterministic approach to later studies of the man and his music.

Overcoming the sentimentalism, dilettantism, and propagandizing power of the Papa Haydn myth has been a welcome corrective. Modern studies of the composer and his oeuvre would be unthinkable without the explosion of the myth. Retracing the multiple referents associated with Papa Haydn, as James Garrett demonstrates in this volume, opens up further complexities. It recognizes the power of language, charts the cultural factors of reception by accounting for variety and diversity in that reception, and illuminates the forces that shaped and were shaped by the Papa Haydn myth itself. Changes in scholarly concern reveal different ways in which Haydn and his music have been studied in different eras and locations, creating a diversity of cross-cultural representations.

The picture of Haydn presented here is a richly complex one, the result of new or revamped theoretical and analytical approaches. Part I probes Haydn the man, his aesthetics, and his public through re-readings of canonic texts that deconstruct received opinion. Further contextualization stems from an understanding of the composer's musical milieu and his interactions with contemporaries, foregrounding the importance of a deeper appreciation of the different locations, languages, and cultures in which Haydn worked. Part II examines two modes of interpreting Haydn's music – one canonical, the other not. Humor (wit, jesting, *Laune*, whimsy, and so on), a trope in Haydn studies, is here applied to close readings of the late symphonies from the perspective of a music theorist. In the following chapter on exoticism, a musicologist explores how selected compositions confront societal anxieties concerning "difference" during the Enlightenment. An overview of a wide range of genres, large and small, instrumental and vocal, forms the core of Part III. Canonical works are explored alongside lesser-known ones, conveying the expansive range of Haydn's musical output during the second half of the eighteenth century and addressing some of their performative contexts. Part IV offers new interpretive angles, ranging from "negotiating" performance through differentiated (and gendered) readings of selected keyboard sonatas, to the changing contexts of symphonic performance and reception based on cultural orientation and technological mediation.

This book reflects an intense collaborative effort from start to finish. In the early stages, Elaine Sisman and James Webster offered valuable guidance. As the project progressed, several authors exchanged written work with one another and benefited from comments and advice offered in the spirit of scholarly exchange. Here the efforts of two contributors – Tom Beghin and Rebecca Green – were truly exemplary. Janette Tilley, a recent graduate of the University of Toronto now teaching at CUNY, prepared all the digitized musical examples with skill and care. In the fall of 2003, the graduate students in my Haydn seminar at the Faculty of Music, University of Toronto, were the first to read and comment on the earliest submissions; they enthusiastically embraced the task and offered astute critical observations. Thanks to Kate Galloway, Dana Hibbard, Eleanor Johnson, Herbert Pauls, Anna Rutledge, Charlène St.-Aubin, and Melissa Thornton for their dedication to this project. (Our rousing performance of Haydn's late part-songs, lubricated by lots of pre-Christmas cheer, will forever be etched in my memory.) Special thanks to Kate Galloway, who continued on as my research assistant, for assembling the bibliography and drafting the initial chronology, to Rosanne King for her indexing skills, and to proofreader Colin Eatock.

To Penny Souster, who first approached me about taking on this project, I offer my heartfelt gratitude. In guiding the book through the planning, review, and contract stage, she ensured a smooth transition to her colleague Victoria Cooper, whose unflagging support, along with that of her assistant Rebecca Jones, production editor Annie Lovett, and copyeditor Michael Downes, have proved invaluable. My ever supportive family – Lou, Tess, and Reid – know how much they are loved.

Toronto, November 2004

Chronology of Haydn's life and career

1732	born March 31 (?) in Rohrau, Lower Austria; baptized Franz Joseph on April 1. Known as Sepperl in childhood, he was the second of five children to survive infancy; his father, Mathias Haydn, was a wheelwright, magistrate, and amateur musician, and his mother, Anna Maria Koller, was a cook at the Harrach family castle in Rohrau.
1737	receives his first formal training while living with a distant cousin, Mathias Franck, in nearby Hainburg.
1739	recruited by Georg Reutter (1708–72), Kapellmeister (musical director) at St. Stephen's Cathedral in Vienna, to join the choir school there; sings treble parts in regular and special services at church and at the Habsburg court, and receives some instruction in theory, composition, and on the violin and harpsichord.
1745	joined at St. Stephen's Cathedral choir school by his younger brother, Johann Michael (1737–1806).
1749	leaves the choir school at St. Stephen's Cathedral after his voice changes.
1750	moves into garret room in the Michaelerhaus (where Metastasio, Porpora, and Marianna von Martínez also lived), and works as an independent musician.
1750s	compositions in the 1750s reflect an acquaintance with the music of his contemporaries in a wide range of genres; during the mid-1750s, Haydn worked at several churches as an occasional singer and violinist, and augmented his income performing in pick-up ensembles for special events at court and in the theater; later in the decade he becomes a close friend of fellow violinist and composer Carl Ditters (1739–99).
1751	writes music for his first stage work, *Der neue krumme Teufel*; comes in close contact with court poet Pietro Metastasio (1714–87).
1753	works as valet and keyboard accompanist for the Neapolitan opera composer and singing teacher Nicola Porpora, from whom he learns much about vocal composition and the Italian language.
1758	begins working as Kapellmeister to Count Morzin, who lived in Vienna during the winter, and in Lukavec, Bohemia in the summer; Haydn's earliest symphonies were written for the Morzin court.
1760	marries Maria Anna Aloysia Apollonia Keller, elder sister of Therese Keller, Haydn's first love.
1761	appointed to the position of Vice-Kapellmeister at the court of Prince Paul Anton Esterházy in Eisenstadt; assists Kapellmeister Gregor Joseph Werner (1693–1766) with church music, and is responsible for all secular music; works closely with violinist Luigi Tomasini, leader of the court

	orchestra, and composes symphonic trilogy on the times of the day – "Le matin," "Le midi," and "Le soir" (nos. 6–8).
1762	death of Prince Paul Anton Esterházy, who is succeeded by Prince Nicolaus "The Magnificent"; composes Concerto for Horn in D major. Gluck's *Orfeo ed Euridice* premieres in Vienna.
1762–66	court moves between Eisenstadt and Vienna; renovations undertaken on an old hunting lodge located on the south shore of the Neusiedlersee – the future palace, Eszterháza.
1765	begins a thematic catalogue of his compositions, *Entwurf-Katalog* ("Draft catalogue"), which he supplemented regularly with additional entries until the late 1770s. Studies C. P. E. Bach's *Versuch* (perhaps as early as 1763), affecting the improvisatory nature of his keyboard works (especially those with varied reprises).
1766	following the death of Werner, Haydn is promoted to Kapellmeister and assumes full responsibilities for the musical life of the court; Eszterháza becomes the summer home of Prince Nicolaus and the court; Haydn purchases a house in Eisenstadt as a home base.
1767	composes *Stabat mater.*
1768	the main opera house at Eszterháza is inaugurated with Haydn's *Lo speziale.* In the late 1760s Haydn learns to play the baryton, the favorite instrument of Prince Nicolaus.
1771	unauthorized publication of Op. 20 string quartets; composes keyboard sonata in c minor, Hob. xvi: 20.
1772	composes the "Farewell" Symphony (no. 45).
1773	the marionette opera house at Eszterháza opens with Haydn's *Philemon und Baucis,* a performance attended by Empress Maria Theresa and members of the Habsburg court.
1774	the first authorized publication of music by Haydn, keyboard sonatas Hob. XVI: 21–26 (dedicated to Prince Nicolaus) by Kurzböck in Vienna.
1775	oratorio *Il ritorno di Tobia* performed at the annual Lenten concert of the Tonkünstler-Societät in Vienna.
1776	beginning of a regular season of opera at Eszterháza, initiated by Gluck's *Orfeo ed Euridice.* Haydn writes a short autobiographical sketch, which is published in an Austrian encyclopedia.
1778	sells his house in Eisenstadt; Artaria & Co. in Vienna expands into music publishing.
1779	on January 1 Haydn signs a new contract with Prince Nicolaus Esterházy allowing him to publish and sell his music and accept outside commissions without the consent of his patron. Fire destroys the Eszterháza opera house and many operatic scores are lost. Soprano Luigia Polzelli (1750–1831) is employed at court.
1780	upsurge in Haydn's commercial activity; Artaria publishes set of six keyboard sonatas by Haydn, Hob. XVI: 20, 35–39, dedicated to the virtuoso Auenbrugger sisters.

1781	Haydn's *La fedeltà premiata* opens the new opera house at Eszterháza; composes Op. 33 string quartets; first set of Lieder published by Artaria in Vienna. Haydn markets his music in England with Forster.
1782	composes the *Missa Cellensis* or Mariazell Mass, and publishes the six string quartets of Op. 33 with Artaria; begins professional relationship with publisher John Bland in London. Joseph Elssler, Haydn's first copyist, dies; he is succeeded by his son of the same name and subsequently by Johann Elssler, who became Haydn's principal copyist by the late 1780s.
1783	composes second cello concerto, in D major. Marriage of Princess Marie Hermenegild to future Prince Nicolaus II.
1784	*Armida*, Haydn's last opera for the court, is staged at Eszterháza to mark the completion of the estate; publishes second set of Lieder with Artaria. First known meeting between Haydn and Mozart takes place at a quartet party in Vienna; Haydn played first violin and Mozart played the viola. Carl Friedrich Cramer publishes first issue of his *Magazin der Musik*, in which he praises the works of Haydn.
1785	becomes a freemason in January and joins the lodge "Zur wahren Eintracht" (True Concord), which Mozart had joined the preceding year; plays string quartets in Vienna with Mozart and friends on February 12; in September Artaria publishes the six string quartets Mozart dedicated to Haydn.
1786	completes the "Paris" Symphonies (nos. 82–87) commissioned for the orchestra of the Concert de la Loge Olympique.
1787	declines invitation to compose an opera for Prague. Death of Christoph Willibald Gluck (b. 1714).
1788	purchases Schanz keyboard.
1789	begins regular contact with Maria Anna von Genzinger, a Viennese aristocrat and amateur pianist married to Prince Nicolaus's physician; composes solo cantata *Arianna a Naxos*. The King's Theatre in London burns down and royal privilege to present Italian opera is transferred to the Pantheon Theatre. The French Revolution begins July 14 with the storming of the Bastille.
1790	Prince Nicolaus Esterházy dies in September; his successor, Prince Anton, disbands the orchestra and opera troupe, leaving Haydn free to seek employment elsewhere; in December he accepts an offer from the German violinist and impresario Johann Peter Salomon (1745–1815) to go to London; enroute he meets the young Ludwig van Beethoven (1770–1827) at the electoral court in Bonn.
1791	arrives in London in early January; first set of "London" Symphonies (nos. 93–98) performed at Hanover Square Rooms with Salomon on violin and Haydn playing fortepiano; composes *L'anima del filosofo, ossia Orfeo ed Euridice*, but the production is halted during rehearsals; Symphony no. 92, the "Oxford," is performed when Haydn receives an honorary Doctor of Music degree from Oxford University in July. Publisher John Bland commissions Thomas Hardy to paint Haydn's

	portrait. Wolfgang Amadeus Mozart (b. 1756) dies in Vienna in December.
1792	leaves London in July; meets with Beethoven again on return trip.
1793	purchases house in the Viennese suburb of Gumpendorf; moves in permanently in 1796. Beethoven moves to Vienna and studies composition with Haydn.
1794	Prince Anton Esterházy dies in January and is succeeded by Prince Nicolaus II; Haydn already enroute to London for a second visit, arriving in February, accompanied by his copyist Johann Elssler. Publishing firm Corri & Dussek founded in London; they published two sets of canzonettas, the Opp. 71 and 74 string quartets, and arrangements of the "London" Symphonies for piano trio.
1795	composes Sonata in E♭ (Hob. XVI: 52) for Therese Janzen; departs London in August; reinstated as Esterházy Kapellmeister with minimal court duties; responsible for the eight wind instrumentalists of the *Harmonie* and small group of string players (primarily for performances at Eisenstadt).
1796	begins collaboration with Baron van Swieten, the imperial librarian and censor and leader of the Gesellschaft der Associirten, an association of noble patrons; Haydn composes Trumpet Concerto in E♭, and the first of his final six masses for Prince Nicolaus II; Leipzig firm Breitkopf & Härtel becomes Haydn's main publisher. British folksong arrangements commissioned by George Thomson.
1797	in January, Haydn granted free admission to all concerts of the Gesellschaft der Associirten, and on December 11 appointed "senior assessor" in perpetuity; the society sponsored the first performances of *The Creation* and *The Seasons.* Haydn made a life member of the Viennese Tonkünstler Societät. Composes the "Emperor's Hymn," which is the basis for a set of variations in the second movement of string quartet Op. 76 no. 3 and later the German national anthem.
1798	first private performance of the oratorio *The Creation* (*Die Schöpfung*) at the Schwarzenberg palace.
1799	first public performance of *The Creation* at the Burgtheater on March 19; oratorio performed again in December as a benefit for the Tonkünstler-Societät. Georg August Griesinger (1769–1845) has initial visit with Haydn as a representative for Breitkopf & Härtel; the publishing firm begins its *Oeuvres complettes de Joseph Haydn.*
1800	Haydn's wife dies in Baden in March.
1801	completes oratorio *The Seasons* (*Die Jahrszeiten*) in collaboration with Baron van Swieten; private premiere on April 24 at the Schwarzenberg palace followed by the first public performance at the Redoutensaal on May 19; two quartets of Op. 77 dedicated to Prince Lobkowitz.
1802	completes last major composition, the *Harmoniemesse*, after which he ceases composing (leaving a third string quartet for Lobkowitz incomplete).
1803	last string quartet (Op. 103, incomplete).

1805	Albert Christoph Dies (1755–1822) meets Haydn; Johann Elsser prepares comprehensive thematic catalogue of Haydn's works (known as *Haydn-Verzeichnis*). Luigi Cherubini writes "Chant sur la mort de Joseph Haydn" when rumors of his death circulated in France and Britain; it was first performed in 1810, nine months after Haydn's death.
1806	Haydn housebound from this point onwards.
1808	makes his last public appearance on March 27 at a performance of *The Creation* conducted by Antonio Salieri at Vienna's old university.
1809	while Vienna under siege by the invading French armies, Haydn dies on May 31 at his home; burial the next day in the cemetery at Gumpendorf; large memorial service in Vienna on June 15.
1810	Griesinger publishes his *Biographische Notizen über Joseph Haydn*; Dies publishes his *Biographische Nachrichten von Joseph Haydn.*
1812	Giuseppe Carpani (1752–1822) publishes his account of the late Haydn in a series of letters entitled "Le Haydine."
1815	Handel & Haydn Society founded in Boston and dedicated to the performance of oratorios.
1818	Handel & Haydn Society presents the first performance of *The Creation* in America.
1820	Haydn's body (minus the head) moved to a tomb in the Bergkirche in Eisenstadt.
1830	Father Heinrich Wondratsch (1793–1881) of the Göttweig Benedictine Abby near Krems completes a thematic catalogue of the library's holdings of Haydn's music entitled the *Göttweig Catalogue.*
1855	Brahms first hears *The Creation.*
1873	Brahms composes *Variations on a Theme of Haydn* (theme falsely attributed to Haydn).
1875	Carl Ferdinand Pohl publishes first volume of Haydn biography (dealing with period up to 1766).
1882	second volume of Pohl's biography (dealing with years 1766–90) appears, coinciding with the 150th anniversary of the composer's birth.
1887	Haydn's biographer C. F. Pohl dies.
1895	adaptation of *Lo speziale* as *Der Apotheker* performed in Dresden (first modern revival of an opera by Haydn).
1904	Haydn's house in Gumpendorf opens as a museum.
1907	Breitkopf & Härtel begins a collected edition of Haydn's works.
1909	special centennial celebrations of Haydn's death in Vienna in May.
1927	Hugo Botstiber completes third volume of Pohl's biography of Haydn.
1932	bicentennial celebrations of Haydn's birth.
1935	museum founded in Haydn's house in Eisenstadt.
1949	Haydn Society founded by H. C. Robbins Landon.
1950	Haydn Society issues first complete recording of *L'anima del filosofo*, conducted by Hans Swarowsky.
1951	first staged performance of *L'anima del filosofo*, in Florence, conducted by Erich Kleiber, and featuring Maria Callas as Eurydice.

1954	Haydn's head reunited with the rest of his remains in the crypt at the Bergkirche in Eisenstadt.
1955	Joseph Haydn-Institut established in Cologne to edit the first historical-critical complete edition *Joseph Haydn Werke* (1958–).
1957	Anthony van Hoboken provides first comprehensive bibliographic account of Haydn's instrumental music and standardizes the composition numbers; catalogue of vocal works completed in 1971; supplement issued in 1978.
1962	H. C. Robbins Landon founds journal *Haydn Yearbook*.
1965	periodical *Haydn-Studien* founded and published by Henle Verlag.
1973	conductor Antal Doráti finishes recording the first complete set of Haydn symphonies with the Philharmonia Hungarica (Decca).
1984	Vienna and the Gesellschaft der Musikfreunde inaugurate an annual festival devoted to Haydn known as *Haydn-Tage*.
1989	Eisenstadt begins mounting regular concerts devoted to Haydn.
1993	Haydn Stiftung founded in Eisenstadt, adjacent to the Haydn museum. (www.haydnfestival.at)

Abbreviations of frequently cited sources

Books

Bartha and Somfai	Bartha, Dénes and László Somfai. *Haydn als Opernkapellmeister.* Budapest: Hungarischen Akademie der Wissenschaften, 1960.
Briefe	Bartha, Dénes (ed.). *Joseph Haydn: Gesammelte Briefe und Aufzeichnungen.* Kassel: Bärenreiter, 1965.
CCLN	Landon, H. C. Robbins (ed.). *The Collected Correspondence and London Notebooks of Joseph Haydn.* London: Barrie and Rockliff, 1959.
Dies	Dies, Albert Christoph. *Biographische Nachrichten von Joseph Haydn.* Vienna: Camesina, 1810.
Gotwals	Gotwals, Vernon (trans. and ed.). *Joseph Haydn: Eighteenth-Century Gentleman and Genius.* Madison: University of Wisconsin Press, 1963. [incorporates translations of Dies and Griesinger]
Griesinger	Griesinger, Georg August. *Biographische Notizen über Joseph Haydn.* Leipzig: Breitkopf & Härtel, 1810; Vienna: Paul Kaltschmid, 1954.
Jones	Jones, David Wyn (ed.). *Oxford Composer Companion: Haydn.* Oxford: Oxford University Press, 2002.
NG Haydn	Webster, James and Georg Feder. *The New Grove Haydn.* London: Macmillan; New York: Palgrave, 2002.
Landon I, II, III, IV, V	Landon, H. C. Robbins, *Haydn: Chronicle and Works.* 5 vols. London: Thames and Hudson; Bloomington: Indiana University Press. Vol. I, *Haydn: The Early Years, 1732–1765* (1980). Vol. II, *Haydn at Eszterháza, 1766–1790* (1978). Vol. III, *Haydn in England, 1791–1795* (1976). Vol. IV, *Haydn: The Years of* The Creation, 1796–1800 (1977). Vol. V, *Haydn: The Late Years, 1801–1809* (1977).

Journals

HS	*Haydn-Studien*
HYB	*Haydn Yearbook*
JAMS	*Journal of the American Musicological Society*
JM	*Journal of Musicology*
JMR	*Journal of Musicological Research*
ML	*Music and Letters*
MQ	*Musical Quarterly*

MR	*Music Review*
MT	*Musical Times*

Others

EK	*Entwurf-Katalog*
Hob. [+number]	Hoboken catalogue number
HV	*Haydn Verzeichnis*
JHW	*Joseph Haydn Werke*

PART I

Haydn in context

1 Haydn's career and the idea of the multiple audience

ELAINE SISMAN

For whom did Haydn write? This simple question, easily enough answered by such obvious recipients as his patrons or the public or particular performers, masks a series of more complex questions about Haydn's career as well as about his muse. How did he balance his own desires with those of his patrons and public? How did he respond to the abilities of the performers, whether soloists, orchestral musicians, or students, for whom he composed? How did he seek to communicate with different audiences, and were his communicative strategies and modes of persuasion always successful? While these questions might be asked of any composer, especially those in the later eighteenth century who had to adapt to an evolving menu of career opportunities, they have special pertinence for Haydn, whose career and works reveal, as well as revel in, the idea of the multiple audience that emerged in this period. This essay will explore the ways in which the shape of Haydn's career, his sometimes inexplicably defensive tone in letters and memoirs, and his musical self-assessments stem from this new source of inspiration. It is perhaps not a coincidence that Haydn, unlike C. P. E. Bach, Mozart, and Beethoven, left no record of disparaging remarks about the public.

Audiences

Let us consider the various shades of meaning associated with the term "audience." Conventionally understood are, in order from local to global, the people who attend a performance; a "readership," in the sense of a book finding its audience; or a group of adherents, a broad following. These virtual dictionary definitions ought to be broadened, given the developing social context, to include those for whom the composer writes: the musicians who will play the music, the patrons and employers who will commission and support it, the publishers who must find it saleable, and the critics who respond publicly and in print. We cannot consider patron, performer, and publisher as transparent windows or mere facilitators between the composer and the wider audience because they materially affected the creation of the works and the works themselves. When Haydn wrote to Artaria in 1789 that he was sending a piano trio that he had "made quite new and, according to your taste, with variations," he may or may not have meant "because that's what people want to play and hear" but certainly Artaria thought so.[1] In the same letter, Haydn sought to interest him in a new Capriccio for piano a year after Artaria's publication of his much older Capriccio in G major (Hob. XVII: 1): "In a most playful hour I composed a quite new Capriccio for the piano, which on account of its taste, singularity, and special elaboration is sure to meet with approval from connoisseurs and non-connoisseurs alike."[2] Haydn's clear-eyed assessment of the appeal of this work, the Fantasia in C (Hob. XVII: 4), reflects the widespread concern on the part of composers and publishers for reaching both sides of the celebrated "binaries" of eighteenth-century cultural forms and musical life – connoisseurs and amateurs, virtuosos and dilettantes – while at the same time considering an entirely different division of his audience, the "present" audience – the known quantity of the local court or city – and the "imagined" audience of a larger musical public that he needed publishers to reach. While it is always difficult to determine what is a sales ploy and what a genuine aesthetic stance, Haydn's interest in the means of reaching the audience remained very high throughout his life.

In 1796, Johann Ritter von Schönfeld's remarkable *Yearbook of Music in Vienna and Prague* gave an invaluable series of listings of performers, composers, patrons, music-lovers, and a host of other categories of people creating musical life toward the end of the eighteenth century.[3] One of the surprising features for the modern reader is that the terms "connoisseurs" and "amateurs" (*Kenner und Liebhaber*) do not make an appearance as a pair.[4] Instead, we read lists, in some cases copiously annotated, of patrons, called "special friends, protectors, and connoisseurs" (*Kenner*); performers and composers, called "virtuosos and amateurs" (*dilettantes*); sponsors of amateur concerts; music-lovers (*Liebhaber*) with big manuscript collections; performers in the imperial Kapelle, as well as performers in courtly house-orchestras, wind-bands, and the national and suburban theaters; composers; conductors who lead from the violin; publishers and music-sellers; and instrument- and organ-makers. It is also surprising to note how infrequently composers used the terms "Liebhaber" and "Dilettante" for "amateur" or "music-lover" in their understanding of the musical public, outside of C. P. E. Bach's big collections of piano music for "Kenner und Liebhaber" published between 1779 and 1785. Mozart famously wrote of "connoisseurs and non-connoisseurs"; his father described the "musical and unmusical public," in which there are "a hundred ignoramuses to every ten true connoisseurs"; J. K. F. Triest used the terms "connoisseurs and half-connoisseurs."[5] And connoisseurs themselves ranged from patrons like Baron van Swieten to other composers; Haydn's biographer Griesinger notes that Haydn as a young man was heard as an accompanist "at Prince von Hildburghausen's [the patron of Dittersdorf], in the presence of Gluck, Wagenseil, and other renowned masters, and the applause of such connoisseurs served as a special encouragement to him."[6] Thus, the term "connoisseur" had several meanings – socially powerful patron, composer, judge – rather than merely designating someone who had studied or who had developed taste.

In a revealing snapshot, when Haydn offered his Op. 33 string quartets by subscription to selected "gentlemen amateurs, connoisseurs, and patrons of music," as he put it to Lavater in Switzerland, he differentiated this method from that of "dedicating his works directly to the public," by which he meant publishing them with Artaria, advice he received from van Swieten.[7] This terminology echoes that of Kirnberger and Sulzer in the article on chamber music in Sulzer's *Allgemeine Theorie der schönen Künste*: "Because chamber music is for connoisseurs and amateurs, a piece can be more learned and more artfully composed than if it were intended for public use, where everything must be simpler and more cantabile so that everyone may grasp it."[8] The "public" comprised many different audiences, and "connoisseurs and amateurs" by no means covered all the alternatives.

Haydn seems to have been acutely sensitive to the principal rhetorical claim of a piece of music: that it must communicate persuasively with an audience through the medium of performance. In eighteenth-century terms, filtered through Haydn's own words, this claim might be rendered: that it instruct, please, and move the passions in the manner appropriate to occasion and venue so that what originated in his own spirit and sensibility would remain in the listener's heart.[9] The role and sound of the performers loomed very large to him, and one must take him at his word when he seemed to describe the best part of his job with Esterházy as the ability to try out things, to see "what would make an impression."[10] One senses that he wrote performers' music as well as listeners' music, from the witty trade-offs in the first string quartet (Op. 1 no. 1, in B♭, in which players almost physically engage with each other) to the expressive details in the Sonata in E♭ for Marianne von Genzinger (Hob. XVI: 49, which he described to her as "very full of meaning") to the soul-irradiating sonorities of the oratorio version of the *Seven Last Words* (especially in the new introduction to Part II). Because he composed at the keyboard, his invention was always linked to sound, and it was both a natural concomitant and a canny career move to ensure that his players enjoyed the works that showed them off to best advantage. With the first symphonic trilogy for Prince Paul Anton Esterházy, nos. 6–8, Haydn hit on the happy idea of quasi-programmatic concertante writing in the tradition of the Vivaldi *Four Seasons* – a score in his patron's library as of 1740 – winning the prince's approbation and the musicians' loyalty.[11] The local success of this style is revealed in the numerous concertante movements in symphonies from the 1760s and 1770s, and the penetration of such related devices as cadenzas, breakaway figurations, and quasi-ritornellos in string quartets and keyboard music (and even the baryton trios). To the end of his career he would feature soloists in sometimes surprising ways and work for sonorous effects to mold an ensemble.

In what follows, I consider first the shape of Haydn's career through the lens of the "success narrative" in which it is usually cast, paying close attention to its problematic undertones that reveal Haydn's changing fortunes and the sources of his unusual mix of confidence and defensiveness. Then, I evaluate several key documents – the most defensive ones – as evidence of Haydn's conceptions of the different strands of his audience. What will emerge are new views of his relationship with performers, of his attitudes towards connoisseurs and critics, and of his enduring desire to be widely understood.

Haydn's career through the looking-glass

Haydn's life story as a rags-to-riches success is easily summarized. Plucked from humble origins, first by a schoolmaster relation and then by the Kapellmeister of St. Stephen's Cathedral, Haydn continued to make auspicious contacts seemingly by accident once on his own in Vienna, while teaching young students. High-spirited street serenading led him to Joseph Kurz, popular theater's "Bernardon," for whose broad style of comic acting and improvisation he provided music. Living in the same building as one of the most famous men in Vienna – imperial court poet Pietro Metastasio – and giving music lessons to Metastasio's pupil Marianne von Martínez, he was quickly introduced to Italian opera composer Nicola Porpora, accompanying his singing lessons. Through these connections he was recommended to his first two noble patrons: for Baron von Fürnberg's summer parties he wrote string quartets and for Count Morzin he undertook directorial duties and wrote symphonies, until another fortuitous introduction led him to the Esterházy princes at the precise moment that Morzin was forced by financial exigency to dissolve his orchestra. Hired in 1761 with a contract regulating his behavior, dress, and responsibilities, Haydn was so successful in pleasing his patrons, first Paul Anton and from 1762 on Nicolaus Esterházy, as well as their musicians, singers, and theatrical troupes, and in acquiring fame abroad, that he was able to negotiate a new contract in 1779 giving him the rights to his own works. Thus he was able to get in on the ground floor with the new Viennese publishing house of Artaria, and to respond to commissions from as far away as Cadíz, Naples, Paris, and London. After the death of Nicolaus in 1790, Haydn spent several years in London and Vienna, enjoying the period of his greatest renown and financial success, and writing the works that would have the greatest continuing impact after his death.

Were we to recast this narrative in terms of the nodal points of sensitivity that underlay Haydn's self-concept and that found their way into several of Haydn's strikingly defensive statements, we might annotate it like this:

Plucked from humble origins, *which forever kept him out of the ranks of the well-connected and made him more than a little sensitive to the courtly birth of composers like Hofmann and Dittersdorf,* first by a schoolmaster relation *who taught him but beat him* and then by the Kapellmeister of St. Stephen's Cathedral, *who gave him scant attention when he tried to compose and beat him when he played practical jokes,* Haydn continued to make auspicious contacts seemingly by accident once on his own in Vienna, while teaching young students, *in a "wretched existence" which embittered him by leaving him little time to study.* High-spirited street serenading led him to Joseph Kurz, popular theater's "Bernardon," for whose broad style of comic acting and improvisation he provided music. Living in the same building as one of the most famous men in Vienna – imperial court poet Pietro Metastasio – and giving music lessons to Metastasio's pupil Marianne von Martínez, he was quickly introduced to Italian opera composer Nicola Porpora, accompanying his singing lessons *and learning the true fundamentals of composition though being beaten and verbally abused.* Through these connections he was recommended to his first two noble patrons: for Baron von Fürnberg's summer parties he wrote string quartets and for Count Morzin he undertook directorial duties and wrote symphonies, until another fortuitous introduction led him to the Esterházy princes at the precise moment that Count Morzin was forced by financial exigency to dissolve his orchestra. *He seems to have been early aware that his reputation would depend on players who sounded good and who enjoyed their work.* Hired in 1761 with a contract regulating his behavior, dress, and responsibilities, *Haydn suffered the nasty meddling of his immediate superior, Kapellmeister Gregor Joseph Werner, and in consequence had to give proof of his diligence to Prince Nicolaus Esterházy. Isolated in the country for most of each year, suffering attacks in the north German press, nonetheless* Haydn was so successful in pleasing his patrons, first Paul Anton and from 1762 on Nicolaus Esterházy, as well as their musicians, singers, and theatrical troupes, and in acquiring fame abroad, that he was able to negotiate a new contract in 1779 giving him the rights to his own works, *though that same year he was outraged by his treatment by the Viennese Tonkünstler-Sozietät over the demand for new works.* Thus he was able to get in on the ground floor with the new Viennese publishing house of Artaria, *whose first three publications responded to or occasioned problems and embarrassments for Haydn,*[12] and to respond to commissions from as far away as Cadíz, Naples, Paris, and London. *The patronage he had praised in his 1776 autobiographical sketch and the originality-producing isolation he praised to Griesinger eventually gave way to feelings of melancholy, loneliness, and involuntary servitude.* After the death of Nicolaus in 1790, he spent several years in London and Vienna, *the latter finally recognizing his achievements*, enjoying the period of his greatest renown and financial success, *even though his Orpheus opera was not produced in London*, and writing the works that would have the greatest continuing impact after his death. *For the last half-decade of his life he was unable to compose at all, his strength and acuity having begun to weaken already about 1800; instead of composing he produced anecdotes and narratives for his biographers, the sober Griesinger, the artist Dies, and the more fanciful Carpani.*

Despite Haydn's fame and public successes, then, he was often conscious that he could not please everyone. In his concern to "make an impression," he needed to win over performers and listeners, publishers and purchasers, connoisseurs and critics. Most of all, he needed to make sure that his work sounded good.

The *Applausus* letter: Haydn and performers

In 1768, Haydn was already full Kapellmeister to Prince Nicolaus Esterházy, yet when commissioned by the abbey of Zwettl in Lower Austria to write a celebratory cantata, called an *Applausus*, for the fiftieth anniversary of the abbot's taking his vows, he wrote a deeply self-conscious letter giving details of performance practice, declamation, and rehearsal time. His conclusion is worth quoting:

> Finally I ask everyone, and especially the musicians, to apply the greatest possible diligence in order to advance my reputation (*Ehre*) as well as their own; if I have perhaps not guessed their taste, I am not to be blamed for it, for I know neither the persons nor the place, and in truth the fact that these were concealed from me made my work very difficult. For the rest, I hope that this *Applausus* will please the poet, the most worthy musicians, and the honorable reverend *Auditorio.*[13]

What Haydn overtly recognizes here is, to paraphrase the old Vidal Sassoon advertisement, if they don't look good, he doesn't look good. Thus the real reason to ingratiate himself with musicians and to write for their strengths is not only to reap the benefits of a happy group of employees but to make his music shine, burnished by the virtuosi at his command: in a good performance, everyone's reputation improves. When a piece is to be heard one time only, the quality of preparation and of the performance itself become crucial. If the audience's experience of the piece lives or dies by the players, then the composer must communicate with the players first, so that their experience as the first audience will guide the rest. Griesinger reported that "through long practice, [Haydn] had learned in general how musicians must be handled and thus succeeded by much modesty, by appropriate praise and careful indulgence of artistic pride so to win over Gallini's orchestra that his compositions were always well performed."[14] Presumably this technique of personnel management had been learned with the Esterházys.

The letter also reveals the extent to which Haydn's self-concept in 1768 is still entirely local, and, perhaps surprisingly, on that basis insecure. To this time, Haydn had always been on the scene to flatter, cajole, and guide musically. Indeed, this letter makes us look anew at the evidence of Haydn's relationships with his musicians in the Esterházy establishment. Although Haydn's works started appearing in print during the 1760s (e.g., the two sets of early quartets published by La Chevardière in Paris in 1764), he was far from imagining his works as destined or even appropriate for venues far removed from his own. Haydn had also come to take for granted a level of skill in orchestral and vocal performance. In *Applausus*, the concertante style of quite a few of his early Esterházy symphonies (as well as of the concertos themselves) is evident in solo turns for organ (no. IVb) and violin (no. VIIb), as well as cadenzas for boy sopranos (nos. IIIb and VIb), tenor (nos. IVb and VIIb), and bass (no. Vb).[15] Moreover, the "Sturm und Drang" style of his contemporaneous Symphony no. 49 in F minor (as well as other works not written in 1768) appears in the wide leaps, frenzied tremolos, syncopations, fast walking bass, and minor mode of the bass aria no. Vb.[16] The tiny organ concerto of no. IVb features a vocal as well as a separate organ cadenza, while the violin and tenor in no. VIIb join for the final cadenza (after the tenor had a solo cadenza in the first A section). *Applausus* contains no fugal movement even in the final chorus but fully three pieces in festive C major trumpet-and-drum style (nos. I, III, VIII). Haydn may well have wondered about local taste because these styles were so fully embodied in his productions of the 1760s that he wondered if they would "travel," in the same way that he later said his operas wouldn't travel well outside of the specific personnel and theater at Eszterháza. Yet by the end of his life, Haydn expressed satisfaction that his works were known in remote places because his goal was to be considered a "not unworthy priest of this sacred art by every nation where my works are known."[17]

The autobiography: an *apologia pro vita sua* for elite readers and connoisseurs

In 1776, Haydn was asked to contribute an autobiographical sketch for inclusion in *Das gelehrte Oesterreich.* He responded in a letter endlessly pored over by scholars, for it is the only account entirely in the composer's own words;[18] together with the interviews conducted by biographers Dies and Griesinger (and possibly Carpani) late in his life, it is the only source for his early years. Its emphases and peculiarities of construction derive from its rhetorical organization,[19] and it is likely that the striking amount of space given to his musical education (the *narratio,* or statement of facts), including the early recognition of his talent, derive from the volume's focus on "learned" achievements. (Of his fifteen years in Esterházy service, he states only that he is "Capellmeister of His Highness, the Prince, in whose service I hope to live and die.") The theme of the "making of a composer" would in any case have been of considerable interest at the time, but the focus stresses his gifts, recognized in unpromising circumstances by more knowledgeable masters, and, more important, the necessity for study to bring them to fruition. Indeed, he still sounds bitter about the necessity to "teach the young" in order to "eke out a wretched existence," noting that "many geniuses are ruined by having to earn their daily bread, because they have no time to study." As Leon Botstein has pointed out, the narrative about his early years appeared to follow certain well-worn tropes about the early lives of artists found in sources from Greek antiquity through the Renaissance, following the "narrative formulas" identified by Ernst Kris and Otto Kurz in their fascinating study *Legend, Myth, and Magic in the Image of the Artist.*[20] These formulas might be summarized as follows: a youth born to pastoral surroundings (an identity as shepherd is not infrequently invented) shows evidence of musical talent already in childhood; this talent is recognized in a chance encounter with a connoisseur who takes the youth's training in hand; the youth rises on the social ladder to achieve great fame. Persistent motifs, including the emphasis on childhood, genius expressing itself early, and the heroic artist triumphing over obstacles, became part of the age-old "legend of the artist." Vasari's celebrated biography of Giotto, in which the shepherd boy noticed by Cimabue in a chance encounter acquires the latter as teacher and mentor, thereafter rising to fame, draws on these older myths while furnishing a model to future generations; Thomas Tolley even wonders if perhaps Baron van Swieten suggested this storyline to Haydn.[21] Haydn's stress on the amount of study involved adds an Enlightenment aspect of self-made moral education, and also appears to suggest that education and patronage does not extend far enough to talented youths.

While Haydn recounted a valuable artistic "lineage" lifting him from folk-harp to Reutter to Porpora to his present eminence, his outsider status remained on display and apparently rankled. One senses that this lies behind his insulting comments to Artaria in 1781 about Leopold Hofmann's recently published Lieder, described as "street songs, wherein neither ideas, expression nor, much less, melody appear"; Haydn wrote that "just because this braggart thinks that he alone has ascended the heights of Mount Parnassus, and tries to disgrace me with a certain high society, I have composed these very three Lieder just to show this would-be high society the difference."[22] A. Peter Brown points out that Hofmann's insider status at court, together with the greater opportunities he was offered from youth on and his earlier established status, may have aroused Haydn's ire.[23] But for all Haydn's supposed comfort-level with people of his own rank and his satisfaction with his remote location (at least before the later 1780s), he felt consistently slighted by the Viennese establishments, including the court and the Tonkünstler-Sozietät. Thus, Haydn sometimes intended his compositions to prove something to at least one segment of his audience, as to the unnamed personage of this letter.

The other lengthy segment of the autobiography concerns Haydn's ill-treatment at the hands of the north German critics (the *confutatio*, refutation of his enemies' arguments), and here Haydn's responses are instructive:

> In the chamber style [referring to all instrumental music not destined for theater or church] I have been fortunate enough to please almost all nations except the Berliners; this is shown by the public newspapers and letters addressed to me. I only wonder that the Berlin gentlemen, who are otherwise so reasonable, preserve no middle ground [*Medium*] in their criticism of my music, for in one weekly paper they praise me to the skies, whilst in another they dash me sixty fathoms deep into the earth, and this without explaining why; I know very well why: because they are incapable of performing some of my works, and are too conceited to take the trouble to understand them properly, and for other reasons which, with God's help, I will answer in good time. Herr Capellmeister von Dittersdorf, in Silesia, wrote to me recently and asked me to defend myself against their hard words, but I answered that one swallow doesn't make the summer; and that perhaps one of these days some unprejudiced person would stop their tongues, as happened to them once before when they accused me of monotony. Despite this, they try very hard to get all my works, as Herr Baron von Sviten [sic], the Imperial and Royal Ambassador at Berlin, told me only last winter, when he was in Vienna: but enough of this.[24]

Haydn's objection to their inconsistency, wondering at their extremes with no "Medium," sounds strikingly like the celebrated letter Mozart wrote to his father on 28 December 1782, in which he claims that the "mean, the genuine in all things, is known and valued no longer" because only extremes reign: "to receive approval, one must write something so easy to understand that a coachman can sing it right back to you, or so incomprehensible that it pleases precisely because no rational person can understand it."[25] In attributing the critics' animus to their inability to perform his works properly and their unwillingness to take the time to learn them, Haydn might have been covertly relying on van Swieten's information on the quality of performances in Berlin, while crediting the diplomat with a less incendiary item. (Swieten was ambassador in Berlin from 1770 to 1777, returning to Vienna for a vacation every winter except in 1776, and this reference to a meeting during the winter of 1775 is the earliest datable account of their contact.[26]) But he might also have been drawing on his own strong sense that he couldn't trust performers he did not himself train. Some of these critiques were after all contemporaneous with *Applausus.* The question of difficulty in performance, although hard to credit when it came to counterpoint and octave doublings, might be right on the money with respect to the "inappropriate" mixtures of comic and serious elements.[27]

Haydn's assessment of his works in performance, that is, his works as experienced by an audience, made him acutely sensitive to the opportunities for misunderstanding. If the picture I have painted elsewhere of Haydn's theatrical style is correct, namely that his profound daily involvement with theater of all kinds at Eszterháza over a period of years affected his musical style and intensified his natural tendencies toward the gesture and the seriocomic mixture, then, as with stage works themselves, his symphonic music could be understood only *as performance*, and thus without proper performance no understanding was possible. We can see the roots of this approach in his first reported interaction with Joseph Kurz, famous for his role as the comic character Bernardon in the popular Viennese theater, when Kurz asked him to accompany his gestures of swimming: to his evident delight, Haydn, perhaps not much older than twenty-one, "fell into six-eight time."[28] The correlation between physical and musical gesture is strikingly evident in Haydn's music, and may be the source of comments like Hiller's: "in springs Hans Wurst, right into the middle of things."[29]

The Auenbrugger letter: Haydn, critics, and "virtuosos and dilettantes"

From the beginning of Haydn's correspondence with Artaria over the publication of the six sonatas dedicated to the Auenbrugger sisters, he was concerned with their reception. On February 8, 1780, he indicated that he hoped to gain honor with the "discerning world," and that he had many critics who were motivated by jealousy.[30] In the very next letter he takes steps to head off such criticism because two of the sonatas share a theme. This letter has never been examined from the perspective of Haydn's communication with the multiple audience:

> Among other things, I consider it necessary, in order to forestall the criticisms of any would-be wits [*Witzlinge*], to print on the reverse side of the title page the following sentence, here underlined:
>
> Avertissement
>
> *Among these 6 Sonatas there are two single movements in which the same idea [Idee] occurs through several bars: the author has done this intentionally because of the difference in realization [Ausführung].* For naturally I could have chosen a hundred other ideas instead of this one; but so that the whole opus will not be exposed to blame on account of this one intentional detail (which the critics and especially my enemies might take the wrong way), I think this avertissement or something like it must be appended, otherwise the sale might be hindered thereby. I submit the point in question to the judicious opinion of the two Misses v. Auenbrugger, whose hands I respectfully kiss.[31]

Haydn suddenly understood that what was intended as a publication for domestic music-making would be noticed by critics, by connoisseurs who understood rhetorical terminology like the "idea" and the "realization," and by his "enemies" – who are these: the unfriendly Berlin critics? rival composers like Hofmann? Haydn's sensitivity to this issue may have been inspired by Christian Gottlob Neefe's essay on musical repetition, published in the inaugural year (1776) of the journal *Deutsches Museum*, or by the trend which it reports, namely, that "it is customary for critics of musical compositions in newspapers, journals, societies, and audiences that they reproach composers [for their] repetition."[32] Neefe divides repetition into two rhetorical categories strikingly similar to those used by Haydn in the "Avertissement": invention (*Erfindung*) and realization (*Ausführung*). For the first, Neefe observes that composers may repeat either their own ideas or someone else's, and that if they repeat their own they are either "poor in invention" and thus "open to censure," or "deficient in memory." Only when it "arises from the necessity of working hard and fast" is it "an error that deserves [our] indulgence." Thus Haydn sought to head off the critics by making the claim that his "repetition," far from being an error, had an appropriate aim.[33]

In fact, the themes to which Haydn refers, the movements they generate, and the sonatas of which they are a part, nos. 36 in C♯ minor and 39 in G of the set dedicated to the Auenbrugger sisters (Hob. XVI: 35–39, 20), differ from each other on several levels, as would have been appropriate for sonatas intended to realize the differences in skill between the two ladies, and, by extension, the larger audience of more and less talented players. First, the form of each movement is somewhat different: each has variations of that theme alternating with episodes, but in the second movement of no. 36 the episodes are both in parallel minor, with the second a variation of the first, resulting in an ABABA form. In the first movement of no. 39, not only are the two episodes in different keys – first parallel, then relative minors, an unusual combination – but the second is unrelated to the first, resulting in an ABACA form.[34] (Common to both movements, however, is the four-measure theme refrain that appears before each variation of A, and the second episode landing on the dominant, without a repeat.) And in no. 39/i the B section (mm. 17ff) is an expressive variation of the A theme, while the C section (mm. 53ff) is a "characteristic" episode. No. 39/i has a more dynamic profile, with sharply pointed dotted rhythms and a higher melodic arch; its mode of execution might be described as quasi-brilliant, as befits a first movement. No. 36/ii is more "rounded," leading to a more graceful yet playful mode of performance, appropriate to a middle movement marked "Scherzando." It contrasts with the moody C♯ minor opening movement. Finally, no. 39/i is more difficult to play, a result perhaps of the unequal talents of the sisters to whom the sonatas were dedicated; contemporary reports reveal that Katharina played better than her younger sister Marianna.[35]

It appears that Haydn, not wanting to execute any missteps with his new publisher and new public, gave them three easier (35, 36, 37) and three more difficult (38, 39, 20) sonatas, in a rational, even didactic, key order (C, c♯, D, E♭, G, c). His letter, long taken as a rationalization for a memory lapse, suggests instead that the set is carefully constructed, exploring different musical topics and shapes in every sonata and finding good reasons to include the earlier C minor sonata (Hob. XVI: 20, the autograph fragment of which is dated 1771) as an expressive conclusion. With his primary focus on the "discerning world," Haydn revealed an interest in dilettantes and students while giving an intellectual basis for the set to connoisseurs and critics.

The "French swill" letter: Haydn, the general public, and posterity

In 1801, Haydn wrote to August Eberhard Müller, the Leipzig Kapellmeister who was making the piano reduction of *The Seasons*, that a particular passage had to be corrected in order to leave out a bit of word-painting. He added rather gratuitously: "NB! This whole passage, with its imitation of a frog, did not flow easily from my pen; I was forced to write down this French swill [*französischen Quark*]. With the whole orchestra this miserable idea disappears rather soon, but it cannot remain in the piano score."[36] The indiscreet Müller showed the passage to J. G. K. Spazier, who had just founded the journal *Zeitung für die elegante Welt*; Spazier's attack on van Swieten's text created a nasty brouhaha between Haydn and van Swieten. Both Griesinger and Dies reported Haydn's complaints about the text and about van Swieten wanting him to use Grétry as a model.[37] The curious features of this incident require some comment, because comparable tone-painting appeared in *The Creation*, a work Haydn seemed rather to admire. Possibly he had already received advance word of critical response to *The Seasons* and would have been pursuing damage control. It is also not out of the question that he was tired of taking suggestions from van Swieten, whose fingerprints are all over *The Seven Last Words* as well as *The Creation*; and van Swieten for his part, two years before his death, took such suggestions as his right. However, what ought to be noted is the placement of the pictorialism in a set-piece rather than in an accompanied recitative. The larger rhythm of the numbers in Parts I and II of *The Creation* creates two-unit or three-unit segments: the laconic words of Genesis are set in simple recitative, moving to more vivid descriptive language, with texts based partly on *Paradise Lost*, in accompanied recitative (the pre-eminent site of word-painting), and then to aria or to the occasional ensemble of soloists enumerating and elaborating the "facts of creation."[38] Choruses of praise, sometimes together with the angelic soloists, round out each "day" of creation. In *The Seasons*, on the other hand, the accompanied recitatives are fewer and farther between, and the set-pieces themselves contain description or action, like the sunrise or successful hunting of a bird. The return to normal after the huge summer storm, itself vividly "painted," occasions cows, quail, crickets, and the frog to be heard – oddly, the frog seems the least intrusive of all! – and Haydn may have objected to the closing Trio and Chorus (no. 18) usurping the role of recitative in this respect while it enacts the most quotidian conclusion in the oratorio. (Even the "tipsy" chorus that concludes Autumn is a tour-de-force of counterpoint despite its text deplored by Haydn.)

The most interesting detail about this controversy is the way it intersects with the question of musical meaning, as different kinds of audiences might understand it. Haydn once again seems to be threading his way between broad appeal and critical detractors (even while poisoning the well), aware that he was reaching the widest audience of his life with the sensationally popular oratorios. Both biographers queried Haydn about the "subject-matter" of his music: what was he trying to express?[39] Haydn told Dies that he "seldom" had a specific topic in mind (or at least as specific as the "coquette" or "prude" with which Dies taxed him), preferring to let his "more purely musical fantasy" prevail; to Griesinger he answered that he had often tried to portray "moral characters" in his symphonies; and to both he recounted the Adagio of an old symphony that featured God arguing with an unrepentant sinner.[40] The widespread sense in Haydn's lifetime that his instrumental music was "about" something reveals how fully characterized and persuasive was his musical rhetoric. Significant in the exchange with Griesinger is that Haydn might have been able to say more about the issue had the biographer showed him score after score, "and that proved irksome to the aged man." One can only conclude that Griesinger *did* try to go through scores with him, and either nothing rang a bell or – a more likely possibility? – Haydn refused to come clean. Why would he risk identifying a background narrative or image or concept or set of characters that might expose him to the same ridicule as the "French swill"? What we may also have here is the discrepancy between a kind of "poetic idea" in a Beethovenian sense – "I have always an image in mind, and work up to it" – which is part of the compositional process, and the meaning that the composer wants the listener to grasp.[41]

But Griesinger had not in fact asked him about instrumental music in particular (only Dies had), merely about his "compositions," so perhaps it isn't surprising that in the two paragraphs after this exchange he goes on to describe the way he illustrated text in the late masses: the Agnus Dei of the *Mass in Time of War* set with timpani "as though one heard the enemy coming already in the distance" followed by all the voices and instruments breaking in pathetically for the text "Dona nobis pacem"; and then a more esoteric example of meaning in the *Schöpfungsmesse*:

> it occurred to him in the [Gloria] that weak mortals sinned mostly against moderation and chastity. So he set the words *qui tollis peccata mundi* to the flirtatious melody of the words in *The Creation*, "The dew-dropping morn, o how she quickens all!" But in order that this profane thought should not be too conspicuous, he let the *Miserere* sound in full chorus immediately thereafter.[42]

Thus, even though Griesinger wove a narrative version of several or many conversations, one must conclude from his presentation that Haydn continued to answer his question about musical meaning, "what he tried to express through musical language," with both obvious and more subtle text-related details in his late masses, details that might be either irrelevant or unrecoverable within the fabric of his instrumental works. As he spoke to his posterity through his biographers, Haydn must certainly have realized that his trademark instrumental qualities of intelligible topical discourse, formal idiosyncrasy, and brilliantly deployed gesture, appreciated on as many levels as there were levels of skill, knowledge, judgment, and taste in his multiple audiences, needed no road maps.

2 A letter from the wilderness: revisiting Haydn's Esterházy environments

REBECCA GREEN

> Well, here I sit in my wilderness – forsaken – like a poor waif – almost without any human society – melancholy – full of the memories of past glorious days – yes! past alas! – and who knows when these days shall return again? Those wonderful parties? Where the whole circle is one heart, one soul – all these beautiful musical evenings – which can only be remembered, and not described – where are all these enthusiastic moments? – all gone – and gone for a long time.[1]

So begins one of Haydn's most remarkable letters, written to Maria Anna von Genzinger in February 1790 shortly after his return to Eszterháza from the Christmas season in Vienna. In this letter we have a rare glimpse of Haydn out of livery as "Capellmeister of His Highness the Prince [Esterházy] in whose service I wish to live and die," as Haydn had styled himself in another well-known letter, his autobiography of 1776.

Eighteenth-century letters are characterized by "ontological ambiguity," eliding public and private, natural and rhetorical in seductive ways, especially as sources for biography.[2] Haydn's autobiographical letter of 1776 is a case in point. Though ostensibly a private letter addressed from one individual to another, the letter was in fact published in *Das gelehrte Oesterreich*, a Who's Who of Austria. By writing to a female interlocutor rather than Monsignor Zoller, for whom the letter was ultimately intended, Haydn invoked contemporary conventions of "cor-respondence" (especially with women) as "writing from the heart," the most sincere and intimate form of communication. Though Haydn apologizes for offering an "artless hotch-potch," the letter is in fact rhetorically accomplished, as Elaine Sisman has demonstrated, and should give us pause before accepting Haydn's reputation as illiterary.[3]

In comparison with the formal humility of Haydn's autobiographical letter, Haydn's correspondence with Maria Anna von Genzinger is spontaneous and passionate, with flashes of humor and rebelliousness familiar from his musical style. The letter continues as follows:

> Your Grace mustn't be surprised that I haven't written up to now to thank you. I found everything at home in confusion, and for 3 days I didn't know if I was *Capell*-master or *Capell*-servant. Nothing could console me, my

> whole house was in confusion, my pianoforte which I usually love so much was perverse and disobedient, it irritated rather than calmed me, I could only sleep very little, even my dreams persecuted me; and then, just when I was happily dreaming that I was listening to the opera, *Le nozze di Figaro*, that horrible North wind woke me and almost blew my nightcap off my head; I lost 20 lbs. in weight in 3 days, for the good Viennese food I had in me disappeared on the journey; alas! alas! I thought to myself as I was eating in the mess here, instead of that delicious slice of beef, a chunk of a cow 50 years old; instead of a ragout with little dumplings, an old sheep with carrots; instead of a Bohemian pheasant, a leathery joint; instead of those fine and delicate oranges, a *Dschabl* or so-called *gross Sallat* [sic]; instead of pastry, dry apple-fritters and hazelnuts – and that's what I have to eat. Alas! alas! I thought to myself, if I could only have a little bit of what I couldn't eat up in Vienna. – Here in Estoras no one asks me: Would you like some chocolate, with milk or without? Will you take some coffee, black, or with cream? What may I offer you, my dear Haydn? Would you like a vanilla or a pine-apple ice? If I only had a good piece of Parmesan cheese, especially in Lent, so that I could more easily swallow those black dumplings and noodles; just today I told our porter here to send me a couple of pounds.
>
> Forgive me, kindest and most gracious lady, for filling the very first letter with such stupid nonsense, and for killing time with such a wretched scrawl, but you must forgive a man whom the Viennese terribly spoiled. I am gradually getting used to country life, however, and yesterday I studied for the first time, and quite Haydnish, too.

While it is tempting to read this letter as a more transparent window on Haydn's personal thoughts and feelings, as we shall see, it is no less constructed than the autobiographical letter. Yet it offers quite a different template for Haydn biography, especially on the question of his geographical and psychological isolation. In order to read Haydn's letters with greater scrutiny for what they reveal about his life, this essay will open the "envelope of contingency that surrounds any letter,"[4] by revisiting the Esterházy environments in which Haydn lived between the ages of twenty-nine and fifty-nine, where he was set apart from the world, and in which he indeed became original.

The Esterházy orbit: Vienna–Eisenstadt–Eszterháza

In her fascinating study of the Esterházy estates, Rebecca Gates-Coon reminds us that "Eszterháza was but one of three locations which together served as the hub of the princely family's activities in the late eighteenth century."[5] Though Gates-Coon describes these three principal locations as the vertices of a triangle, they in fact form a ray extending from the center of the Habsburg Empire into an obscure pocket of Hungary. The Esterházy palace on the Wallnerstrasse was one of the most notable residences in Vienna, the cosmopolitan capital. In the summers the family retreated to their country palace in the German-speaking town of Eisenstadt, situated about thirty miles southeast of Vienna in what is now Austrian Burgenland. Haydn's second prince, Nicolaus, earned his nickname "the Magnificent" in part through the vast renovation of his favorite residence, Süttor, into Eszterháza, located a further forty miles southeast, well inside the border of present-day Hungary.

Haydn's first year with the Esterházys was spent almost entirely in Vienna, where he had already been living for nearly two decades. As Vice-Kapellmeister to Prince Paul Anton, he continued to compose instrumental music while enjoying the security of employment in a noble house which was just around the corner from the Michaelerhaus where Haydn had struggled in poverty just a decade earlier.[6] With the death of Paul Anton in 1762, Haydn inherited a prince even more interested in music, but less enchanted with city life. Prince Nicolaus (and Haydn) soon began to spend more time in Eisenstadt, though Gates-Coon suggests that the prince's imperial duties "required that he make many extra journeys to the capital at all times of year."[7] Haydn did not even visit "Schloss Estoras" until 1766, the year renovations began (they would finally be finished nearly twenty years later). Meanwhile, Paul Anton's widow, Maria-Aloysia Lunati-Visconti, continued to live on the second floor of the spacious Wallnerstrasse palace in Vienna, as was her right according to her marriage contract, and her fondness for music made this house the scene of lively salons attended by noble music-lovers such as Carl Zinzendorf.

Eisenstadt was divided between the jurisdiction of the town itself and that of the Esterházys, whose palace stood at the northwest corner of the town. Theoretically the royal free towns of Hungary had autonomy in matters of town governance, but the Esterházys had the ultimate authority in the county. The title of lord high sheriff (Sopron county included both Eisenstadt and Eszterháza) had been a hereditary possession of the Esterházy family since 1734. Emblematic of overlapping authorities in the town was control of the gates to Eisenstadt. The city gate (*Unterthor*) was situated at the eastern side of town and gave onto the road to Oedenburg and Pressburg, while the castle gate (*Oberthor*) led from the Schlossplatz in front of the palace west towards Vienna. The Eisenstadt palace itself, renovated in 1683 by Prince Paul I, has perhaps been overshadowed in the Haydn literature by the magnificent Eszterháza. Nevertheless, the palace was something to marvel at in 1749 when Thomas Steavens wrote, "This Chateau is situated on an Eminence, at one End of the Village of Eysenstadt, & was built by Prince Paul Esterhasy, Grandfather of the present Prince. It is a vast large

House, built round a Court, & surrounded by a Mote, which you cross over a great Stone Bridge, to enter into the Court."[8]

Despite the presence of the Esterházys, the town of Eisenstadt was not prosperous, due to lack of economic opportunities and its awkward geography, as revealed in this description: "a small town of Hungary, three miles to the left of the road from Vienna to Oedinburgh, with a palace, which is the residence of prince Esterházy, who has large estates in this area."[9] Indeed, the Esterházy family owned over half the urbarial land (worked by peasants) in Sopron county alone. From the *Jagdschloss* of the hunting grounds of the Eisenstadt estate, one had a view of the Neusiedlersee (also known at this time as the Eßterhaser See), on the southwest tip of which the palace of Eszterháza was located.

When Baron Riesbeck visited Eszterháza in the 1780s he observed that "The Neusiedler See, from which the castle is not far removed, makes miles of swamp and threatens in time to swallow up all the land right up to the Prince's dwelling."[10] Though Eszterháza was not particularly distant from Vienna as the crow flies, its geographical situation magnified its distance from the capital. The Neusiedlersee is a highly unusual lake that actually has no basin, but literally rests on the surface. Consequently, the volume of water and the actual area of the lake fluctuates. In the 1720s when the original palace was built, the lake was ebbing until 1740 when it had virtually dried out; by 1786, however, the lake had expanded again to a record high of 198 square miles. Reeds surrounding the lake made it a fine game preserve, but the "small brackish ponds" that filled depressions caused by the winds accentuated its inhospitality to humans. When Haydn used the term *Einöde* to refer to Eszterháza he was perhaps translating the Hungarian term for the marshy plains of the area – *puszta*, which means "wilderness."[11] In twenty-first-century parlance, Eszterháza was off the grid (see Figure 2.1).

Despite the awkward location, many visitors traveled to Eszterháza, especially for the fests held in 1770, 1773, and 1775, at which members of the imperial family were entertained, and during the 1780s when the opera house was at its peak. Haydn also received a number of musical visitors at Eszterháza, including Joseph Martin Kraus in 1783; Michael Kelly and Giuseppe Sarti in 1784; and P. Werigand Rettensteiner in 1785.[12] Which brings us to the question of how these three points on the Esterházy orbit were connected.

Haydn in circulation

"Each letter, however private and personal it may seem, is a letter marked by and sent to the world," write the editors of *Epistolary Histories*.[13] Indeed,

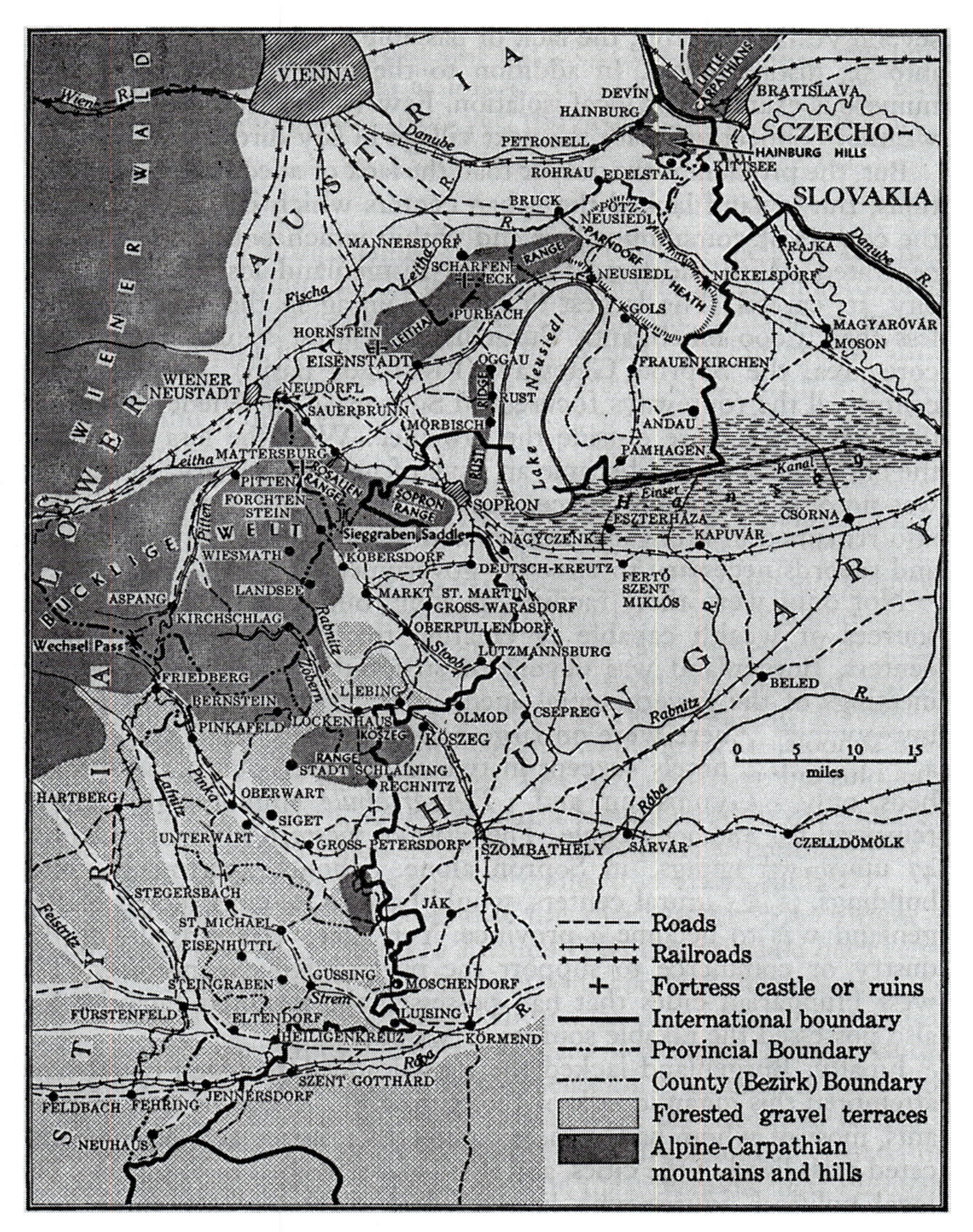

Figure 2.1 Map of Burgenland from Andrew F. Burghardt, *Borderland* (University of Wisconsin Press, 1962.) Reprinted by permission of The University of Wisconsin Press.

the communication of private thoughts and feelings in a letter could only be accomplished by means of insertion in a system governed, maintained, and monitored by the state – the postal system.[14] In his history of this institution Alvin F. Harlow notes that "The function of any state courier service in the Middle Ages was not only to handle dispatches, but to convey government officials engaged upon their sovereign's business. Consequently, when the posts came to be thrown open to public use, it was considered quite as meet for them to carry travelers as letters; and the history of posts all through the seventeenth and eighteenth centuries is also to a considerable extent the history of traveling."[15] This accounts for why a travel guide published in Vienna in 1789, *Geographisch- und topographisches Reisebuch durch alle Staaten der österreichischen Monarchie, nebst der Reiseroute nach Petersburg durch Polen*, also reads like a handbook to the imperial postal system, with detailed information on schedules and fares, even tips and bribes. Its annotated descriptions of the postal routes, with information of special interest to the tourist, can help us imagine what it was like to travel in Haydn's world.[16]

Route no. 6 led southeast from Vienna to Laxemburg, Wimpassing, and Größhoflein; however Eisenstadt is not on this itinerary, presumably because of its awkward location off the main road. The next postal station is Oedenburg (Sopron), described as a town of 11,000 with a thriving textile industry and a bustling meat market. From this strategic destination between two mountain ridges, postal route 6 continued south to Guns and Esseg, whereas Eszterháza lay to the east. Neither of the two main Eszterházy estates was accessible by means of the postal coaches.

In order to facilitate the operation of their numerous estates, the Esterházys maintained their own stations in Vienna, Wimpassing, Größhoflein, Eisenstadt, Oggau, and Oedenburg, staffed by twelve princely hussars. On the occasion of the wedding of Nicolaus's son, Anton, to Countess Erdödy in January 1763, the couple was married in the Hofburg, dined at the imperial table, then traveled to Eisenstadt, and still had time for a Te Deum in the chapel followed by an evening meal of sixty couverts.[17] The dinner hour for the nobility was usually around 2 p.m., and the road from Wimpassing to the castle was illuminated, which suggests that the procession started late in the day. Nightfall was apparently no obstacle to travel; the illumination merely added to the grandeur of the procession.

When Empress Maria Theresa visited Eszterháza in 1773 the *Pressburger Zeitung* reported that she arrived there after a five-hour trip from Vienna, though this is surely an error. Even under favorable conditions the *Reisebuch* estimates six hours to get from Vienna to Oedenburg. The journey from Vienna to Eszterháza must have taken two days, with Oedenburg a crucial stopping point. The Esterházy palace in Oedenburg was the residence of

Prince Nicolaus's son (the future Nicolaus II), and Haydn often rested there, as did Maria Theresa herself on her return trip from Eszterháza.[18]

Haydn's earliest extant letter of an entirely personal nature outlines his travel arrangements for a trip to Pressburg in 1786. He planned to leave Eszterháza with his own horses at 5 a.m. and arrive at Frauenkirchen around 9, where he asked to be met by Count Apponyi's carriage for arrival at Pressburg between 1 and 2 p.m. Despite the length of this journey, he could only stay for twenty-four hours.[19]

Haydn relied on a combination of the Esterházy network and the imperial post to send and receive mail, an apt metaphor of the overlap between his princely obligations and his entrepreneurial interests in the commercial world of Vienna. Though he informed Johann Traeg, "You need only leave your letter at the porter's in the Prince's mansion; a carriage leaves almost daily," he instructed another correspondent, "should you not find any safe and convenient opportunity in the Esterházy mansion, please send them next Monday by the diligence to the following address in Oedenburg: /A Monsieur/ Mons. Baumgartner, Princely Esterházy House-Master/a/Oedenburg/from whom I shall have them collected by my own carriage."[20]

Letters did not always reach their destination, so that manuscripts, money, and even reputations could be lost. A Haydn letter from May 30, 1790, to Maria Anna von Genzinger addresses her concern about a missing letter with the assurance "Your Grace need have no fear . . . because I always have in mind my respect for Your Grace's profound virtue," but there is nothing specifically compromising in the extant letters, even when Haydn is at his most coy: "I'm a poor creature! Always plagued by hard work, very few hours of recreation, and friends? What am I saying? One true one? There aren't any true friends any more – one lady friend? Oh yes! There might be one. But she's far away from me."[21]

The circulation of goods between Vienna and Hungary was hampered by the harsh economic policy of the Habsburgs vis-à-vis Hungary, and Haydn received physical as well as emotional nourishment in his letters from Genzinger.[22] Haydn's life at Eszterháza apparently hinged on extremes of luxury and privation. Descriptions of the Hungarian Paradise invariably dwell on the lavish furnishings, exquisite collections, and dazzling theatrical entertainments that won it so many accolades.[23] However, in a letter of 1781 Haydn requests "when you have an opportunity, please send back the cardboard cover in which the Lieder were packed: such material is not to be had here."[24] As part of the Habsburg strategy to break the resistance of the nobles to taxation, Hungary was shackled with high tariffs, and everything had to be imported from Vienna as domestic manufacturing was practically nonexistent.[25]

Fortunately Haydn received a great deal of goods in kind, including wine, candles, salt, meat, and grain, but luxuries that he had enjoyed in the capital were apparently difficult to obtain in what amounted to a colony. Even beef, one of the main Hungarian exports, seemed to be in short supply at Eszterháza. Despite the thriving meat market in nearby Oedenburg, Haydn complains to von Genzinger of eating a fifty-year-old cow (perhaps a reference to preserved meat, one item that Hungary did export). This is the economic climate in which Haydn is supposed to have bartered string quartets for razors.[26]

The Hungarian Orpheus: Capellmaster or Capellservant?

In 1785 the *Pressburger Zeitung* heralded Haydn as the "Hungarian Orpheus," though his residence in Hungary was but a footnote to the 1784 article in *European Magazine and London Review*, which has "Giuseppe Haydn" born in Vienna.[27] The tension between Haydn's residence in the Hungarian countryside and his cultural citizenship of Vienna is clearly evident in the letter he wrote to Thaddäus Huber, secretary of the Tonkünstler-Societät, in 1779. Protesting the unreasonable conditions attached to his admission, he asks, why? "Perhaps because I am a foreigner (*Auswärtiger*)? In my case, the 'foreign' means only that my person is of no use to the aborigines (*Inwärtigen*): through my works I'm quite aboriginal enough, and if not the composer, oh well, his children are there in almost every concert and provide many nice advantages."[28] Haydn's experience of his identity as foreigner or native, master or servant, was surely influenced by the disparate social, economic, and cultural circumstances of his Esterházy environments: the places he lived in and the people that surrounded him.

Because of the broad definition of the nobility in Hungary, approximately four to five percent of the population could claim noble status at this time, though many of these "gentlemen in sandals" were economically destitute, and lived in circumstances not much better than the peasants. In 1787 there were thirty-seven male nobles living in Eisenstadt, many of whom were unconnected to the Esterházy family, including a circle of Spanish noblemen and women who had settled in the town during the 1770s and 1780s. By contrast, the number of "true bourgeoisie" in Hungary was very low, perhaps only one and a half to two percent. As an officer of the Esterházy estate, Haydn would have been part of this tiny fraction of the population.[29]

Though Eisenstadt was part of Hungary at this time, the town itself was ethnically German, as were the majority of towns in Hungary in the eighteenth century, even Buda and Pest. Eisenstadt also had a sizable Jewish quarter, under the protection of the Esterházy family. Though contact between

Christian and Jew was discouraged, Haydn could not have failed to be aware of this community, as he would have daily passed by the Jewish quarter on his way to and from the palace from his accommodations in the Old Apothecary, which was west of the castle gate.[30]

Shortly after he was promoted to full Kapellmeister in 1766 Haydn purchased a house on the Klostergasse, to the east of the palace. Now he owned property, which included fields, woodlands, and a garden outside the town wall. The documents of the town administration record the activities of a typical householder in Haydn's disputes with neighbors, renovations, lawsuits, and other financial matters. In 1778 he sold the house, presumably due to the growing demands of the opera season at Eszterháza as well as fears of yet another fire.[31]

Despite its modest cultural and economic resources, the town of Eisenstadt provided Haydn with some degree of independence from the Esterházy estate. The same could not be said of the tiny village of Süttor, which was dwarfed by the castle originally named for it. A description from 1760 describes the residents as mostly Hungarian and puts the population at ninety-three (sixty-seven sons) whose professions included mason, weaver, cobbler, blacksmith, glazer, tailor, carpenter, joiner, and cimbalom player.[32] At Eszterháza, Haydn lived with the other musicians, singers, and traveling players in the Musicians' Building, a two-storied building of 250 rooms. It was from his apartment there – his primary residence after he sold his Eisenstadt house in 1778 – that he wrote his letters to von Genzinger.

Though the Esterházys often expressed their nationality as Hungarian nobles, especially when it suited their political purposes, the culture of their palaces was cosmospolitan and followed the fashions of the imperial court. By the 1760s the Esterházys had been effectively assimilated to Habsburg culture. Having converted to Catholicism, they no longer even spoke the Hungarian language and they were princes not of the kingdom of Hungary, but of the Holy Roman Empire. Both Paul Anton and Nicolaus had been educated at the University of Leyden and had married French-Italian and German princesses, respectively. Written communications were in German and Latin,[33] both in town and castle, though Joseph II made German the official language in Hungary in 1784. The majority of Haydn's letters are written in German, though he also wrote in Italian, as well as French and even English. As for Hungarian, Haydn probably had very little contact with the language, especially in Eisenstadt. There is no evidence that it was spoken or written within any of the Esterházy residences. Outside the palace gates of Eszterháza, it was a different matter.

The Hanság marsh, which has posed such a formidable barrier to travel throughout history, also marks an ethnic and linguistic divide between German-speakers to the west and Hungarians to the east (see Figure 2.1).[34]

This may account for Baron Riesbeck's fantastical description of the local population: "On the other side of the castle one doesn't need to make a day's journey to see Tartars, Hottentots, Iroquois and people from Tierra del Fuego living together and going about their various businesses."[35]

Clearly, the Hungarian residents of this region seemed exotic to Baron Riesbeck, a Swiss traveler. Did Haydn share this view? Vienna was a meeting-ground of nations where the languages most frequently heard were German, Italian, and French, but also Hungarian, Slavic languages, and modern Greek.[36] In Johann Pezzl's Vienna "you can often meet the Hungarian, striding stiffly, with his fur-lined dolman, his close-fitting trousers reaching almost to his ankles, and his long pigtail."[37] Nevertheless, Riesbeck was not the only traveler to find Hungary "bafflingly diverse."[38] Prince Nicolaus capitalized on the exoticism of Hungarian culture for the amusement of his guests.

The spectacle of thousands of loyal peasants singing and dancing to their traditional music became a predictable feature of the lavish Eszterháza fests in the 1770s in which the performance of Hungarian ethnicity was an intricate step in the minuet of power between the Empress and Prince Esterházy. In 1766 Maria Theresa had introduced reforms designed to alleviate the hardships of the peasants from their landlords (she is reputed to have thought Esterházy one of the cruelest). That same year peasant unrest in Sopron county had brought a crowd of peasants to the castle door, forcing the Prince to flee, and other reports suggest that relations between the local peasants and their landlord were far from harmonious.[39]

The Esterházy inn provided hospitality to visitors who could not be accommodated in the palace itself, and it also provided one of the few places for Esterházy musicians, grenadiers and other personnel to socialize. The unfortunate tavern brawl on the evening of June 23, 1771, that cost oboist Zacharias Pohl an eye has nevertheless left us with a number of accounts of nightlife at the inn, which consisted of music, dancing, and dice.[40] Though Haydn was often required to mediate disputes between the musicians, he was not in the tavern that night, if indeed he was in the habit of going at all. Clause 3 of his contract stipulated that he "conduct himself in an exemplary manner, so that the subordinates may follow the example of his good qualities; consequently said Joseph Heyden [*sic*] shall abstain from undue familiarity, from eating and drinking, and from other intercourse with them so that they will not lose the respect which is his due but on the contrary preserve it." No wonder Haydn wrote to von Genzinger in 1790 "Always plagued by hard work, very few hours of recreation, and friends? . . . There aren't any true friends any more."[41] For better and worse, Haydn, the "universal genius" hailed by the *European Review*, was now peerless both at home and abroad.

A man of letters

1779 was a pivotal year for Haydn, both personally and professionally. Luigia Polzelli joined the cappella with her husband, and soon became Haydn's mistress. In the opera house there were not one but two Haydn premieres (*La vera costanza* and *L'isola disabitata*) in addition to operas by Paisiello, Astaritta, Anfossi, Gazzaniga, Sarti, Piccinni, and others. Meanwhile, Haydn had received a new contract in January which permitted him to publish his compositions, so despite the demands of an increasingly ambitious opera season at Eszterháza, Haydn also began a correspondence with the Viennese firm of Artaria, which had begun publishing music the year before.

In Haydn's letters of the 1780s we can read of his increasing absorption in Josephinian Vienna, in which censorship was relaxed, publishing flourished, and new institutions like the masonic lodge and literary salon allowed for the exchange of intellectual ideas. Freemasonry was one of the primary vehicles of the Enlightenment in Vienna and the lodge "Zur wahren Eintracht" (True Concord), to which Haydn was admitted in 1785, published a literary journal as well as a scientific review; some of Vienna's most prominent intellectuals and nobles were members.[42]

One of the most prestigious salons was held by Franz Sales von Greiner, whose daughter Caroline Pichler has documented Haydn's presence there, if in a less than flattering light. Her opinion notwithstanding, Haydn seems to have been immersed in a world of letters in the early 1780s. From his letters to Artaria we learn that he was composing Lieder, a new genre for him, perhaps inspired by his contact with Greiner whom he consulted about the texts. He also wrote to the prominent Swiss literary figure, J. C. Lavater, who was a friend of the Greiner household. That his opening greeting, "I love and happily read your works," was intended to flatter does not rule out the possibility that it was also true.[43]

In a letter to Artaria, Haydn promises to sing his Lieder himself "in the critical houses."[44] One such opportunity was the concert that Haydn attended on Christmas Day, 1781, in honor of the visiting Russian Grand Duke and his consort. This concert is notable, not only as the likely first performance of the Op. 33 string quartets, and perhaps the Lieder, but because on this occasion Haydn's music was performed in a noble house outside the purview of the Esterházys' patronage. The Op. 33 string quartets were composed for publication by Artaria, and performed on this occasion by a mixture of Esterházy personnel and Viennese musicians (including Thaddäus Huber, the secretary of the Tonkünstler-Societät to whom Haydn had written in 1779). As the composer, and perhaps also singer, Haydn was recognized on this occasion with a bejeweled enamel box, one of many kudos he would receive over his lifetime.[45]

From minuets at the Redoutensaal to a revival of the oratorio *Il ritorno di Tobia*, Haydn's "children" did seem to be appearing frequently in Vienna, and often the father was present as well. Many of Haydn's letters make reference to his imminent arrivals or recent departures from Vienna. With Mozart, Dittersdorf, and Vanhal he played string quartets, and he counted Councillor Franz Bernhard von Keess, Michael Puchberg, Anton Liebe von Kreutzner, and Count Apponyi among his acquaintances. The *Reisebuch* paints a lively picture of social life in Vienna: the Ballhausplatz by day, and the Redouten by night; the Limonadehütten during the summer and Konzerte von Liebhabern during the winter months. There were plays, operas, even animal baiting, but also "Abendgesellschaften, held daily on certain days of the week in houses of nearly every standing, from the high nobility to the middle class. They begin usually at 7 p.m. and last until 10 p.m. One plays, makes music, dances, or engages in friendly conversation."[46] Haydn and von Genzinger, whose husband was one of Prince Esterházy's physicians, probably met at such an occasion, which sounds very much like "those wonderful parties? (*Gesellschaften*) Where the whole circle is one heart, one soul."

To return to the question of what circumstances prompted Haydn's feelings of isolation, the short answer might be: he began to write letters. In so doing Haydn developed relationships with businessmen, musicians, and amateurs in Vienna, thus enlarging his social and professional circle. The stipulation that he remain at Eszterháza even when the Prince himself was not there clearly hampered these relationships. Even if Haydn and von Genzinger were not lovers, theirs was an especially close friendship, and writing letters, especially with a female correspondent, was an invitation to engage in intimate conversation. Perhaps Haydn felt permitted (or even compelled) to express an affective interiority in his letters to von Genzinger that he did not reveal to his male correspondents.

Though Haydn's letter of February 1790 appears to record the spontaneous expression of his deepest feelings (to represent his self), it is highly rhetorical, beginning with the operatic cadences of a sentimental heroine: "Well, here I sit in my wilderness – forsaken – like a poor waif . . ." In the lament for "those past glorious days" there are echoes of "Dove sono i bei momenti" that Haydn had so recently heard, possibly even in the company of von Genzinger. Certain details of the letter point to the material conditions of Haydn's life that can be corroborated elsewhere. (For example, repairs made to his apartment later that year included a new stove.) But some of his complaints reflect his changing patterns of consumption.[47] The fluidity of Haydn's social status is also apparent in this letter, as his identity began to modulate between the courtly environment of Eszterháza, where his rank was clearly defined, to the emerging middle-class institutions in Vienna where he was negotiating his new role as an autonomous individual. Consequently Haydn's letter to Maria Anna von Genzinger of 1790 and the isolation that it portrays must be read in the context of his recent immersion in the cultural and social whirl of Vienna, where in the Christmas season of 1789–90 he participated in quartet parties, attended the latest Mozart operas (in performance and rehearsal), and indulged in the luxuries of an emerging consumer culture in the company of like-minded friends.

While it cannot be denied that Eszterháza was situated in a geographical wilderness far from the excitement of the capital, neither can one conclude that Haydn was cut off from the musical and cultural developments of his time. Ironically, the evidence of Haydn's experience of isolation comes primarily from his letters, the very existence of which indicates that he was indeed in communication with a growing circle of friends, colleagues, businessmen, and perhaps lovers in Vienna. Haydn's letters literally put him in circulation, in the social, commercial, and musical world of Vienna, as both a producer (of musical compositions) and a consumer (of luxurious commodities). In his letters to Artaria, Haydn asserts his authority over his musical works, but his letters to Maria Anna von Genzinger reveal Haydn as the author of a private life, and as such of a modern subjectivity that is the prerequisite for originality.

Postscript

One year after the letter of February 1790, Haydn's correspondence to von Genzinger records tribulations of a different nature. Writing from London on January 8, 1791, he recounts:

> My arrival caused a great sensation throughout the whole city, and I went the round of all the newspapers for 3 successive days. Everyone wants to know me. I had to dine out 6 times up to now, and if I wanted, I could dine out every day . . . After the concert I was taken to a handsome adjoining room, where a table for 200 persons, with many places set, was prepared for all the amateurs; I was supposed to be seated at the head of the table, but since I had dined out on that day and had eaten more than usual, I declined this honor, with the excuse that I was not feeling very well, but despite this I had to drink the harmonious health, in Burgundy, of all the gentlemen present; they all returned the toast, and then allowed me to be taken home. All this, my gracious lady, was very flattering to me, and yet I wished I could fly for a time to Vienna, to have more quiet in which to work.

Afraid he will miss the mail-coach Haydn signs off in his customary way, "Your Grace's most sincere and obedient servant, Joseph Haydn" but leaves a new return address: Mon[sieur] Haydn, Nro. 18 great Pulteney Street.

3 Haydn's aesthetics

JAMES WEBSTER

[Haydn's] theoretical *raisonnements* were very simple: A piece of music ought to have a fluent melody; coherent ideas; no superfluous ornaments, nothing overdone, no deafening accompaniments and so forth.[1]

Haydn's personality[2]

Until recently, it might have seemed odd to suggest that Haydn possessed anything resembling a coherent aesthetics. Such a notion is incompatible with the traditional image of "Papa Haydn": pious, good-humored, concerned for the welfare of others, proud of his students, regular in habits, conservative; but also naive and unreflective. However, this image is one-sided; it reflects the elderly and increasingly frail man encountered by his first biographers, Georg August Griesinger and Albert Christoph Dies.[3] For a more accurate sense of Haydn's personality, we must turn to his correspondence and other primary sources, insofar as possible from different periods of his life. These are more revealing than has usually been assumed, and convey a tangible sense of the man Haydn: the vigorous and productive composer, performer, Kapellmeister, impresario, businessman, conqueror of London, friend, husband, and lover. Once he is understood as a real person actively engaged in his world, it may seem plausible to inquire into his aesthetic beliefs.

Even the sobriquet "Papa" can be understood in more appropriate ways: as the "father of the symphony," obviously, but also in the sense of "patriarch," as implied by the resolution making him a life member of the Vienna Tonkünstler-Sozietät in 1797 "by virtue of his extraordinary merit as the father and reformer of the noble art of music."[4] Haydn's public career largely exemplified the Enlightenment ideal of the *honnête homme*:[5] the man whose good character and worldly success enable and justify each other; he has been described as the first artist of any kind to achieve European-wide celebrity in his own lifetime.[6] But in private it was a different matter. His marriage was unhappy; he was often lonely and at times melancholy. His character was not simple, but marked by a fundamental duality between earnestness and humor. Although Haydn's modesty was genuine, this too was part of his public persona; in private it was again a different matter. He took great pride in his works, notably including his vocal music.[7] He prized his status as an "original" and was sensitive to criticism. After Mozart's death he

Example 3.1 Example from Haydn's "London Notebook."

willingly accepted the role of greatest living composer; in London he actively defended his "rank" (as he called it) against his rival Pleyel.[8]

Although in no sense an intellectual or a connoisseur of literature, art, or philosophy, Haydn was interested all these subjects. In the 1780s he greatly valued Vienna's artistic and intellectual openness under Joseph II; he recruited important patrons and made close personal friends. His observations in his so-called "London Notebooks" reveal an active interest in every aspect of social life and culture, "high" and "low" alike.[9] In addition to German, he read and wrote Latin and Italian fluently. His library included not only treatises on music but also the complete works of Shakespeare (in English) and of Metastasio and Goldoni, as well as many works of literature and even philosophy; he also owned many engravings.[10] *This* person, I submit, will have had strong aesthetic beliefs. In what follows I focus on Haydn's own ideas, insofar as possible, as expressed in his own words: again, his letters and the London Notebooks permit us to control and augment the often tendentious reports and anecdotes in secondary sources.

Expression

Haydn's musical aesthetics by and large agreed with those current in the second half of the eighteenth century. The traditional foundations of music were imitation and expression,[11] but the purpose of a composition was to "move" the listener. Dies writes: "Haydn's initial aim (this much emerges from his vocal compositions) was always first of all to engage the senses by means of a rhythmically apt and attractive melody. Thereby in a subliminal manner he leads the listener to the primary goal: to move the heart in a manifold way."[12] This orientation assumed engaged listeners, who to be sure approached a composition with many preconceptions, but were prepared to follow its "argument," in a rhetorical sense.[13]

Regarding the necessity for expression, there was little difference between vocal and instrumental music for Haydn. What needs emphasis, because it conflicts with conventional wisdom, is the primacy of vocal music in his mind both generally and in terms of his own oeuvre. He recorded a touching example of vocal expressiveness in the London Notebooks (see Ex. 3.1): "A week before Pentecost I heard 4,000 children sing this song in St. Paul's

Cathedral. In my entire life no music has moved me as much as this reverent and innocent one."[14] Dies commented:

> He noted that the voices sounded like angels; that the descent to low B in the first three measures created a frightening, heartstopping effect, in that the notes died away in the delicate throats of the children and the B could be heard only as a hovering aura; and that in the continuation of the melody the ascending notes gradually increased in life and force and, in that the melody thereby gained light and shade, powerfully affected the expression.[15]

If Dies can be believed, Haydn here adumbrated an informal theory, no less, of the threefold relation between the construction of a melody (or a work), the manner of its production by particular performers in a particular setting, and the resulting effect. The Swedish diplomat Fredrik Samuel Silverstolpe reports his having invoked a correspondence between musical "actions" and the things represented:

> He showed me the aria . . . from *The Creation* [no. 6, "Rolling in foaming billows"] that is intended to portray the motion of the sea and the rocks rising out of it. "Look," he said in a joking tone, "see how the notes run up and down like waves? See too there the mountains, which rise out of the depths of the sea?"[16]

This sense of word-painting reflects the common eighteenth-century notion of a link between the "motions" (activity) within a composition and the "motions of the soul" it arouses or reflects.[17] But expression remained paramount; regarding the contrasting "Softly purling glides the limpid brook" in the major, Silverstolpe continues, "But as we came to the clear stream, oh! I was entirely carried away . . . [He] sang at the piano with a simplicity that went straight to the heart."

If the *Tonmalerei* in the vocal numbers of Haydn's oratorios often seems straightforward, the "Idea" or "Representation of Chaos" (the German *Vorstellung* implies both senses) is another matter. Swieten, who made many suggestions regarding the musical realization of both oratorios, merely commented in passing that "Chaos" might appropriately be rendered by "picturesque features" (*mahlerische Züge*)![18] At any rate Silverstolpe has Haydn address the issue of creating expressive value by technical means: "Eventually Haydn let me hear . . . the representation of Chaos. 'You have doubtless noticed how I have avoided the resolutions that one most expects. That is because nothing has yet assumed form.'"[19]

But instrumental music also demanded expression. Haydn wrote Mme Genzinger regarding the sonata Hob. XVI: 49: "This sonata . . . is meant forever for your grace alone . . . The Adagio . . . is very full of meaning (*hat sehr vieles zu bedeuten*), which I will analyze (*zergliedern*) for your grace at [the first] opportunity."[20] A titillating anecdote suggests that he thought of certain instrumental works as programmatic in a larger or more pervasive sense. In Griesinger's version:

> It would be very interesting to know from what motives Haydn created his compositions, as well as the feelings and ideas which he had in mind and which he strove to express in musical language . . . He related . . . that he had occasionally portrayed moral characters [*moralische Charaktere*] in his symphonies. In one of his oldest, which he however was no longer able to identify precisely, "the dominant idea [is] how God speaks to an unrepentant sinner, and pleads with him to reform; but the sinner in his foolishness pays no heed to the exhortations."[21]

Dies tells a similar story, according to which Haydn specified that the movement was an Adagio.[22] Its identity has been much speculated upon (Symphonies nos. 7, 22, 26 and 28 and the overture to *Der Götterrath* have been suggested), but no consensus has emerged.[23]

The topics of Haydn's "characteristic" symphonies, as they are most appropriately termed, are serious: time and the seasons, religious observance, "ethnically" significant melodic materials, the hunt, and associations with the theater or literary sayings.[24] Regarding ethnic material, Prince Nicolaus Esterházy fostered Hungarian cultural activity; he must have tolerated, and might have stimulated, Haydn's use of such materials in his art music, including several baryton works composed expressly for him.[25] It seems likely that such quotations and thematic references were a central part of eighteenth-century listeners' understanding,[26] possibly even comprising part of the "psychological material" of a given work, to be developed in conjunction with the development of the musical material in the conventional sense.[27] A different aspect of such material was what we would today call its "orientalism," for example the "Turkish" atmosphere frequently invoked in *L'incontro improvviso* of 1775 (similar to Mozart's *Die Entführung aus dem Serail* of 1782).[28]

Finally, Haydn's extramusical associations are linked to musical rhetoric generally. Again, this is most obvious in his vocal music, in which (like Handel) he was a brilliant and enthusiastic word-painter. No more than his "tailoring" his music for his audiences (see below) should this trait be taken as a fault or a "problem" (as was done in the age of "absolute music"). On the contrary, it is but one aspect of what has been called his "musical imagery,"[29] which comprises key associations (e.g., E♭ with the hereafter, as in "Behold, O weak and foolish man" in *The Seasons*), semantic associations (e.g., the flute with the pastoral, as in Symphony no. 6 and elsewhere in the 1761 "times of day" trilogy) and musical "conceptualizations" (e.g., long notes on "*E*-wigkeit" in *The Creation* or "ae-*ter*-num" in the late *Te Deum*).

But rhetoric is a matter not only of "figures" and topics, but also of contrasts in register, gestures, implications of genre, the rhythms of destabilization and recovery, and so on, especially as these play out over the course of an entire movement – all in order to "move the heart."

Melody

The importance of "fluent melody" (*fliessender Gesang*) emerges directly from Griesinger's familiar report (see the epigraph); similarly, Dies mentions melody alone as Haydn's means of "engaging" the listener (beginning of the section "Expression"). Many other sources testify to the importance of melody for Haydn. Robert Kimmerling, who studied with him around 1760 and later became director of music at the Benedictine monastery at Melk, wrote on an edition of Baldassare Galuppi's opera *Il mondo alla roversa, ossia le donne che comandano* (The world upside-down; or, the women who command): "NB: This excellent opera pleased my teacher Joseph Haydn. He recommended it to me . . . for continued study on account of its *good melody.*"[30]

According to Griesinger, late in life Haydn "criticized the fact that now so many musicians compose who have never learned how to sing. 'Singing must almost be reckoned one of the lost arts; instead of song, people allow the instruments to dominate.'"[31] In 1804 he wrote in a similar vein to Karl Friedrich Zelter, the director of the Singakademie in Berlin, praising his efforts to restore "the already half-forgotten art of singing."[32] In such utterances Haydn complains about what we might broadly refer to as the decline of "vocal culture" at the turn of the nineteenth century, both compositionally and in terms of performance.[33] Of particular interest is a much earlier letter praising his own Lieder (while disparaging Leopold Hofmann's "Gassenlieder"), in which he refers to himself as a performer: "I will sing [my songs] myself, in the best houses: a master must see to his rights by his presence and by correct performance (*wahrer Vortrag*)."[34]

Haydn insisted that the accompanying instruments not dominate the melody, especially when the latter is a singer. In 1795 he commented on a performance of Francesco Bianchi's *Acis and Galatea* in London: "The winds are very rich, and it seems to me that if they were reduced one would follow the melody more easily. The orchestra is larger this year, but as mechanical as ever: indiscreet in accompaniment."[35] The phrase "indiscreet in accompaniment" is almost a leitmotif of his attitude on these matters. A tangible manifestation of this principle is seen in Haydn's corrections to August Eberhard Müller's piano-vocal arrangement of *The Seasons*, many of which lighten Müller's over-heavy piano accompaniment[36] – including Swieten's notorious croaking frogs: "in the full orchestra this vulgar passage soon disappears, but it cannot remain in the piano score."[37] It is worth noting that Haydn's attitude on elaborate accompaniments was different from Mozart's, as his music altogether is leaner in texture, indeed often based on only three, or even two, real parts.

Ideas: originality

A central component of Haydn's self-image (as well as his reception) was originality.[38] The concept has several aspects: inspiration, particularly the faculty of inventing novel musical ideas; independence from influences; the concept of genius. Regarding inspiration, Haydn strikingly asserted that its source was improvisation. More precisely, he discovered or invented his musical "ideas" – a more varied and protean concept than mere "themes" – by "fantasizing" (*phantasieren*) at the keyboard, as Griesinger reports: "Haydn always composed his works at the keyboard. 'I sat down, began to fantasize, according to whether my mood was sad or happy, serious or playful, [until] I had seized upon an idea.'"[39] This was not (or was not restricted to) mere "noodling," or the making of cadenzas, but entailed purposeful, compositionally oriented activity. Despite Haydn's current reputation as an exponent of musical "logic," this emphasis on fantasy as a basis for composition is no different in principle from that described by C. P. E. Bach in the middle of the eighteenth century,[40] and insisted on by Heinrich Schenker.[41]

Silverstolpe reported: "I remember that one day he had just rejected and crossed out the finale of a string quartet, in order to write a different finale: 'The previous one,' he said, 'is only an *exercise*; it does not flow freely from the source.'"[42] Here Haydn contrasts merely correct composition with that based on inspiration, which "flows freely"; the implication is that its "source" lies before, or beyond, rational thought. The distinction between artistic creation and mere craftsmanship also informs Griesinger's more familiar anecdote:

> Haydn was informed of Albrechtsberger's opinion that all fourths should be banished from strict composition. "What good is that?" replied Haydn. "Art is free, and should not be inhibited by artisans' fetters (*Handwerksfesseln*). The ear must decide – a trained ear, of course – and I am as competent to make laws in this respect as anyone else. Such affectations are useless; I would rather that somebody tried to compose a really *new* kind of minuet."[43]

These words were not merely laid in Haydn's mouth; in 1779 he wrote to the Tonkünstler-Sozietät in almost identical terms: "The fine arts (*freye Künste*) and the so beautiful science of composition tolerate no *Handwerksfesseln*: the spirit and the soul must be free, if one wishes to be of service to the widows and to attain one's just deserts."[44] Access to artistic "laws" is open to persons who have both training and experience, and taste; their judgments are at once individual and definitive. (The latter point resonates with Kant's theory of aesthetic judgments; see below.) At the same time, the demand for "freedom" testifies to artists' rapidly growing bourgeois aspirations towards the close of the eighteenth century.[45]

Originality on the largest scale is addressed in Griesinger's famous account of Haydn's conditions at the Esterházy court:

> Although Haydn's outward situation was anything but brilliant, it provided him the ideal opportunity for the development of his many-sided talent. "My prince was satisfied with all my works, I received praise; as head of an orchestra I was able to make experiments, observe what makes a [good] effect and what weakens it, and thus revise, expand, cut, take chances; I was cut off from the world, nobody around me could upset my self-confidence, and so I had to become original (*mußte ich original werden*)."[46]

Griesinger sets the stage for his quotation by invoking (falsely) a common trope in discourses about artists: the contrast between their modest outward circumstances and the excellence of their works. (Haydn's situation was scarcely modest; the Esterházy court was one of the richest in Europe, and Nicolaus lavished his full resources and attention on his musical establishment.) Haydn's continuation (as transmitted) is a remarkable rhetorical construction: an elaborate periodic sentence, which postpones the main point until the end.[47] He addresses three aspects of his music-making in turn – social, technical, psychological/aesthetic – and thus implies an essential connectedness among these domains (compare his complex account of the children's melody). He begins modestly, in conformity to his position at court, by placing Esterházy in the subject position ("my prince was satisfied"); even when Haydn names himself, he employs an implicitly passive construction ("I received approval"). Only when he turns to the technical domain does he become the subject: "I could experiment" regarding instrumental balance, effectiveness, large-scale proportions and so forth. None of these points yet pertains to originality as such, except perhaps the final verb: "take chances" (*wagen*). But Haydn still approaches his goal indirectly, via a detour into psychology: it was because he was isolated in the Hungarian "wasteland" (*Einöde*), as he called it elsewhere,[48] that he had no choice but "to become original." Even at this climax he again uses an implied passive, attributing his success in effect to the force of circumstance – but also implying that it was in some sense inevitable, the result of a force of nature. As we shall see, this claim links up to central aesthetic notions of his time.

What Haydn meant by "original" in this context was presumably that he belonged to no "school" and acknowledged few if any models. When Griesinger inquired about a report that Sammartini had been the inspiration for his early string quartets, he brusquely rejected it: "He had heard Sammartini's music, but had never valued it, 'because Sammartini was a dauber (*Schmierer*)' . . . and said that he recognized only Emanuel Bach as his model." On the other hand, Haydn's utterances reveal his awareness that the traditional aesthetics of mimesis (imitation) was gradually being supplanted by the aesthetics of expression, with its demands for "inspiration" and "originality" in a proto-Romantic sense.

Ideas: coherence

Griesinger's account (epigraph) moves directly from melody to "coherent ideas" (*zusammenhängende Ideen*). Haydn returned to this point soon thereafter, immediately after emphasizing his improvisatory methods:

> Once I had seized upon an idea, my whole endeavor was to develop and sustain it in keeping with the rules of the art . . . This is what so many younger composers lack: they string one little idea after another; they break off when they have scarcely begun. Hence nothing remains in the heart after one has heard it.[49]

Here Haydn states that violation of the principle of coherence – whereby the "rules of the art" are principles, not prescriptions or proscriptions – runs the risk of aesthetic failure: if the development is not logical and consistent, "nothing remains in the heart." Silverstolpe's account of Haydn's teaching has the same burden:

> Once, when I visited Haydn, he was looking through a work of a student . . . The longer he read, the darker became his expression. "I have nothing to criticize about the part-writing," he said, "it is correct. However, the proportions are not as I would wish. Look here: this idea is only half complete; it shouldn't be abandoned so quickly. And this phrase is poorly related to the others. Try to give a proper balance to the whole; that can't be too difficult, because the main idea is good."[50]

An important aspect of Haydn's demand for coherence was his self-criticism (see Silverstolpe on the rejected quartet-finale). In March 1792 he wrote Mme Genzinger from London regarding Symphony no. 93, which he had just premiered:

> I cannot send Your Grace the symphony, which is dedicated to you . . . because I intend to alter the finale, and to improve it, since it is too weak compared with the preceding movements. I was persuaded of this myself, and by the public as well, when I produced it the first time . . . notwithstanding, which the symphony made the most profound impression on the audience.[51]

(Note again the lack of modesty.) Griesinger quotes the composer: "From the mass of his compositions one might infer that Haydn must have worked very easily. That was not the case. 'I was never a hasty writer [*Geschwindschreiber*], and always composed with reflection (*Bedächtlichkeit*) and diligence. Such productions are also meant to last.'"[52] Haydn's *Bedächtigkeit* (the modern form) resonates with E. T. A. Hoffmann's famous attribution of *Besonnenheit* (self-possession) to Beethoven. The final sentence is typical of the composer's conviction late in life that his works would outlive him – that he would become a classic. Griesinger quotes him elsewhere: "When a master has produced one or two outstanding works, his fame is assured; my *Creation* will survive, and probably *The Seasons* as well."[53]

Other aesthetic principles

Correctness. We have already noted Haydn's denigration of "artisans' fetters" in comparison to the "rules of the art." In fact, although he naturally set considerable store by correctness in technical matters (compare his initial comment to the student), he was both willing to take liberties and sensitive to criticism of his part-writing. This emerges from numerous comments in both Griesinger and Dies, as well as his own occasional notations of "con licenza" and the like in his autographs.[54] A letter to Härtel regarding the publication of *The Creation* betrays his sensitivity (he underlined the entire quoted passage):

> I only wish and hope that the worthy reviewers won't pull the hair of my *Creation* too strongly. Of course a few passages, or perhaps other little things, may offend somewhat with respect to musical grammar; but every true connoisseur will grasp their motivation – just as I do – and will rise above this bone of contention: "no rule without its exception."[55]

Variety; wit; stylistic mixture. Like all eighteenth-century musicians, Haydn subscribed to the principle of variety within unity. Occasionally he was concerned with variety for its own sake. When composing his second set of lieder in the early 1780s, he wrote his publisher Artaria: "I would very much like to have three new, tender Lied-texts . . . because almost all the others are cheerful in expression – the content could also be sad – so that

I have light and shade, as in the first twelve."[56] The concept of "light and shade," also found in his description of the children singing at St. Paul's, was likewise common in eighteenth-century writings; it can be glossed as the art-historical concept *chiaroscuro*. Insofar as it was positive, the initial reception of *The Seasons* emphasized its variety, in comparison to *The Creation*.[57]

The topic of Haydn's humor is so familiar that I need not dwell on it here, except to emphasize that the governing concept is "wit," with its connotations of intelligence and originality in addition to mere joking and high spirits.[58] One aspect of Haydn's wit relates to variety: his tendency to juxtapose contrasting stylistic levels, something he did all his life. He did this even in church music, as Griesinger reports:

> In the "Creation Mass" it occurred to him, as he was composing "Qui tollis peccata mundi" in the Gloria, that we poor mortals after all chiefly sin only against moderation and chastity. Hence he set the words "qui tollis peccata, peccata mundi" to the playful melody from the passage in *The Creation* [No. 32], "The dew-dropping morn, O how she quickens all!" However, so that this worldly notion would not be too prominent, he had the full chorus burst in with "Miserere" immediately thereafter.[59]

This intrusion of "profane" music into this mass (1801) so offended the Empress Marie Therese (who in general adored Haydn and his music)[60] that she ordered that the passage be changed in the materials used at the *Hofkapelle*. In fact, however, such stylistic mixtures were fundamental to Haydn's music, notwithstanding that they offended critics from the 1760s in Berlin[61] until at least the 1970s,[62] many of whom manifested a deep ambivalence towards Haydn's (and Mozart's) sacred vocal music altogether.

Correct performance; "Delikatesse." Haydn believed that his own participation was necessary for good performances of his music, in part because of what he called its *Delikatesse* (refinement or subtlety). In June 1802 he wrote Prince Nicolaus Esterházy II, asking permission to decline the Grand Duke of Tuscany's request to be supplied with two masses; one reason was that "without my direction they will inevitably lose the greatest part of their value, on account of their subtlety, which would greatly compromise my efforts [on your behalf], and be highly unpleasant to me personally."[63] (The Prince "suggested" that he comply nonetheless.) On another occasion he wrote Mme Genzinger regarding Symphonies nos. 95 and 96: "Please ask Herr Kees on my behalf to have a rehearsal of each symphony, because they are very subtle (*delicat*), especially the finale of [no. 96], in which I recommend the softest *piano* possible and a very fast tempo."[64]

The issue of rehearsals came up often during Haydn's later years; the implication is that many performances were still carried out more or less at sight. This seems remarkable for works as "subtle" as the "London"

Symphonies, although one presumes that in London, under Haydn's direction, these works must have been adequately rehearsed. An indirect confirmation emerges from his notebooks: "On 30 March 1795 I was invited to a big concert in Freemasons Hall by Dr. [Samuel] Arnold and his associates; a grand symphony was to have been performed under my direction. But since they didn't want to offer me a rehearsal, I refused and did not appear."[65] Later he felt it necessary to give instruction to a canon regarding a performance of the *Mass in Time of War* (1796) planned for Ljubljana (in present-day Slovenia):

> [Haydn] sang the beginnings of most of the movements, so that the canon could hear both the various tempos and, here and there, the correct expression. [The canon] should instruct the performers, both individually and as a group; in particular, they should refrain from any sort of ornamentation, which could have no effect other than to disfigure such a subtle [*delikat*] composition: for it already includes all possible expression in itself anyway, just as it is; and the greatest beauty is dependent solely on the correct tempo, [bringing out] the proper light and shade, and precise execution.[66]

The topics covered included tempo, expression, precision, and (again) "light and shade," as well as Haydn's insistence that there be no additional ornamentation. The latter attitude, which admittedly comes from the end of his long career, seems almost Beethovenish.

"*Tailoring.*" Like any eighteenth-century composer, Haydn routinely accommodated, or "tailored" as Mozart would have said,[67] his music to the performers and circumstances for which they were destined. His letter regarding the cantata *Applausus* (1768; Haydn received the commission via a middleman) is often quoted for its detailed instructions on performing practice, but concludes with a less familiar comment: "If with this work I have perhaps failed to divine the taste of the musicians, I am not to be blamed for this, because neither the persons nor the place are known to me; the fact that they were concealed from me truly made my work distasteful."[68] (Less distasteful, we may presume, was the fee of a hundred gulden, equivalent to about a quarter of his annual salary at the Esterházy court.) What is significant here is not Haydn's ill-temper, but his assumption that ordinarily he would compose "for" the performers and the occasion as a matter of course. In 1789 he willingly revised the piano trio Hob. XV: 13 at Artaria's request: "I enclose herewith the third piano trio, which I have composed entirely anew, with variations, according to your taste."[69] The point was not Artaria's taste, of course, but that of the potential market for Haydn's music. Another example of "tailoring" is his systematic differentiation in his London piano works of 1794–95 between a difficult, extroverted style for

Therese Jansen, a noted virtuoso, and a less demanding one for his lover Rebecca Schroeter and other female amateurs.[70] Of course, composing "for" his audiences in this way, whether Prince Esterházy or the anonymous publics who purchased his 1780s instrumental music, entailed no compromise of his artistic integrity or level of achievement.

Haydn's aesthetics; Haydn's style

A word is necessary regarding the relation between these aesthetic principles and Haydn's style as we understand it today. In many ways it can be interpreted as analogous to the duality in his personality between earnestness and humor. He implied as much when saying that he fantasized "according to whether my mood was sad *or* happy, serious *or* trifling" (emphasis added). Of course, in his music these qualities are not unmediated binary opposites but poles of a continuum. Admittedly, since about 1800 Haydn's wit has been the better understood pole. But "wit" signifies intelligence as well as humor, and Haydn's often shades into irony, as was recognized by his contemporaries. Johann Karl Friedrich Triest wrote in 1801: "Haydn might perhaps be compared, in respect to the fruitfulness of his imagination, with our Jean Paul [Richter] (omitting, obviously, the latter's chaotic design; transparent representation is not the least of Haydn's virtues); or, in respect to his humor and original wit (*Laune*), with Lor. Sterne";[71] Jean Paul and especially Sterne are touchstones of irony in fiction.[72] In fact, however, Haydn's irony goes beyond humor: a passage may be deceptive in character or function (the D major interlude in the first movement of the "Farewell" Symphony sounds like a minuet out of context, but it is not a minuet and plays a crucial tonal and psychological role; more generally, both this symphony and no. 46 systematically subvert generic norms); a movement may systematically subvert listeners' expectations until (or even past) the end (the finales of the quartets Op. 33 no. 2 and Op. 54 no. 2); or he may "problematize" music rather than merely compose it (the tonal ambiguity in Op. 33 no. 1).[73]

In any case, earnestness and depth of feeling are equally important in Haydn's art. The slow introductions to the "London" Symphonies are implicit invocations of the sublime (especially clear in no. 103, with its resemblance to the "Dies irae," a passage that may have influenced Berlioz's *Symphonie fantastique*). The sublime then became overt in the Chaos–Light sequence in *The Creation* and elsewhere in the late sacred vocal music.[74] Many works that were later taken as humorous Haydn did not intend as such, including the "Farewell" and "Surprise" symphonies (the drum-stroke in the latter was his "brilliant début" in the 1792 London season, in the context of his rivalry with Pleyel).[75] Similarly, even at his wittiest or most eccentric he never abandons tonal and formal coherence. One should be skeptical of any simplistic correlation between this opposition – earnestness vs. wit – and other common oppositions of Haydn's time; for example, traditional or learned vs. modern or galant style. Still less may we equate it with the distinction "art" vs. "entertainment," and least of all with any supposed differences in artistic quality. Haydn's early string quartets, which are on the "light" side stylistically, are arguably his most polished works of the 1750s; the baryton trios and lyre notturni are finely wrought compositions, as rewarding in their way as the raw expressionism of the "Sturm und Drang."[76]

The principle of variety within unity led Haydn, again in distinction to Mozart, to base a given movement on a single main idea, which his "whole endeavor was to develop and sustain" in manifold, ever-new ways. Thus the so-called "second theme" of his sonata forms is often a variant of the opening theme. To be sure, the working-out usually entails contrasting effects ("light and shade"): the second theme usually differs in treatment, and the recapitulation brings new developments. In his double-variation slow movements the alternating major and minor themes are usually variants of each other; the stylistic dualities in his late sacred vocal music now seem as exhilarating as the similar mixtures in *Die Zauberflöte.* Both novelty and continuity are maintained from beginning to end.

In one respect, however, Haydn did court a union (not merely a juxtaposition) of opposites: his "popular" style that simultaneously addressed the connoisseur. Triest wrote: "If one wanted to describe the character of Haydn's compositions in just two words, they would be . . . artful popularity or popular (easily comprehensible, effective) artfulness."[77] No other composer – certainly not C. P. E. Bach or Mozart, notwithstanding their hopeful appeals to both "Kenner" and "Liebhaber" – could match Haydn's ostensibly simple or folklike tunes, or broadly humorous sallies, that conceal (or develop into) the highest art. One of the best early comments on Haydn's music was Ernst Ludwig Gerber's, that he "possessed the great art of appearing familiar in his themes."[78] That is, their "popular" character is neither merely given, nor an unmediated utterance of "Papa Haydn," but the calculated result (*appearing* familiar) of sophisticated artistic shaping ("great art"). This becomes obvious when Haydn employs tunes from cultures other than his own, as in the "Croatian" theme in the Andante of Symphony no. 103 and the bordun-like theme of the finale of no. 104. In the former, the piquant raised fourth degree is not part of a quotation, but is assimilated into a theme appropriate to a grand symphony. This becomes clear no later than the mini-reprise towards the end of the second strain of the theme, when the melody suddenly turns up in the bass.[79]

Haydn, Kant, and genius

Haydn's aesthetic principles were coherent, consciously held, an active part of his artistic personality. But, when all is said and done, they were conventional: to move the listener by means of melody, original ideas animated by "fantasy," and coherent development. And yet Haydn's art is everything but ordinary. How to reconcile these two aspects? Clearly, although we might be able to infer from his principles what kind of artist he was, it would be a hopeless task to infer what his music sounds like, still less how great it is.

This inability to "predict" Haydn's art from his aesthetic notions of those of his time has an uncanny resonance with his and his contemporaries' beliefs about originality and genius. After summarizing Haydn's *raisonnements* (epigraph), Griesinger continues: "But how to satisfy these requirements? That, [Haydn] admitted, cannot be learnt by any rules; it depends entirely on natural talent and the inspiration of inward genius."[80] This statement amounts to a précis of Kant's often quoted account of genius in the *Critique of Judgment*:

> . . . genius is a *talent* for producing something for which no determinate rule can be given: not a disposition towards a skill at something that can be learned by following some rule or other; hence its foremost property must be *originality* . . .
>
> Genius cannot itself describe or indicate theoretically how it brings about its productions . . . and therefore the author of a production that he owes to his genius does not himself know how the ideas for it come to him, nor has it in his power to think them out at will or according to plan, or to communicate them to others by means of instructions that [would] enable them to generate comparable productions.[81]

Indeed Griesinger himself quotes from this passage in the paragraph devoted to Haydn's *raisonnements*. And Haydn's contemporaries had been referring to him as a "genius" since the 1780s.[82]

Kant's insistence that the chief distinguishing characteristic of genius is originality suggests that we revisit Haydn's "and so I had to become original." This utterance is weary from unreflective hagiographical citation; especially regrettable is its (often unconscious) function in crudely evolutionist interpretations of his career: if he had to "become" original, there must have been an earlier phase in which he was not yet so. My attempt at a less simplistic interpretation (above) is not the only recent one.[83] But I would suggest that Haydn actually got it wrong. Once again he was too modest: his formulation implies that any talented and hard-working composer in the same circumstances might have "had" to become original. But by Kant's precepts, and our sense of things, that is false; nobody else in the history of music could have done what he did. Indeed, if one takes Kant seriously, one must conclude that he did not become original at all! For if he was truly "an original" – a genius, a force of nature – he must have been so from the beginning. And so he was, as connoisseurs of his early music have long argued.

From this point of view, the primary significance of Haydn's aesthetics is what it may say to us. A more accurate and nuanced sense of his artistic beliefs should become part and parcel of an increasingly realistic image of his personality altogether, as it has developed during the last quarter-century. And that image – notwithstanding "persona theory" and postmodern speculations about the "death of the artist" – *is* related to our understanding of his art. It isn't possible to believe in "Papa Haydn" and simultaneously to appreciate the violent expressionism of the "Sturm und Drang," the tonal and gestural subtleties of the string quartets of the 1780s, the boldness and originality of the "London" Symphonies, the sublimity of his sacred vocal music, or the sentiment of his piano music, Lieder, and part-songs. The reverse is also true: the man who composed such music must have reflected on it and on what he was doing, must have had "larger" intentions in mind – as his notions about his own music indicate. Haydn wanted to "move the heart" not only in his own day, but more than two hundred years later, and beyond.

4 First among equals: Haydn and his fellow composers

DAVID WYN JONES

A striking paradox of Haydn's career is that he traveled very little until the two London visits of the 1790s, yet achieved a degree of international eminence that was unequaled in his time. While composers such as Gluck (1714–87), Hasse (1699–1783) and Mozart (1756–91) traveled extensively they never achieved the same durable, self-perpetuating fame that accrued to Haydn during his lifetime. It was without any poetic hyperbole, therefore, that Griesinger was able to write the following encomium near the beginning of his celebrated biography of the composer.

> Haydn was founder of an epoch in musical culture, and the sound of his harmonies, universally understood, did more than all written matter together to promote the honor of German artistic talent in the remotest lands. Haydn's quartets and symphonies, his oratorios and church pieces, please alike on the Danube and on the Thames, on the Seine and the Neva, and they are treasured and admired across the sea as in our own part of the world.[1]

Throughout his biography Griesinger manages to convey the impression that fame was something that happened to Haydn and was not, as in the cases of Gluck, Hasse, Mozart, and others, something that had been actively sought. While this willfully ignores the more opportunistic, ambitious side of Haydn's personality it also conveniently plays into another aspect of the composer's character nurtured by Griesinger: the thoughtful creative figure who was isolated and who achieved greatness alone. On the many years at Eszterháza he was able to quote Haydn directly: "I was set apart from the world, there was nobody in my vicinity to confuse and annoy me in my course, and so I had to be original."[2] Innocence, isolation, and originality are recurring themes in Haydn's posthumous image, qualities that could be set alongside the very different images of the divine, misunderstood Mozart and the difficult, revolutionary Beethoven. A more considered and pluralistic view of Haydn's relationship with his contemporaries yields a picture that is, not surprisingly, much more complex, but also one that fosters a truer understanding of the nature of this fame.

A product of his musical environment

Haydn was scathing about his formal music training at St. Stephen's in Vienna, telling Griesinger that he received only two lessons from Georg Reutter (1708–72), the Kapellmeister. Although some other notable musicians in Vienna are mentioned as potentially significant influences on the young Haydn, including Gluck, Porpora (1686–1768), and Wagenseil (1715–77), the author prefers to stress that Haydn was largely self-taught. Porpora, who was at the end of a distinguished career as a composer of Italian opera, taught singing in Vienna using Haydn as an accompanist. Two decades later Haydn was to credit him with instilling "the true fundamentals of composition."[3] Griesinger makes no detailed comment on Porpora's influence and Wagenseil, too, is mentioned only in passing. The latter omission is particularly unfortunate since Wagenseil's music so frequently anticipates Haydn's earliest works that he can claim to have been a major formative figure. His six divertimentos for harpsichord, Op. 1 (Vienna, 1753) have many formal and stylistic characteristics that were to feature in Haydn's earliest sonatas, while Wagenseil's output of symphonies, over a hundred in number, share the following in common with many of Haydn's earliest symphonies: three movements, thematic material that is predominantly rhythmic rather than melodic, second-subject areas that include a deflection to the dominant minor, slow movements for strings alone, and finales in 3/8.[4]

More significant, according to Griesinger, than any composer resident in Vienna in the mid-century was C. P. E. Bach (1714–88), then employed as a cembalo player at the court of Frederick the Great in Berlin. Griesinger quotes Haydn directly: "whoever knows me thoroughly must discover that I owe a great deal to Emanuel Bach, that I understood him and have studied him diligently."[5] At first this statement seems strange since very little of Haydn's music sounds like Bach, whereas echoes of Porpora and Wagenseil are plentiful. His influence is best sought in two areas, structural procedures and musical orthography. The practice of incorporating embellishment within the compositional process rather than as an aspect of extempore performance practice shows the influence of the north German composer, particularly when there is a formal repetition of a theme or section. Bach wrote an influential treatise, *Versuch über die wahre Art das Clavier zu spielen*, published in two parts, in 1753 and 1762. Haydn would have valued its authoritative treatment of various aspects of music theory and its commitment to vivid performance; when he deliberately changed several aspects of his musical notation in the 1760s, such as notating appoggiaturas in real note values rather in standardized eighth-notes, he did so to reflect Bach's practice.[6]

It was inevitable that in a laudatory biography like Griesinger's Haydn's immediate contemporaries should not figure very much in the narrative, in case they drew attention from the central figure, but broad consideration of the composers who lived and worked in the same musical environment helps to define the expected and the unexpected in Haydn's creative life.

Haydn was one of a generation of Austrian composers born in the 1730s and who were to have active careers up to – and, in some cases, beyond – the end of the century: Albrechtsberger (1736–1809), Dittersdorf (1739–99), Michael Haydn (1737–1806), Hofmann (1738–93), Ordonez (1734–86) and Vanhal (1739–1813). While there is ample evidence that they all knew each other and each other's music, continual interaction, such as one imagines to have existed amongst the composers based at Mannheim, was not a defining feature of their relationship. All pursued careers independent of each other, sustained, in different ways, by the secular and sacred institutions, the abbeys, aristocratic courts, and churches, that provided the bedrock of musical patronage in eighteenth-century Austria. Only Albrechtsberger and Hofmann were supported by the Habsburg court in Vienna, though Joseph and Michael Haydn were favored composers of Empress Marie Therese at the turn of the century.[7] Also characteristic of their careers is how little they traveled. Only Dittersdorf and Vanhal visited Italy, both in their early twenties, and all were content, to a greater or lesser extent, to pursue their musical development within the Austrian territories. Those composers who were employed by sacred institutions, Albrechtsberger, Michael Haydn, and Hofmann, managed to follow a career that was comparatively uniform in character; other composers, notably Dittersdorf and Vanhal as well as Joseph Haydn, were forced to adjust their musical output to changing circumstances, Dittersdorf concentrating in the last years of his life on German opera, Vanhal on piano music, and Joseph Haydn on the opportunities that London and Vienna provided.

While the careers and immediate reputation of these composers were sustained by the characteristics of local musical life there was, too, a distinctive distribution of their instrumental music beyond the Austrian territories. The catalogues of French, English, and German publishers from the 1760s onwards increasingly feature the music of Dittersdorf, Joseph Haydn, and Vanhal in particular, and all were the victims of casual or willful misattribution, with each other and with others.

As regards the output of these composers they all wrote in the instrumental genres of concerto, symphony, and quartet, sometimes prolifically – Dittersdorf is credited with 116 symphonies and Vanhal with fifty-three quartets, for instance – but equally noticeable are a common interest in liturgical music and a comparative neglect of Italian opera.

The central role of the Catholic church in Austrian society is reflected by the large quantity of church music; over 170 masses are attributed to Albrechtsberger, Dittersdorf, Michael Haydn, Hofmann, and Vanhal. Joseph

Haydn's early musical experiences, from a schoolboy at Hainburg to the freelance years in Vienna in the 1750s, were predominantly those associated with the church and, at this stage in his life, he might well have anticipated a career that featured a similar emphasis on church music.[8] In the event, circumstances ensured that church music did not become central to Haydn's creativity until the last phase of his life, when the interest of Prince Nicolaus II encouraged the composition and performance of the six late masses. If the composition of church music was irregular and the number of works fewer than those by Michael Haydn, in particular, surviving sources in the Austrian territories for Joseph Haydn's church music, whether original or contrafacta, is a useful reminder, nevertheless, that for many Austrians up to the 1780s he was as much associated with church music as he was with symphonies and quartets.

The role of Italian opera in the output of these composers is quite different, but, again, Haydn's situation is untypical. Between them Albrechtsberger, Dittersdorf, Michael Haydn, Hofmann, Ordonez, and Vanhal composed only seventeen Italian operas. The reasons for this are general as well as specific. As was the case throughout Europe it was an accepted assumption that idiomatic Italian opera was best provided by Italians, despite the very conspicuous careers in Vienna of Gassmann (1729–84) and Gluck; during the 1750s, the formative years of Haydn and his contemporaries, Vienna was dominated by French rather than Italian opera; and those composers, such as Albrechtsberger and Hofmann, who very early in their professional lives settled into careers supported by sacred institutions, never came into professional contact with the theater. Like his fellow composers born in the 1730s Haydn might well have contemplated a career in which he composed no Italian opera. It was only because of Prince Nicolaus's consuming interest in the genre that it became central to Haydn's existence as Kapellmeister at the Esterházy court.

This commitment to opera is well documented but the peculiar nature of Haydn's relationship with the repertoire and its composers is less commonly remarked upon. Eszterháza had a busy opera house but its resident composer was never to visit Italy and, at first, had limited experience of the genre. Over time, from the late 1760s to 1790, Haydn, as the Esterházy Kapellmeister responsible for adapting and directing over a hundred stage works for the court became thoroughly acquainted with representative works by most of the leading opera composers of the day, including Anfossi (1727–97), Cimarosa (1749–1801), Gluck, Guglielmi (1728–1804), Paisiello (1740–1816), Piccinni (1728–1800), Sarti (1729–1802) and Salieri (1750–1825), but only Sarti traveled to Eszterháza to witness performances of his music.[9] Remote in the Hungarian countryside Eszterháza could not vie with major centers for Italian opera north of the Alps, like London, St. Petersburg, and

Stuttgart. Italian became Haydn's second language, which he spoke with the many singers who came and went (particularly with Luigia Polzelli, his mistress, who stayed), but the world of Italian opera was substantially experienced through the distorting prism of Eszterháza. In the 1780s, when Vienna became a major center for Italian opera and Haydn is known to have attended performances of Mozart's *Così fan tutte* and *Le nozze di Figaro*, for instance, the composer's visits to the city were so short, typically a few weeks either side of Christmas, that sustained interaction with Mozart, as opposed to stunned admiration of his genius as a dramatic composer, was not possible.[10]

In contrast with operatic life at the Esterházy court, very little detail is known about the performances of instrumental music there. According to Haydn's first contract (1761) he was required to "appear daily (whether here in Vienna or in the estates) in the antechamber before and after midday and enquire whether a high princely *ordre* for a musical performance has been given."[11] The repertoire of these musical performances is educated guesswork. Haydn's own compositions were probably more central than they were in the Italian opera house; nevertheless the musical manuscripts that have survived, the occasional document, and what can be reasonably deduced from the practice of other courts suggest that music by other composers, including symphonies and concertos, were regularly played. Haydn's statement that he was "set apart from the rest of the world" was true in a geographical sense – Eszterháza was a day's journey from Eisenstadt, which, in turn, was a day's journey from Vienna – but Haydn was not composing instrumental music in a vacuum.

Developing the tale of two great composers: Haydn and Mozart

Of his immediate contemporaries it might be thought that Joseph Haydn would have maintained most contact with his brother, Michael, who, from 1763, was based at the archiepiscopal court in Salzburg. It seems, however, that contact was minimal, even non-existent, up to 1798, when the two once more became close. Dittersdorf was probably the composer who was most often in touch with Haydn up to the 1780s. Griesinger and Dies both recount the story of the two composers wandering the streets of Vienna at night when they heard some dance music by Haydn; Dittersdorf's own autobiography states that the two were regularly together during the summer of 1763 and the following winter; three of Dittersdorf's Italian operas were performed at Eszterháza in the mid 1770s, *Il finto pazzo per amore*, *Il barone di rocca antiqua* and *Arcifanfano, rè de' Matti*; several symphonies by Dittersdorf were acquired by the Esterházy court; and the two played in a quartet ensemble together with Mozart and Vanhal in the mid-1780s. In a celebrated passage in his autobiography Dittersdorf presented an ostensibly verbatim account of a conversation on music between himself and Emperor Joseph II, during which they assess the relative merits of Haydn and Mozart.[12] For Dittersdorf, Mozart is to be compared with Klopstock ("one must read Klopstock's works over and over again") and Haydn with Gellert ("Gellert's merits are patent at the first glance"); the Emperor's parallel is more materialistic, prompted by the richness of decoration on snuff-boxes: "I compare Mozart's compositions to a gold snuff-box, manufactured in Paris, and Haydn's to one finished off in London." Leaving aside the latent significance of these parallels – for Dittersdorf, emerging well from a bout of verbal sparring with the Emperor was more important than musical acuity – what is striking about the account is that it clearly implies that Haydn and Mozart are the leading composers in Vienna. Although the putative dialogue can be placed in the spring of 1786, it should be remembered that Dittersdorf dictated the autobiography in the late 1790s when such exclusive views were becoming more current.

Haydn, like Dittersdorf, is unlikely to have known much of Mozart's music from before the 1780s. On the other hand Mozart, because he traveled so much, would have encountered Haydn's music quite often, in Vienna (primarily manuscript copies of church and instrumental music) and Paris (mainly publications of quartets and symphonies) in particular, though comparatively little seems to have circulated in Salzburg itself. The cathedral had a copy of the *Stabat mater*, Haydn's most widely distributed work in any genre, and a reconstruction of the content of the library of the family notes the probable presence of only eight works, the six quartets of Op. 17 and two string trios; three of the quartets, nos. 2, 4, and 6, were evidently studied in considerable detail by Mozart, who added performance markings to the parts.[13]

When Mozart moved to Vienna in 1781 he encountered Haydn's music more regularly, both in performance and as readily available manuscript copies and published editions. There is no reason to doubt the impact that the appearance of Haydn Op. 33 quartets made on the younger composer and the sincerity of his remarks concerning the difficulty of composing the set of quartets dedicated to Haydn (K. 387, K. 421, K. 428, K. 458, K. 464 and K. 465). In turn, Haydn's response to hearing some of the quartets is equally genuine: "the greatest composer known to me either in person or by name. He has taste and, what is more, the most profound knowledge of composition."[14] Nevertheless, the elevation of this mutual admiration into the fabulous, a special moment in the history of music, distorts the relationship and ultimately undermines the special creativity of the two individuals involved.

The careers of the two composers in the 1780s were never determined by an admiration for the music of the other; much less did they run in parallel. Indeed in some major respects they were remarkably different. Haydn was a dutiful Kapellmeister; Mozart was a freelance musician. Haydn concentrated on quartets, symphonies, and piano trios; Mozart concentrated on concertos and operas. This was not a strategy of avoidance planned by either composer, merely a reflection of the precise musical environment and circumstances of the two individuals: Mozart was largely responding to the characteristics of musical life in Vienna; Haydn's situation was more complex, partly influenced by his employment at the Esterházy court, partly by Vienna (especially the preferences of the publishing firm of Artaria), partly by a European reputation. For most of the decade Haydn's duties as Kapellmeister meant that he was in Vienna only for a few weeks either side of Christmas. For his part, Mozart never visited Eszterháza and whether he would have done so for the planned performances of *Le nozze di Figaro* in 1790 must remain a moot point. Tantalizingly, the careers of the two composers might have converged in London in the 1790s had the vague plans for Mozart to travel to that city ever come to anything, but this too is speculative.[15]

As Mozart's posthumous image unfolded in the 1790s the role of Haydn as his mentor and his friend becomes ever more evident. The first biography of Mozart, by Franz Niemetschek, appeared in 1798 and was dedicated to Haydn, "Father of the noble art of music, the favourite of the muses." It included several stories that cement the relationship; in particular, it is the earliest known source for the letter that Haydn is said to have written to Franz Roth in 1787 turning down the possibility of writing an opera for Prague. In a footnote Niemetschek characterized the letter as "one of the most beautiful flowers strewn on the grave of the artist who died all too young."[16] Elsewhere in the biography Joseph Haydn is twice coupled with Michael Haydn in Mozart's estimation, an authentic reflection of Mozart's views to set alongside the exclusive Haydn–Mozart relationship that is nurtured by the author.

If the biographical situation is more multifaceted than the exclusive story of two great composers implies, then the musical influence of one on the other is even more complex, and one that, ideally, needs to be projected onto an extensive and stylistically secure knowledge of musical style in general in this period. The relationship between Op. 33 and Mozart's quartets dedicated to Haydn has been probed extensively;[17] a similar but not identical relationship may be sought between Haydn's Symphonies nos. 82–84, published as Op. 51 by Artaria in December 1787, and Mozart's last three symphonies composed in 1788, and between Haydn's Op. 64 quartets and Mozart's quintets in D (K. 593) and E♭ (K. 614). Mozart's increasing interest in monothematic sonata form towards the end of his life, as in the first movements of the piano sonatas in B♭ (K. 570) and D (K. 576) and the overture to *Die Zauberflöte*, may also be attributed to Haydn. On the other hand, it is difficult to nominate individual movements by Haydn that take their cue from a movement by Mozart, and the "London" Symphonies, in particular, are remarkably un-Mozartian. For some commentators the rich wind-band sonority of the trio in Part II of *The Creation*, "Zu Dir, O Herr blickt alles auf," shows the influence of Mozart's *Zauberflöte*, though such sonorities may have been common in Vienna in the 1790s, as is suggested by the extensive repertoire of arrangements of operas and oratorios for the medium that were available.

Universality and individuality

If the impression is that the flow of influence was predominantly one way, from Haydn to Mozart, then that would confirm certain persistent images of the composers: Haydn ploughing a lonely furrow in order "to be original," while Mozart, the eclectic, was avidly gathering musical styles and influences and forging them into consummate individuality. Less exalted, it should be recalled that, though Haydn and Mozart are often coupled together as contemporaries, they were, in fact, a generation apart, an age gap that was more likely to produce a master–pupil relationship. For this reason it is worth broadening the perspective once more to take into account the influence Haydn exerted on some major contemporaries of Mozart, composers born in the 1750s and 1760s who had more than ordinarily successful careers, Adalbert Gyrowetz (1763–1850), Ignace Pleyel (1757–1831), and Paul Wranitzky (1756–1808).

Born in Bohemia, Gyrowetz began to achieve wider acclaim in the early 1780s when his symphonies were played at the Esterházy court; a period of traveling followed before he briefly settled in England where his music was played alongside that of Haydn in the Salomon concerts and where the two composers became firm friends. Gyrowetz finally settled in Vienna, making a successful transition from composing instrumental music to German opera. Pleyel had an equally international career. He had been Haydn's pupil from the age of fifteen to twenty, then traveled first to Italy in the early 1780s before moving to Strasbourg. He renewed his first-hand acquaintance with Haydn in 1791–92 when his music featured in the Professional Concert series in London. From 1795 onwards, when he settled in Paris, commercial ambition as a publisher and a manufacturer of pianos replaced composition as the principal source of income. His publications included the first complete edition of Haydn's quartets, one of the cornerstones of the composer's posthumous reputation. Unlike Gyrowetz and Pleyel, Wranitzky had a career that was spent almost entirely in Vienna and its environs. He almost certainly studied with Haydn in the early 1780s, served as Kapellmeister to Count Johann Baptist Esterházy, a distant relative of Haydn's employer whose main residence was in Pressburg (Bratislava), and became a violinist in the main theaters in Vienna. From 1792 (or 1793) onwards he was the principal violinist at the Burgtheater and a pivotal figure in musical life generally; he was the director of the first, semi-private, performance of *The Creation* in 1798, the first public performance of the work in 1799, and of Beethoven's first benefit concert in 1800 (including the premiere of Symphony no. 1).

Apart from being associated professionally with Haydn at various times in their careers, these three composers composed substantial quantities of symphonies in the 1780s and 1790s, over 120 between them. Whether for Vienna, London, or Paris, the composers were contributing to a tradition that was pre-eminently associated with Haydn and their symphonies frequently ape those of the master from the 1770s onwards, widely distributed and performed. Typically, they will have a slow introduction which, though it may turn to the tonic minor, will not offer a thematic anticipation of the ensuing allegro; the slow movements prefer moderate tempos (Andante or Allegretto) and simple, repetitive themes that are often the subject of variations; minuets alternate tutti scoring in the minuets themselves and solo scoring in trios, with an occasional display of the exotic in instrumental, thematic or harmonic coloring; and finales are more often than not in simple rondo form rather than in sonata form and feature a brisk, evenly phrased theme in 2/4. Contemporary commentators often remarked on the indebtedness of these composers to Haydn. Gyrowetz was taken to task by the lexicographer Ernst Ludwig Gerber for incorporating portions of the finale of Haydn's Symphony no. 86 into a symphony in D major,[18] while Charles Burney was very suspicious of the vogue for Pleyel's music in London at the end of the 1780s: "there has lately been a rage for the Music of Pleyel, which has diminished the attention of amateurs and the public to all other violin Music. But whether this ingenious and engaging composer does not draw faster from the fountain of his invention than it will long bear, and whether his imitations of Haydn, and too constant use of semitones, and coquetry in *ralentandos* [*sic*] and *pauses* will not be soon construed into affectation, I know not."[19] Only Haydn was capable of continually creating individuality from his own style, as the *Morning Chronicle* noted following the premiere of Symphony no. 101 ("Clock") on March 3, 1794: "Every new Overture he writes, we fear, till it is heard, he can only repeat himself; and we are every time mistaken."[20]

Universality and individuality were two balancing opposites, fundamental to the values of the Enlightenment, and Haydn, both in his compositions and, in the last twenty years or so of his life, in his public image, was their unequaled exponent in the musical world. One striking indication of this status was the number of published compositions that were dedicated to Haydn. Traditionally, published dedications were to patrons of a certain social rank, kings, princes, aristocrats, whose connoisseurship was flattered and who, as a result, might be expected to continue their patronage. In dedicating a work to Haydn the motives were clearly different: the imprimatur was not a social one but a musical one, a recognition of the artistic superiority of Haydn and of the striving ambition of the composer who wished to follow in his footsteps. Mozart's dedication of six quartets to Haydn is only one of fifteen known published sets of quartets dedicated to the master, including Pleyel's Op. 2 (1784) and Gyrowetz's Op. 2 (1789).[21] Almost equal in number are the piano sonatas dedicated to Haydn, at least nine examples, including works by Cramer (1771–1858; Op. 23), Eberl (1765–1807; Op. 12), Hummel (1778–1837; Op. 13), and the well-known instance of Beethoven's first published set (Op. 2).

As the eighteenth century drew to a close it could fairly be said of music that it was the Age of Haydn. In his biography of the composer Griesinger was not exaggerating the geographical distribution of Haydn's works; he did, however, lack the historical perspective to point out that this degree of international popularity was unprecedented in music. No other composer, Monteverdi, Bach, Handel, or Mozart, had achieved this universality in his own lifetime. Even in that most international of genres, Italian opera, the eighteenth century never produced a composer who dominated the repertoire in several countries over a significant period of time and whose achievements constituted a commonly accepted challenge.

Dealing with Haydn

Modern chroniclers of this esteem have always presented it in a very positive light, a correction of a historical record that has failed to do justice to Haydn and, within the narrower confines of biography, presenting it as a wholly benign process, one that fits appropriately with the personality of the aging composer. But there was a challenge here too. Was it possible for another composer to achieve the same degree of esteem in his own lifetime? Were the musical challenges that Haydn presented, especially his complete control of a dialectical musical language, ones that could be continued or were they most easily dealt with by avoiding them? Confronting the legacy of Haydn was not the most important determinant of musical development in the first decades of the nineteenth century, as opera and piano music of all kinds gained the attention of the public. For Beethoven, however, Haydn was a presence that he chose to confront, not because it was the most convenient way of securing a musical living in Vienna but because he felt compelled to do so.

From his youth in Bonn Beethoven had been familiar with the music of Haydn. The electoral court owned seventy-eight symphonies, fifty-six quartets and seventy-two trios by Haydn,[22] while one of its officials, Johann Gottfried von Mastiaux, had his own private library of Haydn's music. From November 1792 to January 1794 Beethoven studied with Haydn in Vienna, spending the summer of 1793 in Eisenstadt. Nearly 250 of Beethoven's exercises in strict counterpoint survive, the only extant evidence of Haydn's teaching methods, which were clearly meant to be more rigorous than those he had experienced under Reutter in the 1740s. Beethoven was able to witness at first hand the composition of some of Haydn's latest works, including the Op. 71 and Op. 74 quartets and Symphony no. 101 ("Clock"), and Beethoven's own compositions were encouraged too. There was a promise that Beethoven should accompany Haydn on his next trip to London but for some reason, this never materialized. This unfulfilled promise together with the displeasure of Beethoven's patron, the Elector of Cologne, when he assumed, almost certainly wrongly, that some allegedly new compositions were revised versions of works written in Bonn, were early indications of a troubled relationship between Haydn and Beethoven. It suited the nineteenth century to exaggerate this incompatibility in order to stress the questing originality of Beethoven, and many of the difficulties in the relationship were accordingly misinterpreted, exaggerated, or simply fabricated.[23]

But even a casual reading of Beethoven's correspondence and other documents relating to his life shows that Haydn and his status were constant preoccupations; Mozart's name, in contrast, never features in this way. When Artaria accused Beethoven of double-dealing over the publication of the string quintet in C (Op. 29), the composer defended himself by stating that Haydn had always acted like that.[24] Writing to Prince Nicolaus Esterházy in the summer of 1807 about the Mass in C, Beethoven expressed real apprehension about its reception "since you, most excellent Prince, are accustomed to have the inimitable masterpieces of the great Haydn performed for you."[25] More generally Beethoven's life-long wish, idealized certainly, was to be a Kapellmeister, partly for financial reasons, partly because he recognized that at its most supportive it would have nurtured his individuality as it had done Haydn's.[26]

It was Haydn's looming presence that led Beethoven to focus on the quartet and the symphony as the two genres that were ineluctably progressive. Like Haydn, Beethoven came to revel in sonata form as musical drama and he similarly expanded Haydn's resourcefulness in variation and rondo forms. The surface volatility of Beethoven's music, especially orchestral music, with its abrupt contrast of dynamics, insistent rhythms and exaggerated accentuation, also owes much to Haydn. Most compelling, the strong sense of compositional unity across a multi-movement work that is associated with Beethoven has its origins in Haydn's music.[27]

While absorbing and transforming this inheritance was the driving force behind much of Beethoven's creativity, occasionally a finished composition fell short of its stimulus. Beethoven's nervousness about the Mass in C was fully justified; even though it was composed after the "Eroica" Symphony, the "Razumovsky" quartets and *Leonore* (the first version of *Fidelio*), it is a very deferential work, uncomfortably conscious of Haydn's six late masses and, in the end, lacking their striking individuality. An earlier, more frequently discussed example, is the First Symphony, a work that sits very comfortably within the Haydn symphonic tradition as practised by Gyrowetz, Pleyel, and Wranitzky. But within two years of its first performance Beethoven had completed the Second Symphony in which this tradition is boldly and unprecedentedly reinvigorated. It is not known whether Haydn ever heard a performance of this symphony but he would surely have admired its inventiveness, not least in the finale. A sonata rondo, like most of the finales in the "London" Symphonies, it even has the Haydnesque semitones, rallentandos, and pauses that Burney complained about in Pleyel's music, but content and structure combine to produce a movement of ruthless musical energy and integrity.

One of the most self-consciously auspicious musical developments in Vienna in the first decade of the nineteenth century was the setting up of a new subscription concert series, the Liebhaber Concerte, in the winter of 1807–8, which, in the event, lasted only one season.[28] Organized by a group of aristocrats, it was deliberately designed to feature well-rehearsed performances of the best of Viennese music. With prescient discrimination the twenty concerts were dominated by the music of Haydn, Mozart, and Beethoven. The series ended on March 27, 1808 with a special performance of *The Creation* to honor Haydn's seventy-sixth birthday.[29] As well as various members of the aristocracy, Beethoven, Gyrowetz, Hummel, Salieri (who directed the performance), and other composers were present, and the weeping Beethoven is supposed to have kissed Haydn's hand. Heinrich Collin, the author of *Coriolan*, wrote a three-verse commemorative poem and Giuseppe Carpani a sonnet. Most enduringly, the artist Balthazar Wigand recorded the scene, much reproduced in books on Haydn and on CD covers of recordings of *The Creation*. With appropriate artistic licence Wigand makes Haydn the focal point of the picture, seated in the middle, the point of convergence for two informal lines of individuals waiting to present their compliments; except for four trumpet players and a timpanist, who are declaiming a fanfare, the orchestra and choir look towards Haydn. The symbolism of the occasion was overwhelming: the cumulative concert in a series that articulated the greatness of Vienna as a musical city; the artistic discernment of the aristocracy; the power of music as high art; Haydn, Mozart, and Beethoven as its leading exponents and the honored centrality of Haydn. While many of these characteristics were to become familiar threads in the historiography of music, Haydn was soon to cede his pivotal role to Beethoven. One hero replaced another; two would have spoiled the story.

Clearly the heroic agenda of the nineteenth century had the effect of devaluing Haydn. It also obscured the complexity of Haydn's relationship with his contemporaries, generally underplaying the characteristics of his musical environment. But if in any revisionist history the process of accommodating this plurality ignores the very impulses that led Wigand, Griesinger, Niemetschek, Mozart, Beethoven, and many others to stress the individuality of Haydn then this, too, would not do justice to the composer. Critical perspectives that embrace these two standpoints best suit Haydn for, in the most fundamental manner, he was the first among equals.

PART II

Stylistic and interpretive contexts

5 Haydn and humor

SCOTT BURNHAM

Like a clown stepping onstage, some of Haydn's finale themes need only appear to prepossess the listener toward the humorous:

Example 5.1 Symphony no. 102, finale, mm. 1–12

This highly sectionalized theme, with its internal rhymes on clipped triadic figures, comes on like irrepressible doggerel. (The melodic triad is a comic resource when used in this way – not as declamatory scaffolding, or as pleasantly flowing concord, but as throwaway patter.) The surprise tumble onto an A major triad at the end of the fourth two-measure phrase begins to act on the promise of antic possibility. From here the theme abandons its doggerel rhyming and climbs into and through d minor, ending on F major. And now, just as the plot seems to be thickening, we are hustled back to the opening utterance for a repeat of everything we have just heard.

The premature repetition, coming a full four measures early, plays a fairly obvious practical joke on the listener.[1] But a more subtle comic effect obtains here as well. By being made to repeat when it does, the returning theme confirms the F major harmony not as a relative major to that fleeting suggestion of d minor but as a dominant to the original key of B♭. Hence the listener is forced into a retroactive interpretation of the obliquely conjured F major triad as a pivotal dominant, essential to the normative syntax of such a theme and its repetition (the A section of a binary-structured theme often ends on a dominant). Haydn thus makes a conventional repetition into a comic event, and he creates the irony of a slapdash presentation of a harmony turning out to be the very thing demanded by convention. One could also interpret the return of theme and tonic as on schedule, but the preceding move to the dominant as elliptical and premature. For this latter scenario, picture the opening of the theme relaxing in the wings, waiting for its usual cue to return; startled to hear the dominant arrive four measures early, it now must rush out onto the stage. In the end, these two readings run to the same: the absolutely literal enforcement of normative syntax – acting on the material appearance of an F major triad as though it were the hinge-pin dominant – comically destabilizes the theme.

Such a theme can hardly fail to be heard as humorous: its doggerel dialect is already funny, and it is so designed that its repetition brings about a practical joke as well as a subtle, ironic joke. But even themes with completely regular phrasing and an unremarkable harmonic plan can have a comic effect:

Example 5.2 Symphony no. 98, finale, mm. 1–8

Gretchen Wheelock brilliantly remarks that this theme possesses "the earmarks of a limerick."[2] This effect resides in its brief, speech-like subsections, its AABA design, and the way that the last phrase collects and closes the opening two sections. There is a babbling brightness to this theme, with its steady-stream eighth-note triadic figures and agogic rhymes. Its terse, choppy patter seems to parody the Classical-style penchant for appositely paired phrases: the often decorous reliability of such pairings is here downgraded to a clownish predictability.

That one habitually hears such phrasing in Haydn's finale themes could convey the sense that one is in fact hearing the unbuttoned default setting of Classical-style phraseology – that after the willed dramatic adventures and lyrical focus of the preceding movements, the finale drops the tone to something like a vernacular. The origin of many of Haydn's finale themes in the genre of the popular contredanse only reinforces this sense, as does the prevalence of rondo, or rondo-like, forms, in which thematic returns sound like comic refrains. Melanie Lowe has argued convincingly that Haydn's style can be heard to move to this lower valence at several different levels – at the global level of a multi-movement design, at the level of a sonata-form exposition, and at the very local level of a typical theme.[3] At each of these levels, utterances in the high style (declamatory or lyrical) move to utterances in a lower, more popular style. This pervasive sense of downhill motion through social registers is a comic trajectory much relished in the eighteenth century. The music discussed in this chapter comes primarily from finales, as the most characteristic site of the comic vernacular and as the gathering end term in this downhill trajectory.[4] With the help of selected passages from a variety of instrumental genres, I will review the kinds of material manipulation that have most often been heard as humorous: repetition, contrast, motivic amplification, and the special treatment of returns and endings. The chapter concludes with some speculation about the nature of the comic spirit in Haydn's compositional ethos.

Repetition and contrast

Comedy relies on exaggeration for its most pronounced effects. The best way to create comic exaggeration in music is through simple repetition. One of Haydn's favorite comic ploys is to extend phrases internally by repeating melodic figures, such that the music seems to get stuck on a pattern. The effect is either one of distracted daydreaming or mechanical malfunctioning; in either case, the prevailing illusion of sovereign human agency is severely compromised, with humorous results.[5]

Repetition can also sound like much ado about next to nothing:

Example 5.3 String Quartet in C, Op. 33, no. 3, finale, mm. 1–8

This rondo theme comes on like a hyperactive clown, making frantic business with a minimal prop, the interval between G and E. The sixteenth-notes offer only a first degree of elaboration, blurring with added commotion the G–E eighth notes.[6] Meanwhile, the accompaniment emphasizes the nullity of the melody with its own empty multiplication (quarter-note iterations become eighth-note iterations).[7] At the other end of this movement, the coda foregrounds vacuity to an even greater degree, adding antiphonal and inversional exchanges that absurdly profile the simple figure:

Example 5.4 String Quartet in C, Op. 33, no. 3, from coda of finale, mm. 147–56

In this lively conversation on a trivial tag, as in the theme itself, we hear irrepressible energy animating stinted material. This combination of high energy and low stakes is funny.

For Wheelock, the finale of Op. 33 no. 3 serves as an example of another kind of high and low: she hears the coda as "a mockery of imitation and inversion as artful contrapuntal devices" and suggests that the movement as a whole may be "a comedy of errors in which the lowborn attempt to imitate (or perhaps mock?) the witty conversation of their betters."[8] Interpenetration of the socially high and low was of course a rich and readily available source of fascination in Haydn's day, propelling much of the comedy and drama. (Cheeky servants have been around since Menander, but this gambit finds a new edge in the waning of the age of monarchy.) Whether in Haydn's coda we laugh at the trivial being profiled (the lowborn putting on airs) or the means of profiling being trivialized (the highborn deflated), disparity is the perceived result, comic energy the spark that jumps the gap.[9]

Such contrasts occur at various levels of form and articulation and involve either similar material developed in different directions or very different material directly juxtaposed. Here's an example of the first case, at a very local level. The passage in question occurs before the last big cadence in both the exposition and the recapitulation of the finale from Symphony no. 98. Note how the threefold fanfare on a B♭ major triad is answered:

Example 5.5 Symphony no. 98, finale, mm. 115–24

We hear the same harmonic function (subdominant, or pre-dominant), in two stylings – the first is a dramatic fanfare on a brassy major triad, the second an almost querulous questioning on a chromatically inflected minor triad. That the latter version is also subject to the same threefold repetition makes it both a symmetrical device that balances the fanfare and a comic device that undermines it: with an irony perhaps peculiar to Haydn this figure is both called for (i.e., structurally necessary) and uncalled for (i.e., nose-thumbing mockery).[10]

Different stylings of similar material can also serve to articulate the affective contrast between different formal sections. The allegro theme of the first movement of Symphony no. 98, while preserving the intervallic and rhythmic outline of the initial utterance of the preceding slow introduction, can be heard to puncture the dramatic pretense of that opening: ponderous minor is answered by lapidary major, as sententious thirds, fifth, and diminished seventh in the second half of the phrase become untroubled fourths and fifths tripping along to the tonic. A more immediate juxtaposition can be found between the same two formal sections in Symphony no. 103, in which the pitches of a portentous bass line pointing ominously to the dominant of c minor are instantly reinterpreted at the onset of the allegro as a blithe melodic figure in E♭ major – bass line becomes upper-voice melody; minor-mode inflection of a dominant becomes major-mode inflection of a third; and an imposing closing gesture becomes a fleet new beginning (see mm. 35–42.) The nineteenth-century music theorist J.-J. de Momigny programmatically interpreted the allegro theme of Symphony no. 103 as gently mocking the emotional intensity of its slow introduction, in his scenario of a congregation of country folk gratefully emerging into the light of day after a long period of confinement spent praying for the respite of a fearsome storm of Biblical proportions. The slow introduction represents the scene of prayer inside the temple; the allegro theme is the sound of relieved people teasing each other about how scared they had been.[11]

We need not hear such examples exclusively as some sort of abasing parody. They can also be perceived as the rapid succession of two faces of the same material, and thus as the witty development of a musical idea. Fundamental to both possibilities is the composer's ability and inclination to "act" his material in different ways, to push the material into different characters – a comic impulse at bottom but not convulsively so. (Here the French word "comédien" comes to mind, as an umbrella term for comedian and for actor.) The comic gesture here is one of witty juxtaposition, so often the scratching post of a frisky intelligence.

In larger contexts, humorous contrasts can create long-range continuity, by effecting a kind of formal logic. In the finale of Symphony no. 98, big arrivals tend to be overdramatized in a manner bordering on parody and are often followed by a jaunty theme that bounces along without a care:

Example 5.6 Symphony no. 98, finale, mm. 86–94 (beginning of second theme from exposition)

To follow a momentous arrival with a new theme is part of the typical strategy of thematic exposition in this style.[12] But in this case, Haydn makes that strategy decidedly funny, for the extreme stylistic deflation is comic. Moreover, this steep contrast becomes a running joke throughout the movement. The development section particularly emphasizes the contrast – each time we hear the jaunty theme it comes as the comically nonchalant reaction to some bit of trumped-up drama, often turning its heel on that drama by setting out in a surprise key. This disparity is enhanced by the scoring: a solo violin carries the nonchalant theme throughout the development section, becoming, in Wheelock's words, a "whimsical persona."[13]

At the extreme end of the spectrum of comic contrast is the shock of the utterly incongruous. Here the effect is one of jarring discontinuity. The most famous example of such a shock is no doubt the "surprise" of the "Surprise" Symphony, but a far more outrageous example takes place near the end of the slow movement of Symphony no. 93, in the section from mm. 71 to 81. Nothing in the movement prepares the listener for the grotesque explosion of the bassoon's low C in m. 80. After hearing the dotted descent of scale degrees 3-2-1-7-6-5 in the flutes and violins, then 8-7-6-5-4-3 in the oboes, we are set up to expect a concluding 6-5-4-3-2-1 (as the last in a series of descents by sixth to each of the stations of the tonic triad). But at this point, the music seems lulled to sleep on the subdominant harmony (this pre-dominant harmony being a favorite site for distraction in Haydn's music): after seven increasingly drowsy repetitions of 6–5, the 6 cannot even be coaxed down to the 5, and the music gradually closes its eyes.[14] But not for long – the bassoon sounds its vulgar klaxon, and the entire orchestra responds, disgorging the long withheld 6-5-4-3-2-1 descent with irreverent trills. To bring such sounds into the precincts of a surpassingly beautiful slow movement is to be capable of anything. Taking a longer view, however, we find that even this supremely disruptive moment enjoys an ironic and almost paradoxical effect, for it turns out to be the very thing that puts this movement back on track and allows it to conclude.

Upbeats

Another means of comic exaggeration in Haydn's music is the amplification of an isolated motive. The most common instance in the Haydn finale is that of the upbeat figure. In the finale themes from Symphonies nos. 98 and 102, a pronounced upbeat is present in almost every two-measure subsection, as a kind of energizing push, the hand that spins the merry-go-round. Haydn's first move in the next section of the theme from the finale of Symphony no. 102 is to detach the initial upbeat figure and to alternate iterations of that upbeat with two-measure sections of the theme (see Ex. 5.7). Then he further isolates the upbeat figure, both by paring it down to one iteration at a time and by leaving it hanging in a higher register. The figure then does a solo turn in that register – a mincing vamp on the high wire – before prancing down to articulate the big dominant that will usher in the return of the theme's opening.

This kind of motivic isolation is less about motive as seed of a long-range thematic process and more about motive as a kind of character tic that can be isolated and exaggerated for comic effect.[15]

In Haydn's rondo (or rondo-like) finales, any theme marked with a strong upbeat is certain to have one or more of its returns brought about through a playful treatment of that upbeat. In the finale of Symphony no. 98, a tutti section leads to the first big dramatic cadence, on the dominant (mm. 36ff). All this sound is followed by three isolated iterations of the transposed upbeat figure from the outset of the theme, at a soft dynamic and in the middle register of the first violins (one figure per measure, leading to the downbeats of mm. 40, 41, and 42). A fourth iteration then follows an octave higher, regaining the appropriate register for a return of the theme, now in F. The isolated upbeats work well as a way to initiate the section in F; they not only drain off the energy of the preceding section, but they create a vamping count that sounds like the first return in a rondo design (which itself entails a joke, for we are clearly in the dominant here). But these

Example 5.7 Symphony no. 102, finale, mm. 12–30

three isolated upbeats are as nothing compared to what's in store for the big return to the theme later in the movement. At the end of a development section that has lurched through a motley assortment of keys, including A♭ major, C♯ minor, A major and E♭ major, each new key helping to profile the comedic contrast described earlier between hyperbolic intensity and jaunty nonchalance, Haydn brings the music to the home dominant of B♭. Then this passage ensues:

Example 5.8 Symphony no. 98, finale, mm. 222–35

The solo violin takes the three vamping upbeats from before, compresses them into a measure and a half ("and a one and a two and a three") and then sequences them upwards ("and a one and a two and a three"), all of which results in a four-measure phrase. The figure is then broken down into single eighth-note upbeats spanning four measures ("and one, and two, and three, and four"), and then these eighth-note upbeats are compressed into two measures ("and one and two and three and four"), finally stepping up into the return of the theme in the tonic key. The harmonic content is also being built up here, such that the home key's dominant seventh is assembled third by third, with much final marching in place on the crucial seventh itself. The entire passage – with all its motivic fragmentation and reconstruction, its rhythmic expansion and compression – comes off as a comically belabored approach to the returning theme.[16] A text underlay for the passage might thus read something like this: "Here it comes, here it comes, here it comes. Here it comes, here it comes, here it comes. It comes; it comes. It comes; it comes. It comes, it comes, it comes, it comes . . ." Sharpening the gag in the original London performance is the fact that the leading line in this retransition, the solo violin, would have been in the hands of the orchestra's leader, J. P. Salomon, Wheelock's "whimsical persona" of the development section. One can imagine the potential for humorous mugging between Salomon and Haydn, who manned the continuo – in fact, Haydn trumps Salomon's sally with his own solo in the coda.[17]

Haydn never tires of this kind of teasing postponement, and it is around this modest premise that he stages some of his most elaborate comic scenes. The mainspring of such action, which can be wound so as to unspool in greatly varying spans of time, is the ever-expedient upbeat figure. For the upbeat is the most immediately tangible means of predictability in this style – an upbeat, after all, is always followed by a downbeat. An upbeat engages the directly predictable, arouses the reflex twitch of expectation. To detach and isolate upbeats is to detach and isolate musical predictability – and with predictability comes comic opportunity.

Returns and endings

But the comedy of the return in Haydn is not always a matter of these upbeat teases, deliciously deferring the inevitable. Sometimes he painstakingly prepares the opening pitch or interval of a returning theme, again with the comic effect of amplifying the trivial. In the finale of the String Quartet in C, Op. 33 no. 3, Haydn prepares the theme's initial minor third G–E with a dramatically paced chromatic ascent to G in the upper voice, as the dominant of c minor. Then, after undergoing five smorzando repetitions of a melodramatic turning figure, this pedal G is coaxed by degrees down to E, alternating first with F♯ and then with F♮. Thus the G is dramatically built up and then comically undermined – it arrives as the final term in a chromatic ascent, and it then chromatically "decays" into its comic form as part of the chattering minor third from the outset of the theme.

In addition to having fun with thematic returns, much of Haydn's choicest humor is pledged to beginnings and endings. Haydn's humorous ploys at these junctures are legion, and the best-known include cases where a beginning has all the characteristics of an ending (the finale of the String Quartet in D, Op. 76 no. 4, which begins with a series of energetic V–I cadences) or where the ending and the beginning turn out to be identical (the elaborate and oft-discussed joke at the end of the finale of the String Quartet in E♭, Op. 33 no. 2). Other times, Haydn waves the double bar line in front of the listener like a matador's cape, goading a charge to the finish. In the finale of Symphony no. 90, for example, the machinery of closure is put into effect prematurely, as a rousing ending in the home key of C takes place way too soon after the onset of the recapitulation. The listener is pulled up short by this conclusion, which is followed by four measures of silence (again simulating closure, and surely filled with the anxiety of an audience wondering whether to applaud) and then the first theme is quietly resumed – in D♭! Or take again the ending of the "Joke" Quartet, Op. 33 no. 2, which feigns closure at several points before actually ending (with the very beginning of the theme).

In Symphony no. 46 Haydn brings joking about closure to another level altogether by returning to music from a previous movement within the coda of his finale. Here a finale full of flapping loose ends gets tucked into the statelier music of the preceding minuet movement, whose motivic resemblance to the finale theme allows it to sound as the charmed last chapter of that theme. But the returning minuet music does not in fact close the piece. Instead, it trails off on a bewitching harmony, ceding the last words of the symphony to the finale theme, whose garrulous squandering is now ruthlessly exposed.[18]

What is at stake with returns and endings? Why are these the most frequent spots for extended comedy in Haydn's music? As the indispensable stations of any plausible musical process in this style, endings and returns are the most open to comic manipulation – like a reliable straight man, they will always be there, rooted to the spot. Playful adjustments to their expected arrivals are guaranteed to work, because the most marked constraints of the style gather at returns and at endings; the audible cues of their imminent presence number among those most likely to be recognized by all kinds of listeners.

Return and closure in fact permeate Haydn's musical language at all levels, from the local rhetoric of paired phrases to the global ethos of the development and renewal of thematic material. In such a pervasively articulated, hyper-discursive style, generally predictable at the micro level of an upbeat, or at the successively larger levels of a consequent phrase, the ending of a period, the unfolding of an exposition, the return of an initial theme, or the close of an entire movement, opportunities for a play on expectations arise at every turn. And because Haydn always eventually fulfills the underlying protocols of his musical language, his style can be playful without being iconoclastic, witty without being subversive.

Punch lines

Leon Botstein relates this property of Haydn's music to a broader effect of his music: the encouragement in Haydn's own time of what Botstein calls "philosophical listening," a kind of imaginative hearing that moved from the transient particularities of the material surface to the underlying "systematic 'truth' of musical structure," an abstract, rational substrate that is always fulfilled. This systematic truth "was revealed through the elaboration of the musical material in the work and was underscored by the structure of endings and the very shape of musical memory, which is why wit, surprise, and delayed or interrupted expectations within a piece were part of the compositional strategy."[19] Like the sallies of verbal *esprit* so valued in the age of Enlightenment, Haydn's playful disruptions ultimately confirm the sovereignty of Reason.

To make one suddenly aware of one's expectations about beginnings, middles, and ends is to transform things that are so fundamental as to be taken for granted into things whose inevitability is not only commented upon but staged: in being teased about our expectations, we re-experience the expected events as, in fact, inevitable. We can be teased about such events precisely because they will not be withheld in the end – each playful episode teasingly ensures us that the contract with Reason will be fulfilled yet again, just as a teasing parent stages the onrushing renewal of his or her affection for a child by seeming to withhold it. The happy ending of a generic comedy is never actually put in question, no matter how extensive the series of setbacks delaying its eventuality, and the enjoyment of the observer rests in seeing just how all those complications will be ironed out.

But if this scenario of Haydn's artful confirmation of Reason seems too comfortably rooted in an untroubled conception of the Enlightenment, more ironic visions of Haydn's art also stand in the offing. Recall again his penchant to make necessary cadences funny, or to transform formally mandated contrasts into comic oppositions. By turning such inescapable events into opportunities for comedy, Haydn could be construed as practicing a kind of sublimated gallows humor, seeming to transcend unavoidable constraints by joking about them. (A penniless Oscar Wilde on his deathbed reportedly looked at the hideous wallpaper in his sordid Parisian hotel room and commented, "One of us is going to have to go.") The very fixity of convention and closure encourages the fluid freedom of Haydn's wit, which dances around and above these constraints but could never dance without them. Haydn's practice of foregrounding the articulative junctures of his music, whether at the level of the phrase or the entire movement, plays as well into the comic imperative of making visible what is usually kept backstage. By amplifying the articulative elements that keep his musical language ordered and coherent, Haydn draws one's attention to the inevitable mechanism of the language. This has prompted Mark Evan Bonds' substantial comparison of Haydn's music to the supremely self-reflexive literary art of Laurence Sterne.[20] If Sterne can be said to have created a kind of meta-novel, Haydn can be heard to have composed a kind of meta-music; both foster an ironic sense of aesthetic detachment.

Daniel Chua plays this theme with double stops, construing Haydn's music as a profound example of Romantic irony, in that its very language is predicated on "catching itself out" and is thus foundationally ironic.[21] If Botstein proposes an Enlightenment Haydn and Chua a Romantic Haydn, Marshall Brown adds further nuance, placing Haydn on a middle road somewhere between Romanticism and Enlightenment: "[Haydn's] humor is something less than ironic formal self-consciousness . . . and something more moody than Enlightened tolerance – rather more like the fretful rubbing of a subdued, not very troublesome, yet irrepressible psycho-social instability."[22]

But whether we take in this music as fretful or playful, as wittily rational or self-consciously ironic, Haydn's musical material projects a distinct sense of being genially *deployed* at every turn. This aspect of his style can be heard in the continuous and knowing development of thematic motives. And it can be heard in both the profiling and the lability of articulative punctuation – the instant availability of all manner of partial stops, full stops, extensions, and elisions, audible in the unfolding irregularity of a single phrase or in the elaborate delay and preparation of a returning theme. Finally, it can be heard in the ready profusion of different musical dialects, be they noble or rustic, exalted or vulgar. There is an overriding sense that Haydn can do whatever he wants with his material – extend, elide, interrupt, shift, combine, contrast, play – because the energy and originality of his art present themselves most readily as an irrepressible impulse to manipulate.

This emphasis on genial manipulation tends to distance the musical material itself, to treat it more as means than as end.[23] But while such distancing is necessary to the comic artist, to the consummate "comédien," it may well be what has kept Haydn's music from being as generally beloved as that of Mozart or Beethoven. For Haydn's is primarily an art of wit rather than of Mozartean sensuousness or Beethovenian moral force. His music is clearly not as sonorously gauged as Mozart's (or even Beethoven's). Mozart's music in particular emanates sonority, the machinery of its style unobtrusively supporting beautiful utterances and textures. Haydn just about reverses this disposition: his thematic material less often sounds as its own *raison d'être*, more likely serving as an occasion for witty doings that throw the spotlight on the very machinery one rarely notices in Mozart. And Haydn's overall thematic process also stands apart from Mozart and Beethoven. While

Beethoven shares with Haydn a consuming knack for motivic development, he often indulges this practice in order to create a compelling totality in which themes are reduced to motives so as to be heard as parts of a whole that will be still greater. Nor can Haydn be said to present a Mozartean plenitude of ravishing themes. Instead of a concatenation of memorably expressive melodies or an inexorable motivic teleology, Haydn's thematic logic is distinguished by a kind of vital intelligence that prevails throughout.

Both Mozart and Beethoven play more readily to Romantic and post-Romantic constructions of subjectivity – their music is often heard to emanate from and to address interiority, to resonate in the great inward spaces of the post-Enlightenment subject. In the wake of this powerful alignment, a full appreciation of Haydn's art seems a lost sensibility. This loss is witnessed today by the automatic and condescending relegation of Haydn's instrumental music to the opening of concert programs, as though enacting the ingrained critical habit of treating Haydn as an innocent predecessor of composers whose music descends more deeply into the realms of human experience. The Haydn we are left with is a warm-up act, treating the audience to accomplished witticisms while stealing no thunder from the acts to come.

It wasn't always this way. Haydn was clearly the headline act for those audiences in London who listened eagerly to his newest symphonies. And though we can hardly hope to recover their worldview, one last attempt to describe the effect of Haydn's musical humor may help rekindle a sense of what all the excitement was about. At the end of her book on wit and humor in Haydn, Gretchen Wheelock develops the handsome idea that Haydn dramatizes "the interplay of composer and listener."[24] The listener is drawn into an active role when he or she becomes self-conscious about expectations. When those expectations are thwarted and then fulfilled, the listener is in effect both straight man and insider, progressing from someone who is joshed to someone who gets the joke. This is a consequential progression: to be caught out and then brought back inside, to move from being fooled to being informed, from being manipulated to being aware of being manipulated, from enacted object to understanding subject – this shift in perspective forces a sudden recognition of consciousness. And this brief shock of recognition is no vertiginous glimpse into a solipsistic abyss but rather a surging confirmation of the self-transcending dimension of self-consciousness. This is one reason why a good laugh can be so reconstituting: we seem to get rebooted, all systems again activated and ready to go.

Haydn's comic energy encourages this playful exercise of intelligence and consciousness. Subtle shifts in listener perspective can occur at almost every shift of the music, resulting in listening that stays engaged with the detailed progress of the music as if absorbed in a game or a lively conversation.

The modest chuckles that arise from an audience listening to Haydn are the sound of pockets of awareness being released, a bubbling aeration of conscious musical competence.

It is fun to imagine listening to Haydn in the manner of those London audiences that so enjoyed his final symphonies, to hear his music not as appetizer but as the main course, to be taken along on his supreme entertainments, putting ourselves in his hands but also putting our own sensibilities into every turn of the ride, primed for wit, eager, ready, open, wondering only: What will he do next?

6 Haydn's exoticisms: "difference" and the Enlightenment

MATTHEW HEAD

In Persia, a sofa married an easy chair; the Indians of the Molucca Islands fashion wigs from wire; in China, a Muscovite man gave birth, while a satrap in the Indies was impaled for making love – so reads aloud Sempronio, the pharmacist in Haydn's *Lo speziale* (1768), from his newspaper.[1] The librettist, Carlo Goldoni, at once indulges and ridicules his period's fascination with the fabulous, unnatural, and irrational incidents in far-flung climes reported in journalism and travel writings. Goldoni parodies Sempronio's gullibility, and implies that the pharmacist's preoccupation with world news renders him oblivious to events closer to home. As Sempronio reorganizes the war-torn world with the help of a compass and globe, his unqualified assistant mixes and muddles the potions that his master will dispense. Sempronio's fanciful internationalism blinds him to Mengone's designs on his ward, Grilletta. Indeed, Sempronio's fascination with the exotic makes him an easy target when Mengone sues for Grilletta's hand in the exalted costume of a Turkish ambassador. Mengone is not the only suitor to don Turkish disguise in the hope of winning over Grilletta's reluctant guardian. Masquerading as an ambassador to the "King of Moluccas," Volpino (a frequent visitor to the pharmacy) offers Sempronio a job in Turkey as the King's pharmacist. Volpino's related aria "Salamelica, Semprugna cara" (Act III) begins with Italian-derived gibberish, standing in for Turkish, while the last two lines refer ungrammatically to singing and dancing, as if in celebration of the impending wedding.

What music would suit this scene? Haydn might well have wondered, for there were few conventions governing the musical depiction of Turkey (then the Ottoman Empire) at this time. The question is important because a distinctive feature of composition during the European Enlightenment is that composers found ways of representing cultures, and music, different from their own. These experiments in exoticism sought, in Locke's definition of the term, to evoke "a place, people or social milieu that is (or is perceived to be) profoundly different from accepted local norms in its attitudes, customs and morals [through] musical features typical of, or considered appropriate to, the people or group in question."[2] Exoticism, then, is concerned with difference. This difference need not involve geographical

Example 6.1a *Törökös*, notated 1786

Example 6.1b *Lo speziale*, "Salamelica" (Volpino), mm. 1–15

distance – the Other was sometimes close at hand. Haydn was particularly interested in representations of the Gypsy (properly speaking Romani) music making that surrounded him during his long career at the Hungarian court of Esterházy.[3] Similarly, from his first stay in London (1791–92) Haydn was involved in a substantial project of providing accompaniments to the popular and historical tunes of Scotland and the Celtic fringes of the British Isles.[4] As Locke implies though, and several commentators have stressed, exoticism is a fiction told about difference – it conjures an illusion – but it does not seek an authentic presentation of another type of music.[5]

Exoticisms are most often derived from earlier exoticisms, rather than from first-hand contact with the music and culture at issue. Thus we might expect Haydn to score Sempronio's aria with the type of "Turkish" music employed in Viennese ballet and Singspiel of the 1750s and 1760s by Joseph Startzer and C. W. Gluck. Viennese Turkish exoticism involved the addition of percussion instruments – specifically the bass drum, cymbals, and triangle – to the orchestra to create a noisy, military sonority in fast, duple-meter, march-like passages. Haydn himself used this type of exoticism in the overture to his "Turkish" opera *L'incontro improvviso* (1775) and the second movement of his Symphony no. 100 ("Military").[6] But in Volpino's "Salamelica" Haydn struck out on his own and set the aria with a type of Hungarian popular dance itself called "in the Turkish style" (*Törökös)* (see Exx. 6.1a and b). This dance developed in Hungary during the period of

Ottoman (Turkish) rule and was performed at weddings in central Hungary by dancers in pseudo-Turkish costumes. Thus it is deeply appropriate for the dramatic context. Haydn's aria shares with the *Törökös* duple meter and a melodic motif in which scale-degrees 1 and 3 rebound. To these Haydn adds a folksy harmonic progression from chord V to IV that, in the context of court opera, breaks the rule of syntax according to which the subdominant chord prepares, but does not follow, the dominant.[7]

Sempronio, at least, is impressed. On hearing the aria he exclaims "what witty, spirited people! What a fine country Turkey is!" Such a positive impression, Goldoni implies, is based entirely on greed – the prospect of the Sultan's riches coming Sempronio's way convinces him of the value of the nation. Such blinding self-interest, not Turkey, is sent up in this scene – exoticism is a mechanism that highlights a character flaw.

Haydn: an Austrian composer?

The openness of Haydn's score to the *Törökös*, which is introduced wholesale, is characteristic of the composer's engagement with difference. Haydn's music incorporates a rich variety of national, popular, and folk melodies from northern and central Europe. Crucially, he does not crudely "Other" such materials, that is, he doesn't present them simply as exotic curiosities. Instead, he treats them as topics and as melodies that can participate fully in the musical discourse.[8] The relationship between exoticism, as a construction of difference, and the national, regional, and peasant colors of Haydn's music is not clear-cut. The designation "exotic" depends on where and who you are within Europe. The boundaries of "Europe" and the nature of "European" were as flexible in Haydn's day as they remain today. For Haydn such materials belonged to the contexts in which he grew up and worked. For European audiences removed from Haydn's Hungarian context, the appearance of, for example, two Croatian folk tunes in the second movement of Symphony no. 103 (mm. 0^2–8 and mm. 26^2–34) was presumably exotic with specific regard to ethnicity and nationality. But Haydn understates their exoticism, domesticating them to the metrical and harmonic terms of their new context. These tunes provide the two principal themes for a variation movement and thus achieve a high degree of integration in the fabric of the movement. Indeed, this movement invites the audience to imagine that even such "advanced" and technologically sophisticated music as Haydn's "London" Symphonies is grounded in, and elaborates, traditional and folk melody.

The national, regional, and ethnic affiliations of Haydn's music are far more mobile, inclusive, imaginative, and complex than his canonization as a

Teutonic master suggests. That canonization began during his own lifetime and often took the form, within Austria and Germany, of a nationalist appropriation of the composer as a pioneer of autonomous instrumental music. In his centennial "Remarks on the development of the art of music in Germany in the eighteenth century" (1801), Johann K. Fr. Triest asserted jingoistically that Haydn's name was everywhere spoken with reverence, "that London and Paris are competing in their praise of one of his most recent works" and that "everything is united in him to make him the greatest of all instrumental composers."[9] Georg August Griesinger began his biography of the composer with a claim that Haydn was a national treasure whose music, universally admired, spread the fame of Germany "in the remotest lands": "Haydn's quartets and symphonies, his oratorios and church pieces, please alike on the Danube and on the Thames, on the Seine and on the Neva, and they are treasured and admired across the sea as in our own part of the world."[10]

There is scant evidence that Haydn saw himself and his music as representing German-speaking lands abroad. Such a role would have made little sense to the composer. Until 1790, his music was the legal property of his patron, a Hungarian prince; after 1790 Haydn worked in a freelance capacity, not as a representative of State. Haydn was born at the boundary of Austria and Hungary, in a multiethnic, primarily German-speaking area populated by rural Austrians, Hungarians, Croats, and Slovakians. Haydn subscribed to the supra-national, cosmopolitan ideals of the bourgeois Enlightenment. A member of the Viennese freemasonic lodge "Zur wahren Eintract" (True Concord) from 1785, Haydn took the organization's ideal of universal brotherhood seriously, setting Gellert's "The Love of Enemies" and "The Philanthropist" as canons. The notion of a Republic of Letters, uniting the middling strata of society around the globe through a shared print culture, expressed this international ideal, and Haydn may have been thinking along such lines when he stated that "my language is understood throughout the whole world."[11] The Enlightenment rendered sectarian and national hostility unfashionable, at least in art and the conversation of the educated.

The exotic as a mask for self-critique: *L'incontro improvviso*

In 1775 Haydn set the "Turkish" abduction opera *L'incontro improvviso* with its tale of the Sultan of Egypt's transformation from tyrant to forgiving, tolerant ruler. This positive image of the Ottoman Sultan was an operatic convention. The Sultan's transformation was implicitly a lesson to European (not Ottoman) monarchs on the need for reforms to despotic rule, and so illustrates the function of exoticism in later eighteenth-century culture as critique of European society as much as a set of stereotypes about Europe's Others (overseas and at home). In either case – as masked self-representation or stereotype about other kinds of people – exoticism was always based on Europe's "concerns about itself."[12] Exotic peoples were not viewed, or represented, in their own terms, a fact that some critics link directly to imperialism and colonization.[13]

As an opera centering on the imprisonment of a Persian princess, Rezia, in the seraglio (harem) of the Sultan of Egypt, the exotic setting focuses attention on the European ideal of liberty. Women's freedom to choose their partners – the contemporary European discourse of romantic love – was dramatized by the harem setting. Since all characters of the opera are non-European, the opera does not stabilize a distinction between East and West, but, again, universalizes its (distinctively European) preoccupations. The Eastern setting is a mirror-like representation of Europe in which an older despotic-feudal order is pitted against an emerging bourgeois realm that took "romantic love" between men and women as a sign of its broader ideals of liberty and sensibility. "Music" is thematized in the opera and emerges as a medium of these ideas. Rezia asks Ali to sing again a song about her eyes that he used to sing before they were separated, a song that develops into a duet as if to symbolize the role of "music" in romantic love ("These eyes are one of love's shafts," Act II). The finale celebrates the Sultan's largesse in freeing the lovers – his transformation into an Enlightened despot – and, to this end, employs the *batterie turque* (those additional percussion instruments mentioned above), a clever scoring that characterizes the Sultan as at once European and Turkish.

A possible exception to this rosy picture of exoticism as progressive is met in the character of the Calender. The Calender is a fake dervish who begs for alms and lives well off people's misguided generosity. He befriends, and then betrays, the escaping lovers and, alone of all the cast, is excluded from the opera's happy ending. Such exclusion compromises the opera's discourse of universal humanity and indicates that a specifically non-European "Other" helped to define the European Enlightenment's vision of global brotherhood by establishing a limit to that inclusivity. (Osmin, in Mozart's *Die Entführung aus dem Serail*, and Monostatos in *Die Zauberflöte* share the same fate as the Calender.)[14] However, the Calender was also read in this period as a masked critique of monasticism within Europe. That is, othering goes hand in hand with self-criticism. Haydn's contemporary Zinzendorf, referring to Gluck's setting of the libretto in 1764, described the Calender as "a very biting satire against monks."[15]

Example 6.2 "Castagno, castagna," *L'incontro improvviso*, mm. 1–16

Haydn's music can be heard to describe the Calender's greed, self-interest and deceit, as much as his ethnicity or his purportedly Islamic faith. The Calender sings a stage song to accompany his begging on a nonsense text, "Castagno, castagna" (Ex. 6.2). This, he claims, is "an old secret chant by Mahomet from the Koran," a claim the audience is not invited to take seriously. Haydn's music, possibly inspired by Gluck's earlier setting, is designed to make the Calender's false piety sound grotesque and primitive. A grotesque character, constructing the Calender as morally corrupt, is conveyed by the ungainly leap between first-inversion chords (V and I) in mm. 8–9, and a sinister rather than appropriately spiritual or pious chromatic turn around the dominant pitch, mm. 3–6. The second theme of the song (mm. 29–36) gets "stuck" on scale degrees $\hat{1}$ and $\hat{2}$, and, at this point, all instruments except the violin 2 play in unison, a quasi-monophonic texture that signals primitivism.

The particularity of all things: exoticism and humor

Haydn's exoticisms are closely tied to his humor. Exoticism is sometimes the occasion for musical farce as discussed above, with reference to the Calender of *L'incontro improvviso*. But the connection between exoticism and humor runs deeper. Haydn's musical humor sometimes highlights the arbitrary nature of musical conventions and, in doing so, denaturalizes what would otherwise remain "normal" – just the way things are. The tricks Haydn plays on his listeners reveal that compositional conventions are culturally specific practices not immutable laws. For example, Haydn's "false" recapitulations unveil the historical and regional contingency of sonata form as a practice and shock the audience into an awareness of the constructed nature of

Example 6.3a Keyboard Concerto in D major, Hob. XVIII: 2, mm. 25–30

Example 6.3b Keyboard Concerto in D major, Hob. XVIII: 2, finale, mm. 150–55

their musical expectations. This is precisely the same narrative strategy Montesquieu employed in his *Persian Letters* (1721), an epistolary novel that describes Paris from the vantage point of the outsider, in this case, two Persian visitors. Such distancing and ironizing strategies render particular, even foreign, what otherwise passes for normal. Haydn's music employs both humor and exoticism to illustrate the Enlightenment formulation that (in Irish philosopher George Berkeley's words of 1713) "it is an universally received maxim, that everything *which exists is particular.*"[16]

Sometimes the exotic and the humorous are indistinguishable, as in the "Hungarian-Gypsy Rondo" of the Keyboard Concerto in D, Hob. XVIII: 2 (*c.*1780). The predominant topic is that of a Hungarian gypsy popular dance characterized by 2/4, no anacrusis, tonic pedals, and a melodic figure in which the tonic rebounds with its upper fifth, the latter with a ♯4 acciaccatura (see Ex. 6.3a). Other notable Hungarian dance figures in the movement include the repeated scalar descents from 5 to 1, with each note trilled (see mm. 150–58), a gesture that sounds pantomimically threatening in this context (Ex. 6.3b). After the opening tutti, closing in the tonic D major, the solo presents its main theme in the "wrong" key, e minor, followed by a "correction," the theme stated immediately a step lower in the tonic (Ex. 6.3a). This "wrong-key" humor constructs the keyboard solo as a loose cannon and so contributes to the exoticism of its materials, which are in danger of breaking out of the conventional formal framework. The intertwined humor and exoticism of the movement invoke an idea of freedom, specifically the breach of musical protocol.

Such uses of exoticism and humor exemplify the critical temper of the Enlightenment – the resistance to the authority of received ideas (religious, legal, philosophical, scientific, aesthetic, and compositional) insofar as that authority was based solely in convention and the power of institutions.

Example 6.4 String Quartet Op. 20, no. 4, Menuetto: Allegretto alla zingarese, mm. 1–6

Haydn's Menuetto: Allegretto alla zingarese ("in the gypsies' style") from the String Quartet Op. 20 no. 4 (1771) illustrates the use of exoticism to critique compositional "rules" and learned style (see Ex. 6.4). Ignoring for a moment the syncopations that disrupt the meter of this movement, the minuet (a courtly, elevated topic) is treated here in the manner of academic counterpoint. The absence of rests, preponderance of tied and suspended notes, restriction of rhythmic values to duple division of the quarter-note pulse, or its duple augmentation, and the constantly thick, four-part texture; the learned imitation in the second section (mm. 10–13) between violin 1 paired with viola, and violin 2 (paired with cello), suggesting canon at the distance of one beat – all these evoke the serene world of Fux's *Gradus ad parnassum* (1725), a treatise on counterpoint that Haydn is known to have studied (and used in the lessons he gave Beethoven). But Haydn introduces another ingredient: syncopation (the *fz* markings on weak beats). Through his title, Haydn identifies this single gesture as exotic – as relating to Hungarian Gypsy music-making – such that its disruptive effect on scholarly counterpoint and courtly dance is attributed to an outsider. But this is effectively a mask for the composer's own breach of decorum. Syncopation is an important element of the composer's Gypsy style, but the intensive, and itself academic use of that element alone distances the piece from the actual representation of Gypsy music-making as a whole.

What was Haydn up to in this movement? He does not just send up the Gypsies as "incompetent" by the (metrical) rules of art music; nor simply launch an attack on decorum. Neither is Haydn indulging in the pleasures of becoming vulgar – he indulged this elsewhere, in the trio of the String Quartet Op. 33 no. 2 with its indication to the first violin to slide between widely-spaced notes, on one string, in the manner of folk or peasant fiddle-playing.[17] One possibility is that Haydn is dissolving boundaries between social-musical categories as part of a current discourse on universal brotherhood and global conviviality. Haydn does not single out any one social-musical type for parody; rather, each topic in the movement defines itself through the other and is, through such definition, exposed as particular. The point that Haydn seems to want to make is that Gypsy music is not so different after all and that its principles (here, specifically, the principle of syncopation) is universal and can be coupled (if only imaginatively within the idealistic discourse of music) with Western art music. This ties in with the Enlightenment's idea of universal human nature, according to which differences of dress, language, social organization, and manners were superficial and masked a common humanity. As Roy Porter encapsulated the idea: "amongst the values dearest to Enlightenment thinkers was cosmopolitanism. Claiming that reason shed the same light all over the world, the *philosophes* commonly insisted . . . [on] a single universal standard of justice, governed by one normative natural law . . . [and on] a single uniform human nature, all people being endowed with fundamentally the same attributes and desires, 'from China to Peru.'"[18]

Such ideals were criticized as naive and homogenizing even within the eighteenth century, and I am not upholding them here so much as attempting to show that they provide a meaningful context for Haydn's music.[19] Insofar as Haydn's movement reduces Gypsy music to a single element it is vulnerable to accusations of excessive domestication and rationalization of cultural difference. The fact that the "gypsy" topic is one of disruption suggests both danger and the need for external control. However, global and international thinking in the eighteenth century were often associated with the period's dominant idea: progress. Knowledge of people different than oneself was deemed progressive because such knowledge overcame isolation, ignorance and prejudice. The economist and philosopher A.-R.-J. Turgot exclaimed in his *Observations:* "the human mind becomes more enlightened, isolated nations draw nearer to each other, commerce and politics connect all parts of the world, and the whole mass of the human race, alternating between calm and agitation, good and bad conditions, marches always, though slowly, toward perfection." The hot-air balloon pioneered in France was imagined to provide a means of resolving international conflict and making war a thing of the past. In his futuristic novel *L'An 2440* (*The Year 2440*), Sebastien Mercier predicted that "Chinese mandarins [would] take routine flights to Europe to discuss matters of philosophy."[20] While this dream is still unrealized, it is thought that Haydn's music made its way to Peking during the composer's lifetime as part of a British trading delegation led by Lord Macartney in 1793.[21]

Something of this dream of global conviviality can be sensed in Haydn's music itself, particularly when different national and ethnic references are combined in a single piece. For instance, the second movement of the Piano Trio in A major, Hob. XV: 18 (by 1794) is an untitled *siciliano* with detached, staccato articulation in piano and cello. The finale is an untitled polonaise in which Haydn also uses a Hungarian Gypsy motif, the *Kuruc* fourth as a cadential flourish (m. 8). Thus he mixes exoticisms together. This may suggest an instance of the carelessly generalized and imprecise exotic but can also be heard as an imaginative effort to cross boundaries and confound categories. Music lent itself to such experiments and could effortlessly suggest that national boundaries are unnatural, in the sense of man-made and culturally specific.

Celtic-Germanic primitivism

In the last two decades of his life, Haydn was an active participant in a Celtic-Germanic "primitivism" that defined, and championed, a form of controlled wildness and naturalism in art. This is most apparent in his providing accompaniments to traditional Scottish and other Celtic melodies, for the London-based publishers William Napier and George Thomson.

Haydn's knowledge of Scotland was probably honed on the greatest publishing sensation of the century: James Macpherson's English "translations" of the poetry of a (fictional) third-century Celtic bard Ossian (the translations were later exposed as Macpherson's own creations). Ossian was widely read in Germany. Goethe included an extract from Ossian/Macpherson in his novel *The Sorrows of Young Werther* (1774) and Herder's polemic statement of Teutonic primitivism was titled "Essay on Ossian and the Songs of Ancient People" (1771). Herder celebrated the perceived primitivism of Ossian's poetry, which he understood as its formal incoherence and direct relationship to lived experience. In Ossian, Herder found an example of Rousseau's theoretical idea of the freedom and liberty of mankind in the state of nature:

> The wilder, that is the more living, the more freely active a people is, the wilder, that is the more living, more sensuous, freer, fuller of lyrical action must be its poetry. The further away from artificial, scholastic modes of thought, speech, and writing a people is, the less its songs will be made for paper and be dead literature. The essence and purpose of these songs depends alone on the lyrical, living, as it were dance-like character of song, on the living presence of the images, on the connection and as it were dire urgency of the content and feelings.[22]

Music, as performance, could recreate this freedom, could conjure, at least as an illusion, a liberating regression from scholasticism and writing to spontaneity and voice. A dissertation by the critic William Tytler on Scottish music, prefixed to Napier's first volume of songs (Haydn made his first appearance in vol. II), emphasizes the connection to Ossian. While historically inaccurate, the dissertation provides a context of meaning for Haydn's settings. First, Tytler asserts that Scottish songs are the musical equivalent of the poetry of Ossian, an expression of "the genius of the Scots." The antiquity and Scottish authorship of the music are asserted and, on this basis, Scotland is said to contend with Italy as the seat of solo song. Indeed, in a novel twist, it is asserted that the Italians lacked melody – their music was all contrapuntal artifice until, at the turn of the sixteenth to the seventeenth centuries, Gesualdo set about imitating the direct emotional effect of Scottish melody! The secular origin of Scottish melody is asserted (these songs are not derived from hymns and chants), with the figures of the bard, strolling harper and minstrel of old summoned as icons. Scottish melody is validated as the most direct continuation of Greek music and its mythic power over the emotions. Opposed to fashion and novelty, Scottish song is concerned with love and with melancholy. This Rousseau-inspired aspect of the description is encapsulated in the remark that "as the Scottish songs are the *flights of genius*, devoid of art, they bid defiance to artificial graces and affected cadences [ornamentation]." Scottish songs are said to possess "simplicity and wildness," a neat encapsulation of the north European primitivist aesthetic.[23]

What is the function of the setting provided by Haydn? According to the advertisement to Napier's second volume, Haydn renders the songs "worthy of National Patronage," by which is meant the dedication to the Duchess of York and the English purchasers of the volume.[24] Haydn's name is part of the imperialist framing of Scotland for the English drawing room.[25] Haydn's contemporary biographer Griesinger employed a vocabulary of civilizing improvement to describe Haydn's role: "Haydn values them; the melodies are shrill and often bizarre, but through his accompaniments and several improvements these relics of ancient national song are rendered very acceptable."[26] This vocabulary recalls the eighteenth century's interest in modernizing and improving nature through landscape gardening. But these imperialist and civilizing aspects of the project do not necessarily represent Haydn's own relationship to Scottish melody.

The settings themselves suggest that Haydn respected the originals, in the sense of wishing to preserve in his setting as much of the melody's original character as possible. Instead of Haydn "modernizing" the melodies, he employs modern music to illuminate the beauty of the originals. This extended to Haydn's self-suppression: the effacement of his own authorial identity. The accompaniments support but do not swamp the melodies. Haydn employs pedals, doubles the melodies in thirds and sixths, provides rests in the continuo to allow the voice to enter solo at the beginning of phrases, and, in general, supplies a continuo of anonymous late Baroque character that does not compete perceptually with the melody. The harmonizations are simple, with modulation and applied-dominant chords used only when the melody requires them (rather than when the melody can accommodate them, as in Bach's chorale harmonizations). Rhythmically,

Example 6.5 "O'er Bogie" (Napier no. 16), mm. 1–5

the accompaniment does not interfere with the distinctive snaps, syncopation, and dance rhythms of the melodies. Haydn accepts, rather than alters the melody when it does not lend itself to a standard harmonic progression. For example, in "O'er Bogie" (Napier, no. 16) the harmonic progression at the cadence in m. 4 proceeds I, IV, vi, in accordance with the melody's cadential "Scottish" twist to the submediant (complete with "Scotch snap" rhythm) (see Ex. 6.5). Indeed, the song ends on the submediant chord, indicating Haydn's willingness to adapt the resources of modern harmony to the requirements of Scots melodic tradition.

In the Thomson settings the instrumental parts are more elaborate, and here Haydn actively frames "the primitive" melodies. But equally well, Haydn can be heard to unite antique, national song with the resources of modern instrumental music – again breaking down boundaries and working towards inclusivity. In his preface, Thomson identifies the picturesque aesthetic effect that arises from such variety, citing the contemporary aesthetician Uvedale Price on how complexity gives delight and pleasure.[27] The "artful combinations" in the accompaniment heighten the enjoyment of simple melodies, Thomson argues, citing Price's "An Essay on the picturesque" (1794).

In sum, Scottish melodies served as (imaginary) points of origin for contemporary Austro-German and British music. They were at once exotic (ancient, from the Celtic fringe of Britain, rustic, artless) and native – the present's living past and a model for the values of Teutonic art: not bound by scholastic rules, wild, now beautiful, now sublime. The frequent analogies made by contemporary critics between Shakespeare and Haydn overlap with this discourse on north European ruggedness.[28] The ambiguity of Haydn's settings as staging of the Other and tribute to (a fictionalized) Self, as exhibition of the primitive and honoring of the paradigmatic, point up the ambiguities of exoticism in the "Classical" period.

Hungarian Nationalism and the Gypsy Trio

If we read Haydn's exoticisms literally as representations of the musical others named in their titles we risk missing much of their cultural meaning. Haydn's exoticisms are often instances of Self-definition through imaginative affiliations across national, ethnic and class boundaries. A final example of this is also Haydn's best known essay in exoticism: the "Rondo in the Gypsies' style" from the Piano Trio in G, Hob. XV: 25 (by April–May 1795).

The episodes of this ABACA form are influenced by the *Verbunkos*, a type of music played by Gypsy bands for the recruitment of Hungarian men into the army (an army that served the Austrian State). The *Verbunkos* was a hybrid form; it combined Western-European "art" music with Gypsy styles. The first published examples, from 1784, were by Joseph Dengraf (actually titled *Ballet Hongrois*). However the *Verbunkos* was widely disseminated through performance, appearing at social dances in Hungary, and Haydn's knowledge of the form did not depend upon published examples. A comparison of the published *Verbunkos* repertory with themes from the episodes of Haydn's "Gypsy" Rondo reveals a close relationship. Indeed, the first theme in the C episode, mm. 121–28, is a *Verbunkos* fingerprint (see Ex. 6.6).[29]

The use of a *Verbunkos* idiom in the episodes, but not the refrain (a contredanse) frames "the Other" and puts it on show. But the proportions, and construction, of the episodes lend them weight and de-emphasize the refrain (mm. 0^2–34) such that the apparent hierarchy is not necessarily maintained in performance and listening. The first return of the refrain is brief, while the two episodes, sharing the Hungarian Gypsy topic, are long and polythematic (see figure 6.1). The episodes "join forces" through their shared topic.

As a representation of Gypsy music-making, Haydn's episodes evoke tropes of frenzy and wildness. This is particularly evident in the ascending, scalar idea, over stamping accompaniment, that – implying *crescendo* – "erupts" in a syncopated Gypsy anapaest and a flourish of shorter note values in a high register (mm. 121–28). This is the melodic type that Haydn draws from the *Verbunkos*, representing a new element in his treatment of the Hungarian Gypsy style. Encompassing comic and serious extremes, Haydn's episodes contain moments of grating dissonance (where the cello

Example 6.6 Piano Trio in G, Hob. XV: 25, Rondo in the Gypsies' Style, mm. 121–28

Section	Length in measures, counting repeats
A¹	52
B	60
A²	26
C	40
A³	25
Coda	17

Figure 6.1 Weighting of sections in Haydn's Gypsy Rondo

adds acciaccaturas a half-step below the roots of the piano chords, mm. 59–62), and intoxicated slurred figures (the drunken, syncopated motif in the violin alternating D and C♯, mm. 133 and 137). The overarching trope is of irrationality – the music implying (but not itself succumbing to) frenzy. The rhetorical technique of the episodes is "primitive"; ideas are forcefully repeated, with or without variation. Forceful attack from all players lends a visceral quality. Again, Haydn elevates the primitive on the basis of its immediacy, "manly" force, expressive intensity, and rejection of courtly decorum.

Alongside this reading, however, we need to consider Haydn's circumstances at the time of the work's composition and publication. The trio was probably composed in and for London – it was written no later than April/May 1795. The trio's connection to London is further suggested by its dedication to Rebecca Schroeter with whom Haydn enjoyed an affair during the winter of 1791–92. Haydn may have been representing – or constructing – himself as exotic through music that suggested not just Gypsy music-making but his ersatz homeland, Hungary. This possible self-Othering forms a counterpoint to Haydn's adaptation to the English-Handelian oratorio tradition to which he was the self-styled heir in *The Creation* and *The Seasons.* For English audiences, the Hungarian Gypsy style would have been unfamiliar and thus the impression of exoticism and difference particularly intense. Furthermore, the *Verbunkos* circulated in Europe as a sign of the vigorous Hungarian national movement, largely unknown to Haydn scholarship.[30] Haydn's Rondo is probably "about" not only the music-making of the Gypsies but also the Hungarian nationalism that such music had come to represent.

This possible musical engagement with Hungarian nationalism provides a context for understanding an otherwise anomalous piece in Haydn's output: the Hungarian National March (Hob. VIII: 4), composed on Haydn's own initiative (not on commission) for the military musicians at Esterházy in 1802.[31] The March contains a couple of "Gypsy," that is – for Haydn – Hungarian motifs: the *Kuruc* fourth (complete with ♯4 acciaccatura) in m. 4 and the *sf* syncopation in m. 12, although it is otherwise without exotic coloring.

Conclusions

Haydn's exoticisms express the Enlightenment's rhetoric of universal brotherhood – the rejection of intolerance and prejudice based on national, class, and religious differences. They do this through the way in which exoticisms are presented compositionally, as well as through the choice of texts and libretti. While critics have noted that eighteenth-century exoticism is marked with the rhetorics of imperialism and orientalism (in the Saidian sense), Haydn also stresses kinship, identification, and the dissolution of boundaries. A common trope in Haydn's various exoticisms is that of the primitive. This trope served, rhetorically, as a mode of European self-critique. Along with other Enlightenment figures such as Rousseau and Herder, Haydn valued this constructed primitivism as a critique of bourgeois and courtly politeness. While popular, national, pastoral, and folk melody are domesticated and framed according to Haydn's own compositional vision, they are nonetheless accorded aesthetic and philosophical significance.

Haydn's exoticisms are almost always meta-musical. They involve the presentation or representation of another type of music, be that Hungarian

Gypsy bands, Turkish Janissary music, Celtic traditional song, or even the stage-air of the greedy Calendar. The musician figures within, and on the margins, of Haydn's exoticism and forms a category that cuts across national, religious, and class differences. Haydn seems well aware of the fact that music (along with clothing, language, and food) is one of culture's most potent signs of ethnicity itself. His music discloses the particularity of Viennese "Classicism" through his humorous denaturalization of conventions coupled with a complex negotiation of regional and national styles.

PART III

Genres

7 Orchestral music: symphonies and concertos

DAVID SCHROEDER

During the span of almost forty years that Haydn wrote symphonies, the nature of the genre changed dramatically, from a type of composition that served various musical and social functions of the *ancien régime* to a highly defined genre that would stand at the center of musical life for the next two centuries. New concert societies late in the eighteenth century broadened the class-base of the symphonic audience, and Haydn proved extraordinarily adept at making the transition. Throughout his career he gradually reshaped the nature of the symphony, and in the end provided an enduring model for future practitioners of the genre. Symphonies teemed in Vienna during the mid-eighteenth century, and composers such as Matthias Monn, Wagenseil, Dittersdorf, and Hofmann provided much originality. Nevertheless, we owe the emergence of the symphonic tradition primarily to Haydn, and even major composers of the twentieth century, Prokofiev among them, have acknowledged that debt. As a composer of concertos Haydn's achievements are less striking, although because of the prominence of the symphonies we tend to underestimate the concertos.

Because Haydn's symphonies still speak to us with a relevance that has traversed two centuries, we sometimes forget that in the eighteenth century vocal music was considered pre-eminent.[1] With opinion such as this as the common currency, it should not surprise us that Haydn, in his autobiographical sketch from 1776, listed only vocal works among those he considered his finest.[2] Late nineteenth-century writers such as Eduard Hanslick contributed to another misconception about eighteenth-century symphonic works, in their insistence on these as absolute or pure music. Unlike Hanslick, eighteenth-century commentators, including Haydn's biographers Georg August Griesinger and Albert Christoph Dies, were deeply concerned about the social or spiritual functions of symphonies.[3] Griesinger wished to know "from what motives Haydn wrote his compositions, as well as the feelings and ideas that he had in mind and that he strove to express through musical language." Haydn replied that "he oftentimes had portrayed moral characters in his symphonies. In one of the oldest, that he could not accurately identify, 'the dominant idea is of God speaking with an abandoned sinner, pleading with him to reform. But, the sinner in his thoughtlessness pays no heed to the admonition.'"[4] Studies in moral characters proliferated during the eighteenth century, best known from *The Tatler* and *The Spectator* of Addison and Steele, introduced in Germany by Mattheson in *Der Vernünfftler*, and later popularized by Haydn's professed hero, Christian Fürchegott Gellert. Haydn had presumably read enough of Gellert's writing to be aware that his description of God and the sinner, with its religious orientation, deviated from the standard descriptions of moral characters.[5]

Dies also raised the issue, having heard several times about the possibility that Haydn "sought in instrumental pieces to work out some verbal problem or other selected at will," including character representation. Haydn's answer of "seldom" has provided fodder for the absolutists: "In instrumental music, I generally allowed my purely musical fantasy free play." The one exception to this occurred in the Adagio of a symphony, in which "I chose as a theme a conversation between God and a heedless sinner."[6] If Haydn could no longer identify the symphony, recent commentators have been more than prepared to try.[7] Of even greater interest is his response that he seldom attempted character representation, and that he usually indulged in "purely musical fantasy." That reply does not square with the facts, and it may have been a ploy to avoid the story of the sinner, preferring in 1806 that readers of Griesinger and Dies should regard his symphonies in the light of the most current thinking on the subject.

The symphonies themselves reveal a composer deeply concerned about expression and wishing to engage his audience, whether in the court of his patron or in a more public forum, in a provocative manner on issues both sacred and secular. To achieve this, Haydn occasionally quoted vocal music in his symphonies, including arias, street songs, and folk tunes; he used opera or liturgical music as models for symphonies; and, he had aspired to emulate certain types of literature, especially dramatic works, but also novels, other types of prose, poetry, or more generally the principles of rhetoric.[8] The answer to Griesinger about portraying moral characters likely was accurate, although he probably did not intend this in an overtly programmatic manner. The moral essence of a symphony for Haydn meant something different, with earlier works assuming sacred characteristics or positions similar to those emerging from opera, and later works closer to the enlightened views of his friends and associates such as Metastasio, Greiner, Born, Sonnenfels, and no doubt even Nicolaus Esterházy. From these he gained a sense of the secular enlightened notions of morality, involving not only tolerance or principles of altruism, but also the more subtle sense of furthering moral goals through achieving higher levels of refinement. Near the end of his life he could say with confidence from an enlightened moral perspective, "I also believe I have done my duty and have been of use to the world through my works."[9]

Central to Haydn's view of the symphony stood the effect it should have on his audience, a view that changed over time. Because of the nature of his employment and the contractual agreement he had with the Esterházy family at the early stages of that employment, his audience initially differed from that of his symphonist colleagues. While the works of Hofmann, Dittersdorf, and others would have been performed at the Burgtheater and elsewhere in the early 1760s, Haydn's contract limited the performance of his symphonies to his patron, initially at Eisenstadt and later at the new palace in Eszterháza, although that did not necessarily deter performances at other venues (primarily through circulating orchestral parts). Haydn may have been expected to fulfill certain types of social functions with his early symphonies, such as celebrating his prince's birthday, as Giuseppe Carpani in *Le Haydine* claims of no. 25, but that did not prevent him from putting his mark of higher purpose on these works. In sorting out the differences among various types of composition – and Haydn's own definition of what constituted a symphony was surely broader than ours, including overtures if not other types as well[10] – the most fundamental distinction would have been between public works designed for a listening audience and more private types intended primarily for the enjoyment of players.

Belonging to the public category, the symphony and concerto had an affinity to opera and oratorio. Like opera, the symphony necessarily had to arouse the audience's interest. That could be done by focusing on individual players in a concertante style, or through the appeal of orchestration. Haydn's Eisenstadt orchestra of the early 1760s lacked the richer resources of the larger public orchestras, but that did not prevent him from becoming a superb orchestrator. In his early symphonies, Haydn's style of orchestration may have seemed like making a virtue of necessity, but he soon moved away from the standard sounds of strings, horns, and oboes, where winds merely doubled strings or provided static harmonizations. He exploited the distinctive sounds of the winds alone or in combination, and of course used instruments to define topics as well, such as trumpets and drums for military purposes, and horns for the hunt.

Increasingly he saw the engagement of his audience in dramatic terms, building procedures into his symphonies that in some respects allowed these works to parallel drama for the stage. Frequently that drama resists abstraction, becoming definable by quoting well-known pieces of music, or by quoting styles that all would recognize. In his progression towards greater sophistication he moved further away from actual quotation, but at the same time discovered musical principles that heightened drama even more intensely. With his new audiences in Paris and England, he prepared listeners for more complex works by first giving them pieces easier to digest, as happened during his second London season (1792), with no. 98 easing listeners into the more complexly dramatic no. 94. In no. 98 the minor thematic material of the slow introduction becomes the major theme of the Allegro of this monothematic movement. In no. 94 complexity already permeates the introduction and the effect of this on the rest of the first movement goes far beyond thematic material, to levels of counterpoint, chromatic passages, and other destabilizing factors.

It has been difficult for some, including writers during his time, to accept that Haydn would often write symphonies intended to appeal to popular taste. Griesinger observed that "strict theoreticians found much to take exception to in Haydn's compositions, and they cried out especially over the debasement of music to comic fooling." Haydn explained that this did not trouble him, since "a narrow adherence to the rules oftentimes yields works devoid of taste and feeling."[11] For the best minds of the eighteenth century, taste and feeling always trumped the rules, and here Haydn had over half a century of literary tradition to support him. That tradition went back at least as far as the Third Earl of Shaftesbury, whose *Characteristics of Men, Manners, Opinions, Times* Haydn had in his personal library.[12] Shaftesbury, perhaps even more influential in Germany than England (certainly swaying Gellert and Haydn's friend Ignaz von Born), had laid the groundwork for the enlightened conception of the fusion of aesthetics and morality, and in his scheme of things nothing superseded the relationship of author and audience. Writers needed to appeal to their public, but that did not mean pandering to it in their efforts to persuade. Humor played a central role in any strategy to persuade, and Shaftesbury advised writers to "recommend wisdom and virtue in a way of pleasantry and mirth."[13]

Drama in a symphony must necessarily unfold in the context of musical forms or procedures. In part this concerns the format of a symphony, notably the number of movements and their arrangement. When he started writing symphonies in the late 1750s, the idea of a musical/dramatic thread running through the movements was simply not part of the aesthetic. We associate this primarily with Beethoven, but credit for initiating this type of integration of a work goes to Haydn, not only in late symphonies, such as nos. 101 or 104, but much earlier, certainly by 1772 with Symphony no. 45 in f♯ minor, the "Farewell."[14] Concerning the number and order of movements, Haydn appears not to have done anything revolutionary, as he alternated between three and four movements in his early symphonies, using the so-called *da chiesa* format in some, starting with a slow movement; eventually he settled on a four-movement format, and in late symphonies preferred to start with a slow introduction.

The four-movement format has remained the norm, whether movements interconnect or not. Each movement, in most cases with exclusively distinctive characteristics, sets its own tone, means of evocation, and dramatic appeal, and overall this resulted in something highly satisfying and engaging. Boundless possibilities existed for originality within individual movements, and over time the possibilities for changing approaches to the movements themselves could be striking. Slow movements use melodies of a vocal nature, revealing great beauty, but could just as easily upset that with comic twists, as in no. 93. Third movements, minuets and trios, were under no obligation to behave as minuets, often gravitating more to the character of rustic dances, and equally having the potential to disrupt the triple time with metric ambiguity or other types of distortion,[15] as in no. 94 where figuration periodically shifts the bar line or sets up duple patterns. Finales could range broadly from rondos to sonata form, or find a hybrid approach combining elements of both. We generally recognize Beethoven as the one to shift the weight of works from the first movement to the finale, but Beethoven could take a number of Haydn's late symphonies as his model for this new aesthetic, especially no. 101. Haydn recognized in his own approach that as the drama of all movements became more intense, the finale often required greater substance to bring the work to a fitting close.

Just as Haydn cannot be called the father of the symphony since he did not invent the genre, he similarly did not originate the idea of sonata form, but what he did with it, compared with any of his contemporaries, can only be described as breathtaking. No one understood better than Haydn the dramatic capacity of sonata form, and this took on new and striking features in the late symphonies written for Paris and England. Here slow introductions may be highly integrated with what follows, not only in first movements, but also beyond. Expositions often define polar opposition, not necessarily between first and second themes (many symphonies are monothematic), but possibly between stable thematic material and unstable transitions. Developments take the principles of thematic working and modulatory exploration to new heights. They may also obscure the arrival of the recapitulation with a *fausse reprise*, as happens with the unprepared tonic return of the opening theme in the first movement of no. 91, or the return in the wrong key in the first movement of no. 102. Recapitulations generally do not simply play a role of settling the material of the exposition down in the tonic key; Haydn treats recapitulations as places for dramatic issues to be resolved through an intelligible process. That solution, often revealing parallels to the procedures of drama for the stage, should not go unnoticed by the listener, since it may very well adumbrate through purely musical means a principle central to the Enlightenment.

Pinning down the exact number and chronology of symphonies by Haydn has proved difficult. The most persistent problems arose from Haydn's great popularity and, in the absence of firm copyright laws, the inclination of unscrupulous publishers to issue symphonies written by others in his name. Currently the number stands at 106, two more than Eusebius Mandyczewski identified for his 1907 catalogue to accompany the complete edition proposed by the publisher Breitkopf & Härtel. The original list of 104 is still in use, although one or two remain suspect and in some cases the proposed order of composition badly misses the mark.[16] All of this has hampered the preparation of a collected edition of the symphonies; the Breitkopf project faltered after forty-nine symphonies. Although the Haydn Society of Boston added more volumes in the mid-twentieth century by avoiding duplication of the earlier attempt, they too failed to complete the project. The *Joseph Haydn Werke*, the scholarly edition of Haydn's complete works, remains in progress.[17] Thanks to H. C. Robbins Landon, co-editor of the Boston attempt, an excellent edition of the complete symphonies exists, published in both miniature and performance scores between 1965 and 1968.

Concertos

Compared to the richness of the symphonies, Haydn's concertos, most of which were written before 1770, seem like poor cousins, and relatively few have survived.[18] With our inevitable inclination to compare Haydn and Mozart, we have judged the concertos harshly, perhaps unfairly so, considering Mozart's achievements with the medium. Unlike Mozart, who wrote his piano and violin concertos for himself, Haydn, with the exception of early keyboard concertos, wrote his on commission or for the members of his orchestra. He saw no need to invest himself in these three-movement works for soloist and orchestra or to engage the listener as Mozart had, preferring the symphony to achieve that; in fact, in Vienna during the middle of the century, unlike Italy, audiences and hence composers had a marked preference for symphonies.

Haydn's output of concertos, while not comparable to symphonies or string quartets, was nevertheless substantial, and was originally thought to be much larger than has proved to be the case since he did not write many of those attributed to him. He wrote keyboard concertos for organ, harpsichord, and eventually for clavicembalo or fortepiano, which became a serious concert instrument around 1770. For strings he wrote concertos for violin, cello, his patron Nicolaus's favorite baryton (although these are all lost), and even the violone, or contraviolone (the immediate ancestor of the double bass). His wind concertos include those for flute, bassoon, horn, two horns, and trumpet, although most of these too are lost.

His earliest concertos for organ (or harpsichord) and orchestra from *c.*1750s onwards were perhaps used in his capacity as leader of the orchestra at the Barmherzige Brüder church in Vienna or organist at the chapel of Count Haugwitz. After the Esterházy appointment he wrote only three keyboard concertos, now for harpsichord or piano, and the last of these, in D (Hob. XVIII: 11), emerged as his finest, with its distinctive thematic material and superior treatment of sonata-ritornello writing. His concertos for string instruments all belong to the Esterházy years, those for violin in all likelihood written for virtuoso lead violinist Luigi Tomasini, and those for cello for Joseph Weigl. Weigl's friendship with Haydn may have had some bearing on the high quality of the Concerto in C (Hob. VIIb: 1), a work believed to be from the early 1760s that remains firmly lodged in the cello repertoire, along with the Concerto in D (Hob. VIIb: 2) from 1783, despite its more conservative approach. The Concerto for Horn in D (Hob. VIId: 3) of 1762 has an Allegro first movement instead of the usual Moderato, and places extraordinary demands on the player. The most unusual of his concertos are the five for lira organizzate, commissioned in 1785–86 by King Ferdinand IV of Naples. Ferdinand played this instrument, similar to a hurdy-gurdy with a miniature organ lodged in it, with great skill, but since Haydn knew nothing of it, the commission presumably had to be accompanied by instructions on its range and capabilities.

Haydn wrote the Trumpet Concerto in E♭, his last known concerto, in 1796 for his friend Anton Weidinger. At the time the clarino trumpet remained the standard instrument, but various inventors, including Weidinger, were tinkering with keyed trumpets. By 1796 no one had perfected the instrument, and even though Haydn, recently returned from England, may have wished to give Viennese audiences a taste of his new orchestral prowess, the concerto could not be performed. After its eventual premiere in 1800, the *Wiener Zeitung* announced that Weidinger wished "to present to the world for the first time . . . an organized trumpet which he has invented and brought – after seven years of hard and expensive labor – to what he believes may be described as perfection: it contains several keys and will be displayed in a concerto specially written for this instrument by Herr Joseph Haydn."[19] Haydn endowed this concerto with brilliant passages ranging from trumpet fanfares to moving cantabiles, all with a rich orchestral sound underlying the solo line.

Early symphonies

Griesinger tells us that "in the year 1759 Haydn was appointed in Vienna to be music director to Count Morzin," and that he composed his first symphony in this position.[20] He identifies this work as no. 1, which squares with Haydn's own records, but the date appears to be out by one or possibly two years. Remaining with Morzin until the prince had squandered his small fortune and had to disband his little orchestra, Haydn wrote at least fifteen symphonies, establishing himself as a leading symphonist by 1760. These early works, sometimes compared with those of Johann Stamitz and others in Mannheim, probably have more in common with Gassmann, a leading composer of symphonies in Vienna until his death in 1774, and even more with Italian opera overtures. No clear line distinguished overtures and symphonies at this time, and the pre-eminence of Italian opera determined the primary influence.

This, along with comparisons with string quartets, led some to speculate that Giovanni Battista Sammartini exerted a strong early influence on Haydn, although Haydn denied this.[21] The earliest symphonies variously use the overture three-movement format of fast–slow–fast, the expanded four-movement possibility with added minuet, and the approach of starting with a slow movement, using the baroque *di chiesa* style. These pre-Esterházy works are the most neglected of Haydn's symphonies, but their emerging confidence reveals that the striking new approach at Eisenstadt did not emerge from a vacuum.

Haydn's appointment in 1761 to the position of Vice-Kapellmeister to the Esterházy family secured his career as a music director and composer. Post-Enlightenment thought has tended to disparage the working conditions that Haydn accepted in his first contract, signed May 1, 1761, but the language contained nothing unusual for the time. Amid clauses about his responsibilities to Ober-Kapellmeister Gregor Joseph Werner, as well as clothing, conduct, supervision of the musicians, and care of the instruments, his compositional obligations stipulated that he should not "communicate such new compositions to anyone, nor to allow them to be copied, but to retain them wholly for the exclusive use of his Highness."[22] For a composer not yet thirty years of age and eager to work, the terms of the contract suggested much more opportunity than restriction.

After the relative economy of means in the Morzin symphonies, Haydn could move to a grander style for the Esterházys, as his works could now reflect the splendor of the court and benefit from the quality of the band of musicians available to him. While some of the twenty-five symphonies composed between 1761 and 1767 distinctly served to entertain, others opted for a more learned style or combined the two types. Few of these use three movements, as the four-movement symphony now became the standard.

Initially Haydn had a very small ensemble with which to work, no more than thirteen to fifteen players, typically six violins, one viola, one cello, one bass, two oboes, two horns, one bassoon, and occasionally one flute.[23] Horn parts could occasionally be augmented beyond the usual two, as nos. 13, 31, 39 and 72 use four horns. The musicians themselves all played at an exceptionally high calibre, necessary for performing music on demand at short notice. Haydn had the contractual authority to manage them as he saw fit, but he also immediately realized he needed to secure their loyalty. His first three symphonies for the ensemble, nos. 6–8, "Le matin," "Le midi," and "Le soir," achieved this brilliantly as each one features solo obbligato parts that display individual members of the ensemble to great advantage. According to Dies, Prince Paul Anton "gave Haydn the four times of day [*Tagszeiten*] as a theme for a composition;"[24] whether or not the ideas came from the prince, the works themselves were highly original and charted new territory.

No. 6, "Le matin," opens with an adagio introduction in which a rhythmic rising figure in the first violin is joined by the second violin and then full orchestra, moving from pianissimo to fortissimo, representing the rising sun. The opening allegro theme, marked by two measures of quarter notes in the flute followed by a rapidly rising D major scale, provides material on which other movements can draw. The finale most notably uses this material, also starting with solo flute, now opening with the rising D major scale. Like the first movement, the second also begins with a slow introduction and moves from pianissimo to forte. No. 7, "Le midi," has a second movement that features a duet between solo violin and cello. Marked "recitativo" at the beginning, and with regular shifts from adagio to allegro, it appears to be in the operatic style of a *scena*, and the vocal style of the solo strings reinforces this impression.

While opera underlies parts of no. 7, the operatic association in no. 8 becomes much more explicit, as Haydn took bold new dramatic steps. Daniel Heartz has drawn connections between a number of passages in the first movement of "Le soir" and Gluck's "Je n'aimais pas le tabac beaucoup," a song featured in *Le diable à quatre*, an opera revived in 1759 and well known to Viennese audiences.[25] In a fascinating and plausible reading, Richard Will takes this further, suggesting that Gluck's song triggers a dramatic association with the opera itself, and that the movement portrays the relationship between two of the characters from the opera, the cobbler Jacques and his wife Margot, giving us a domestic, conjugal drama. Her interest in tobacco becomes the issue, after her husband forbids her to use it, and the presentation of contrasting themes representing male and female characters, along with their working-out and resolution, offers up a specific drama.[26] From this early stage Haydn perceived the symphony as a composition that could appeal to an audience in a similar way to opera, by being dramatic, and it could best do so with actual references to opera.

Other works from his first five years in the service of the prince also reveal dramatic features, if not as overtly as no. 8. This can involve exchanges of the comic and serious, as happens in the dialogue-like exchanges in the finale of no. 13. Reference to familiar material could also take various guises, including horn calls associated with the hunt, in no. 13, and even more dramatically in no. 31, the "Horn Signal" Symphony (1765), which also features military and posthorn calls. Around the same time Haydn introduced liturgical associations, as in no. 22, "Le philosophe." Heartz describes its opening Adagio as a kind of chorale prelude, with a walking bass that looks back to Bach and the Lutheran tradition, and belongs to the tradition of the "church symphony."[27] No. 30, the "Alleluja" Symphony (1765), takes this even further, since it incorporates near the outset a liturgical melody, and continues with the sacred tone.[28]

The minor mode, church, and theater

Much has been written about the symphonies of 1768–72, a disproportionate number of which are in minor keys, and by now the epithet "Sturm und Drang" has more or less been abandoned as a suitable description for them. While they may have striking features that distance them from the earlier 1760s, neither the minor keys nor the content suggest that they arose from some personal crisis that Haydn may have experienced. Some have found it useful to define these works in the context of a pre- or early-romantic trend, but that has only served to dislodge them even further from the century in which they originated. The term "Sturm und Drang" arises from a novel by F. M. Klinger, from a decade later than the symphonies the term applies to, and the nature of this literary phenomenon bears no resemblance to the content of Haydn's symphonies. Some of the more recent attempts to characterize these as church symphonies or theater symphonies hit closer to the mark;[29] since this group includes both types as well as some that fit into neither, the right epithet remains elusive.

No work defines the church symphony as well as no. 26, the "Lamentatione," which not only incorporates a Gregorian chant familiar to virtually every churchgoer in eighteenth-century Austria, but also turns the symphony into overt drama. In the first movement Haydn quotes the *Cantus Ecclesiasticus Sacrae Historiae Passionis Domini Nostri Jesu Christi* at length, setting up a Passion drama in the same manner as the liturgical source.[30] To prepare the listener for this theme, labelled "Chorale," agitation permeates the opening sixteen measures of the first movement, appropriately in the key of d minor and with syncopation. Continuing this spirit in the second movement, Haydn quotes a lamentation of Jeremiah from the same liturgical collection. The source material in the first movement, with texts for the Evangelist, Christ, and the Vox populi (see mm. 17, 26, and 35 respectively), in conjunction with the lamentation in the second, turns the symphony into a kind of vocal work without words. The instrumentation also supports this, as the source material always sounds in the oboe and violin II parts.[31] Liturgical gravitation and theater occur in the same work. Another work from this time, no. 49, "La passione," similarly directs the listeners' thoughts to Holy Week, and thematic material here may also have plainchant origins.

As unusual and daring as some of the symphonies in minor keys are, nothing surpasses no. 45, the "Farewell" (1772), for originality and provocation. The familiar story said to have inspired the symphony, related by Dies in great detail,[32] tells of the musicians wishing to leave Eszterháza and return to their families in Vienna. They persuaded Haydn to give a musical message to Prince Nicolaus, and he accomplished this in the finale, with instructions for the musicians to blow out their candles and leave when their parts end, leaving only two violins to complete the work. There appears to be no compelling reason why Dies did not get most of the details correct, but his story ignores even greater musical significance than the farewell drama staged in the coda of the finale. Aside from the cyclical nature of the work already noted, the first movement proves to be highly dramatic and provocative in its disruption of formal expectations.[33] The exposition lacks a second group, which arrives in the development with a new theme. The development develops nothing, as that falls in the recapitulation. With this manipulation of expectation, the Prince's curiosity may have been as piqued by this movement as by the finale.

For many past writers on Haydn, the symphonies of the 1770s, completely lacking in minor keys, seem like a return to the symphonic dark ages of celebratory appeal and enforced popularity. Nothing could be further from the truth. In exploring the expressive possibilities of his symphonies, Haydn had earlier quoted all sorts of source material, aligning symphonies with liturgical drama or opera, and devising new levels of complexity in thematic working, tonal exploration and formal flexibility. Minor keys had offered interesting possibilities, but we clearly overrate their expressive power. Just as Mozart could present the deepest feelings in major keys in a work such as *Le nozze di Figaro*, Haydn now proceeded in major keys, with no deterrence to his achievement of beauty or the sublime. The next decade proved every bit as critical to his development as the previous one, and with the marked increase of his operatic activities, especially with the new and intensive phase beginning in 1776, it comes as no surprise that his symphonies gravitate more towards opera and the theater in general.

A useful characterization of the symphonies from this time has been provided by Elaine Sisman, with special focus on no. 60 (1774), "Il distratto," made up of the six-movement incidental music (overture, four entr'actes and finale) for the performance of the comic play *Le distrait* by Regnard.[34]

The possibility exists that Haydn wrote other incidental music at this time, perhaps even for Shakespeare's *Hamlet* or Goethe's *Götz von Berlichingen*, and that various symphonic movements served the combined purpose of symphonies and operatic overtures or incidental music for plays. That the first movement of no. 63 is an altered version of the overture to *Il mondo della luna* helps to make the point, and it may be the case, although not all agree, that the "La Roxelana" epithet for no. 63 points to incidental music.[35]

The movements or entr'actes of no. 60 parallel the appropriate parts of *Le distrait* to which they correspond, and this begins as early as the overture, which, in the apparent distractedness of aspects of the music, presumably introduces us musically to the absent-minded protagonist. Transitional material appears to lose its way, as though Haydn lost track of where he was, and derailment of the forward drive continues throughout the movement, culminating with an apparent quotation from the opening of the "Farewell" Symphony,[36] a movement that sets the standard for derailment. This and other works from the 1770s and early 1780s leave no doubt that Haydn believed a symphony could engage an audience very much as an opera could, or even literary works for the stage.

Along with the greater dramatic appeal of his symphonies came a new ability to reach audiences beyond the Eszterháza estates, in the form of a new contract he signed on January 1, 1779, which dropped the restrictive language of his original contract. Now he could accept outside commissions, sell his music to publishers, or arrange for performances elsewhere. Nicolaus may have had various reasons to loosen things up after almost two decades of faithful service from his Kapellmeister, and not the least of these may have been that Haydn had become an international sensation, another jewel in his patron's crown well worth displaying widely. If the prince's interest in symphonic music flagged at this time, concert organizations throughout Europe could not get enough of Haydn, and he could now write works specifically for them. In 1782 he wrote a set of three, nos. 76–78, aimed towards a publisher or a concert organization, probably in England.[37] With no. 78 he wrote a symphony in a minor key for the first time in a decade, and another minor one came shortly thereafter, no. 80, also belonging to a set of three. The serious d minor opening of this work stands in marked contrast to the lighter second group beginning at m. 25, and especially the closing theme with its comic Scotch snap rhythm (mm. 57–64). This contrast of comic and serious had by now been elevated to a dramatic principle.

During Haydn's Esterházy tenure the size of his orchestra steadily grew. While still at Eisenstadt he drew extra players from the church orchestra or other local musicians, building an orchestra of close to twenty players, but at Eszterháza that number increased as the violins were augmented, and eventually flute, trumpets and timpani became regular fixtures. During the 1770s and 1780s the orchestra included more virtuoso players, and turnover occurred frequently; by 1780 Haydn could depend on having at least twenty string players at his disposal, and sometimes more.

Paris and English symphonies

By 1785 Haydn found himself no longer needing to reach out to an international audience since that audience approached him with commissions, in the first instance from Count d'Ogny for six symphonies to be performed in Paris by the Concert de la Loge Olympique. Now he could write for a particular audience, certainly sophisticated,[38] with the knowledge that justice would be done to his works from the fine orchestra of fifty-five to sixty members. The concert society, as the name implies, was a masonic organization, and since Haydn's own initiation to the lodge "Zur wahren Eintracht" took place at exactly this time, he may have had additional impetus to present these works in a certain way. His enlightened attitudes appear to have been influenced by his masonic friends such as Greiner, Sonnenfels, and Born, and these symphonies may have seemed the ideal place to put these principles into practice.[39] These symphonies surpass his previous ones not only in their musical breadth and scope but also in their new focus on an intelligible dramatic process. In no way should that belittle earlier works, as these symphonies clearly acknowledge a debt to their predecessors; in fact, one of them, no. 85, "La Reine," more or less quotes the opening of the "Farewell" Symphony, in f minor instead of f# minor, perhaps drawing a connection with a work that points forward.

The order of composition remains unclear; the Parisian publisher Imbault issued them as 83, 87, 85, 82, 86, and 84, although Haydn recommended something else to his Viennese publisher Artaria, who opted to give them in two sets of three as 82–87. No. 83 appears to be one of the first, and its first movement reveals admirably if bizarrely the new approach taken by Haydn in engaging his audience in a process of focused and active listening. He sets up the drama epigrammatically in the first four notes of his g minor theme – G–B♭–C♯–D – reverting to something sounding as though it could come from plainchant, thus giving it an even stronger focus. Within these four notes consonance and dissonance pull against each other, the notes on the beat giving a tritone while the first, second, and fourth notes provide the tonic triad. The first three notes, emphasized by forzato marks, offer a broken diminished chord, and resolution on the fifth degree comes as a weaker afterthought.

Example 7.1 Symphony no. 83, first movement, mm. 176–93

The dramatic problem contained in these notes becomes the focus of the movement, and Haydn highlights the issue in the recapitulation, strikingly drawing the listener's attention to it, demonstrating overwhelmingly that this section will serve a critical dramatic function.[40] With the fermata over a whole-note diminished chord at m. 181, he arrests all forward progress, bringing us to the precise point of dramatic resolution. After the fermata he states the problematic tritone figure twice and then gives the solution in the oboes (Ex. 7.1), thereby demonstrating one of the most fundamental enlightened principles in purely musical but dramatic terms: opposing forces can coexist, and in human terms the principle of tolerance has been put forward.

The great success of the "Paris" Symphonies led to another commission from d'Ogny, nos. 90–92, and nos. 88–89 also capitalized on his new currency. Another commission at this time takes us back to earlier church symphonies, orchestral pieces programmatically representing the last words of Christ, written for the cathedral in Cadíz, Spain. In a letter to William Forster he emphasized the premium he placed on their accessibility to the listener: "Each Sonata, or rather each setting of the text, is expressed only by instrumental music, but in such a way that it creates the most profound impression even on the most inexperienced listener."[41] With the *Seven Last Words* he embraces programmaticism at an extreme level, without falling into the traps of trite representation,[42] achieving what he considered his most successful work.[43]

An invitation to Haydn from the violinist and concert producer Johann Peter Salomon to come to London and present six new symphonies and other works became feasible after the death of Prince Nicolaus in 1790. On 15 December he and Salomon left Vienna, reaching Dover on New Year's Day 1791. Unlike his commissions from Paris, with everything transacted from afar, he now could live in the city for which he would write the symphonies – a matter of great significance. Always conscious of his audience and the need to adapt his works to it, he now acquired an awareness of English musical culture from professionals such as Salomon, from his many new friends, and from attending concerts. In letters back to Vienna he spoke of revisions made to conform to English taste, including the previously written Symphony no. 91, of which he claimed to "have to change many things for the English public."[44] In the same letter he noted the need to make changes to one of the symphonies written for London, presumably no. 93: "I intend to alter the last movement of it, and to improve it, since it is too weak compared with the first. I was convinced of this myself, and so was the public, when it was played the first time last Friday."[45] How he measured this, one cannot say, but the idea itself suggests interesting possibilities for his approach to the English symphonies in general.

Intent on gaining the approval of this audience in whose midst he now resided, to say nothing of coming out ahead of his former pupil Pleyel at the rival Professional Concerts, also at Hanover Square, he appeared to follow a fairly consistent strategy in his six symphonies written for his first two London seasons, 1791–92. One notes a general progression from works with a more popular appeal to those that challenge the listening skills of the audience more intensively. That challenge, as with early symphonies, does not reveal itself in musical complexity alone, but also, as no. 83 had, draws the listener into contemplation of enlightened principles. For the first season of twelve subscription concerts, advertised by Salomon to the "nobility and gentry," he opened with an existing work, no. 92, and then moved to new ones, nos. 96 and 95 (the only English symphony in a minor key and lacking a slow introduction). The 1792 season challenges listeners even more with the innovations of nos. 93, 98, 94 and 97. In 1791 Haydn had a full orchestra of about forty players at his disposal at Hanover Square, including two each of flutes, oboes, bassoons, horns, trumpets, as well as timpani. By the final season that number had grown to sixty, and included clarinets.

He returned to Vienna in 1792, but back in England for the 1794 season, he challenged his audience with new levels of complexity, such as a linkage between the slow introduction and transitions in the first movement of no. 99, thematic connections among the movements of no. 101, or the unstable arrival of the new key in the first movement of no. 100. Haydn had shrewdly insisted that his symphonies appear only on the second half of concerts, allowing his to surpass the works heard first. In 1794, with nos. 99, 101, and 100, reviewers were stunned by the originality of these works. One in the *Morning Chronicle* on March 5 expressed concern that the composer might repeat himself, but "we are every time mistaken. Nothing can be more original than the subject of the first movement; and having found a happy subject, no man knows like HAYDN how to produce incessant variety, without once departing from it."[46] In earlier works Haydn had established that the slow introduction did much more than provide a rhetorical opening

Example 7.2 Symphony no. 103, first movement, mm. 2–5 and 73–74

Example 7.3 Symphony no. 103, first movement, mm. 79–82

to what would follow. Thematic material, tonal procedures, and even metric ambiguity now linked introductions to subsequent material, and in no. 101 he goes well beyond that. Thematic links now travel across the Minuet and the highly complex finale.

Audiences in 1795 must have been as taken by nos. 102, 103, and 104 as audiences remain today, and all of these place high demands on the listeners' focused attention. Complexity begins in the slow introductions, sometimes with contrapuntal working of thematic material, and this carries forward to the rest of the first movement and beyond. This counterpoint can be intense in transitions and even more so in developments, as in no. 102 (mm. 209–16), where as many as four or five previously heard motifs or themes interact simultaneously. Slow introductions in these late symphonies often set a distinctive character, using features of funereal music from both folk and liturgical sources to establish striking contrasts with the bright material in fast sections to follow.[47] In no. 103, for example, immediately after the opening drumroll, the first four notes model those of the "Dies irae" plainchant. As the line unfolds, it sets up an odd metric ambiguity, written in a triple meter, but with nothing to suggest that duple would not be just as appropriate (Ex. 7.2a). In the exposition the dominant key arrives at m. 73 almost unnoticed, and the extraordinary treatment of thematic material here seems equally obscure. The contour of the line in mm. 73–74 parallels the Adagio introduction almost precisely, evoking its funereal character, but at the same time the rhythm suggests a cheerful dance (Ex. 7.2b).[48] This

Example 7.4 Symphony no. 103, first movement, mm. 201–14

dance character anticipates the dance-like theme which follows, at m. 79 (Ex. 7.3).[49] And like the metric ambiguity of the introduction, the dance character places a triple meter against the written 6/8 held in the lower strings and bassoon.

When material similar to the introduction appears at m. 111 of the development, it again can easily slip by unnoticed – a situation reversed in the recapitulation. Now twelve measures of new fortissimo material lead to a fermata, giving the listener no choice but to be alert. With the return of the drumroll and the first two phrases of the Adagio introduction, Haydn commands our full attention. At m. 214 the 6/8 Allegro con spirito returns, bringing back the notable material of mm. 73–74, making it impossible to ignore what may have gone unnoticed earlier (Ex. 7.4). Here Haydn surely takes the listener by the hand, following Shaftesbury's dictum, giving a lesson in listening. Now he offers an extraordinarily sophisticated fusion of opposites, allowing them to coexist in this most potent two-measure line, again reinforcing the notion of tolerance. With these late symphonies Haydn reached not only the highest possible achievement of musical mastery, but he also set the standard for music addressing social and spiritual issues at the deepest possible level.

8 The quartets

MARY HUNTER

Haydn's sixty-eight string quartets[1] span essentially his whole compositional life, from the "Opus 0" and "Opus 1" works of the late 1750s and early 1760s to the unfinished "Opus 103" of 1803. (The traditional opus numbers are retained here for convenience.) They naturally reflect the changes both in Haydn's own compositional habits and in the status and meaning of the string quartet during that near-half-century. The works do become increasingly grand over time, but the extent to which many of the traits of the later quartets are discernible – albeit *in nucis* – in the early ones is quite remarkable. Haydn's compositional modes in these works range from galant to learned and passionate, from intensely original and inward looking to approachably public, and from folklike to sublime. Although this oeuvre mirrors many of the stylistic concerns of the period and of Haydn's music overall, the features that most distinguish the quartets are their use of "conversational" textures and devices, their persistent elevation and seriousness, which is intensified rather than undercut by their pervasive wit, and their strikingly tactile and performative use of the medium.

Origins and sources

Works specifically for two violins, viola, and cello with this last as a solo participant rather than as the written-out representative of a continuo group,[2] were already by *c.*1760 not unusual in southern Germany, Austria, and Bohemia, as well as in Italy, albeit in a rather different style.[3] In France, the *quatuor concertant*, or *quatuor dialogué* – a genre distinguished by its conspicuously evenhanded distribution of thematic material to all the parts – was also on the rise.[4] The oft-repeated story of Baron Fürnberg's request for the Haydn works eventually known as Op. 1 – namely that he wanted some music for a particular combination of players (Haydn himself, Fürnberg's estates manager, the local pastor, and the cellist J. A. Albrechtsberger)[5] – suggests that the medium at least was in some sense familiar, and that the genre was viewed as congenial for friendly, if not completely amateur, music-making. Nevertheless, despite the undoubted pre-existence of the medium, it is not inaccurate to portray Haydn as "inventing" a version of the string quartet that laid the compositional, aesthetic, and cultural foundations of the genre both for subsequent composers (most famously Mozart, who dedicated his first six mature quartets to Haydn) and for Western musical culture more broadly.

Haydn's quartets were so influential not only because they are great works in a genre whose time had evidently come, but also because they were so immediately and widely published. Parts for all the quartets regularly appeared in at least three countries as soon as the first print or copy was made available. Indeed, the early publications were in fact unauthorized by Haydn: it was not until the Op. 33 set of 1781 that Haydn was contractually permitted to sell his works to publishers and thus to have some control over the disseminated text. But authorized or not, the first publications, all in parts, sold vigorously, from which the logical conclusion is that across Northern Europe there were significant numbers of players both eager and able to tackle this often challenging music. From Op. 9 onwards the quartets were typically published in the sets of six or three designed by Haydn in conformance with longstanding practice for both small and large-scale instrumental works. The original opus numbers were, however, often not the ones familiar to us now, and in any case differed from one publisher to the next. In addition to the nine sets of six (Opp. 9, 17, 20, 33, 50, 54/55, 64, 71/74, 76) there are three independent works: "Op. 0" (*c.*1760), Op. 42 (1785), and the unfinished Op. 103 (1803). Op. 77, a set of two, was evidently intended for Prince Lobkowitz as a full opus, but was, for reasons unknown, never completed.[6]

By and large the sets were published with the individual works in the order familiar to us today, though Opp. 54 and 64 had alternative orders well into the nineteenth century. The published order, however, was typically not the order in which Haydn composed the works, but rather an arrangement calculated to make the best impression on potential buyers.[7] There are certain compositional features common to all the sets: in none of the nine sets of six are there two works in the same key, and all sets but Op. 20 include one work in the minor mode (Op. 20 includes two). In addition, each of the nine sets of six has a more or less distinct compositional "character," as if Haydn was looking at a particular set of compositional strategies from six points of view. Op. 20, for instance, is famous for its fugal finales and its "Sturm und Drang" intensity. In Op. 33 the minuet and trio movements are all entitled "Scherzo," (joke) and as many commentators have noted, the set as a whole is particularly full of witticisms. The Opp. 50 and 54/55 sets include works of striking and conspicuous originality, and the Op. 71/74 set is often noted for its public character, which includes the "noise killing" opening measures – which of course also have a variety of internal structural functions.[8] Op. 76 includes the longest and most obviously grand works of all, with extraordinarily solemn and reflective slow movements (including, most famously, if not most sublimely, the variations on the "Kaiser" hymn in the slow movement of no. 3). At the same time, the sets are by no means monolithic: within Op. 76, for example, the grandeur of the Kaiser hymn movement and the long-breathed opening of the "Sunrise" quartet, no. 4, are offset by the exoticism and grotesquerie of the finale to the "Quinten" quartet, no. 2 in d minor, and the apparent naivety of the opening variation movements in nos. 5 in D and 6 in E♭.

The circumstances prompting Haydn to write any given set of quartets are, apart from the story about Baron Fürnberg, not terribly clear. The early works, and Opp. 9, 17, and 20, are not dedicated (except by implication, to Prince Nicolaus), were published only in unauthorized editions, and we do not know what external factors, if any, stimulated their composition. Op. 33 has no dedication, but was written directly for publication soon after the famous change in Haydn's contract, which removed the condition that Haydn's work belonged to Prince Nicolaus.[9] Op. 50 was dedicated to King Friedrich Wilhelm II of Prussia, a keen (and evidently accomplished) cellist. Opp. 54/55 and 64 were sold to the violinist and perhaps over-entrepreneurial merchant Johann Tost, who may or may not have arranged for their publication in Paris. Op. 71/74 was written with the impresario and violinist Johann Salomon in mind, for Haydn's second visit to London, quartets from Opp. 54/55 and 64 having been of interest in public concerts before and during the first London visit.[10] The late quartets (Opp. 71/74, 76, and 77) have dedications (to Count Apponyi, to Count Erdödy, and to Prince Lobkowitz, respectively). Erdödy, at least, is said to have "ordered" – i.e., commissioned – his set.[11] Whatever the circumstances of commission, Haydn had excellent players – especially first violinists – for whom to write, and it is generally assumed that the earlier works (up to and including Op. 33) would have been written with Eszterháza concertmaster Luigi Tomasini in mind. It is possible but by no means certain that Tost was the violinist Haydn had in mind as a first performer of Opp. 54/55 and 64. It is not clear whom (if anyone) he might have intended as the first performers of the last works; there is a reference to a performance of Op. 77 at Eisenstadt in October 1799: it is not out of the question that Luigi Tomasini (and possibly his sons Alois and Anton), who were part of the Eisenstadt orchestra, might have performed.

Given the striking absence of clear circumstantial stimuli for the composition of the quartets, it is tempting to think of them as a private compositional laboratory, as "art for art's sake," prompted only by the desire to work out particular generic and compositional problems.[12] There is surely something to this, but the notion of the compositional hothouse is enriched and complicated both by Haydn's desire to sell these works as broadly as possible, and by their brilliantly tactile use of the medium: even if they were a kind of laboratory, intended as much for himself as for an unknowable audience, it is hard to believe that Haydn did not have both the sounds of particular players and the interests of particular kinds of buyers in mind as he wrote.

Unlike Haydn's large-scale or public works – symphonies, masses, operas, oratorios – the quartets did not have highly publicized premiere performances. The occasions for which they were written were more generic than particular, and the kinds of occasions differed sharply in Vienna and London. As many commentators have noted, string quartets are not found on the programs of any public concerts in Vienna during Haydn's lifetime; nevertheless, production and consumption of quartet publications during the latter part of the century in Vienna were extraordinarily strong.[13] This suggests an active private life for this genre. The notion of the quartet as a private genre, in conjunction with the pervasive (and contemporary) notion of the quartet as conversation, might suggest that this genre belonged in the parlour, with its connotations of domesticity and femininity. This may have been the case for lighter *quatuors concertants*, and perhaps for *quatuors brillants*, which would have required only one truly excellent player. But in fact the few records of Viennese quartet occasions that have so far been unearthed[14] suggest that the performers of quartets such as Haydn's tended to be at least partly professional, overwhelmingly though not uniformly male,[15] and the whole enterprise self-consciously high-minded in a way that other kinds of chamber music (chamber music with piano, and Lieder, for example) were not, or at least not so consistently. Ludwig Finscher points out that the study score seems to have been invented for Haydn's quartets;[16] there is no evidence that Haydn himself was in on this invention (though of course his autographs, like those of other quartet composers, were in score); but the notion of a venue in which a relatively small audience could follow a performance along, and for which performers could have studied the work in a more holistic and disinterested way than a single part might allow, fits extraordinarily well with the many refined compositional devices – and many of the witticisms – in these works. It also connects with the increasingly pervasive notions about "true" quartets (as opposed, presumably, both to quartet arrangements and to aesthetically lighter works for the medium);[17] Haydn's quartets in Vienna both helped form, and responded to, this construction.

The place of quartets in London musical life was quite different from that in Vienna. There were, of course, also private quartet parties, but quartets – increasingly of the broadly structured *brillant* type – were also heard in public concerts, by a large audience accustomed to programs mixing all genres of music from symphony to solo aria.[18] Thus it is not surprising that part of Haydn's London lionizing consisted of performances (by Salomon and his quartet) of pieces from the Opp. 54/55 and 64 sets.[19] It also fits that certain kinds of obvious effects (e.g., staccato homophony, pregnant pauses, unison passages) in Op. 71/74 (written for public performance in London), either make their first appearance, or are particularly frequent in these works.

The nature of the genre

Genre as a topic

By the end of Haydn's life the string quartet was considered a genre distinct from and superior to other kinds of chamber music. Griesinger's introduction to his biography of Haydn lists the quartets second, immediately after the symphonies.[20] And Dies's summary of Haydn's early life notes that he "wrote quartets and other pieces that won him increasing favor . . . until he was known all over as a genius."[21] This elevation of the string quartet above other chamber genres was perhaps incipient in Johann Georg Sulzer's notion in his 1772–79 dictionary that four-part chamber music writing was absolutely the most difficult kind of composition,[22] but he does not specify the string quartet in particular. It is not clear exactly how and when the string quartet found its high place, but it is generally agreed that Haydn's work in this genre crucially affected the change in status. The qualities of the canonized string quartet included not only the special sound of four solo string instruments, but also the "conversational" relations among the four parts (that is, the sharing of important material among the parts), the intellectualism of the music, which, in Haydn's hands especially, often emerged as wit, and the mixture of this intellectualism with performative display.

A survey of Haydn's quartet oeuvre suggests that other genres – the *quatuor concertant* and the *quatuor brillant*, the concerto, the solo sonata, as well as aria, recitative, hymn, fugue, and various versions of minuet – all fed into Haydn's emerging sense of the string quartet. Often in his earlier quartets these other genres function as models that pervade most or all of a movement. For example, concerto-like opening movements, in common or cut time, beginning with a single clear melodic line that articulates a strongly periodic melody over a steady accompaniment can be found in Op. 9 no. 3, Op. 9 no. 1, and Op. 17 no. 2; these movements tend to continue in a concerto-like mode, with the three lower parts in largely accompanimental, filler, or rather mechanically concertante roles. Although first-violin virtuosity is a feature of almost all the quartets from earliest to latest, in the later works concerto-like moments (especially "brilliant-style" cadences) tend to be sutured to non-concerto-like material. Similarly, the famous finales of Op. 20 nos. 2, 5 and 6 are thoroughgoing fugues; in later quartets fugato passages tend to occur either in development sections, or in finales as a kind

Example 8.1a Op. 74, no. 1, first movement, mm. 3–6

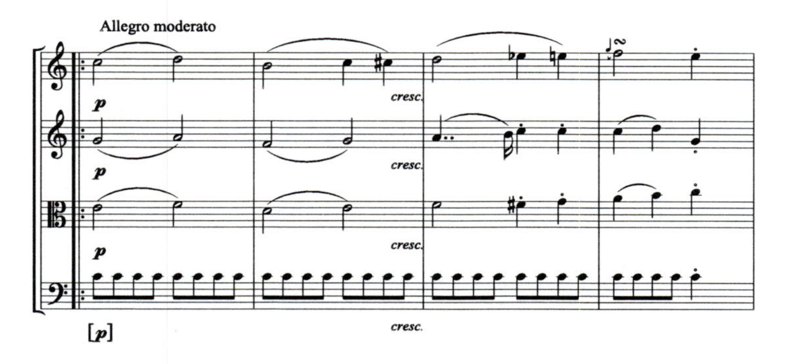

of foil to the strikingly light or jolly opening material. This general chronological trend notwithstanding, already in the finale of Op. 9 no. 4 we see Haydn enjoying the comic possibilities of juxtaposing a fugal texture with lighter material.

Vocal models also abound throughout the quartets, especially in the slow movements, but the earlier quartets are more likely than the later ones to retain the model throughout a movement. The slow movement of Op. 17 no. 5 consists entirely in an alternation of arioso and recitative. While the recitative is a literal copy of the vocal model, the arioso, like most such moments in Haydn, evokes song in a more generalized way, using the full range of the instrument and idiomatically instrumental figuration. Other vocal models invoked include full aria, chorale or hymn, and even in one instance (Op. 64 no. 2) a quasi-sacred cantus firmus.[23] In the later quartets Haydn is more likely to invoke a vocal genre and then transform it into something purely instrumental: the slow movement of Op. 76 no. 1, for example, starts out as a hymn, but juxtaposes this with quintessentially quartet-like conversation between cello and first violin around a pulsating accompaniment in the inner parts.

By the later quartets, not only had Haydn absorbed elements from a host of different genres into his string quartets, and not only was he quite accustomed to juxtaposing and interweaving them, but the quartets' "ownership" of these different idioms and textures could become a topic in itself. The first movement of Op. 74 no. 1 is a wonderful example of genre as the topic of a movement.[24] It begins almost symphonically, after the characteristic "noise-killer" introduction of this public opus, with the three upper parts in slow motion over a Trommel (or drum) bass in the cello (see Ex. 8.1a). The transition is much more conversational, or "truly" quartet-like, with material passed among all the parts, but subtly altered each time (see Ex. 8.1b). A concerto *topos* emerges to clinch the modulation to the dominant and the exposition closes with a *quatuor concertant*-like passing around of unremarkable passage work (see Ex. 8.1c). A fugato appears in the recapitulation,

ex. 8.1a
ex. 8.1b
ex. 8.1c

Example 8.1b Op. 74, no. 1, first movement, mm. 18–29

Example 8.1c Op. 74, no. 1, first movement, mm. 49–54

and the movement ends with a symphonic unison version of the opening material and a repeat of the concertante codetta. It may be no accident that this display of generic inclusiveness – with all genre-markers discrete and unmistakeable – occurs in the set written specifically for public performance in London; it is in its way an assertion of the by then well-understood power of the quartet.

Even in the earliest quartets the minuet was a genre sufficiently well established that it could immediately be played with. The compositional issue in this case seems to have been not so much "how do the relevant characteristics of this genre translate to the string quartet," but "what is a minuet anyway?" Gretchen Wheelock has argued that it was both an easily recognized dance and the classic composition-teaching medium, both of which "templates" Haydn used with endless invention.[25] Wheelock points out the ways in which Haydn plays with the expected regularities of dance meters and phrases: hemiolas and uneven phrase lengths are rife. In addition, the courtly minuet, with its more or less equal three beats, turns easily into the country dance Ländler, with its waltz-like emphasis on the first beat, and its characteristic slurring of the first two beats. Haydn often exploits this slippage, either in the contrast between Minuet and Trio, or within the minuet itself. The minuet's role as teaching tool is often invoked in its use of canon (the majority of Trios have at least one canonic moment), and its direct use or suggestion of a two-voice texture, which can be as obvious as the famous canonic movement in the "Quinten" quartet, Op. 76 no. 2 or as subtle as the beginning second strain of the minuet in Op. 17 no. 3, which starts with a brief two-voice imitative entry for the two violins, seems to be going to bloom into four parts, then tightens back into two parts again, this time with each part played by two instruments in octaves.

Conversation

The metaphor of the quartet as a conversation "among four reasonable people," as Goethe famously put it,[26] was in the air as Haydn was writing his quartets. It had been used for various kinds of chamber music throughout the eighteenth century, but between the 1770s and the early nineteenth century it became particularly attached to the string quartet.[27] And indeed, the quartet as a genre, certainly, if not exclusively in Haydn's hands, was in part "about" the conversations possible when four people play music together in a given situation; primarily among the four parts (and secondarily among the players of those parts), but also between the players and the audience, and between the composer as represented in the "work itself" and the listeners. "Conversation" in the quartet is often taken to imply a kind of textural democracy; that is, the four parts having comparably important roles in the presentation of the musical material, and taking turns, at least to some extent, in leading the discussion.[28] But eighteenth-century descriptions of the quartet as conversation suggest that the metaphor was also useful because it invoked an ideal of clarity or rationality in the disposition of roles, as much as, if not more than, democracy. Some writers took the idea of roles to the logical extreme, assigning the four instruments dramatic characters. Giuseppe Carpani, an early Haydn biographer, heard in his quartets a first violin who was a spirited and likable middle-aged man; a second violin who was his friend and whose main function was to keep the conversation going, rarely drawing attention to himself; a learned and sententious cello who often lent gravity to the utterances of the first violin; and a viola figured as a charming but chattering woman with nothing important to say, who could at least occasionally let the others draw breath.[29] Other writers relied less extravagantly on the metaphor. Music theorist Heinrich Christoph Koch described the galant style of quartet writing as follows: "While one voice takes the leading melody, the two others [aside from the voice serving as a bass] must continue with complementary melodic material that will reinforce the expression without beclouding the leading melody."[30] One could imagine the real-life conversational equivalent of Koch's "complementary melodic material" as the body language of an interlocutor, subtly shaping the main speaker's utterance. But whether or not there is an exact parallel in verbal communication, the picture that Koch paints here is of a discourse where all the participants know their roles and where those roles collaborate in clarifying the current hierarchy of events.

The ending of the first movement of Op. 64 no. 2 in b minor is a case where Haydn achieves both "democracy" and "clarity," and uses the variety of textures at his disposal to articulate the structural function of his material (see Ex. 8.2). The excerpt begins with the tonally stable version of the first theme (as in Op. 33 no. 1, the earlier b minor quartet, this one begins as though it could be in D, b minor's relative major); the unison emphasizes the "grounding" function of this material. No sooner has Haydn established this idea, though, than the texture changes [at (1)] to first-violin domination with corroborating pairs of notes in the two inner parts. This phrase elides at (2) to what sounds like pre-cadential wind-up. The first violin repeats a motive derived from the opening of the movement, and the cello both provides a steady rhythmic drive and articulates the dominant pedal – a classic "supporting" role. The viola at (3) joins the cello in pushing, staccato, to the third beat – a support to the support, perhaps bringing out something latent in the lowest line. The second violin starts this phrase [at (2)] by seeming to stick obstinately, if subsidiarily, to the slurs from the previous measure, perhaps "agreeing" to be supportive, but demurring enough not to

Example 8.2 Op. 64, no. 2, first movement, mm. 92–104

want to join the staccato bandwagon. At (4) the second violin's independence turns out to have been prescient, as its three-note figure, fitted with a turn, converses directly and relevantly with the first violin. The second has thus transformed itself from mere sidekick to the supporters into the co-leader of the conversation. However that moment in the sun is (as always) short-lived, as the first violin and cello together push the argument off its dominant pedal and towards an extended cadence in which the first violin takes on a kind of diva role. The cello here keeps the rhythm going, lending life to the first violin's long notes, and the two inner parts provide "mere" harmonic filler – inglorious but essential. At (6), the beginning of the series of short cadences that end the movement, the viola resumes (though in a different rhythm) its staccato accompaniment from (3), but since there is no cello line, this motive takes on the "first-supporter" role that the cello had before. But the line is a little more mobile than the cello's at (2), and the new timbre of the viola as bass line lends it a level of independence (perhaps akin to an addition to the argument rather than a simple agreement). The second violin takes over this role briefly, "chattering" in the background with the viola, but as the cadence looms, the cello takes over the role of bass line, and all the lower parts line up to accompany the first violin (see Ex. 8.2).

Words do not adequately capture the subtlety of the discourse in this excerpt, but among its miracles is that the thread of the argument is never in doubt despite the complexity of the texture. The movement as a whole is constructed from only a couple of motives, and this passage very clearly explicates, diverges from, and then returns to those motives; in addition, the first violin is clearly the part that carries the discursive thread, despite the activity in the other parts. These measures constitute only one example among many such moments of compositional virtuosity in this oeuvre.

Wit and humor

However confined the immediately imagined performance venues for most of Haydn's quartets, it is clear that they are directed not only to the players but also to non-playing listeners. Gretchen Wheelock has noted of the last movement of Op. 33 no. 2, the "Joke," that the famous undercutting of the ending by fragmentation of the theme, general pause, and use of the opening motive as a cadence directly invokes the idea of an audience, since the players, even if sightreading, would be able to see the full workings of the music at this point.[31] This famous joke is all about expectation – when will the piece end, and how can the listeners tell when to clap or otherwise indicate their acknowledgment of the end? Many, if not most, of Haydn's witticisms in the quartets play on the listeners' (and often also the players') expectations, though most do not do so as baldly as the end of Op. 33 no. 2. General pauses of a measure or more (particularly in evidence in Op. 71/74) are obvious examples of such play.[32] More subtle play on expectations can involve the function of a phrase: the "how do you do" beginning of Op. 33 no. 5, for example, is a classic cadential motive; such "beginning/ending" jokes are quite prevalent in the earlier quartets. The play on expectations can also be about the genre: the dissolution of the strenuous contrapuntal beginning to the finale of Op. 9 no. 4 into something much lighter (see above) plays on the listeners' expectations of the aesthetic and social level

Example 8.3 Op. 71, no. 3, second movement, mm. 1–8

both of this movement in particular and of finales in general. Witticisms that play on the listeners' expectations can also involve structural stereotypes: the first movements of the quartets (especially those before Op. 50) are full of false or otherwise ambiguous or elided moments of recapitulation. And in the *grazioso* binary theme of the slow movement in Op. 71 no. 3, the first strain, which "should" go to the dominant, F major – and even does, briefly, at the beginning of m. 7, gets diverted to d minor – a very peculiar ending for a theme that started out so innocuously (see Ex. 8.3). Because jokes such as these rely on the listeners' (and players') structural and generic expectations for their appreciation; because, in other words, the recipients of the works need to contribute something quite specific in order "properly" to receive them, many of the witticisms in these quartets can be said to contribute to their overall ethic of conversation, with the interchange here occurring between the composer on the one side and all qualified players and listeners on the other. The subtle and technical nature of many of these witticisms also demarcates an "inner circle" of aficionados perhaps analogous to the ideally exclusive circles in which "true" conversation took place.

Some jokes in the quartets, however, address a less exclusive audience. There are many moments when the sound alone is the humor. Sound *qua* sound is a preoccupation throughout these works: they are carefully marked with dynamics and articulation, and Haydn uses double stops, open strings, and "una corda" designations (i.e., playing high on a low string). He also plays with the sonic qualities of the relations among the parts: close harmonies, high instruments playing a bass line, "too many" instruments playing a busy accompaniment, drones, octave and at-pitch doublings, and different instruments playing the tune. Even in this astonishingly varied palette, some sounds stand out as humorous. The obsessively gurgling bariolage (alternation of an open string with regularly stopped notes, often on lower strings) in the finale to the "Frog" quartet, Op. 50 no. 6, is one such example;

the extraordinary high and homophonic staccato passage for the three upper parts towards the end of the slow movement of Op. 71 no. 3 is another. Haydn sometimes uses pizzicato to provoke a laugh: the completely plucked end of the already flamboyantly rambunctious finale to Op. 33 no. 4 is funny partly because it reintroduces from the first four beats of the work the question of beginnings that sound like endings and vice versa, but partly also because ensemble pizzicato is in this context an astonishing sound.

Performativity

If the witticisms in the quartets play up the relation between the composer and his audience, the sonic humor draws some attention to the material qualities of the instruments for which these works were written. But Haydn's quartets also make performance unusually prominent, both as a physical act and as a more abstract *topos*. Concerto-like moments occur in most of these works at one point or another, as they do in Mozart's quartets. These moments raise the *topos* of performance by evoking what we might think of as the typical concert violinist. Haydn also evokes the Hungarian Gypsy fiddler[33] in a number of places: among which are the development section of the opening movement of the "Kaiser" quartet, op. 76 no. 3, where the Hungarian melody[34] is emphasized by crude drones in the lower parts, and the finale of Op. 20 no. 4, where the second violin adds the obligatory tinkling grace notes to the exotically repetitive sixteenths of the first violin.[35] In addition to depicting different "ideal types" of performers, however, Haydn also writes passages that draw attention to the players' manual efforts. These include extreme and speedy string crossings and bariolage, which draw attention to the player's bow arm, often in ways disproportionate to the compositional interest of the passage. In addition, Haydn occasionally specifies fingerings that highlight the player's left-hand technique – again often in ways that exceed the structural or melodic needs of the passage. Examples include the conspicuous slides in the trio of the "Joke" quartet, and a number of passages that use the higher reaches of low strings in surprising or conspicuous ways – as in the closing group of the first movement of Op. 64 no. 4.

Attention to performers and performance is not incommensurate with wit. In a number of instances Haydn plays with the disjunction between sight and sound, or between what the audience might assume the composer wrote, and what the performers must actually do. For example, the Trio of Op. 9 no. 4 is in three independent parts (itself a pun), but is played by only the two violins (the first violin plays in double stops throughout). And in the middle (G♭ major) section of the slow movement of Op. 74 no. 2, the second violin has the tune, in a relatively high register, with the first playing not filigree decorations on top, but rather a typical second violin part: long notes in the middle register. These kinds of witticisms about performance roles and expectations are completely absent from Mozart's and largely absent from Beethoven's quartets, and suggest the extent to which Haydn was concerned not only with humor, nor, indeed, only with art in the abstract, but also with the variety of interactions possible in a fully composed work played by four people with three different instruments and an undetermined number of attentive listeners.

9 Intimate expression for a widening public: the keyboard sonatas and trios

MICHELLE FILLION

The keyboard was an enduring focus of Haydn's activity and achievement. Composition began for him with improvisation at the keyboard, and he later likened himself to "a living keyboard" touched by imagination.[1] As a performer he was by his own admission no "wizard";[2] yet he mastered the harpsichord and clavichord in his youth, and skillfully navigated the passage to the fortepiano as it became increasingly available in the 1780s. These three instruments inspired around sixty solo sonatas (Hoboken work-group XVI), a handful of incidental pieces (Hob. XVII), at least forty keyboard trios with violin and cello (Hob. XV), and an odd dozen divertimentos and concertinos for keyboard and accompanying strings (Hob. XIV).[3] This impressive body of work runs the gamut from the solo and accompanied *Clavier* divertimentos and partitas of the 1750s and early 1760s to the London pianoforte sonatas and trios of 1794–95, bringing him from the loneliness of his attic garret on the Michaelerplatz to a pan-European market. This essay examines how Haydn's keyboard music – while remaining essentially a vehicle for private sentiment – widened its appeal to reach an international audience of publishers and patrons.

The literature in English on Haydn's keyboard music and its performance includes distinguished full-length studies by Brown, Somfai, and Harrison, and three fine essays on the solo music (Sisman) and the piano trios (Rosen and Sutcliffe).[4] This essay differs from the latter in its brevity, to be sure, but also in its examination of Haydn's accompanied and solo keyboard music in a single, integrated sweep. Whether solo or accompanied, Haydn's keyboard music was intended for performance in the home and private salon – and most often by women, for whom the keyboard had become a centerpiece of their education and socialization.[5] The sonatas and the still-neglected piano trios profit from a comprehensive view of their reciprocal responses to a common set of compositional, aesthetic, and social issues. Keyboard music emerges from this survey as a constant throughout Haydn's long career, as would befit the set of instruments that served him as muse and alter ego.

Genesis of a public style (*c.*1750–74)

Haydn's keyboard sonatas, trios, and accompanied divertimentos before the mid-1760s emerged from the culture of Austrian keyboard music around the Habsburg *Hofklaviermeister* Georg Christoph Wagenseil.[6] Haydn tailored these works to "the needs and capacities of his pupils,"[7] from beginners (the little sonatas Hob. XVI: 7–10 are still a mainstay of every young pianist's formation) to accomplished musicians. The largest solo sonatas (Hob. XVI: 2, 6, 13–14) are brilliantly conceived for the harpsichord, and exude a rugged vitality and breadth of expression unmatched by Wagenseil's works. The Sonata in B flat (Hob. XVI: 2), with its vigorous opening fanfare and powerful Largo slow movement in the relative minor, ending with one of the most memorable minuets in Haydn's early music, can easily hold its own in a modern recital (Sviatoslav Richter had it in his repertoire).[8] Haydn's early trios likewise profited from the example of his contemporaries (especially the works of J. A. Steffan), but here too his originality prevails. The finest of these works bring together elements of the trio sonata, string trio, and keyboard sonata with optional string accompaniment in a manner unmatched in the works of his Viennese contemporaries.

Several of the larger sonatas and trios may have served as teaching material for two of Haydn's most distinguished harpsichord students in the 1750s, Marianne von Martínez and the Countess Maria Christine Thun.[9] The superb trios in E major and f minor (Hob. XV: 34 and f1) may have figured at Count Fürnberg's famous quartet parties,[10] while the four-movement trio in G (Hob. XV: 41) found its way into the music collection of the Habsburg Archduchess Maria Elisabeth.[11] The speculation that the brilliant Capriccio in A, Hob. XV: 35, with its unusual concerted violin part, may have been composed in the mid-1760s for the Esterházy court would make it one of the last of the series of early trios.[12] Although Haydn's Esterházy contract of 1761 precluded the selling or dissemination of his works, much of this music circulated widely beginning in the 1760s. These early manuscript copies and editions may have earned Haydn no income, but they brought his keyboard music into homes in Austria, the German states, Holland, France, and even London.

Beginning around 1766, in a series of keyboard sonatas that include Hob. XVI: 18–20 and 44–46, Haydn's keyboard style underwent a decisive change. If these works have been overshadowed in the literature by the path-breaking and far more numerous symphonies and string quartets of 1768–72, this is partially because seven of these sonatas are lost and known only through incipits in Haydn's own catalogue of works (Hob. XVI: 2a–e, g–h); the latter include two in the minor mode and one in the unusual key of B major also used in the Symphony no. 46. Recent scholars have avoided the traditional association of this music with the literary "Sturm und Drang," seeking motivation for its charged emotionality and imposing manner in Haydn's appointment as Kapellmeister in 1766 and his new responsibilities for church music and opera. In the case of the keyboard music there is an additional likely catalyst – Carl Philipp Emanuel Bach.[13] It is now believed that Haydn's momentous discovery of Bach's *Essay on the True Art of Playing Keyboard Instruments* with its musical appendix of *Probestücke* took place shortly after 1763. Brown traces the first impact of the *Versuch* in the Capriccio *Acht Sauschneider müssen sein* (Hob. XVII: 1) of 1765 and the sonatas beginning with Hob. XVI: 45 of 1766.[14] Bach's influence on these works may be found in their new profusion of finely calibrated ornaments and appoggiaturas, Haydn's distinctive adaptation of the "varied reprise" (the practice of writing out sectional repeats with ornamental variations), and the elevation of embellishment and articulation to vital structural elements.[15] The enhanced expressiveness, rhythmic intricacy, selective reinstatement of neo-Baroque counterpoint, and new dramatic weight accorded each movement of the sonata cycle are Haydn's own. Finally, the shift to the standard five-octave range (F_1–f^{111}) around 1768 may indicate a new instrument following the fire in his home in August of that year.[16]

The magnificent Sonata no. 20 in c minor of 1771 is justifiably the most played of this sequence. Its numerous dynamic indications (many but not all of which derive from the 1780 Artaria print) have made it the focus of an ongoing controversy regarding its intended instrument, clavichord or fortepiano.[17] The Sonata no. 46 in A♭, with its intricately embellished opening movement and profound Adagio in D♭, is no less impressive. The Sonata no. 44 in g minor is often eclipsed by these companions, partly owing to its two-movement form. Yet its Moderato opener combines the function of a sonata-form first movement with the depth of a slow movement in full *empfindsamer* style. Its nervous rhythmic surface and intense introversion make it ideally suited to the clavichord. The g minor sonata demonstrates the sturdy originality of Haydn's adaptation of the Berlin Bach to Austrian practice.

The Viennese edition of six harpsichord sonatas (Hob. XVI: 21–26) in 1774, dedicated to Prince Nicolaus, is Haydn's first authorized print. This collection initiates Haydn's consciously public keyboard style: in it the severity of his previous sonatas yields to a more ingratiating manner. Reminiscences of the mid-century Viennese keyboard divertimento (especially nos. 21 and 26) alternate with playful, vivacious music that may reflect his heightened activity beginning in 1773 with comic and marionette opera. The Sonata no. 23 in F major demonstrates the new dramatic appeal to both connoisseurs and amateurs. Its brilliant opening movement – easier than it sounds – features nimble fingerwork and toccata-like episodes ideal for the harpsichord (especially mm. 68–77), alternating with glimpses of the "pathetic" mode of the earlier g minor sonata (at mm. 29–32 and 61–68). Its sharp contrasts of *Affekt* are further played out in the following movements: a delicate pathos reigns in the delectable *siciliano* in f minor, while the Presto finale is a *buffo* romp.

Transition to a fortepiano idiom (1780–90)

On January 1, 1779 Haydn's new Esterházy contract took effect, permitting him to sell his music for profit at home and abroad.[18] The timing was propitious. The Viennese firm of Artaria had recently entered the music publishing trade, and in April 1780 Haydn initiated their long association with a set of six keyboard sonatas, Op. 30 (Hob. XVI: 35–39, 20). At the publisher's behest it was dedicated to Katharina and Marianna von Auenbrugger, Viennese salon pianists admired by Haydn for their masterful playing and "genuine insight into music"[19] – qualities required of the performer of this diverse opus. Haydn was delighted at the choice, and would endorse the marketing practice of female dedicatees in his subsequent keyboard prints. A shrewd compilation of old and new, Artaria's Op. 30 was superbly crafted for the marketplace. It includes the sternly conservative Sonatas nos. 36 in c♯ minor and 38 in E♭, three brilliant works in modern style in C, D, and G (nos. 35, 37, and 39), concluding with the large Sonata no. 20 in c minor of 1771. The collection exemplifies the striving for balance – between delight and edification, tradition and innovation, commercial expediency and artistic value, the capacities of the amateur and the discrimination of the connoisseur – which would inspire Haydn's keyboard collections for the next fifteen years. Their alternative scoring "for harpsichord, or forte-piano" is borne out in the music, which reflects Haydn's increasing engagement with the touch-sensitive piano.[20] Although Haydn's keyboard prints retain the dual-scoring convention to the end of his career, the fortepiano would soon supplant the earlier instruments as his medium of choice.

The set of three short sonatas (Hob. XVI: 40–42), published by Bossler in Speyer in August 1784, is Haydn's first authentic foreign print of keyboard music. It initiated a phase of intensive engagement with this medium in a widening international arena. The next six years, until Haydn's departure for London in January 1791, would also see his focused return to the keyboard trio after an almost twenty-year hiatus. The resulting thirteen trios (Hob. XV: 5–17) and two additional solo sonatas (Hob. XVI: 48–49) were disseminated in authorized first editions by Haydn's London publishers Forster and Bland, Breitkopf of Leipzig, and Artaria in Vienna, making Haydn the pre-eminent keyboard composer of the decade. Moreover, in consolidating the achievements of the string quartets, Opp. 33 (1781) and 50 (1787), and the "Paris" symphonies nos. 82–87 (1785–86) and 90–92 (1788–89), they likewise adopt a more popular style. By the last of these works, his gradual shift to the fortepiano would be complete.

The three Bossler sonatas are small in size alone. They are dedicated to Princess Marie Hermenegild Esterházy, who had married the future Nicolaus II in September 1783; it is the first of a number of dedications to her, including the late masses. They are often referred to as *Damensonaten*[21] for their modest size and two-movement design featuring variation and ABA forms. Yet the women for whom this set was intended, beginning with this young Princess, must have been intelligent, cultivated readers of the rhetoric of social behaviour.[22] From the *innocente* double-variation opener of the first Sonata no. 40 in G, the collection is *faux-naïf* in its diverse humor, subtle harmony, nervous rhythms, and melodramatic outbursts (see its *minore* variation, mm. 61–72). An early reviewer also deemed these sonatas "more difficult to perform than one initially believes. They demand the utmost precision and much delicacy in performance"[23] – none more than the Sonata no. 42 in D. It begins with one of Haydn's most refined sets of keyboard variations on an elaborate Andante con espressione theme. The generous articulation and dynamic markings are woven into its very fabric, demonstrating his growing accommodation with the fortepiano.

Haydn's initial return to the keyboard trio in 1784 seems to have been prompted by market pressure. At first, preoccupation with the operas *Orlando paladino* and *Armida* prevented him from responding to repeated appeals for accompanied keyboard sonatas from Vienna and abroad, beginning in 1782.[24] With the premiere of *Armida* behind him in 1784, he responded – apparently half-heartedly – with three trios for Forster (Hob. XV: 3–5), the first two of which were pawned from Pleyel,[25] and the third (Hob. XV: 5), a retrospective work owing much to the early trios. But his interest was piqued, and in 1784–85 he composed two sets of trios for immediate publication: for Vienna, Artaria's Op. 40 (Hob. XV: 6–8), and for London, Forster's Op. 42 (Hob. XV: 9–10, with the earlier Hob. XV: 2).

By 1785 Vienna had followed the rest of Europe in embracing the culture of accompanied keyboard music.[26] The keyboard sonata with violin accompaniment and the trio with added cello were by far the most popular scorings. The string parts were often markedly simpler than the brilliant keyboard part – suitable for performance by musical servants or children – and the cello normally doubled the keyboard bass line. This form of social *Hausmusik* gave accomplished female musicians the performance opportunities denied them in the male-dominated string quartet. A vignette of one such performance appeared in 1798 on the title page of Artaria's Op. 80 print of Hob. XV: 10.[27] It depicts an elaborately coiffed and corseted

Example 9.1 Hob. XV: 7, third movement, reduction of mm. 50–103

woman at the keyboard, surrounded by bewigged male string players in more unassuming attire.

Haydn favored the trio scoring over the duo sonata with violin (the two-movement sonata for keyboard and violin Hob. XV: 32 of 1794 may be his only authentic work in that scoring[28]). Perhaps the dictates of fashion contributed to his taste for two-movement cycles without slow movement in the trios of the 1780s (as Emanuel Bach had lamented in a letter to Breitkopf in 1785, "the Adagio movement . . . is no longer fashionable"[29]). Whatever their concessions to popular taste, Haydn's accompanied sonatas are constructed with consummate skill, and demand no less of the interpreters. The violin parts require an accomplished player capable of carrying off the lyrical solos in subsidiary themes of the large outer movements (as in Hob. XV: 9/I), variations (Hob. XV: 7/I, var. 3), rondo episodes (Hob. XV: 15/III), and the many delectable slow movements. The cello parts are far from optional, leading rather than following the keyboard left hand by virtue of its singing voice and sustaining power. And all three players must bring considerable understanding to bear on the signal musical demands.

The rondo finale of the trio Hob. XV: 7 in D, the gem of Artaria's Op. 40, is a case in point. Given the complexity of its huge retransition (mm. 51–102), it is no wonder that Haydn plotted its course in a meticulous sketch.[30] As outlined in Ex. 9.1, this passage traces an overall rising minor third progression, ending at m. 88 with a stunning enharmonic shift underscored by the teasing upbeat taps. The ensuing false recapitulations in B major and b minor overshadow the concealed tonic reprise at m. 103. Its coda, introduced by a long ad libitum lead-in for the piano (mm. 147–51), transcends the "accompanied sonata" texture by featuring soloistic writing for all three instruments, including cello (see mm. 175–80). The two-movement trio in A (Hob. XV: 9) also reveals a stunning grasp of modern piano trio texture, including frequent solos for high cello in duo with the violin, and a written-out cadenza *en trio* in mm. 55–64 that caps the coda of its first movement.

Haydn again took up the keyboard in 1788 following an intense period of symphony and quartet composition. In August, finding himself in need of "a little money," he offered to write *six* quartets or piano trios for Artaria; the number is significant, implying an expected decision in favor of the quartet. The publisher's request for trios in the customary set of three reflects the continued commercial draw of the accompanied sonata. In order "to compose [these] Sonatas particularly well," Haydn purchased a fortepiano by the Viennese builder Wenzel Schanz in October.[31] Now lost, it was likely a five-octave instrument (F_1–f^{111}) with knee-operated damper mechanism and a moderator for soft contrast.[32] Haydn repeatedly endorsed the Schanz fortepiano for its light touch and comfortable action, as well as its value over the more expensive Walter pianos favoured by Mozart.[33] Although Haydn's keyboard music of the earlier 1780s had already demonstrated more than passing acquaintance with the piano, this purchase is the earliest confirmation that he had a fine working instrument for daily use. The results are immediately evident in the exuberant works of the following months, the trios Hob. XV: 11–13 (Artaria's Op. 57), the Sonata in C for Breitkopf (Hob. XVI: 48), and the wonderfully madcap Fantasia (Hob. XVII: 4). By 1790 his transition to the piano was complete, as attested on the autograph of the Sonata in E♭ (Hob. XVI: 49), '*per il Forte-piano*'. In his letter of June 27, 1790 to his dear Viennese friend Maria Anna von Genzinger, to whom the sonata was dedicated, Haydn excused its unsuitability to the harpsichord with the disclaimer that "I was no longer accustomed to it."[34]

The trios Hob. XV: 11–13 and the contemporary sonata Hob. XVI: 48 radiate the pleasure of his new instrument in their exploration of texture, color, and embellishment (see the fine double variation set that opens the latter sonata). The legacy of the "Paris" Symphonies is likewise reflected in their dramatic surprises, "Sturm und Drang" outbursts, and jolly, folk-like themes, not to mention a fully symphonic minuet (in Hob. XV: 11) and superb rondo finales (in Hob. XV: 12 and Hob. XVI: 48). (Perhaps the unprecedented critical and financial success of these symphonies encouraged him to widen the expressive scope of his keyboard music.) For all their improvisatory play, these works convey a deep seriousness. Two of these trios are in the minor mode, and all three exploit a full gamut of learned devices. Most impressive is the Trio no. 12 in e minor, the only three-movement work of the set. Its sonata-form opener parallels the play of light and dark in the corresponding movement of the Symphony no. 83 in g minor ("La Poule"), while its spacious Andante in E major anticipates the slow movements of the London piano trios. All three movements feature rigorous contrapuntal developments, none more than the Rondo finale. Perhaps with an eye to market appeal, Artaria asked Haydn to revise the third trio in c minor (Hob. XV: 13) by substituting a set of double variations with a relaxed C major second theme for the original opening movement.[35] Yet even its jaunty finale in C major has its learned moments (e.g., the canons at mm. 106–19 that recur in a distant A♭ in the coda, mm. 233–39). The 1789 review in the *Allgemeine deutsche Bibliothek* praised the set for its superior construction, originality, and seriousness, while warning the reader of the "frequent excursions into distant keys – which often require many accidentals, even double ones."[36]

With Haydn's keyboard works of 1789–90, his late keyboard style is fully realized.[37] All but one (Hob. XV: 17) are in three movements, with substantial slow movements that form the heart of the work. Of these the "Genzinger" Sonata in E flat (Hob. XVI: 49) is deservedly prized as a model of the Classical style; like the largest of Mozart's late sonatas it was published singly. The Adagio e cantabile slow movement is a gem of sensibility in its scrupulously articulated varied reprises (the Henle edition by Georg Feder is the most faithful to the autograph). Although composed with Frau von Genzinger's "delicate hand" in mind, the hand crossings in its b♭ minor middle section provoked her gentle complaint in a letter to the composer.[38] Yet the technique was hardly uncommon by this time (see its first movement, mm. 42–48). Perhaps it was the unusual voicing that challenged her abilities: a rotary pattern is played softly and evenly by the right hand, while the left alternates between ringing bass octaves and the long, penetrating melodic gestures in the upper register. Such textural layering would become a norm of Romantic piano music beginning with Beethoven's "Moonlight" Sonata, but was uncommon in 1790.

The four trios of 1790 are likewise admirable. The three substituting flute for violin (Hob. XV: 15–17)[39] are a welcome addition to the repertoire for that instrument. The remaining trio Hob. XV: 14 in A♭ was selected by Haydn for performance in London at the Hanover-Square Concert of April 20, 1792 (with a thirteen-year-old Johann Nepomuk Hummel at the pianoforte and Johann Peter Salomon on violin),[40] making it the first and only known public performance of a Haydn keyboard trio during his lifetime. The work is superbly suited to the concert hall. The grand sonata-form opening movement is a fitting complement to a program that included the Symphonies nos. 93 and 94. The close of its exposition momentarily derails on a "wrong" note at mm. 67–69, a B♮ that heralds the extended enharmonic shift to B major in the development section (at m. 117). Recurring as an E♮ in the recapitulation, this detail prepares the remote E major tonality of the exquisite Adagio in ABA form. Its B section in the parallel minor features a poignant violin aria surrounding an extravagant keyboard "improvisation," its pizzicato strings melding bewitchingly with the fortepiano's silvery upper register. It connects without break to the "Rondo" finale (in sonata form!) by way of another enharmonic shift (from the dominant of g♯ minor) that recalls the identical process at the end of the development of the first movement (m. 163). Thus the Trio no. 14 joins the select rank of Haydn works that explore a compositional issue across an entire work.[41]

Vienna and London, 1793–1803

The first London trip deflected Haydn from the piano, and when he rejoined his Schanz in July 1792 the relationship was slow to rekindle. For the moment his concerns lay elsewhere – composition of the quartets, Opp. 71 and 74, his challenging student from Bonn, and the sudden death of Frau Genzinger in January 1793 at the age of forty-three. The single major keyboard work of the Viennese interlude is, however, a splendid anomaly. The Variations in f minor (Hob. XVII: 6) were written in 1793 for Barbara von Ployer, a superb pianist who had studied with Mozart. Haydn's first intention for this double-variation set may have been as the first movement of a two-movement cycle in the manner of the recent Hob. XVI: 48 or Hob. XV: 13, for its autograph is entitled "Sonata." In the process of probing his two themes, a solemn aria with dotted anacrusis, and its lyrical F major complement with swirling arabesques, the movement broke free. It also acquired a massive new closure, initiated by a circling back to the original f minor theme (at m. 146) and opening out into a rhapsodic coda of overwhelming intensity (mm. 168–205), which subsides into a closing meditation on the dotted figure. The ironic title on the presentation copy, "Un piccolo Divertimento," belies the work's grandeur. Stunningly original in both architecture and use of the piano, this work is a milestone in the Romantic variation style.

The bounty of piano music from Haydn's second London trip, for which he embarked in January 1794, is exceptional. The London musical environment – with its plethora of professional pianists and cultivated amateurs, fine instruments by Broadwood and others, and publishers eager for his newest piano music – was surely a powerful stimulus. By the time he left London in August 1795, he had probably completed thirteen large trios (Hob. XV: 18–29, 31) and the last three sonatas (Hob. XVI: 50–52).

The trios nos. 18–29 were published in London in sets of three (Table 9.1):

Table 9.1

	First edition	Publication date
Hob. XV: 18–20	Longman & Broderip, Op. 70	November 1794
Hob. XV: 21–23	Preston, Op. 71	May 1795
Hob. XV: 24–26	Longman & Broderip, Op. 73	October 1795
Hob. XV: 27–29	Longman & Broderip, Op. 75	April 1797[42]

The first two sets were dedicated to Esterházy princesses: Hob. XV: 18–20 to Marie Anna, the recently widowed Dowager Princess; and Hob. XV: 21–23 again to Maria Hermenegild. These works were possibly offered in partial appeasement for their Kapellmeister's extended absence.[43] The remaining sets were tokens of affection for London friends. The genial trios Hob. XV: 24–26 were written for Rebecca Schroeter, the attractive widow whose piano lessons with Haydn during the first London trip had ripened into a tender romance; the Schubertian Sonata in D, Hob. XVI: 51, may also have been written for her.[44] The largest and most brilliant of the London works, the trios Hob. XV: 27–29 and the sonatas Hob. XVI: 50 and 52, were written for Therese Jansen, an excellent pianist whose marriage to Gaetano Bartolozzi in May 1795 Haydn had witnessed.

The remaining were private works, published singly after a gap of several years. The curious two-movement trio Hob. XV: 31, the finale of which ("Jacob's Dream!" in E♭) had been a gift to Jansen in 1794, was completed the following year with the addition of its opening rondo in e♭ minor and the suppression of its fanciful title. It remained unpublished – perhaps in her private collection – until 1803, when Traeg issued it with a dedication to another distinguished pianist friend, Magdalena von Kurzböck.[45] Shortly afterward, Haydn recast this work as a violin–piano sonata as a gift for Madame la Maréchale Moreau, a Parisian piano virtuoso of Creole descent. As a result, it gained the reputation as Haydn's "Dernière Sonate" in early editions. This honor belongs rightly to the large trio in E♭ major (Hob. XV: 30), written in Vienna in 1796 and published by Artaria without dedication the next year.

This repertoire was almost exclusively written for and dedicated to women. These works are generously endowed with moments – and entire movements – of the greatest tenderness and sensitivity (such as the Poco Adagio from Hob. XV: 22 for Marie Hermenegild or the first movement of Hob. XV: 24 for Schroeter). They also feature numerous ABA forms with varied reprises, used not only for slow movements but also as first movements (Hob. XV: 29) or finales (Hob. XV: 20, 24, and 26). Rondo or double-variation forms, musical emblems of the feminine, also appear in place of the sonata-form first movement in Hob. XV: 19, 23, 25, and 31. There are forays into the pastoral (Hob. XV: 21/I) and naïve modes (Hob. XV: 29/II, played *innocentemente*), the *style hongrois* (Hob. XV: 25/III), as well as popular dances such as the Ländler (Hob. XV: 20/III, trio), tarantella (Hob. XV: 19/III), and German dance (the finales of Hob. XV: 29–31). Yet these are also grand works, often original to the point of eccentricity. They feature a full array of virtuosic devices, including hand-crossings, double thirds, legato octaves, rhapsodic figuration in irregular rhythmic groupings, metrical displacements, and cross-rhythms. Even more daunting are

Haydn's signature excursions into the "well-known learned style" and his frequent "chromatic passages and . . . diversions into the most distant keys – even those needing double flats," as described in an early review of Hob. XV: 30.[46]

The last E♭ Sonata (Hob. XVI: 52) is a case in point. From its heroic, rolled opening chords and incisive double thirds, it is a work of power and originality. No wonder it has dominated the concert stage and the critical literature, eclipsing all Haydn's other London piano music except the trio in G major (Hob. XV: 25) with its famous Gypsy rondo. Yet the very features that made *the* E♭ sonata so beloved – brilliance, sublime wit, wide emotional palate, daring harmony (especially its E♭/E tonal axis), and architectural sweep – are matched by other equally formidable works of this time, especially the trios Hob. XV: 26–30 and the C major Sonata (Hob. XVI: 50) – but none more than the trio Hob. XV: 22, its stylistic sister in the same key of E♭. In the wider context of the London piano music, the Sonata no. 52 emerges, not as an isolated wonder, but as an integral part of a coherent project inspired by the London pianoforte.

The sonata-form opening movements of the London works are spacious in design and leisurely in pace. They explore the limits of late eighteenth-century chromaticism, setting the stage in this regard for Beethoven and even Schubert. The development sections are the chief locus of harmonic innovation, often introduced by way of startling false recapitulations in outrageously distant – and sometimes enharmonic – keys. The first movement of the C major Sonata no. 50, for example, underscores its false recapitulation in flattened VI at m. 73 with an uncanny "open pedal" effect, a popular device in English keyboard prints of the time.[47]

The slow movements are the glories of these works. Several look back to the sonatina-form Adagios from earlier Viennese sonatas in their intricate rhythmic surfaces, especially the slow movements of two "Esterházy" trios (Hob. XV: 19 and 23) and the Sonata no. 50 in C (the latter revised from Artaria's 1794 single-movement version with generous addition of articulation and dynamic markings). Others look back further, to the Italian chaconne (Hob. XV: 20) or the air *en passacaille* (Hob. XV: 28). The latter is so reminiscent of the Andante from Bach's Italian Concerto that one wonders whether it commemorates a performance by Mrs. Bartolozzi, a student of the Bach-loving Muzio Clementi. The most heartfelt are in Romantic song form (ABA), often with extravagantly varied reprises and central episodes in the parallel mode. They regularly highlight lyrical violin solos, as found in Hob. XV: 18 and 25. If one slow movement rises above the others, however, it is the exquisite Adagio in F♯ major from the last of the Schroeter trios (Hob. XV: 26). The recent consensus is that it preceded the F major version in the

Symphony no. 102,[48] possibly making the latter a secret public message of affection for his English sweetheart.

Wider circulation of Haydn's keyboard music began with the publication of the twelve-volume *Oeuvres complettes de Joseph Haydn* between 1800 and 1806 by the firm of Breitkopf & Härtel.[49] Consisting almost entirely of music for or with piano (including thirty-four solo sonatas, thirty-two trios, and a large sampling of songs), and with most of the early works excised, it established the corpus of Haydn's keyboard music that held sway until the end of the nineteenth century. It also brought Haydn's keyboard music squarely into nineteenth-century middle-class homes, where it was reduced to the largely pedagogical role of a *Gradus ad Beethoven*. There, too, it quickly succumbed to the emerging reductionist view of Haydn's compositions as a world of "childlike happiness" that, in the words of Robert Schumann, was "as clear as sunlight . . . bereft of any sense of ennui with life."[50] Haydn's keyboard music has still not fully recovered from its association with the parlour, practice room, and teaching studio.

Even today, only a handful of Haydn's sixty-odd piano sonatas are regularly heard in recital. To be sure, they offer challenges in performance on the modern piano, but their sturdy texture make them somewhat more adaptable than Mozart's. The piano trios are too rarely played, and still remain one of the best-kept secrets of Haydn's instrumental music. The problems of balance between modern strings and piano are considerable, but they are more than simply "accompanied keyboard sonatas." As Dean Sutcliffe has demonstrated, their violin and violoncello parts fulfill an essential and manifold role in their chamber texture beyond the obvious violin solos and passages of string pairing.[51] Even where the strings essentially double the piano, they often emerge more prominently than would appear in the score. Moreover, the delicate balance among the players is superbly calibrated to the sound characteristics of the instruments of Haydn's time, to which modern players can aspire by careful attention to ensemble, stage placement, and choice of instruments. The 1789 review of the trios Hob. XV: 11–13 still holds true today: "when played cleanly in all parts and with the proper expression, they yield the greatest enjoyment that this kind of music can provide."[52]

10 Sacred music

JAMES DACK

That music survives from the past with the inevitable loss of its original context is a truism that might be challenged above all by sacred music, on the grounds that a liturgy provides a timeless context within which music composed for its service can continue to fulfill its original purpose. Indeed, the Catholic liturgy that emerged from the Counter-Reformation after the Council of Trent (1545–63) – the Tridentine Rite, a normative form of late medieval Roman Use[1] – persisted until the reforms of the Second Vatican Council (1962–65), providing for four centuries a constant framework of worship (local variations and emphases of practice aside) for which music could long remain in use. As many a set of manuscript parts from the repertories of religious establishments in the former Habsburg lands of central and eastern Europe attests, Haydn's sacred music continued to be performed within the Catholic liturgy throughout the nineteenth century, a tradition often reflected in the nature of the performing material (a core of original eighteenth-century parts, supplemented by various accretions) and the recording of dates of performance on the reverse of the organ part or folder. Yet today Haydn's sacred music is seen to have suffered a loss of context more far-reaching than that undergone by some other genres of his output. The late masses for instance – works large enough to form independent musical entities – are performed as concert pieces, crossing boundaries of genre, style, and purpose between "church" and "chamber" more fundamental than the contextual changes affecting, say, the string quartets and symphonies. Moreover, the transference of a mass to the concert hall has its problems, for the unbroken sequence of movements in the same tonality places on aesthetic sensibilities a strain not encountered in the liturgical context; and a sense of propriety may be jarred by the secular performance of liturgical texts. Some pieces have appeared too prolix (the *Missa Cellensis in honorem Beatissimae Virginis Mariae*, which rivals Bach's Mass in B minor in length) or peculiar (the *Stabat mater*, with only two of its fourteen movements in an above-moderate tempo and half in the minor mode) to have been taken up with any frequency as concert music, while others are simply too small to establish that independent existence.

The historical and liturgical contexts[2]

Haydn's sacred music encompasses his entire career, falling approximately in three distinct periods: the early years until his appointment as Esterházy Vice-Kapellmeister at Eisenstadt in 1761; from 1766, on his succession to full Kapellmeister after the death of his predecessor Gregor Joseph Werner, until the mid-1770s, by which time Prince Nicolaus Esterházy's passion for opera at Eszterháza had made it Haydn's principal concern; and the late years from 1796. His output comprises a presumed total of fourteen masses, from all stages of his career; the large-scale *Stabat mater* (1767) and late *Te Deum* (1800); and from the early and middle periods numerous other smaller works together with a somewhat indeterminate group of *contrafacta* (adaptations of existing compositions for sacred use).[3] Works can be divided according to their setting of liturgical or non-liturgical texts and – not a direct correlation – whether they were performed within the liturgy or outside it in connection with the liturgical season. At least until the introduction of Joseph II's ecclesiastical reforms from 1783 – in the usual account of Haydn's church music dividing the earlier from the later works – his sacred music reflects a liturgy and associated practices shaped by a peculiarly Habsburg synthesis of church and state, in which the liturgy of a propagandist Catholic church emerging triumphant from the Counter-Reformation was overlaid in the early eighteenth century by the victory of Habsburg over Turk. Under Charles VI (1711–40) the combination of secular pomp, public display of imperial piety, the Viennese enthusiasm for pilgrimages and processions, and a veneration of the Blessed Virgin Mary of medieval intensity was at its height. This *pietas austriaca* – preserved by Empress Maria Theresa (1740–80), albeit under some retrenchment and softening into rococo – continued to echo through Haydn's church music, not only in the evocation of imperial power and signalling of a particular grade of liturgical ceremony by the C major clarini and timpani of the first *Missa Cellensis* (1766), composed in connection with the pilgrimage church of Mariazell, but also in Haydn's intimate and devout settings of Marian texts.

An awareness of liturgical context can restore to Haydn's sacred music a dimension otherwise missed. For example, the grave simplicity of the four *Hymni de Venerabili* (*c.*1767) is explained and enhanced when they are imagined performed in turn to accompany the processional display of the Host at four altars during the celebration of Corpus Christi, the last and one of the most important festivals of the liturgical year, observed with particular emphasis in Vienna and its surrounding regions.[4] Titles may indicate the liturgical purpose (*Missa Sancti Nicolai*, "Cantilena pro adventu"), although a title may accommodate use on various occasions ("in honorem Beatissimae Virginis Mariae") and masses in particular were appropriated to other purposes. For instance, Haydn apparently used either the *Missa Sancti Nicolai* or the *Missa in honorem BVM* ("Große Orgelsolomesse") later as a *Missa Sancti Josephi.*[5] On the other hand, the presence of a liturgical text should not be taken to mean a direct location in the liturgy. For example, the thirteenth-century verse meditation "Stabat mater" was adopted in the liturgy as late as 1727 for use on the Feast of the Seven Sorrows of the BVM on the Friday of Passion Week. Haydn's *Stabat mater*, however, was identified with the following Holy Week, in particular Good Friday. In all likelihood Haydn directed the first performance of the *Stabat mater* from the organ in the Eisenstadt castle chapel on Good Friday, April 17, 1767, following the tradition of Good Friday oratorios composed by Werner, and the work is known to have received Good Friday performances on at least two further occasions.[6] Likewise, Haydn's settings of two Marian antiphons – the *Ave regina* and the two *Salve regina*s – might find their liturgical place, according to season, at the end of Vespers or Compline (although in the Tridentine Rite they could follow any Office).[7] The tradition of Marian devotion known to Haydn, however, suggests their alternative use in a votive observance (one outside the normal course of the liturgy) dedicated to the Virgin. As for pieces with non-liturgical texts, the "motets" and *contrafacta* in particular found a liturgical place as substitutes for the Proper offertory of the mass, as perhaps did Haydn's Advent arias during that season, although again, on account of their characteristic extolling of the Virgin Mary, a votive use seems possible. Similarly, Haydn's only authenticated pastorella ("Herst Nachbä") and possibly one or two others may have been performed as the offertory of Christmas mass or even outside the liturgy within a traditional observance centered on the crib of the Nativity.[8] Dialect texts presenting in dramatic fashion (not without a touch of comedy) the shepherds' amazement on hearing the angels' news, and their seeking out and adoration of the Christ Child, set to an intentionally homespun and allusive musical style, suggest that Haydn's pastorella(s) were destined beyond the court, an inference supported by the location of surviving sources; nevertheless, a capacity on the part of the Esterházys for indulgence in a popular tradition both entertaining and edifying should not be entirely discounted.

c.1749–65

Sacred works contribute all that is known of Haydn's first attempts at composition. It was perhaps inevitable that the "Kapellknabe" drilled in the liturgy under Reutter at the Stephansdom should try his hand first in church music;

the contrast with the genres first essayed by Mozart is instructive. Haydn's earliest works in their likely order were the disputed *Missa "Rorate coeli desuper"* (1749 or earlier?), the *Missa brevis* in F (Haydn's later dating: 1749) and the *Lauda Sion* in C (*c.*1750?), preceded, if we take the accounts of Griesinger and Dies on trust, by some boyish attempts that again indicate a first location in sacred music.[9] The transmitted *Missa "Rorate,"* if authentic,[10] gives ample evidence of Haydn's early deficiencies in technique, as he admitted later: "I wrote diligently, but not quite correctly."[11] Gross errors in part-writing and other solecisms argue against the authorship of Reutter, the principal other contender, but a competence of the figured organ bass invites speculation that Reutter might have offered some instruction. Individual pairings of parts work well enough – soprano and organ bass, violins and organ bass, violins and soprano – to suggest piecemeal composition without an understanding of the complete texture. A peculiarity of Haydn's writing for voices, particularly noticeable in the early works, is the low pitching of the tenor, often undercutting the bass and apparently subverting the position of the voices within the harmony. Haydn's procedure can be justified by a linear understanding of the part-writing and the restitution of the harmonic bass by the instrumental bass (violone), sounding an octave lower. The technical lapses of the early works are less important than the indications of artistic substance, as in, for example, the "melody, and a certain youthful fire"[12] of the *Missa brevis* in F, with its affective use of harmony ("Et incarnatus"), control of formal structure (Benedictus) and assured writing for the violins.

Probably none of Haydn's instrumental works of this time rivals the achievement of what may justly be called his first masterwork, the *Salve regina* in E, which Haydn later dated from 1756. It demonstrates full command of the current Italianate style in Viennese church music (acquired, on Haydn's own testimony, from his experience as general factotum to Nicola Porpora)[13] in the service of an affective and expressive setting of the Marian text. Haydn's characteristic and lifelong choice of E major for music of deep intensity is established here, as is his manipulation of formal paradigms to effective ends. A remarkable feature of the second movement ("Ad te suspiramus") is the extraordinary sequence of parallel fifths, broken only by dissonant "second inversions," for the setting of "gementes" ("mourning"), in the long chromatic descent "in hac lacrimarum valle" (mm. 32–47). In the closing movement ("O clemens"), the surprising turn to the minor (m. 60) turns the final ritornello into an unexpected course that includes a rapid alternation of solo and tutti invocations of the Virgin (mm. 63–69), thereby expressing a heightened anxiety not dispelled until the final plagal cadence.

1766–81

The six years immediately following Werner's death in March 1766 saw Haydn's most sustained period of engagement with sacred music. As director of the modest musical forces of the Eisenstadt castle chapel, Haydn apparently assumed the role of solo organist on occasion[14] and composed works both for the chapel and for other destinations. According to Haydn's original contract of employment, authority over the sacred music at the Esterházy court had been reserved for Werner;[15] now Haydn's change in status to full Kapellmeister appears to have prompted him to an overt statement in the genre. Year by year (except for 1770, when he was apparently overcome by a serious illness)[16] Haydn produced a major sacred work: the first *Missa Cellensis* in 1766, the *Stabat mater* in 1767, *Missa "Sunt bona mixta malis"* in 1768, *Missa in honorem BVM* ("Große Orgelsolomesse") in ?1769, the *Salve regina* in g minor (again with a solo organ part) in 1771, and finally, the *Missa Sancti Nicolai* in 1772. This may be seen as part of a larger desire at this time to explore all branches of composition, which in sacred music posed challenges in the setting of text, large-scale musical structure, supra-movement coherence, mastery of a range of styles and techniques (including fugue and *stile antico*) and, not least, measuring up to tradition.

Haydn no doubt drew on a repertory of large-scale *missae cum clarinis* in C major for the first *Missa Cellensis.* What is so astounding about this work – Haydn's most ambitious in any genre to date – is its mastery of the required range of styles and techniques: choral movements in Baroque ritornello structure (Kyrie I), modern symphonic style ("Gloria in excelsis") and *stile antico* ("Gratias"); solo ritornello arias ("Christe," with choral interjections; "Laudamus"; "Quoniam"); affective movements for chorus and solo voices ("Qui tollis"); and choral fugues (Kyrie II; "In gloria") carried out on the largest scale and with the greatest assurance, all the more impressive in that these were among Haydn's earliest essays in fugue. The "Domine" initiates in Haydn's sacred music a type of movement in 3/8 meter with moderate to brisk tempo and usually based on a ritornello procedure. This typical movement of mid-century Italianate church music becomes in Haydn's hands an extended, freely developing structure, incorporating the entry of the solo voices by turn, various solo combinations, and chorus. The achievement represented by the *Missa Cellensis* is no less remarkable if, as there is evidence to suggest, it was composed in more than one stage between 1766 and *c.*1773, first as a Kyrie–Gloria pair (an Italianate *missa solemnis* of the time) in 1766, and gaining the other movements later.[17]

The structural coherence and expressive import of "through-composition" proposed for the *Salve regina* in g minor[18] is preceded in the *Stabat mater* by a comparable manifestation of a long-range design that both binds the piece together in musical terms and projects an interpretive setting of the text. At the immediate level the text drew from Haydn, who hoped to have "expressed adequately words of such great importance,"[19] an affective response and musical symbolism of Baroque intensity (for example, in the first movement, the solo tenor's opening *messa di voce* stasis on "Stabat," "Neapolitan"-inflected and chromatically descending line for "dolorosa," C♯ at "crucem," brokenly "tearful" falling thirds for "lacrymosa," and long chain of suspensions for "pendebat"). Beyond that, the progression of the text – i.e., from the depiction of the Mother of Christ at the foot of the Cross ("Stabat mater dolorosa") through the appeal to sympathy ("Quis est homo") and the request to participate in her grief ("Eja Mater") to the prayer for her aid in the Day of Judgment ("Flammis orci ne succendar") and the gaining of salvation ("Quando corpus morietur . . . Paradisi gloria") – is paralleled by a sequence of movements linked for the most part by tonalities falling by a third. The process is inflected by other tonal relationships, so that the home G minor, together with its heightened affective import of "Neapolitan" and "augmented sixth" harmonies, recurs at crucial points in the text: at the return of standing by the Cross (no. 9: "Fac me vere tecum flere . . . Juxta crucem tecum stare," in which an additional coincidence is the unique movement-heading Lagrimoso, recalling the opening two lines of text "Stabat mater dolorosa, juxta crucem lacrymosa"), and for the anticipation of death (no. 13). This is transformed at last to radiant G major for a vision of Paradise (no. 14) in *stile antico*, interrupted by the joyous roulades of the solo soprano.

Various traditions of Austrian church music are addressed in turn by the following three masses: classic *stile antico* (*alla cappella*) in the *Missa "Sunt bona mixta malis,"* which even in its apparently fragmentary state presents Haydn's most extended essay in this style; the mass with *concertante* organ part in the "Große Orgelsolomesse," which uses for the first time in the masses a secular instrumentation of horns and cors anglais in line with the Esterházy musical forces; and the *missa brevis* in the *Missa Sancti Nicolai.* Here Haydn appears to have exploited labor-saving strategies associated with the genre – the repetition of music for subsequent sections of text, notably that of the Kyrie for "Dona nobis pacem," and the simultaneous setting of successive lines of text in the longer movements, as in the Credo – in combination with certain features of a large-scale mass, among them an expanded instrumentation (again secular, with horns) and vocal solos, in order to compose, perhaps in some haste, a setting appropriate to the celebration of Prince Nicolaus's nameday on December 6, 1772.[20] After 1772, Haydn's composition of sacred music decreased as the opera house at Eszterháza claimed ever more of his attention: chief among the few works from these years is the *Missa brevis Sancti Joannis de Deo*

("Kleine Orgelsolomesse"; *c.*1773–77), in which the extreme brevity of the Gloria (thirty-one measures, Allegro di molto), achieved by declaiming lines of text simultaneously, led Haydn's brother, Michael, to provide a version "un poco più prolungato" (118 measures). Yet practicality does not deny art in this miniature mass: the Adagio Kyrie has a breadth beyond its twenty-five measures; the Benedictus presents an exquisite pairing of the solo soprano and concertante organ part; and the Adagio Agnus Dei eschews the common procedure of a *missa brevis* "Dona ut Kyrie" for an independent setting of "dona nobis pacem," effecting a peaceful close (violins *perdendosi*, pizzicato bass *senza Organo* and each voice in turn pianissimo).

1782–1802

Haydn's claim that the Op. 33 string quartets (1781) were "written in a new and special way" might equally be made for the second *Missa Cellensis* (1782), in that the latter shows a greater kinship with Haydn's subsequent masses than with his earlier ones. Indeed, the *Missa Cellensis* might well be termed the first of "the last seven masses," contrary to the traditional proposition of a stylistic gulf between the earlier and last six masses, reflecting the fourteen years' hiatus that was shortly to follow in Haydn's composition of sacred music (1782–96). Not that the *Missa Cellensis* has no connection with its predecessors; for example, comparison with the *Missa Sancti Nicolai* shows a similar employment of recapitulation as a means of structure. But in the *Missa Cellensis* the strategy appears with greater subtlety. Whereas the opening "Gloria in excelsis Deo" of the Gloria of the *Missa Sancti Nicolai* effects a literal return to close the first section of the movement (mm. 1–2 become mm. 35–36), in the Gloria of the *Missa Cellensis* the opening musical substance returns appropriately for "glorificamus te" (mm. 35ff.), with rhythmically adjusted vocal parts inserted into the repeated instrumental texture. In the Credo – here the parallel with the *Missa Sancti Nicolai* is exact – a musical recapitulation accompanies "Et resurrexit," with the text compressed in *missa brevis* fashion (mm. 112ff.). The *Missa Cellensis* also carries forward other features of Haydn's earlier sacred works, notably the Baroque affective style in the Credo for "Et incarnatus . . . crucifixus." On the other hand, it displays characteristics of the late works, including a menacing Benedictus (a trait already present in the first *Missa Cellensis*), a fugue in 6/8 meter for "Et vitam venturi saeculi, amen" and, most immediately striking, a Kyrie with an Adagio introduction leading to a Vivace in symphonic style.

Tradition has it that Haydn composed his last six masses for the annual celebration of the nameday of Princess Marie Hermenegild Esterházy, wife of

Prince Nicolaus II. Although all six were performed in this connection, only the last three – the "Theresienmesse" (1799), "Schöpfungsmesse" (1801), and "Harmoniemesse" (1802) – can be said with certainty to have been composed for the occasion. The relationships of the first three with the Princess's nameday are more complicated, colored by the fact that the usual day for the celebration – not the nameday itself, the Nativity of the BVM on September 8, but, appropriately enough, the following Sunday, the movable Feast of the Most Holy Name of Mary – continued to be the day the Viennese commemorated victory over the Turks in 1683: and this at a time when Austria was again at war.[21] Thus the first performance of the *Missa Sancti Bernardi d'Offida* ("Heiligmesse"), in all likelihood on Sunday September 11, 1796, in the Bergkirche at Eisenstadt, would have enjoyed the coincidence in that year of the saint's day – thus fulfilling the primary designation of the first of the six masses – with the double celebration of a historic military victory and the Princess's nameday. The explicit and implicit references to war in the *Missa in tempore belli* ("Paukenmesse," 1796) and *Missa in angustiis* ("Nelsonmesse," 1798) suggest an original connection not with the Princess Esterházy but with external events, and both masses received only belated performances in Eisenstadt in honor of the Princess's nameday on September 29, 1797, and September 23, 1798, respectively. The association of the latter mass with Nelson or his defeat of Napoleon's fleet at Aboukir Bay in the summer of 1798 is spurious.

By 1796, and after Joseph II's restatement of the relationship between church and state, the musical component of the Baroque amalgam of imperial show and liturgical ceremony was no longer a valid stylistic mode for a large-scale mass. Even so, the comparison of Haydn's last six masses with his late symphonies, although valid in many respects of style and structure,[22] should not obscure the fact that the late masses were conceived as sacred music and performed liturgically, albeit on special occasions when attention no doubt focused on the musical part of the proceedings. In these masses Haydn continued to draw on Viennese traditions, both in the musical representation of vivid textual images – in particular, those of the Gloria and Credo – and in matters of structural organization. Gloria and Credo, for example, follow an established Viennese tripartite pattern, with a central section for "Gratias . . . qui tollis" and "Et incarnatus . . . crucifixus" respectively, each with a major point of internal articulation as indicated. Some movements are overlaid with strategies of thematic return that make fair claim to a symphonic comparison, but also draw on ritornello procedure: the Gloria movements of the *Missa in tempore belli* and *Missa in angustiis*, for example, are particularly tightly organized in this respect. Kyrie movements, often proposed as "sonata" structures with a slow introduction comparable with a symphonic first movement, demonstrate the tension that exists, if liturgical propriety is to be preserved, between a tripartite text ("Kyrie . . . Christe . . . Kyrie") and a musical structure with the fundamental bipartite logic of departing from the tonic and returning to it: each Kyrie presents a different solution to the crucial placing of "Christe eleison." In setting the text Haydn exploits a variety of relationships between solo and tutti voices and instrumental forces, ranging from a texture that is primarily instrumental in conception to one that is primarily vocal. For example, the Kyrie of the "Theresienmesse" begins with an Adagio, which in its opening measures might well preface a symphony. In mm. 4–11 the vocal parts are inserted into this predominantly instrumental texture, first entering on a dominant octave, as if horn parts; only from m. 11 do the vocal parts begin to take precedence, with instrumental accompaniment. The ensuing Allegro (mm. 29ff.) begins as a thoroughly vocal fugato, the instruments *colla parte.*

The "Harmoniemesse" (1802), Haydn's last completed work and one of his most richly scored, aptly lends itself to interpretation as the summation of his late synthesis of vocal and instrumental styles. The Poco adagio Kyrie, although a complete sonata movement itself, can be perceived as a massive prelude to the Gloria, an extension of the Adagio introduction-Allegro of other Kyrie movements to a supra-movement relationship that indeed heightens the liturgical reality of the direct following of the Gloria on the Kyrie. Harmonic shifts in the Kyrie to tonal regions a third distant (including at the recapitulation, bars 83–84, a reinterpretation of the old Baroque ploy of the "hiatus return," here from the chord of D major to B♭ major) and the subdominant-inflected coda contribute to the peculiar stasis and extraordinary breadth of this movement. The central "Gratias . . . qui tollis" of the Gloria once more invokes the 3/8 movement – by now a thoroughly old-fashioned type – and begins in E♭ with the entry of the solo voices in turn normally enough, within a ritornello structure. With "Qui tollis" (tutti), however, the movement breaks out of the ritornello frame into a continuous expansion that builds to a shattering crisis on "miserere" (m. 231, "Neapolitan" chord) and soon after collapses into a cadence in g minor – an "open" ending that again invokes coherence at a higher level. And in the "Et incarnatus . . . crucifixus" traces of Baroque symbolism – triplet movement in the accompaniment and an emphasis given to wind instruments invoking the traditional *topos* of the Nativity – are veiled by a musical expressivity that projects the state of becoming Man (mm. 100ff.); the agony of the Crucifixion (mm. 112ff., in particular, the F/G♭ dissonance between the brass and other parts in m. 115, followed by the climactic and paradoxical C major for "passus" in mm. 118–19); and a particular pathos in the recall of the opening *topos* to accompany the final "passus et sepultus est" (mm. 128ff.).

Dissemination and reception

Three major forces governed the initial dissemination of Haydn's sacred music: its liturgical purpose limited it to Catholic areas of Europe, specifically the Habsburg dominions; dissemination was in manuscript parts, the normal mode of distribution of sacred music during the eighteenth and nineteenth centuries; and manuscript distribution was subject to the influence of regional centers, large and small, and the still little-known dynamics of commercial copying. Only the *Stabat mater* stands apart from these general conditions through its printed publication in London (Bland, 1784) and Paris (Sieber, 1785) and absorption into the tradition of the Protestant oratorio. In the main, Haydn's sacred music spread west from Vienna along the line of the Danube, only faltering when meeting the regional influences of Salzburg in Upper Austria and Munich in Bavaria. It traveled north into Habsburg (then again Catholic) Bohemia and Moravia, until reaching the Protestant lands of Saxony and Prussian Silesia, eastward into Hungary and south through Styria, Carinthia, and other Habsburg domains. It made little headway, however, in Italy, Spain, and France. The continued manuscript dissemination of Haydn's sacred music in the Catholic Habsburg heartlands during the nineteenth century indicates its defiance of the historicist campaign of the *Allgemeiner deutscher Cäcilienverein* (founded 1868) to promote the composition of sacred music in the "true church style" of Palestrina, a classicism – save for its Romantic overtones – anticipated by that traditionally espoused by the eighteenth century in the occasional composition of sacred music in *stile antico*.

Outside the natural habitat of his sacred music an incipient classicizing of Haydn himself is discernible at the beginning of the nineteenth century in the project of the Leipzig firm Breitkopf & Härtel to publish the masses in score. This dissemination in an unusual format can be seen as the beginning of the later reception of Haydn's sacred music, for the venture represented a notable change of attitude after Härtel's refusal of Haydn's offer of his masses for publication in 1799.[23] Six masses were published between 1802 and 1808 and a seventh in 1823,[24] with the *Stabat mater* in 1803. In England Christian Ignatius Latrobe (1758–1836) and Vincent Novello (1781–1861) promoted Haydn's sacred music through the publication of movements from the masses and other pieces in vocal score with keyboard (organ) accompaniment. Novello's complete series of Haydn's masses (1822–25) and their continued reprintings throughout the nineteenth century and beyond were of primary importance for their establishment in the English musical canon.[25]

Breitkopf & Härtel's publication of the first *Missa Cellensis* (no. 5, 1807) as the only earlier mass in the series brought to critical attention hitherto largely unknown aspects of Haydn's art as a composer of sacred music. The contrapuntal movements of the mass and what was deemed its appropriately serious spirit received repeated commendation in the Leipzig *Allgemeine musikalische Zeitung.* A review of April 20, 1808, found that, compared with the masses published previously, this setting was not compromised by "their more glittering coloring and lighter style in general, the sharper contrasts, surprises and other means of achieving what one now terms brilliant effects."[26] Already in Haydn's day voices had been raised against the claimed theatrical style of modern church music, and the implied unease in Leipzig opinion with respect to the later masses has resonated through the reception of Haydn's sacred music ever since in a range of predominantly adverse opinion, which reaches its nadir in assessments such as "the masses of Haydn . . . lack dignity, solemnity and depth, and may be fitly termed pleasing toys of the Papacy."[27] At best, apologists have sought to deflect the charge that Haydn's sacred music was unfitted for the liturgy by pleading "the *topos* of rural innocence" – a cheerful "Volkstümlichkeit" that informed Haydn's background, character, and attitude to the composition of church music – and citing in support Haydn's reported comment that when he beheld God his heart leapt for joy and therefore his music did likewise.[28]

Some have admitted the liturgical unfitness of Haydn's sacred music but have pointed nevertheless to its artistic qualities. Others have claimed both inappropriateness to intended function through the improper setting of texts and deficiencies in musical and aesthetic substance, raising the charge of naive musical representation, taking exception, for example, to the Agnus Dei of the *Missa in tempore belli,* in which "the [anxious] beating of the heart is portrayed by the timpani" or, in another interpretation, "Haydn has the timpani imitate the distant thunder of cannon."[29] Any response, of course, requires an assessment of the standpoint of its author. For example, one writer, presumably with ruling concepts of peace and humble prayer in mind, found the opening of the "Dona nobis pacem" of the *Missa in tempore belli* unacceptable "when . . . (after much military drumming of the timpani and similar blaring of trumpets) finally in a formal fanfare with all possible racket of timpani, trumpets, C-clarinets and other noisy apparatus, [Haydn] sighs to the Lamb of God in the following way"[30] (Agnus Dei, mm. 40–56). Rather, Haydn, who in his sacred music was well able to invoke Burke's sublime of astonishment verging on terror,[31] as the climax of the Benedictus of the *Missa in angustiis* demonstrates, presents here in the *Missa in tempore belli* "the horrid sublimity" of war[32] and the anguished cry for salvation. It would appear that the point was not lost on Beethoven, who in all likelihood knew this mass and included a comparable representation in the "Dona nobis" of the *Missa Solemnis.*

Any history of the reception of Haydn's sacred music leaves us with questions of how we might address this repertory today and indeed how Haydn's sacred music might speak to us. Certainly in 1776 Haydn rated his operas and sacred music above his instrumental works and late in life reportedly expressed pride in his masses.[33] Indeed, in 1790 it was claimed "around the year 1780 [Haydn] attained the highest level of excellence and fame through his church and theater works."[34] Such assessments compel a revision of the traditional narrative of Haydn's oeuvre and the place of his sacred music within it. These are historiographical issues; and the restoration of the contextual dimension, both historical and liturgical, to Haydn's sacred music and the recovery of some sense of the central importance it had in eighteenth-century perceptions are exercises in informed historical imagination. Beyond that stand those of Haydn's sacred works that continue to be part of current musical experience despite their loss of original context – which ultimately proves unimportant – and yet others that might be retrieved, as it were, from their status as historical documents. Such works confront us as ahistorical and immediate artistic and aesthetic presences. Relieved of time-bound questions of function and appropriateness, they reveal their continuing validity as bearers of whatever meanings we find in them, as musical creations, particular realizations of sacred texts, or conveyors of spiritual or philosophical import.[35] Readings are not mutually exclusive, and all belong to the larger critical inquiry into what Haydn's music might mean for today.

11 The sublime and the pastoral in *The Creation* and *The Seasons*

JAMES WEBSTER

Haydn's oratorios

When Haydn returned to Vienna from London in 1795, he had become a cultural hero. Many of his remaining works originated in collaboration with the cultural-political establishment and were staged as "events" of social and ideological as well as musical import. As a result, his compositional orientation changed fundamentally: he composed little instrumental music except string quartets, devoting himself instead primarily to masses and oratorios. He had composed one earlier oratorio, *Il ritorno di Tobia* (1774–75); the libretto (by a brother of Boccherini) narrates the story of the blind Tobit from the Apocrypha, whose sight is restored by his son Tobias. Haydn fashioned a magnificent example of late Baroque Austrian-Italian vocal music, comprising chiefly long bravura arias; most of the recitatives are expressive *accompagnati*. In 1784 he modernized the work, shortening some of the arias, adding two magnificent new choruses, and revising the instrumentation; in this form it has been revived with success.

Haydn's remaining oratorios date from the late Vienna period. He collaborated on all three with Baron Gottfried van Swieten, the imperial librarian and censor and the resolutely high-minded leader of the Gesellschaft der Associirten, an "association" of nobles that subsidized oratorios and other large-scale works. *The Seven Last Words of Christ our Saviour on the Cross* (winter 1795–96) is not a true oratorio, but a reworking of Joseph Friebert's choral adaptation of Haydn's programmatic orchestral work of 1786. Swieten altered the text, incorporating numerous passages from Karl Wilhelm Ramler's famous *Der Tod Jesu* (set by Telemann and Graun as oratorios). Although a great success during Haydn's lifetime, it is less popular today than the original: it is not a full-length work; it comprises eight consecutive adagios which, paradoxically, seem more monotonous with chorus than for orchestra alone; and the sentimental, grafted-on text does not successfully combine with the pre-existing music.

By spring 1796 Haydn and Swieten were pursuing bigger game. On Haydn's departure from England Salomon had given him a libretto (now lost) entitled *The Creation of the World*, supposedly written for Handel but never set to music.[1] Back in Vienna, Haydn showed it to Swieten:

"I recognized at once that such an exalted subject would give Haydn the opportunity *I had long desired*, to *show* the whole compass of his profound accomplishments and to express the full power of his inexhaustible genius";[2] the emphasized phrases imply that Swieten's purpose was not artistic alone, but cultural-political as well. The Associirten guaranteed Haydn five hundred ducats (later raised to six hundred; this was approximately four times his annual salary as Esterházy *Kapellmeister* up to 1790), and subsidized the copying and performance. Haydn, whose enthusiasm for the project was bound up with his experience of "mass" performances of Handel's oratorios in London, conceived the remarkable idea of disseminating the work in both German and English (it is apparently the first original bilingual composition); Swieten translated the libretto into German and later adapted the English prosody to Haydn's musical setting. Hence the work should be performed in English for English-speaking audiences, in a text based on that of the first edition (which Haydn self-published); although formerly much maligned, it is now known to correspond closely to the lost original.[3] Swieten also made suggestions regarding the musical setting, many of which Haydn adopted.[4] He began the composition apparently in autumn 1796 and completed it in winter 1797–98. The Associirten at first produced the work in private, on April 30 and May 7 and 10, 1798; the first public performance took place on March 19, 1799, with a very large complement of 180 performers.[5] The work soon became a staple especially of charity performances, many conducted by Haydn himself. He and Swieten began planning *The Seasons* apparently in spring 1799; Haydn probably composed the music from the autumn of 1799 through the winter of 1800–1. The private premiere took place on April 24, 1801, the first public production on May 29.

The Creation and *The Seasons*: reception

In the years immediately following its premiere, *The Creation* "made history" on a pan-European scale in a way equaled by no other composition in the history of Western music.[6] Its reception both in Vienna and elsewhere was almost uniformly positive and often wildly enthusiastic; the few dissenting voices emanated primarily from the high-minded "literary" culture in Weimar and Berlin and the conservative Handel faction in London.[7] This success was owing to multiple factors: its commission by the politically conservative but artistically forward-looking Viennese music-loving nobility, its production as an "event" of high cultural-political significance, its sublime subject, its appeal to both connoisseurs and ordinary listeners, Haydn's unrivaled stature as the greatest living composer, the grandeur, boldness, and originality of his musical setting, and its appearance at a crucial cultural-historical moment, on the cusp between Enlightenment and Romanticism.[8]

The initial reception of *The Seasons* was also highly favorable. Four days after the premiere, Haydn wrote Clementi in London: "In the meantime I inform you that the music to my *Four Seasons* has been received with the same unanimous approval as *The Creation*; indeed many go so far as to prefer it, on account of its [greater] variety"; the following week he wrote Pleyel in Paris that it had enjoyed an "unparalleled success," and he believed that it would join *The Creation* in assuring his lasting fame.[9] Griesinger concurred, writing to Härtel on April 25 of "the general enthusiasm with which the work was received. The voices that had been raised against it (mostly *a priori*) were converted."[10] This suggests that it was not an inevitable fate of reception that would soon marginalize *The Seasons* in comparison to *The Creation*. However, negative critics were soon heard, who emphasized two points in particular: the subject was perceived as "lower" than the exalted one of *The Creation*; and the text was judged aesthetically dubious, and its many pictorialisms indefensible.[11]

Haydn himself reportedly contributed to both strands of criticism. Regarding "high" and "low," Dies writes,

> The Emperor [Francis II] . . . asked him . . . to which of his works he himself gave first place, *The Creation* or *The Seasons*? "To the former," Haydn replied. "And why?" "In *The Creation* angels speak and tell of God, but in *The Seasons* only Simon speaks."[12]

This distinction, which soon became a commonplace, was indirectly reflected in the authentic titles: *The Creation: an oratorio*, but merely *The Seasons*.[13] Regarding word-paintings, Haydn indiscreetly criticized Swieten's croaking frogs (in the last number of Summer) to August Eberhard Müller ("This Frenchified trash was forced on me") and Griesinger ("This passage actually belongs in Grétry").[14] Griesinger describes him as ridiculing the absurdity of the choral hymn to "toil" (*Fleiß*): "As he came to the passage 'O Toil, O noble toil, from thee all virtue flows!' he commented that he had worked hard all his life, but it had never occurred to him to set 'toil' to music." But Griesinger added privately to Härtel, "Haydn has the Midas touch, and knows how to turn dross (*Drek*) into gold."[15]

The resistance to pictorialisms soon began to affect *The Creation* as well, leading to an ambivalent reception in the later nineteenth and much of the twentieth century not fundamentally different from that of *The Seasons*.[16] This was no accident. Notwithstanding the differences just described, the two works do not belong to different genres and indeed are not "opposites."

The Creation too is not an oratorio in either primary sense: a religious drama entailing characters and a storyline; or a lyric, cantata-like work intended for performance in divine service.[17] The dominant modes in both are narrative, contemplation, and celebration, to which *The Seasons* adds many scenes of country life. Both works reflected and revalorized the enlightened-conservative sensibility of the Viennese elite at the turn of the nineteenth century. Both are essentially deistic in outlook; both "speak" of high *and* low, sacred *and* secular, in a way that only Haydn's "popularizing artistry" or "artful popularity" could articulate. Most importantly, both are organized in terms of a mixture of two aesthetic modes ordinarily thought of as contrasting: the sublime and the pastoral. (Beethoven aptly characterized both librettos as *Lehrgedichte*, "didactic poems," a characterization that Swieten would surely have endorsed.)[18] Although the sublime seems dominant in *The Creation*, the pastoral is also essential; conversely, notwithstanding the obvious pastoral status of *The Seasons*, the sublime is central to it as well. Indeed I shall argue that the two works together implicitly tell a single story, one that *The Creation* introduces, but only *The Seasons* can conclude.

The Creation: sublime

The libretto derives primarily from Chapter I.1 of Genesis, Milton's *Paradise Lost*, and the Book of Psalms. It falls into three parts, of which the first two are based on the six Biblical "days" of creation, while the third represents Adam and Eve in Paradise (see Table 11.1).[19]

In Parts I and II, although there are many variations and the First Day is altogether different, each remaining Day (or pair of Days) is based on the following ideal sequence:

> Prose narrative from Genesis (recitative), leading to . . .
> Commentary in verse (aria or ensemble)
> Narrative (recitative), leading to . . .
> Chorus of praise

Thus the typical eighteenth-century alternation of recitative and set-piece is preserved. Both the narrative function and the concerted solo numbers are distributed among three archangels: Gabriel (soprano), Uriel (tenor), Raphael (bass). At the same time, each Day as a whole points towards a triumphant chorus as climax. On a larger scale, a similar progression is found within each of the first two parts, whose respective final choruses – "The heavens are telling" and "Achieved is the glorious work" – are the longest and grandest of all.

Table 11.1 *Plan of* The Creation

Movements	Subject matter	Principal keys
Part I		
1–2	Overture: The Representation/Idea of Chaos	c
	First Day: creation of heaven, earth, light	c–C
	No. 2 (Chorus with soloists): "Now vanish before the holy beams"	A–c–A
3–4	Second Day: division of the waters	
	No. 3 (Raphael): "Outrageous storms"	F–V/C
	No. 4 (Solo [Gabriel] and chorus): "The marv'lous work beholds"	C
5–10	Third Day: land and sea; plant life	
	No. 6 (Raphael): "Rolling in foaming billows"	d–D
	No. 8 (Gabriel): "With verdure clad"	B♭
	No. 10 (Chorus): "Awake the harp"	D
11–13	Fourth Day: sun, moon, stars	
	No. 12 (Uriel): "With splendour bright – With softer beams"	D–G–V/C
	No. 13 (Chorus with trio): "The heavens are telling"	C
Part II		
14–19[1]	Fifth Day: birds and fish	
	No. 15 (Gabriel): "On mighty pens uplifted"	F
	No. 16 (Raphael): "Be fruitful all, and multiply!"	d
	No. 18 (Trio): "Most beautiful appear" →	A–V/A →
	No. 19 (Chorus): "The Lord is great"	A
20–28	Sixth Day: large animals; man and woman	
	No. 21 (Raphael): "Strait opening her fertile womb"	(B♭–)D
	No. 22 (Raphael): "Now heav'n in fullest glory shone"	D
	No. 24 (Uriel): "In native worth"	C
	Nos. 26–28 (Chorus–trio–chorus): "Achieved is the glorious work"	B♭–E♭–B♭
Part III		
29–30	Adam's and Eve's awakening; praise of the Lord	
	No. 29 (Uriel): "In rosy mantle appears"	E–(G)–
	No. 30 ("Lobgesang"; duet and chorus): "By thee with bliss"	C
31–34	Adam's and Eve's love; praise of the Lord	
	No. 32 (duet): "Graceful consort–The dew-dropping morn"	E♭
	No. 34 (Chorus with soloists): "Sing the Lord"	B♭

[1] Nos. 18–19 are run-on.

This music invokes the sublime, but in no ordinary eighteenth-century manner. A new sense of the musical sublime was arising, analogous to Kant's newly formulated category of the "dynamic sublime," and manifested in works such as Mozart's and Haydn's late symphonies, *Don Giovanni* and *Die Zauberflöte*, and Beethoven's Third and Fifth Symphonies. Squarely in the middle of this repertory stood Haydn's late oratorios and masses, in which the dynamic sublime is a central element.[20] Haydn's remarkable "Representation" or "Idea" of Chaos (the German *Vorstellung* entails both senses) is not literally "chaotic," but paradoxical.[21] This is essential to the sublimity of his First Day. The Creation of Light is overwhelming not in its own right, but because it resolves the disjunction and mystery of the entire Chaos music, as it resolves an unstable c minor into the radiant purity of C major. It culminates a progression across three separate movements (overture, recitative, chorus), from paradoxical disorder to triumphant order; it offers a perceptible and memorable experience of that which is unfathomable, unthinkable: the origins of the universe and of history. The remainder of Part I takes place as it were during the reverberation of this event. The most familiar number is "The heavens are telling," also in C; its ending made a great impression on Beethoven, who "troped" it at the end of the first movement of his Second Symphony.[22] Many other choruses in *The Creation* include sublime moments, especially those that end the two remaining parts.[23]

The Creation: pastoral images

Because the sublimity of *The Creation* can thus be taken for granted, I shall focus on its "other" mode, the pastoral.[24] To be sure, it is not an Arcadian idyll, nor an idealized portrayal of country life (as in *The Seasons*) or action set in an artificial venue where ordinary social constraints do not apply (as in *Così fan tutte*), nor a "heroic pastoral," as Charles Rosen has called Haydn's late instrumental music.[25] Still, in any work whose governing mode is the sublime, features other than the divine or supernatural occupy a lower stylistic level, and thereby imply the pastoral.[26] In *The Creation*, moreover, many numbers adopt the pastoral mode overtly: the descriptions of plant and animal life (of "nature"), and the representation of Adam and Eve in the Garden of Eden.

Haydn's music emphasizes this aspect to the full, nowhere more effectively than in his word-paintings. One of the most telling defects of the aesthetics of "absolute music" was its prejudice against such phenomena.[27] Fortunately, Swieten and Haydn – like Handel and his librettists – were still blissfully unaffected by this prejudice, so that today we may once again enjoy Haydn's illustrative sallies without guilt. These invocations of the natural world – not only in Gabriel's invocation of plant life in "With verdure clad" (no. 8), but also the non-animate ones such as "Rolling in foaming billows" (no. 6) – are pastoral through and through. They not only idealize nature but, even though there are still no human characters, present images that seem immediately familiar to *us*; Carl Friedrich Zelter wrote that *The Creation* "shows us the beauties of Paradise, of a magnificent garden, or of a new-born world."[28] Haydn illustrates each verbal image before the text is sung; the slightly paradoxical result is to concentrate our attention precisely on the musical image, because we are not yet certain what it signifies and therefore cannot "lock in" its association until we hear the "confirming" text. The illustrations themselves are plastic, in the best sense: vivid, tangible *Gestalten*, of a directness and immediacy that even Tovey's most "naive" listener can appreciate.

As noted above, these effects soon became anathema to "absolute" musicians. But it is famously a characteristic of pastoral that its naivety is only apparent; those sweetly mourning shepherds know more than they can say. And it was notoriously the fate of pastoral that from the mid-eighteenth century to the mid-twentieth, critics by and large marginalized it as a "conventional" or "artificial" genre (parallel to the traditional denigration of comedy in comparison to tragedy). The analogy with Haydn's word-paintings is telling. Formerly considered naive, or merely humorous, in fact they reveal profound compositional shaping and even psychological insight. In part, this is owing to Haydn's genius in integrating the word-paintings into coherent larger-scale progressions. The "softly purling limpid brook" in D major at the end of no. 6 is deeply moving after the heaving seas and mountains in the minor, as is the ghostly moon in the quiet subdominant after the triumphant sunrise in D; the densely contrapuntal low strings of "Be fruitful and multiply!" vividly suggest "teeming" creatures of the deep. In the catalogue of animals (no. 21), the large and vigorous lion, tiger, stag, and horse descend by fifths from B♭ to an alarmingly distant D♭; after a pause, the sheep and cattle appear in a drastically contrasting key (A major), tempo and orchestration, featuring the pastoral solo flute. Equally important, however, is the word-paintings' role in articulating the optimistic deism of *The Creation*, because they induce us to identify with nature while it is still the original "Arcadia." Parts I and II of Haydn's oratorio, despite their sublimity, are profoundly pastoral as well.

The Creation: Adam and Eve

Part III abandons Genesis and the biblical Days, but continues to draw on *Paradise Lost* and the Psalms. Adam and Eve are introduced by Uriel's accompanied recitative no. 29, "In rosy mantle appears," which features three flutes (again) and is set in a radiant E major; both signify the innocence of the Garden of Eden. The astonishing tonal contrast with the end of Part II in B♭ was perhaps prefigured in no. 2, with its confrontation of Hell in c minor and the "new-created world" in A major, and in no. 21, with the pastoral sheep in A following D♭. Adam and Eve sing only two numbers, but they are among the longest in the entire work. First comes a gigantic "Lobgesang" (hymn of praise: no. 30) in C, comprising a slow hymn, a long, moderately fast rondo describing how all living things praise the Lord, and a choral fugue and climax. Then follows a love-duet (no. 32 in E♭), in two parts: a slow cantilena in 3/4 ("Graceful Consort!") and a fast 2/4 contredanse ("The dew-dropping morn"). The tone is secular, indeed in the second section downright earthy. The oratorio then concludes, as had Part II, with a choral fugue in B♭.

Although Part III has been widely criticized, I believe that to understand it as pastoral exposes the criticisms as misguided. These proceed on either or both of two related grounds: aesthetic, with the claim that the change from "high" to "low" style is inappropriate or anticlimactic; and dramatic, with the claim that the move forward in time from pre-human history to the Garden of Eden violates unity and propriety. Tovey went so far as to end his performances with the "Lobgesang," which he called "the greatest design Haydn ever executed, and the sublimest number since the 'Representation of Chaos.'"[29] Indeed he praises the "Lobgesang" as the "inevitable outcome" of the c minor Chaos, invoking the "symphonic order in which [Haydn] was supreme," thereby implicitly invoking the now outmoded notion of "tonal planning" in large-scale vocal works.[30]

Siegmund Levarie objected, stating rightly that Adam's and Eve's "earthy" and "human" aspect in no. 32 is related both to Haydn's own serious and playful styles in his late masses, and that Adam's and Eve's love-duet resembles Singspiel in its contredanse rhythms and playful alternations between the singers.[31] He too reads *The Creation* in terms of an overall tonal plan, but one that *moves*, from the "divine" C to the "human" B♭, a move that he interprets as an allegory of the Fall:

> To Haydn, man . . . has to be shown in both his aspects as partaking of divinity and succumbing to worldly pleasures . . .
>
> The "fall" from the tonic is well laid out . . . Part III . . . settles the descending trend definitively below the tonic, on E flat and B flat.[32]

But Adam and Eve are not "succumbing to worldly pleasures." In the Garden of Eden (if only wishfully in the pastoral), sexual love is chaste, as Milton insisted:

> Hail, wedded love . . .
> . . . sole propriety
> In Paradise of all things common else! . . .
>
> Far be it that I should write thee sin or blame,
> Or think thee unbefitting holiest place,
> Perpetual fountain of domestic sweets,
> Whose bed is undefiled and chaste pronounced . . .[33]

Swieten and Haydn portrayed Adam and Eve as human in both senses: as created in the image of God, and as our parents; but they did not portray them as subject to the fall, certainly not in this love-duet. Indeed it was precisely this "earthy" tune that Haydn notoriously – gloriously – recycled in the "Creation Mass" (see chapter 3). *The Creation* originated in a conservative but optimistic context of belief in rational understanding and human progress, in which the dominant religious sense was deistic rather than dogmatic. It does not address differences of class or the existence of human misery, but subsumes them in a larger vision which, in one of those miracles that only art can convey, rings true despite everything. It is one of the last visions of Enlightenment, beside which can be set only *Die Zauberflöte* and (in a later, Utopian mode) Beethoven's Ninth Symphony.

The Seasons: pastoral and sublime

Although *The Seasons* was not called a "pastoral" by Swieten, Haydn, or their contemporaries, or by any modern commentator before the mid-1990s,[34] its status as such is self-evident. The basic pastoral conceit is the view, on the part of sophisticated persons, that country life (or "Arcadia") is morally superior to the evil city and the artificial court.[35] Within the pastoral tradition the "four seasons" comprised one of the oldest and most widespread topics, doubtless because of the powerful analogy between the sequence spring–summer–autumn–winter, and the stages of a human life-span or "ages of man," from childhood, through adulthood and maturity, to old age and death. In addition, the "rhythm of the seasons," at once cyclical and teleological, fosters our identification with Nature; for the devout Christian the eternal renewal of spring symbolizes the hoped-for entry into Heaven. These aspects alone suffice to refute the absurd if widespread notion that *The Seasons* is merely a succession of pictures. Relevant as well is the topic of the "labors of the months," cultivated since antiquity: sowing the seed, driving the cattle to summer pasture, gathering the harvest, the hunt, the vintage, spinning by the fire, and so forth.[36]

Swieten's libretto is based on James Thomson's pastoral epic of the same title (1726–28, rev. 1740), in the German translation by Barthold Heinrich Brockes. He drastically shortened Thomson's very long poem and transformed the anonymous poetic narrator into three peasants – Hanne (or Jane; soprano), Lucas (tenor), and Simon (bass) – whose utterances combine descriptive passages, idealizations of country ways, and a late-Enlightenment (if not already proto-Biedermeier) tendency to moralize.[37] As in all pastoral, their simplicity is only apparent: behind the moralizing and the genre-scenes lies, again, an enlightened deism. They sing both the narrative recitatives and the arias, and also participate in many of the choral movements. Some of the choruses are overtly pastoral as well. Following

Table 11.2 *Plan of* The Seasons[1]

Movement	Subject matter	Principal keys
Spring		
1–2[2]	Overture: the passage from winter to spring → recitative →	g → c–V/g →
	Chorus: "Komm, holder Lenz"	G
4	Genre-aria (sowing the seed; Simon): "Schon eilet früh der Ackersmann"	C
6	Prayer (chorus with trio): "Sei nun gnädig"	F
8–9[2]	Song of joy (trio with chorus): "O wie lieblich" →	A–C–G–V/G →
	Chorus with trio: "Ewiger, mächtiger, gütiger Gott!"	B♭
Summer		
10	Introduction: dawn; recitative	c–C
11	Genre-aria (shepherd; Simon): "Der munt're Hirt" → recitative[3]	F → D
12	Chorus: "Sie steigt herauf–Heil, o Sonne, Heil!"	D
14–15	Recititative (Lucas): "Die Mittagssonne brennet"	A–E
	Cavatina (Lucas): "Dem Druck erlieget die Natur"	E
16–17	Recitative (Hanne): "Willkommen jetzt, o dunkler Hain"	C–B♭
	Aria (Hanne): "Welche Labung für die Sinne"	B♭
18–19[2]	Recitative (Hanne): "In banger Ahnung"[4] →	D♭–V/c →
	Chorus: (storm): "Ach, das Ungewitter naht"	c
20	Trio: "Die düst'ren Wolken trennen sich"	F–V/E♭
	Chorus (begun by trio): "Von oben winkt der helle Stern"	E♭
Autumn		
21	Introduction: the husbandman's satisfaction at the abundant harvest	G
23	Trio with chorus: "So lohnet die Natur"	C
25	Genre- and love-duet (Hanne, Lucas): "Ihr Schönen aus der Stadt"	B♭
27	Genre-aria (hunting fowl; Simon): "Seht auf die breiten Wiesen hin"	a–A
28–29[2]	Recitative (hunting hares; Lucas) →	e–V/D →
	Genre-chorus (hunting the stag): "Hört das laute Getön!"	D–E♭
31	Genre-chorus (the vintage): "Juhhe, der Wein ist da!"	C
Winter		
32	Introduction: thick fogs at the beginning of winter	c
33–34	Recitative (Simon, Hanne): "Nun senket sich das blasse Jahr"	c–D♭–A
	Cavatina (Hanne): "Licht und Leben sind geschwächet"	F
36	Aria (Lucas): "Hier steht der Wand'rer nun"	e–E
38	Genre-aria with chorus (spinning-song; Hanne): "Knurre, schnurre"	d
40	Genre-aria with chorus (Hanne): "Ein Mädchen, das auf Ehre hielt"	G
42	Aria (Simon): "Erblicke hier, bethörter Mensch" → recitative[3]	E♭ →
44	Double chorus with trio: "Dann bricht der grosse Morgen an"	C

[1] The numbering is taken from the Peters full score (Leipzig, n.d.), reprinted New York: Dover, 1986. Simple recitatives are not listed; for the chief parallel passages in Thomson, see Landon V, 95–113.
[2] Nos. 1–2, 8–9, 18–19, 28–29 are run on, in "progressive" tonality.
[3] Run on from the preceding aria.
[4] Run on from preceding simple recitative.

the overture, which depicts winter's violent retreat, "Komm, holder Lenz" invokes spring with affective immediacy. The succession of keys and affects, a stormy g minor leading to the liltingly diatonic 6/8 G major, is an earthly analogue to the progression from Chaos to Light in *The Creation.* Pastoral as well is the evensong at the end of Summer: along with the animals, we too find deserved rest, as "the evening bell" and "bright star invite us to soft repose."

The many "genre" scenes, as I call them owing to their parallels to the "labors of the months," are equally pastoral. The arias include Simon sowing the seed (no. 4), with Haydn's quotation of the Andante of the "Surprise" Symphony (which annoyed the censorious Swieten); the "happy shepherd" (no. 11), with an amazing horn obbligato in F; and the extended sequence of the lost wanderer, Hanne's spinning-song, and her tale of the duped nobleman (nos. 36–40), by which we pass the dead of Winter. In pastoral style too is the duet (no. 25) for Hanne and Lucas in B♭; they begin separately, with the obligatory put-down of citified ways, but then astonishingly break into a heartfelt slow hymn in a remote C major ("What happiness is true love!"), and conclude in a rapid 2/4 contredanse scarcely distinguishable from that of Adam and Eve.[38] The two genre-choruses, both at the end of Autumn, are stupendous: first the hunt, from sighting to chase to kill to celebration (the horns quote numerous actual hunting-calls, and also assist in representing the baying of the hounds), and in progressive tonality from D to E♭; then the drinking chorus in C, with increasingly uncertain harmonizations of a prominent high note for the raising of glasses, a dance in 6/8 that leads to an inebriated fugue, and a breathless windup that may have inspired the end of Verdi's *Falstaff.*

However, other choruses in *The Seasons* are overtly religious; some entail invocations of the sublime as effective as any in *The Creation.* Indeed all the choruses except nos. 2, 20, and 29 lead to a fugue or fugato, which however is rarely the climax, the latter being withheld for a sublime moment at the end.[39] In Spring, the response to Simon's happy planting is a beautiful "prayer" for life-giving rains (no. 6), in which the fugue recalls "Quam olim Abrahae" from Mozart's Requiem; while the concluding "Ewiger, mächtiger, gütiger Gott" (no. 9) is perhaps the most massive chorus Haydn ever composed (it is run on in "progressive" tonality from the preceding trio). The brilliant depiction of summer heat is sustained through six numbers (nos. 14–19), finally exploding in Haydn's greatest storm, whose awe-inspiring sublimity was duly noted in contemporary reviews. Equally pertinent is its resolution into the peaceful sublimity of "natural religion" to conclude Summer; this succession strongly influenced Beethoven's "Pastoral" Symphony.[40]

If Haydn's implicitly pastoral word-paintings in *The Creation* no longer require defense (see above), this is doubly so for *The Seasons,* whose very purpose entails depictions of natural phenomena. In Summer, for example, the cock crows at daybreak (no. 10), Lucas sings of the vegetation "fainting" under the burning midday sun (nos. 14–15), Hanne (no. 16) describes twittering birds, "whispering aspen leaves," a "murmuring brook," "buzzing insects," and a "shepherd's pipe" – and, after the storm, the "fattened" cattle

Example 11.1a *The Seasons*, no. 42, "Erblicke hier, bethörter Mensch," mm. 54–62

moo themselves to their stalls, the "happy" crickets chirp, and the notorious frogs croak. On the other hand Hanne's pastoral aria in B♭ (no. 17) outdoes Gabriel's in *The Creation* (no. 8, in the same key): there, an archangel's invocation of nature, in a single tempo and chaste sonata form; here, an almost operatic *scena* in two tempi, with demonstrative virtuosity towards the end.

In Winter, the implicitly sublime orientation of the entire work becomes explicit, in two ways. First, the text (finally) draws the analogy between the rhythm of the seasons and the rhythm of our lives. "The face of the earth is now a grave," sings Lucas in no. 35, and in Simon's famous aria (no. 42) the pathetic fallacy takes over entirely (Swieten paraphrases Thomson's Winter, ll. 1028–35):

> Behold, fond Man!
> See here thy pictur'd Life; pass some few Years,
> Thy flowering Spring, thy Summer's ardent Strength,
> Thy sober Autumn fading into Age,
> And pale, concluding Winter comes at last,
> And shuts the Scene. Ah! whither now are fled,
> Those Dreams of Greatness? those unsolid Hopes
> of Happiness? those Longings after Fame? . . .

Swieten's sixth line is more graphic: "And shows you the open grave." Haydn's two-tempo aria reflects the change of topic at "Whither now are fled?" when the 3/4 Largo in E♭, with its associations of the hereafter, yields

Example 11.1b *The Seasons*, no. 44, "Dann bricht der grosse Morgen an," mm. 27–34

to an impatient 2/4 Allegro molto, which astonishingly breaks off "wie ein Traum" (like a dream) on an insubstantially high, unresolved 6–4 chord for the winds, and Simon's long-held "Nur Tugend *bleibt*" (Only virtue *remains*) – Haydn's last pictorialism – persists beyond the orchestral cadence into the final recitative.

Then in C major glory the final chorus ushers us into heaven.[41] It features a prominent accompanimental motive from Simon's passionate regret of a life now past (see Ex. 11.1). Such overt motivic links are unusual in Haydn;

this one signifies the essential role of "virtue" in assuring our salvation, owing not least to its prominence during the question-and-answer passage in the minor (mm. 30–48; reminiscent of *Die Zauberflöte*), in which good works are praised as the means to salvation. On another level, the force of this chorus derives from its tonal relations to the beginning of Winter, a dark, halting prelude in c minor portraying "thick fogs" – psychological as well as meteorological – and to Simon's aria in E♭, the relative major of c minor. In fact, both Winter and Summer begin in c minor, and of course Chaos itself originally gravitated there. In *The Seasons* the *Ur*-progression from Chaos to Light, c–C, is repeated first in two "earthly" versions, g–G (Spring) and c–E♭ (Summer), but in Winter it is literally re-presented as c–C; the oratorio concludes with Haydn's greatest representation of the sublime as an end, as salvation. Of course, these key-usages were primarily a matter of association, the dictates of vocal range, and the need for variety. Nevertheless, they suggest reading Haydn's two great oratorios as a kind of diptych: taken together, *The Creation* and *The Seasons* represent the history of the world, from the beginning of time and the Creation of Light, to the Day of Judgment and the end of time.[42]

What comes in between is – pastoral. In many ways *The Seasons* outdoes *The Creation*: it is longer, more virtuosic, with more run-on movement-pairs, more varied, more comprehensive. As a whole, the two works are thus complementary not only topically, but compositionally as well. Haydn's style, like his personality, remained mixed to the end. In subsuming the natural cycle of the world into the divine order of eternity, *The Seasons*, like so many pastorals, transcends its ostensibly "lower" subject. It is one of the final glories of a tradition that is more than high enough.

12 Miscellaneous vocal genres

KATALIN KOMLÓS

When the Leipzig publisher Breitkopf & Härtel decided to print the collected works of Joseph Haydn in 1799, the firm actually meant the complete edition of the keyboard works. Clavier music was highly marketable, satisfying the insatiable demand by amateurs making music in the drawing room, and Breitkopf hoped to expand and increase their market through this medium. The twelve volumes of the final product – ambitiously titled *Oeuvres complettes de Joseph Haydn* (1800–6) – comprises solo and accompanied sonatas (trios), and solo and part-songs with keyboard accompaniment. Interestingly, accompanied songs were still considered keyboard rather than vocal music at the time, just as they had been in various German collections since the mid-eighteenth century. Volumes VIII–IX of the *Oeuvres complettes* include nearly all the German Lieder, the English canzonettas, the cantata *Arianna a Naxos*, and the thirteen part-songs for three or four voices – exactly the repertory discussed in this chapter.

What was Haydn's most popular music around 1800, however, would later become the most neglected. Viewed as precursors to the great song repertories of Franz Schubert and Robert Schumann, and damned for their inferior texts, Haydn's songs were regarded as unworthy of a composer possessing his talents and abilities.[1] Like the solo keyboard sonatas, which since the 1970s have formed part of the regularly performed sonata repertory and are no longer viewed as inferior predecessors to the sonatas of Mozart and Beethoven, Haydn's songs are gradually being rediscovered by present-day singers and keyboardists. More and more they are being appreciated again for their small-scale dimensions, intimate range of expression, and understated pleasures.

Solo songs

Lieder für das Clavier, Hob. XXVIa: 1–24

The genre of the Lied, cultivated in Germany since the 1750s, was slow to appear in Vienna. In the music of the German *Empfindsamkeit*, easy clavichord pieces and songs were published together in the same albums (*Musikalisches Allerley*, 1760; *Musikalisches Mancherley*, 1762; etc.), and enjoyed great popularity. Composed on religious or fashionable

Anacreontic/pastoral poems, the score of the short, mostly strophic songs looked exactly like the solo pieces, except that it included text between the two staves; that is, the vocal part was not printed on a separate staff, but merely doubled the right-hand keyboard part.[2]

In the very different intellectual climate of Vienna, new literary and musical trends began to emerge towards the end of the reign of Empress Maria Theresa. The Deutsche Nationalsingspiel, founded by Joseph II in 1778, and the Viennese aspiration for the partial Germanization of a basically Italian and French-oriented musical culture contributed to the awakening interest in German poetry and art. That same year the Viennese publisher Joseph Edlen von Kurzböck began printing a series of German songs by Austrian composers, each album titled "Sammlung Deutscher Lieder für das Klavier," issuing four volumes up to 1782. Three collections were composed by the *Hofklaviermeister* Joseph Anton Steffan alone (1778; 1779; 1782), and the content of the 1780 volume was shared between Karl Friberth and Leopold Hofmann. Following Kurzböck's initiative, Artaria decided to join the enterprise. Hoping to capitalize on his other success, the publisher asked Joseph Haydn to provide two volumes of German songs for publication. The resulting two collections – *XII Lieder für das Clavier*, I and II – were printed in 1781 and 1784 respectively.

It has been noted repeatedly in the literature that Haydn was not particular in his choice of text, possessed poor literary taste, and was content to set inferior poetry in his Lieder. The truth is that all contemporary Viennese Lieder repertory drew from a similar supply, with texts extracted from almanacs, pocket-books, lady's journals, and the like. This kind of simple, slightly sentimental poetry was favored in Viennese salons, and seemed the evident choice for musical settings.[3] Haydn's two dozen songs use texts selected from the *Wiener Musenalmanach*, *Göttinger Musenalmanach*, *Vossische Musenalmanach*, and *Ramlers Lyrische Blumenlese*, and among the poets are G. Leon, J. G. Jacobi, C. F. Weisse, J. A. Weppen, Stahl, G. A. Bürger, F. W. Gotter, W. L. Gleim, G. E. Lessing, and J. E. Engel. Haydn's letters indicate that his main advisor in the matter of selecting suitable texts was the Court Councillor Franz von Greiner, a freemason and amateur poet himself who kept an elegant literary salon in the Mehlgrube. He had advised Steffan and Hofmann before Haydn, so it is not surprising that the Kurzböck and Artaria song collections draw on the same poetic repertory. Several of Haydn's song texts were set not only by his contemporaries Steffan and Hofmann, but also by Johann Holzer, Leopold Kozeluch, and – later – Beethoven.[4]

In the two sets Haydn achieves a great variety of character, inspired by the diverse nature of the texts. The love songs are predominantly male utterances (nos. 3, 7, 15, etc.), while several other songs depict country life, or reflect an

Arcadian/pastoral manner (nos. 8, 10, 14). There are contemplative essays as well as humorous ones, often with a mischievous story (nos. 4, 12). The only religious text is in the second set (no. 17, "Geistliches Lied"), by an unknown author. "I assure you that these Lieder perhaps surpass all my previous ones [single German songs by Haydn survive from both before and after the publication of the Artaria sets] in variety, naturalness, and ease of vocal execution," wrote the composer with self-confidence to his publisher in May 1781.[5] Haydn was conscious of the competition, too, and wanted to prove his equality if not superiority in the medium, especially compared to the unpretentious "street songs" of Leopold Hofmann.[6] His songs exceed those of Hofmann in every artistic respect, and, when compared to those of his other rivals, reveal more detailed attention and sensitivity to textual accent, poetic structure, rhetoric, and affect.

The musical world of the twenty-four Lieder is a microcosm of Haydn's art. Short, strophic songs alternate with longer, more complex ones, and the gamut of expression spans from the deeply melancholic to the jolly and frivolous. Composed around the same time as the Op. 33 string quartets and the "Bossler" sonatas (Hob. XVI: 40–42), these miniatures share similar stylistic qualities with the instrumental works, and several Lieder anticipate a good deal of later Haydn, including the refined lyricism of the English canzonettas on the one hand, and the familiar, folklike idiom of *The Seasons* on the other. The pathos, the multicolored harmonic palette, and the elaborate keyboard accompaniment of some of the odd-numbered songs (nos. 5, 9, 11, 17, 19, 21) presage the character of the London compositions, whereas "Eine sehr gewöhnliche Geschichte" (no. 4) became a model for Hanne's cheerful song in the Winter section of *The Seasons* (no. 40, "Lied mit Chor"); indeed, it seems that Haydn remembered not only the metric profile, the G major key, and the folksong-like character, but some definite melodic turns as well when composing the great oratorio twenty years later.

English canzonettas, Hob. XXVIa: 25–36

It was in completely different circumstances and in a different country when Haydn set out to compose a series of songs again. And this time the texts were even in a different and foreign language. In contrast to Vienna, where the Lied was a fresh genre for composers around 1780, domestic vocal music had been in great vogue in England through the latter half of the eighteenth century. Hundreds of volumes of songs, ballads, airs, canzonets, pastorals, romances, ariettes, elegies, sonnets, etc. had already been published for the amateur clientele. Canzonetta, or canzonet, designated two discrete genres that existed side by side: Italian canzonettas, written (as a rule) for two treble voices and *basso continuo*; and English canzonettas for solo voice, with pianoforte or harp accompaniment. Notable composers of the former type were Johann Christian Bach, William Jackson, and Charles Burney, and collections of canzonettas with English text were published by Samuel Arnold, Stephen Storace, J. G. C. Schetky, and William Shield, among others.[7]

Haydn arrived in England in January 1791 and accommodated himself and his art to the new conditions in an amazingly short time. His first London lodging in Great Pulteney Street, opposite John Broadwood's pianoforte shop, was a short distance from the house of the famous surgeon, Dr. John Hunter, in Leicester Square. The active social life the distinguished guest participated in must have soon taken him to the weekly salon of Dr. Hunter's wife, Anne Hunter (1742–1821), a talented and cultivated woman with exceptional literary gifts. Eventually, a close understanding developed between Anne Hunter and the composer, perhaps not unlike the one that drew Haydn to Marianne von Genzinger in Vienna. Without Anne Hunter's influence and poetic inspiration, it is unlikely Haydn would have tried his hand at composing English songs. Indeed, circumstances suggest that Anne Hunter passed on to Haydn all her verses during the first London sojourn.[8]

Haydn's English songs comprise two sets of canzonettas – *VI Original Canzonettas*, I–II (1794 and 1795) – and two further single songs, published separately. Of the two sets, the first is more compact: all the lyrics are by Anne Hunter (an interesting case of collaboration between Haydn and a woman, one who was not merely a dedicatee), and all the music is newly composed. In the second set the texts are by various authors, and the closing piece is a transposed version of an earlier song, originally with German words.[9] The melancholy text of "The Wanderer," the second song of the second set, is by Hunter, whereas the third is attributed to Metastasio and the fourth is by Shakespeare, two of the most recognized poets of great tragedy in the eighteenth century. Two other individual songs, "The Spirit's Song" and "O Tuneful Voice," were once again inspired by Anne Hunter's popular poetic fantasy, the latter text marking Haydn's departure from England.

The world of Haydn's canzonettas is entirely different from that of the earlier German Lieder. For starters, the English songs are printed on three staves, with a separate line for the vocal part, and they are considerably longer than their predecessors. Here Haydn makes explicit on paper what might very well have been an improvisatory practice in performance in Vienna *anno* 1781 – i.e., keyboard embellishment. Furthermore, the predominantly strophic structure of the former repertory gives way – especially in the second set – to a wider variety of form. Besides through-composed models we find fine examples of the "veränderte Reprise" principle, as in the second stanza of "The Wanderer" where variation is achieved by contrapuntal means in the keyboard part. In the ABA ternary form of "The Spirit's Song" the ominous chromatic ascending motive returns in a descending form in the reprise.[10]

Two basic types of contemporary English songs, the pastoral, and the sea song, are represented among Haydn's canzonettas, and still another fashionable mode, *elegy* characterizes certain Hunter songs. "Fidelity," the closing piece of the first set of canzonettas, relates to the *furioso* f minor arias of Arianna and Berenice ("Misera abbandonata" in *Arianna a Naxos*, Hob. XXVIb: 2; and "Perché, se tanti siete" in *Scena di Berenice*, Hob. XXIVa: 10), but the soaring end in the key of the *maggiore* proclaims the final triumph of love over storm and affliction.[11] "The Spirit's Song," likewise in f minor, is a real *ombra* scene in a highly rhetorical style, while the setting of Viola's words from Shakespeare's *Twelfth Night* is a pure distillation of musical poetry.[12]

Keyboard parts

The German and English songs offer an excellent opportunity to compare Haydn's earlier and London keyboard writing styles. The "Clavier" designation of the former repertory could have meant clavichord, harpsichord, or fortepiano equally, depending on availability, personal inclination, or circumstances of the performance, whereas the instrumental language of the canzonettas reflects the strong influence of the English pianoforte on Haydn's keyboard idiom. The German Lieder, in keeping with contemporary Viennese practice, are notated on two staves, the keyboard right hand simply reinforcing the vocal part. At least one half of the German songs are provided with instrumental preludes that, in some cases, are quite substantial, whereas postludes are less frequent. These carefully worked-out solo introductions, with their delicate line, or sprightly gait, define the *Affekt* of the song. The proximity of the sonatas Hob. XVI: 40–42 is palpable in the decorative art of these short keyboard essays, and they display a sensibility that calls for the expressive resources of the Viennese fortepiano.

In the English canzonettas, the instrumental part takes primacy. The genre is close to Haydn's "accompanied sonata" conception, in which the keyboard part is the essence, and the non-keyboard part (in this case, the voice) is the addition. Influenced by the full, resonant tone of the late eighteenth-century English piano, Haydn's keyboard writing went through a real metamorphosis during the London years. Thick textures, a sustained cantabile style, use of the entire range of the keyboard (low register in particular), and novel kinds of playing techniques are manifest not only in the solo sonatas and the trios, but in the keyboard parts of the songs as well. "Sailor's Song," clearly the most "British" piece among the canzonettas, has the most robust piano texture.[13] A certain heaviness is required by the character of the song, which is produced by thumping beats, and many eight-part chords. Quite another world is the last of the second set of canzonettas, "Content," and the single song "O Tuneful Voice." Together, they represent a pre-Romantic type of song, with homogeneous triplet accompaniment – as in the case of "O Tuneful Voice" – in the manner of the early cavatinas of Rossini and Bellini.[14]

Several documents indicate that Haydn liked to perform his songs himself. "When they are ready, I shall sing them myself in the critical houses," he wrote to Artaria in July 1781, concerning the first set of the German Lieder. Later in England, Haydn, who possessed a light tenor voice, sang his canzonettas to his own accompaniment in royal and aristocratic circles.[15]

Cycles or not?

Apart from a few single pieces, Haydn arranged his songs in sets of six, or twelve (2 × 12 German Lieder; 2 × 6 English canzonettas). To have works printed in sets was contemporary practice, but Haydn took particular care to plan his opuses in a well-ordered sequence, be they string quartets, keyboard sonatas, or trios.[16] Since songs are very short compositions, variety in a series of them must have seemed even more important than in the instrumental genres. Haydn's German songs, for instance, create organized cycles not in the sense of the coherent nineteenth-century *Liederzyklus*, but as strings of little pieces of diverse musical and literary character. His correspondence with Artaria reflects concern for variety in the sets. "I would like . . . to receive three new, gentle Lieder texts, because almost all the others are of a lusty character. The content of these can be melancholy, too: so that I have shadow and light, just as in the first twelve," Haydn wrote in October 1781.[17]

The composer's ideal is realized more successfully in the first set. Here lyric/sad and fast/humorous songs succeed each other, and the tonal plan is based on the consistent alternation of flat-side and sharp-side keys. The dramaturgy of the second set shows less variety; here slow tempos prevail, and two consecutive songs are written in the same key. Research undertaken by Marianne Helms, however, indicates that the original order may have been altered due to publication necessities.[18] This would explain the *lapsus* in diversity, for Haydn still aspired to achieve a well-conceived tonal plan for his second set, as his letter of February 3, 1784, to Artaria indicates: "I shall send you the missing Lieder next Friday or Saturday; I would only ask you to let me know the key of the final printed Lied, and how its text begins, so that I can decide the keys of the ones to follow."[19]

The English canzonettas were also conceived as sets. Both start with a sea song, and contain two pastoral-like songs in 6/8 meter and another in a minor key, and both also display a fine variety of poetic mood and character. (As noted above, the second set is slightly less homogeneous – an odd concurrence with the German collections.) There is a great difference, however, between the endings of the two sets. "Fidelity" gives a most effective close to the first set, while the concluding canzonetta of the second set, "Content," is one of the gentlest, most lyrical essays among all the songs. The ethereal pianissimo and più adagio of the last bars seems like an anticlimax at the end of an impressive series. Perhaps pressed by time, Haydn selected an older song to complete his set, but it is equally possible that he fancied a dreamy, poetic ending. In support of the latter possibility is the fact that the very last of the German Lieder, "Auf meines Vaters Grab," is a quiet song.

What are the consequences of the cyclic conception for performance? Haydn's comments suggest that the songs should be sung together as sets; otherwise, how could the alternation of "shadow and light" be perceived, or why should the choice of key for subsequent songs matter? Perhaps it was enough for Haydn to realize these ideals on paper alone. Order and variety in sets was a natural part of Haydn's artistic aesthetic. He did not expect musicians to play six string quartets or six keyboard sonatas in a row, nor should the songs be compared to multi-movement instrumental works. If not performed as complete cycles, then smaller groups might be devised from them, based on variety of *Affekt* and character, thereby maintaining the principles of shadow and light.

In Haydn's time Clavier music (solo or accompanied) and song-repertory was written primarily for *Liebhaber* (dilettantes). In cultivated homes *Hausmusik* represented the main attraction of social life, and music-making was unthinkable without singing. Today, that situation can well be transposed to chamber concerts, or small musical gatherings, set in an intimate milieu. This is the ideal environment for the performance of Haydn's secular vocal music, together with instrumental works in a mixed program. A "Haydniade" of this sort should create the same kind of atmosphere as the legendary "Schubertiades" did in their time.

Solo cantata – *Arianna a Naxos*, Hob. XXVIb: 2

The mythological story of the Cretan princess, Ariadne, inspired several opera composers from Monteverdi to Richard Strauss. Nearly contemporaneous with Haydn's work is Georg Benda's melodrama *Ariadne auf*

Naxos (1775), representative of a rare genre, which had a marked influence on the twenty-two-year-old W. A. Mozart.[20] Haydn's *Arianna* is a descendant of the dramatic Italian Baroque solo cantata, but in place of *basso continuo* support it has an elaborate, fully worked-out fortepiano accompaniment. The keyboard part is tailored so idiomatically to this instrument that later orchestrated versions (*not* by Haydn) seem tame, indeed awkward, in comparison.

We do not know what motivated Haydn to compose this solo cantata with keyboard, nor can we identify the author of the Italian text. The autograph, now lost, bore the date 1789, and the work was published by Artaria in 1790, with the following sub-title: "Cantata a voce sola, accompagnamento del clavicembalo o fortepiano." Biographical evidence suggests that it was intended for the the Viennese salon of Marianne von Genzinger, wife of Prince Esterházy's doctor Peter von Genzinger. Haydn was a frequent guest at the musical gatherings of the Genzinger family in the Schottenhof, where his works were often performed. Apparently he gave voice lessons to the sixteen-year-old daughter, Josepha ("Pepperl"), and "Fräulein Pepperl" is mentioned several times in Haydn's letters to Frau von Genzinger, invariably in connection with the interpretation of the composer's "favorite *Arianna*."[21]

Arianna a Naxos is a masterly psychological portrayal of a forsaken woman. The *scena*, built on the alternation of recitatives and arias, traces the dramatic development of the heroine's emotions through solitude, despair, desire of death, and rage. The grand soliloquy opens with an extensive section containing a contemplative recitative prefaced by a substantial fortepiano introduction – the only self-contained movement in the work. It continues with a slow aria, a middle recitative, and a closing compound aria (Larghetto, F major – Presto, f minor) joined together by attacca, as in a through-composed process.[22] Most remarkable is the *stile concitato* character of the central section, where the agitated, dramatic mixture of *recitativo* and *arioso* recalls the violent passion of Monteverdi's dramatic vocal music.

In a recent article Julian Rushton ponders whether *Arianna* was meant for amateur or professional performance.[23] While the sole accompaniment of the fortepiano and the modest range (b–g♭″) and technical level of the vocal part suggest a *Hausmusik* function, the work appears to have initiated a new chapter in the history of the cantata in London, where it was received with great success at both private and public concerts. The castrato Gasparo Pacchierotti with Haydn at the keyboard performed *Arianna* at a "Ladies' Concert" in February 1791 held "at Mrs. Blair's in Portland Place." Reporting on the event, the critic of the *Morning Chronicle* could hardly find sufficient superlatives for his praises:

> The Musical World is at this moment enraptured with a Composition which Haydn has brought forth, and which has produced effects bordering on all that Poets used to seign of the ancient lyre. Nothing is talked of – nothing sought after but Haydn's Cantata – or, as it is called in the Italian School – his Scena . . . It abounds with such a variety of dramatic modulations – and is so exquisitely captivating in its larmoyant passages, that it touched and dissolved the audience. They speak of it with rapturous recollection, and Haydn's Cantata will accordingly be the musical *desideratum* for the winter.[24]

The production was repeated some days later at a public concert in the Pantheon. And perhaps to encourage private performance, the English publisher Bland printed it in 1791.

Popularity of the cantata increased during the 1790s through a bewildering variety of performances for different occasions, far and wide. For instance, it was sung during a Holy Week service at one of the *ospedali* in Venice in 1792, with sacred Latin text as a *contrafactum*, and Anna Ascher, soloist of the Kärntnerthortheater, sang it at a morning Augarten concert in Vienna in June 1798, as did Lady Hamilton when she and Admiral Nelson visited Haydn in Eisenstadt in September 1800.[25] During their visit, Lady Hamilton and Haydn spent many hours making music together, and as a memento of her visit the composer presented her a manuscript copy of "The Spirit's Song."

Part-songs – Hob. XXVc: 1–9, XXVb: 1–4

In the second half of the 1790s Haydn wrote thirteen part-songs for three or four solo voices with keyboard accompaniment. This unexpected group of late compositions has no precedent in Haydn's earlier oeuvre, provoking the question: what prompted the aged composer to initiate a new genre? Perhaps acquaintance with the English glee inspired Haydn to create a German equivalent.[26] James Webster believes that the *Mehrstimmige Gesänge* "adumbrate the characteristic nineteenth-century Viennese genre of social music for vocal ensemble."[27]

The autograph bears the date 1796, the beginning year of composition for a projected series of two dozen pieces; however, no more than thirteen were completed by 1799.[28] The part-songs were printed in volumes VIII–IX of the *Oeuvres complettes* by Breitkopf & Härtel in 1803. Haydn himself regarded them highly, and at his request Breitkopf issued a separate edition entitled *Drey- und vierstimmige GESAENGE mit Begleitung des Piano-Forte von Joseph Haydn.* He intended his part-songs for solo voices, describing them as "vocal quartets."[29] The keyboard accompaniment has a curious division in the autograph: nos. 1–9 are provided with figured bass, and only nos. 10–13 have a fully written-out keyboard part. The Breitkopf first edition substituted pianoforte accompaniment for the rather old-fashioned *basso continuo* (the realization is not by Haydn), and the printed order of the pieces departs from the original sequence of the autograph.[30]

Haydn's primary source for German poetic texts was the popular collection *Lyrische Blumenlese* [Lyrical flower harvest], a potpourri of verses by various German poets edited by Karl Wilhelm Ramler. Haydn selected texts (by Götz, Lessing, Gleim, and Weisse) with subjects ranging from the serious and mock-serious to the humorous and the ironic.[31] The later group of part-songs turns to the religious texts of Christian Fürchtegott Gellert, with nos. 9–10 and 12–13 setting poems from the *Geistliche Oden und Lieder* (1757), a volume that inspired many composers from C. P. E. Bach to Beethoven.[32]

These thirteen pieces, although little known, represent the highest craftsmanship of Haydn's late style. Homophonic and polyphonic writing appear side by side, with abundant counterpoint enriching the texture of each song; for instance, nos. 7, 8, and 13 begin with strict fugal imitation, and no. 7 features thematic inversion. Beautiful sonority is achieved in the homophonic sections through the spacing of the chords, enhanced by rich harmonies. The songs also employ a wide array of original devices for the musical representation of the text, ranging from the *madrigalesque* to the highly rhetorical. Certain passages in no. 3 ("Alles hat seine Zeit") recall the elaborate vocal textures of the late-sixteenth-century Italian madrigal (Marenzio in particular; see Ex. 12.1), while the various *figurae* applied for verbal emphasis in nos. 9, 11, 13, and elsewhere speak an eloquent rhetorical language.[33] (For example, *abruptio* in no. 9 at mm. 20–21, 47, 60–61 on the word "keiner"; *repetitio* in no. 11 at mm. 14–15 and 42–43 on the word "Schönheit"; *exclamatio* in no. 13 at the double invocation "Herr!" at the beginning, and again in mm. 37–38, 59–60, and 87–88.) Humorous texts also inspire lively word-painting (no. 4), or facetious dialogue (no. 11).

With regard to the general mood and musical character, one of the most special pieces is no. 9, "Betrachtung des Todes" (Contemplation of Death). The only setting in a minor key, this trio foreshadows – like late Haydn often does – the subjective musical expressivity of the first Romantic generation. Haydn translates the content of the text into the language of music through subtle harmonies and key-changes – the uncanny turn from C major to c♯ minor at the word "Irrtum" ("error," in mm. 22–24) creating a most startling modulation. Here the distant relationship of two chords/keys with a "common third" (that is, major *versus* semitone-higher minor) mirrors similar special effects in Schubert's music. Novel harmonic constructions are later introduced, such as a Neapolitan six–five chord in the last chromatic

Example 12.1 Part-song "Alles hat seine Zeit," mm. 21–25
[text translation: "be enthusiastic with me"]

Example 12.2 Part-song "Betrachtung des Todes," mm. 49–54
[text translation: "and no one perceives the error"]

passage preceding the coda (mm. 49–54; see Ex. 12.2). Transience of life – the subject of Gellert's poem – is poignantly present in the spiritual quality of this music.

Among Gellert's *Geistliche Oden und Lieder* the aged Haydn found two odes that may have resonated with him directly. "Danklied zu Gott" and "Abendlied zu Gott," both thanksgivings, are addressed to God at the end of earthly life. Approaching the age of seventy, Haydn may have identified with the simple, sincere thoughts of the Protestant poet, choosing these texts for the last two of his part-songs. Haydn's devout religious feelings, so overt in the great masses of the past period, are here sublimated in more personal, hymn-like settings. "Abendlied zu Gott," one of Gellert's better-known poems, begins with an invocation to "Herr" that is doubled and intensified by a full chordal exclamation in long notes with fermatas. The word "Treue" is first highlighted by a leap in the soprano register at bar 43, and later with a melisma at bars 101–6. This piece might very well be understood as Haydn's "Vor Deinen Thron tret' ich hiermit" (Before Thy throne I now appear) – a final offering to the Creator similar to that of Johann Sebastian Bach after *Der Kunst der Fuge.*

13 Haydn in the theater: the operas

CARYL CLARK

Haydn wrote over two dozen works for the theater *c.*1751–96,[1] a thirty-five year period that began and ended with German Singspiel composition. Italian opera dominated, however, especially from 1762 to 1791, the years encompassing Haydn's employment at the Esterházy court and his first London visit. Representing all the major operatic genres prominent in the second half of the eighteenth century – including intermezzo, opera buffa, opera seria, *dramma giocoso*, and Singspiel (for traditional and marionette opera stages) – this repertory demonstrates Haydn's development from fledgling dramatic composer to that of fully competent *Opernkapellmeister*. Because of the paucity of surviving sources, it is difficult to make a knowledgeable assessment of the composer's early forays into Singspiel for the German stage in Vienna during the 1750s and of other works in his native language written for the marionette theater at Eszterháza. This chapter concentrates on Haydn's Italian operas, the major interest of his primary patron and of opera audiences in general during the second half of the eighteenth century.

Context

Before learning to play the violin or the keyboard, Haydn was taught to sing by his father. Recruited at the age of eight to sing in the choir school at St. Stephen's Cathedral in Vienna on the strength of his pure, sonorous voice and exceptional mastery of the vocal trill, Haydn sang at church services there twice daily and at numerous religious and other local functions. He later claimed to have learned more from singing and hearing the music he was making than from formal lessons. Narrowly avoiding castration to preserve his soprano voice,[2] Haydn was unceremoniously dismissed from the choir school when his voice changed around the age of sixteen, leaving him to seek other employment in his adopted city.[3] As an adult Haydn possessed a light tenor voice, which he used when making *Hausmusik* with friends in a variety of social settings. But he once commented to Griesinger that, "singing must almost be reckoned one of the lost arts; instead of song, people allow the instruments to dominate"[4] – a remark tinged with irony given the course of Haydn historiography, since posterity has rarely remembered Haydn as an opera composer. Even though some of his earliest compositions were for the stage, including the lost Viennese Hanswurstian comedy *Der krumme Teufel* (*c.*1751) and possibly several German comedy arias (or "Teutsche Comedie Arien") for Singspiele performed in Vienna in the 1750s, and although he devoted nearly thirty years to composing and producing opera for the Esterházys and was later commissioned to write an opera for London, the leading center of Italian opera production in this period, Haydn's operas circulated within a small sphere (mainly in German translation), and his last opera never did reach the London stage. Conceived and designed for local conditions[5] and subsequently silenced by cultural and aesthetic currents, Haydn's operas fell into oblivion, with the predominant interpretive positions established during the long nineteenth century continuing to shape perceptions of his operatic oeuvre to this day.

Certainly his patron was the catalyst behind Haydn writing so many theatrical works. Prince Nicolaus, the wealthiest and most powerful member of the Hungarian nobility, first staged operas at the family palace in Eisenstadt in conjunction with court celebrations. But after building an opera house on his eponymous estate, Eszterháza, in 1768, and a marionette theater in 1773, the Prince required Haydn to engage in theatrical activity on a regular basis. Even though Haydn never traveled to the country where opera was born nor regularly saw staged productions outside of Eszterháza, with the exception of limited exposure in Vienna, operatic composition and adaptation, including manuscript preparation, transcription, vocal instruction, rehearsal, and direction, played a central role in his career, especially after the institution of a regular operatic season in 1776 and continuing through to the death of Prince Nicolaus in 1790.[6] The majority of Haydn's theatrical works date from the middle Esterházy years – from the opening of the opera house in 1768 with *Lo speziale* (The Apothecary) and the intense puppet opera years of the mid-1770s through to *Armida* of 1784 – a sixteen-year period during which he composed ten Italian and five marionette operas and oversaw the development of a repertory theater. Haydn was provided with all the necessities for producing opera, including two opera houses equipped with production, theatrical, and musical personnel.

The operatic establishment at Eszterháza functioned very differently from the typical Italian opera house of the period. Most operas were imported, with Haydn, the resident composer, supplying the only new works, although even these were on pre-existent librettos whose texts were adapted to the changing exigencies of the local opera troupe.[7] As a private theater owned and funded by an aristocratic patron, the Esterházy opera house did not depend on box-office receipts for survival. Salaried personnel, including singers, orchestral players, poets, designers, carpenters, seamstresses, etc., including Haydn, the de facto manager, all worked for the ideological "director," the Prince, whose primary objectives were self-celebration and entertainment. Outside of special court occasions such as weddings and state visits, when members of the aristocratic household and special high-ranking visitors attended performances, it is not entirely clear who frequented the four-hundred-seat theater or how often the Prince occupied his oval box on the first floor opposite the stage.[8] Frequently members of the aristocracy and sometimes foreign travelers attracted to this isolated cultural hub were among the audience, and members of visiting theatrical troupes and other artisans or some of the approximately thousand employees at court may also have attended the opera on occasion, especially in the 1780s, when performances were twice weekly and the season extended from March to December.[9] Comparatively little is known about the grotto-like marionette theater or its workings, although it too functioned as a place for entertainment and princely glorification.[10]

Occasional operas: 1762–76

Haydn's *Acide* (1763), a *festa teatrale* on a libretto by Ambrogio Migliavacca, formed part of the festivities in conjunction with the marriage of Count Anton, Prince Nicolaus's eldest son and heir, to Countess Marie Therese Erdödy. Although subsequently revived in 1774, surviving materials from both versions still do not constitute a complete work – its fragmentary state destining it for concert performance today. Arias for the main characters – Acide, his beloved Galatea, her friend Glauce, and rival Polifemo – are all in da capo form, still the standard format for seria arias in this period; nevertheless they reveal Haydn's early penchant for high tessitura and flashy coloratura when writing for the court's leading tenor, Carl Friberth, a member of the Esterházy chorus since 1759 and creator of the title role. In the final scene, a new character, Tetide, arrives to restore Acis to life after being slain by Polyphemus, permitting a happy ending, as called for by the occasion.[11] The groom, then aged twenty-five, would eventually be Haydn's third Esterházy patron from 1790–94.

The similarly fragmentary *La marchesa Nespola* (1763) was inspired by the *commedia dell'arte*, although here the sources suggest that the nine individual arias were inserted into a spoken play that mixed Italian songs with German dialogue, typical of the works performed by Giralomo Bon's theatrical troupe, which was on long-term contract at the court during this period.[12] Several smaller operas known only by their titles entered in the composer's draft worklist or *Entwurf-Katalog* may also have been performed during the mid-1760s.[13]

Although the earliest documented performance of *La canterina* (The Songstress) is February 16, 1767 in Pressburg, this charming little intermezzo was most likely performed the preceding July in Eisenstadt for the nameday celebrations of Count Anton. Adapted from a mid-eighteenth-century Neapolitan intermezzo,[14] *La canterina* has no overture and is cast in two parts, each with a concluding quartet.[15] It features four characters based on Italian comic character types: Gasparina, the clever *virtuosa* of the title who, with the counsel of her *finta madre*, Apollonia (sung by the tenor Leopold Dichtler, perhaps in falsetto, since the role is notated in the soprano clef), humors two suitors – the young merchant Don Ettore (a trouser role played by the soprano Barbara Dichtler, Leopold's wife), and the singing master Don Pelagio. A coded and complex scene in part one, hinging on the erotics of dominance and submission associated with the music lesson in opera (think of similar scenes in Rossini's *Il barbiere di Siviglia* from 1816 and its precursor by Paisiello from 1782), depicts the elderly master, seated at the keyboard, instructing his young female student in singing an aria he has composed to an outmoded text from Apostolo Zeno's *Lucio Vero* (Venice 1700). His meta-performance introduces a direct musical discourse that ironizes the self-reflexive act of "singing" in opera while simultaneously poking fun at the Maestro's fatuous behavior, particularly in the revving up of his lustful intentions displayed in the repetitive, mechanical passagework and vapid scales of the disproportionately long orchestral introduction preceding his accompanied recitative (see Exx. 13. 1a and b). His fingers moving magically across the keyboard, conjuring up the orchestral music we hear – his empty virtuosity doing little to bolster Haydn's reputation as an opera composer! – he holds his protégée hostage to his fumbling and "dolci lumi," reinforcing the status of the female singer as learner. Part of the opera's appeal at court may have related to the terms of Haydn's 1761 employment contract, which stipulated he was "obliged to instruct the female vocalists, in order that they may not again forget (when staying in the country) that which they have been taught with much effort and at great expense in Vienna,"[16] – a task for which he had gained invaluable experience as a vocal accompanist in the studio of Nicola Porpora in Vienna in the early 1750s.

Lo speziale (The Apothecary), a comic opera in three acts that inaugurated the opera house in Eszterháza in 1768, is the first of three works by Haydn on libretti by the well-known Venetian social satirist Carlo Goldoni. Initially set by Fischietti and Pallavicini the preceding decade, it was stripped of its original *parte serie* to reduce the cast from seven to four characters, creating an intensification of the comic action. A beautiful young ward, Grilletta, coveted by her caretaker, the lecherous old apothecary, Sempronio, his young assistant, Mengone, and another suitor, Volpino, is eventually betrothed to the apprentice, with whom she shares age and social rank, following a ruse to trick the apothecary into seeking fame and fortune in the

Example 13.1a Accompanied recitative, "Che mai far deggio," from Act I of *La canterina* (1766), mm. 1–13

Example 13.1b Accompanied recitative, "Che mai far deggio," from Act I of *La canterina* (1766), mm. 29–34

East. The music for the third act is lost except for a parodic *alla turca* aria and the concluding quartet. The missing music was imaginatively reconstructed by the Viennese music critic Robert Hirschfeld for a performance in German as *Der Apotheker* in Dresden in 1895, later conducted by Mahler in Hamburg (1896) and Vienna (1899), making it the first modern revival of a Haydn opera.[17] The opera abounds in word-painting for comic effect, as in "Per quell che ha mal il stomico" where Mengone demonstrates cures for cramps, constipation, and diarrhea, and employs disguises to similarly farcical effect, e.g., Mengone and Volpino as notaries in the Act II finale, and Volpino as an emissary from Turkey in Act III (see also chapter 6).

Le pescatrici (The Fisherwomen), written to celebrate the marriage of the prince's niece, Countess Lambach, to Count Pocci, in September 1770, is the second Goldonian comedy Haydn set and his first true *dramma giocoso.* Here, the noble and lowly born appear together on stage, however, only the brother and sister pairs – Nerina and Frisellino, Lesbino and Burlotto, who are in love with each other's opposite – perform in the dramatically static sectional finales. Set in a small Italian fishing village, the story revolves around the discovery that Eurilda, raised as the daughter of the old fisherman Masticcio, is actually of noble birth and therefore worthy of betrothal to Prince Lindoro, the young hero who has come in search of the missing princess of Benevento. Interestingly, the role of the young lover was sung by a baritone (Christian Specht), since the two available tenors, Dichtler and Friberth, who played the fishermen, were comedic, indicating just how stretched the resources of the opera troupe were during its early development. The libretto printed for this lavish production indicates "nine scene changes with seven separate sets including a beach with a ship."[18] Was this vessel the one Lindoro arrived in before singing his stormy aria in d minor "Varca il mar" evoking his rough ocean voyage? Although the conclusion of this aria is missing from the autograph score (and approximately a quarter of this score is missing entirely), there are sufficient syncopations, rushing semi-quavers, and wide vocal leaps associated with the storm and stress style remaining to convey the hazards of travel at sea. While the buffo antics of the fishing couples might seem inappropriate for a dynastic wedding, the depiction of noble love in a pastoral setting allied to Eurilda's refined sensibility and awakening sexual passion – all within the flexible and fashionable framework of a musical comedy designed to display Prince Nicolaus's up-to-date tastes – suggests that "the aristocracy were ever more comfortable with representation of a more complicated hierarchy of social interactions."[19] Indeed, following an E major chorus redolent of ocean breezes ("Soavi zeffiri"), the opera closes with an ensemble blessing the marriages of three couples. Choral forces make an auspicious entrance on the Esterházy stage in this work, further testament to the growing operatic enterprise.

The "burletta per musica" *L'infedeltà delusa* (Infidelity Outwitted) on a libretto by Marco Coltellini premiered July 26, 1773, during the grandiose nameday celebrations honoring Prince Nicolaus's widowed sister-in-law. It was performed again in early September along with the marionette opera *Philemon und Baucis* for the celebratory state visit to Eszterháza of another widow, Empress Maria Theresa. Perhaps the experience of witnessing this delightfully comic chamber opera on a libretto by her former house poet (Coltellini had worked at the Vienna court from 1766–72) in conjunction with the grandiosity of the celebrations prompted the Empress's (apocryphal) remark: "If I want to hear good opera, I go to Eszterháza!"[20]– although it is debatable how much opera she was accustomed to experiencing at this time and what her basis of comparison may have been. Operas staged within the context of special festivities at Eszterháza in the early 1770s were part of a totalizing theatricality of sequential courtly entertainments that included staged productions in both opera houses, and elaborate banquets, shooting parties, fireworks displays, pantomimes, tattoos, and concerts held in the dining rooms, ballrooms, and extensive grounds surrounding the palace. "A series of such celebrations, stretching over several days, may be regarded as a single pageant which had the aim of dazzling the participants by the wealth of spectacle and accumulation of entertainments."[21]

The first of Haydn's operas to survive entirely intact, *L'infedeltà delusa* opens with a pastoral-style *introduzione* in F major (Moderato cut-time; Allegro 3/8) depicting the rural country setting and wafting summer evening breezes. Languorous horns and sonorous oboes in consonant thirds and sixths lend atmospheric color to the opening vocal quartet, but with the arrival of the faster section, we learn that all is not as tranquil as it appears. The old peasant farmer, Filippo, wants his daughter Sandrina to marry the wealthy farmer, Nencio, who is coveted by the clever Vespina ("little wasp"); however, Sandrina, who wants to marry for love not money, desires Vespina's brother, the penniless Nanni. Vespina assumes four different identities in Act II – that of an old woman, a German servant, a marquis, and a notary – to win Nencio for herself. Haydn creates a parade of comic orchestral gestures to depict Vespina's disguises – an old woman's limping, the revelry of the drunken, dancing, jovial German, and the mock-seriousness of the marquis, whose regal dotted rhythms in the opening horns are mocked by the violin's Scottish snaps in the opening ritornello of "Ho tesa la rete." Haydn, whose Italian operas are normally in three acts, here writes a two-act work in which the Act II finale returns to the opening key of the opera (the Italian overture begins and ends in C major) and contains both the dramatic climax and *dénouement* of the action. Filippo and Nencio learn of their double duping when Vespina reveals the full extent of her machinations, and the drama concludes with a double wedding that reinforces a stable society: Sandrina weds her beloved Nanni, and Vespina wins Nencio.

The German puppet opera *Philemon und Baucis*, which opened the new marionette theater during the state visit of 1773, was preceded by a short prologue entitled *Der Götterrath* (The Council of the Gods) and concluded with an allegorical representation glorifying the Habsburgs. All three parts are missing music. The narrative concerns a poor husband and wife, Philemon and Baucis, whose son, Aret, and his betrothed, Narcissa, perished during a terrible storm (depicted in the tempestuous d minor overture and opening chorus). They share their story of woe with a pair of disguised visitors – the gods Jupiter and Mercury (speaking roles) – seeking refuge from the storm, and are ultimately rewarded for their generosity. We might well ask who was glorifying whom in this seemingly unpretentious little work performed by lifeless mute dolls manipulated by craftsmen pulling strings, when, after a grandiose display of homage – in which the Habsburg coat of arms descended from the clouds accompanied by allegorical representations of Glory, Clemency, Justice, and Valor, followed by Fame, and kneeling in veneration below it the Hungarian Nation with Love, Obedience, Devotion and Fidelity – "the rear of the new theater began to sink . . . and the illustrious audience saw the splendid illumination in the garden [with] fireworks."[22] The Prince certainly knew how to impress his guests!

For another state visit to Eszterháza in 1775 Haydn composed *L'incontro improvviso* (The Unexpected Meeting). This time the architecture of courtly entertainment designed to impress Archduke Ferdinand, Habsburg governor of Milan, and his consort lasted four days and included a huge masquerade ball, a performance of Symphony no. 60 "Il distratto" (The distracted man) featuring theatrical pantomime, an all-night illumination of the garden, and the feudalistic rallying of thousands of Croatian and Hungarian peasants dancing and singing folksongs – a live display of local exotica. Even the exoticism associated with the spectacle of Haydn and his musicians performing in Oriental costume in the Chinese Pavilion collaborated with the Orientalist themes and location, Janissary marches, and chanting dervishes of *L'incontro improvviso*, an abduction opera fashioned from Gluck's *La rencontre imprévue* (Vienna 1764) by court singer and librettist, Carl Friberth. This fascination with "Turkish" and "abduction" subjects – including chance meetings, thwarted rescue, and royal clemency – and French *opéra comique* reflect recent trends in theatrical works performed in the imperial city. Prince Ali of Balsora (a role Friberth wrote for himself) and his buffo servant, Osmin, undertake a madcap search and rescue effort in Cairo for the Persian Princess Rezia (written for his wife Magdalena Friberth), who has been abducted by the Sultan and is being held prisoner in his harem along with Balkis and Dardane. Haydn has ample opportunity to depict the exotic East using so-called Turkish-flavored music, i.e., leaping melodies, reiterated thirds, chromatic inflections, and percussion effects, as in the idiotic alms begging song sung by the dishonest dervish, "Castagno, castagna" (discussed in chapter 6). Another representation of difference or "otherness" occurs in the evocation of a hot, sensuous locale in the sumptuous trio for the three female captives, "Mi sembra un sogno" (Andantino 3/8 in E♭ major). The passionate yet effortless vocalizing of the three sopranos, intertwining with a pair of haunting English horns accompanied by muted strings, captures the timeless allure of the steamy seraglio and their dreamy anticipation of rescue, all the while playing on European society's larger concerns about liberty, freedom, and choice, especially in matters of government and marriage.

1776–80: the new season – a period of growth and experimentation

In 1776, the same year that Joseph II dismissed the Italian opera troupe and orchestra and instituted the German National Theater project in Vienna, Prince Nicolaus reformed operatic life at Eszterháza in other substantive ways: instituting a repertory theater for the production of Italian opera, with twice-weekly performances alternating with concerts, spoken plays, and German-language productions in the marionette theater. These institutional reforms, linked as much to the Prince's decreasing interest in the baryton as to Haydn's growth as an opera composer, were initiated in March with a production of the greatest reform opera of all time, Gluck's *Orfeo ed Euridice* (1762). This opera's extensive use of chorus and ballet must have stretched the resources of the court's modest opera troupe, even with the hiring of seven new singers.[23] The five other Italian operas performed between April and October that year were lighter theatrical fare, including three intermezzi by Haydn's old friend Dittersdorf, requiring only four vocalists each, a *dramma giocoso* by Sacchini, *L'isola d'amore* (1766), that circulated widely in the 1770s, and Piccinni's *La buona figliuola* (1760) to a libretto by Goldoni, arguably the most famous opera buffa of its day. Add to this Haydn's composition of (possibly) five marionette operas in the 1770s – *Philemon und Baucis* (1773), *Hexenschabbas* (?1773; lost), *Dido* (?1775; lost), *Die Feuerbrunst* (authenticity uncertain), and *Die bestrafte Rachbegierde* (1779; lost) – and we begin to understand the Prince's grand design as staking a claim for Eszterháza on the wider European stage. Thereafter, Haydn was responsible for staging numerous operas at court, all of which required careful editing, revision, and reworking to meet local conditions.

Haydn's first Italian opera in this new context was *Il mondo della luna* (The World of the Moon), the three-act Goldonian *dramma giocoso* composed for the wedding celebrations of Prince Nicolaus's second son to his niece, Maria Anna Weissenwolf,[24] and performed twice more in repertory alongside operas by Gassmann, Paisiello, and Dittersdorf.[25] This work has the most complex sources of any opera by Haydn, with some parts completely rewritten more than once. Although the tenor Guglielmi Jermoli and his wife, Maria, are described as singing the roles of Ecclitico, the doctor turned bogus astrologer, and the pert maid, Lisetta, the couple left the Esterházy employ in July 1777 prior to the wedding, necessitating further revisions.[26] In this private domestic comedy replete with *commedia dell'arte* overtones, Ecclitico hatches a plan to convince the gullible Buonafede into believing he has been transported to the moon (in reality Ecclitico's garden) where, by the end of the opera, he is swindled out of his two daughters and maid: Flaminia is betrothed to Ernesto (they are the *parti serie*), Clarice to Ecclitico (the *parti buffe*), and Lisetta (whom Buonafede himself fancies) to Cecco, Ernesto's servant. The exotic locale is admirably depicted in the first act by three short pantomimic intermezzi, during which Buonafede observes lunar life through a telescope (representative of his over-sized lust), and in the second by a sinfonia and several ballets, the first of which is a minuet based on the sinfonia and features offstage echoes. The dances may have been crafted for and performed by the Schmalügger ballet troupe, which was in residence at Eszterháza that summer.[27] In the topsy-turvy world of the moon, Cecco masquerades as the emperor, spouting pithy one-liners that lampoon contemporary society . . . rather satirical fare for the assembled wedding guests. Presumably Prince Nicolaus wished to align himself not with the old-fashioned patriarchal figure, Buonafede (good faith), but with the masterminding Ecclitico, creator of the magical lunar world and ingenious representative of the next generation (in direct contrast to the rigid authoritarian Empress Maria Theresa and her co-regent son, Joseph). Certainly Ecclitico's all-knowing ways and role as master of ceremonies in the lunar charade mirrored that of the Prince as Apollo, the sun god, and source of light for the moon's reflected glory.[28]

Haydn's growing penchant for long-range tonal planning is here evident in the alignment of E♭ major with "la triforme dea" idolized by the false astrologer's apprentices in the opening chorus, and the return of that key at the outset of the first act finale where, having drunk a magic elixir, Buonafede believes he is flying to the moon. The beauty of this finale's opening music "lifts the dramatic moment above straightforward dramatic irony and puts the audience on the knife edge between empathy and ridicule."[29]

Indeed, the fake "magic" precipitates dramatic change (similar to mesmerism in the first act finale of *Così fan tutte*), setting up the masquerading on the moon in Act II. The earthly rootedness of C major, set up in the sonata-form overture later recycled as the opening movement of Symphony no. 63,[30] returns in the grand bravura aria "Ragion nell'alma siede," allowing Flaminia to demonstrate her *seria* roots as well as her capacity to love the noble Ernesto.[31] Her impudent sister, Clarice, is the perfect mate for the cocky Ecclitico, as shown in their sexually explicit duet in Act III where they engage in erotic fondling.

La vera costanza (True Constancy, 1779; rev. 1785) marks Haydn's foray into the popular subgenre of opera buffa known as *comédie larmoyante*; however, the version we know is a reconstruction from 1785 since the original score and parts were incinerated along with many costumes, instruments, and other performing materials when fire destroyed the opera house on November 19, 1779. Adapted from a libretto by Francesco Puttini first set by Pasquale Anfossi (Rome 1776), *La vera costanza* explores the sufferings of a virtuous sentimental heroine named Rosina, who, having secretly married above her social class five years earlier, was abandoned some two months afterwards by her husband, Count Errico, whose son she later bore. The Count's aunt, Baroness Irene, and her suitor, Marchese Ernesto, in attempting to rescue Count Errico from his errant ways, try to foist the doltish Vilotto onto the poor heroine. The comic, delusional antics of Vilotto are a foil to those of the Count, whose inner torment shows him to be every bit the emotional equal of the heroine, despite their differences in gender and social status.[32] Masino, Rosina's fisherman brother, and Lisetta, the baroness's maid and comic counterpoise to the young heroine (Lisetta even addresses herself as "poverina" in her first aria), complete the cast of this touching work, which was renamed *Laurette* in its unauthorized adaptation into a French-language *opéra comique* by Peter Ulric Debuisson for Paris in 1791.

Rosina is a rare heroine in comic opera. She is a forsaken wife *and* an abandoned mother, forced by social norms and a deep sense of constancy and moral propriety to bear her burden in secrecy. She engages all our sympathies when spurned and ridiculed by a disturbed spouse and his righteous aunt, buffeted by the advances of a buffoonish suitor, and subjected to cruel jokes and misunderstandings, all the while remaining committed to her estranged husband and their child. Following a long heart-to-heart dialogue with Lisetta, Rosina recounts how she fell in love with the gentleman suitor in the Andante opening of her aria "Con un tenero sospiro," only to plunge into despair in the following Allegro section when she recalls how he betrayed her; despite the character's heightened emotional state, her vocal line is restrained, befitting her class and station in life (in contrast to the coloratura a high-born *seria* heroine might employ).[33] The opening ritornello depicts her tentative steps, submissive nature, and emotional fragility – hallmarks of the sentimental heroine – through its timid upbeat gesture broken by rests and leading to a noble dotted-rhythm figure that is forsaken as soon as it is sounded, overcome by soft sighs. In the aria immediately preceding hers, the Count employs a grandiose heroic style when instructing Vilotto in the art of love as military warfare, underscoring the unequal power dynamics of their relationship. "A trionfar t'invita" is a triumphal multipartite *aria di guerre* enlivened by timpani and horns in C, since the Esterházy orchestra had no trumpets.

In her second-act aria, "Dove fuggo," a confused and distraught Rosina calls out: who will help me? where can I turn? how can I save my son? Her frenzied state and frayed emotions tumble forth in a breathless f minor Presto featuring sudden shifts in dynamics, driving repeated notes, syncopated rhythms, turbulent passagework, and dramatic pauses associated with the tempestuous "Sturm und Drang." As contemptible as the Count may seem at first, he also has a sentimental side, as shown in the semi-delusional mad scene where he assumes the role of an emotionally distraught Orpheus in search of his beloved, wronged Eurydice – a scene lifted directly from Anfossi's opera. A dejected Rosina then attempts to flee with her small son, who appears on stage for the first time. Bidding farewell to her home in a slow-moving aria, whose pathetic cantabile melody is exposed by muted string accompaniment, she seeks temporary refuge in the ruins of a nearby tower as the others search for her. This dramatic juggernaut is held in check through the predictable comic shenanigans at the outset of the second act finale, until the Count enters all alone and, sensing an inexplicable aura, meets a crying child in search of help for his mother. That the catalyst for recognition, remorse, and reunification is his own son makes for a touching theatrical moment, ultimately persuading everyone that Rosina and the Count are worthy partners. Unbridled sentimentality, with its heightened capacity for feeling, equated with virtue, gave rise to a deeper understanding of realism and emotional expression in the theater mirrored by an increased respect for the individual in society. An awakened social conscience promoted a sense of compassion and benevolence towards the downtrodden in later eighteenth-century society, including widows, orphans, unwed mothers, and other outcasts.[34] When the original Rosina of 1779, Barbara Ripamonti, sang the role again six years later at the Esterházy revival, the opera's overarching themes of constancy, marital fidelity and parental obligation would have reverberated at a court where both Prince Nicolaus and his Kapellmeister had mistresses – especially with Haydn rumored to be the father of Antonio Polzelli, born in 1783 to Luigia Polzelli, the soprano who sang the part of Lisetta in this revival.[35]

L'isola disabitata (The Desert Island; not yet published in *JHW*) was librettist Pietro Metastasio's contribution to the mid-eighteenth-century intellectual debate about the relative merits of civilized society versus nature in the formation of character. Performed at the marionette theater for Prince Nicolaus's nameday on December 6, 1779, some two and a half weeks after a disastrous fire destroyed the main opera house, the opera's idealized setting helped reinforce the notion of an isolated pastoral location, retreat, or refuge where aristocrats might escape to ponder, reflect, and undergo knowledge transformation.[36] What better birthday gift could the Prince give himself when constructing his own metaphorical desert isle than a modest-scale opera that would permit personal reflection on his own Enlightenment journey, one determined by rank, privilege and a university education (in contrast to that of his humble-born Kapellmeister, who, through hard work and dedication, sought to develop his innate musical talent). To set up the drama Haydn crafted an intellectually engaging overture with a harmonically rich slow introduction, an anguished g minor fast movement, "Sturm und Drang" style, which is suddenly interrupted by a lyrical minuet in the relative major that invokes memories of happier times, followed by a truncated reprise of the minor-mode Vivace assai. To complement Metastasio's exquisitely crafted verse and lofty subject-matter, Haydn set all the recitatives to orchestral accompaniment, as if to endow the dialogue with a timbral halo that would encourage heightened yet natural delivery of the flexible arioso melodies and contribute to greater text intelligibility (in a era before surtitles or simultaneous translations!).

L'isola disabitata, a two-part *azione teatrale* combining traits of opera seria and Greek drama (unity of time and place, and a single set) with touches of light comedy, traces the experiences of four characters representing classical stereotypes. The story opens with Costanza (soprano) and her younger sister, Silvia (soprano), marooned on a bucolic desert island following the abduction of the former's husband, the noble Gernando (tenor), by pirates thirteen years earlier. Believing herself to have been abandoned intentionally, Costanza laments her cruel fate and contemplates suicide in the manner of a mythological heroine. Her sister, who was so small at the time she no longer has any memory of the outside world, grows up on the idyllic tranquil island to be a happy, untroubled child of nature in the mold of Rousseau. When Gernando returns with his friend Enrico (bass) to search for his beloved, Silvia immediately falls in love with the latter before realizing he is one of those men whom her sister, based on personal experience, has instructed her not to trust. She observes Enrico from afar as he delivers a dashing aria, "Chi nel cammin d'onore," whose martial horn fanfares portray him as a man on a mission. An innocent Silvia wrestles with her new emotions in "Fra un dolce deliro," enhanced by solo flute and bassoon. When they finally meet in Act II, their flirtatious conversation is riddled with a melodic gesture that accompanies their growing attraction and Silvia's development from a naive girl into a feeling young woman – a subtle permutation made possible within the context of continual *recitativo accompagnato* texture. In her simile aria "Come il vapor s'ascende," inserted for Luigia Polzelli who created this role at Eszterháza, Silvia compares the burning fire that increases within her heart to vapor rising in the air. Having derived strength from the young couple's awakening love, the older couple's sorrow turns to joy upon their reunification, preparing the way for a vaudeville finale – a nod to French style in a rationalist-inspired work. Solo vocal statements alternate here with concertante solos for violin, cello, flute, and bassoon that imitate the registers of the singers while simultaneously championing the prowess of the Prince's opera troupe, orchestral players, and composer. With this final proclamation of the power of love and music, Haydn heaped praise on his patron and court while thanking him for his own good fortune and continuing education at Eszterháza despite his growing feelings of isolation there . . . feelings alleviated by his recent acquaintance with the twenty-nine-year-old Italian soprano for whom he carefully crafted the role of the innocent young lover.

1781–84: the new opera house featuring grander works on fantastical themes

The inauguration of the new opera house in February 1781 with *La fedeltà premiata* (Fidelity Rewarded) represents a shift towards grander productions at Eszterháza. The opera's self-conscious staging of a hunt asserts princely hegemony while emphasizing the transformation of an abandoned hunting lodge into a monument to princely power. In Giambatista Lorenzi's complicated yet delightfully parodic pastoral libretto, first set by Cimarosa in 1779, a curse plagues the land of Cumae, necessitating the yearly sacrifice of two faithful lovers to the sea-monster until a brave soul offers his life instead. Since to be seen in love would invite a death sentence, all couples try to avoid detection by Melibeo, a priest in the temple of Diana, whose task it is to locate the sacrificial couple but who abuses his power by overlooking some lovers while framing others. To conceal her identity, the shepherdess Fillide (fidelity) assumes the name Celia (from *celare*, to hide) and denies her love for the noble Fileno. Rebuffed, Fileno turns his affections toward the nymph Nerina who, in turn, fancies Lindoro, a temple employee and brother of Amarante. Melibeo's affections reside with the vain and arrogant Amarante, but when her favor turns toward the newly arrived Count Perrucchetto, the jealous priest contrives to have the Count brought forward with Celia as the sacrificial victims – an obvious mismatch since it unites the *prima seria* with *primo buffo*! When Fileno courageously offers his life to save that of his beloved Celia, the Roman goddess of the hunt, Diana, arrives miraculously to enforce justice, uniting Fileno with Celia and Amarante with Count Perrucchetto, while striking dead the evil Melibeo.

The opera's hunting theme is vividly depicted in the "caccia" style overture, later reused as the finale of Symphony no. 73, subtitled "La chasse." A swift-paced movement in D major and 6/8 meter, it incorporates an actual horn signal known as "L'ancienne vue" later adapted for the appearance of Diana near the end of the opera,[37] indicating the extent to which the practices, protocols, and other visual and aural associations of the hunt were part of an eighteenth-century audience's interpretive lexicon. An avid hunter whose extensive parklands at Eszterháza contained a Temple to Diana, Prince Nicolaus was likely flattered by the rich semiotic coding depicted in the central scene of Act II, which stages an actual hunt. It features a chorus of male and female *cacciatore* celebrating the day's take with a galloping Presto in D major incorporating prominent horn fifths. Parodic depictions of traditional hunting prowess and procedures – as when the vulnerable Perrucchetto is pursued by a bear, or falsely claims to have killed the wild boar that was deftly dispatched by Fileno, or speaks of being victimized by Amarante's winged arrow (Cupid) – represent the cowardly Perrucchetto as the dramatic foil to the brave Fileno. Haydn's arsenal of musical jokes includes loud horn blasts signaling cuckoldry and a jealous lover in Melibeo's first aria, and a parody of the furies music from Gluck's underworld scene in *Orfeo ed Euridice* (Vienna 1762; Eszterháza 1776) during the presentation of the sacrificial victims in the Act II finale.[38]

The social and cultural encoding of the hunting frame also extends to the opera's gender dynamics.[39] Fileno's engagement with the literal and metaphorical hunt depicts him as a deft marksman who is strong, steadfast, and selfless, whereas Celia's faithfulness renders her defenseless and powerless. Like a passive fawn or doe, she continually hides, denies, and evades her love to avoid detection, subjugating her own self-interest to save her lover. Unattainable, she is all the more desirable, giving Haydn latitude to portray musically Celia's helplessness, frailness, and emotional instability. In the muted horn solo that initiates the Largo section midway through her Act I aria, "Deh soccorri un infelice,"[40] where Celia pleads for Nerina to rescue Fileno, the faded melody intrudes into her memory as the voice of her distant beloved, representing the loss of her hunter/lover. Even the tirades and protestations of the Amazon-like huntress, Amarante, are calculated to lure, wound, and snare a man of rank and position. And the betrothal ceremony Diana presides over at the end of the opera has its origins in the ritualistic distribution of prizes over the body of a slain beast (Melibeo) at the conclusion of a successful hunt. Diana, protector of wild nature and the goddess of virginity, dictates the moral code for society and ensures its stability and security – a role assumed by the Prince in his own hunting domain.

Orlando paladino (Knight Roland) of 1782 was adapted by Nunziato Porta, the recently appointed house-poet and director of the opera, from the comic libretto *Le pazzie d'Orlando* by Carlo Francesco Badini (set by Guglielmi for London 1771) and from his own librettos for Prague (1775) and Vienna (1777).[41] It joins a long history of musical dramatizations of Ariosto's sixteenth-century chivalric epic, *Orlando furioso* – including well-known settings by Vivaldi and Handel – in which the knight-errant, Orlando, is driven to insanity by his passionate yet unreciprocated love for Angelica, who loves Medoro. Haydn's *dramma eroicomico* unites serious and comic elements; mental instability and madness are represented as ambiguous states capable of evoking laughter and pity, derision and sympathy, especially in the antics of the delusional title character, his Leporello-like squire and sidekick, Pasquale, and his rivals, the young African Prince Medoro and the boastful and brutish Rodomonte. Powers of persuasion, bewitchment and enchantment reside with the women: Angelica, Queen of Cathay, the sorceress Alcina, and the shepherdess Eurilla. Meant to be the theatrical focus of a Russian royal visit to Eszterháza in the fall of 1782, which never materialized, the opera instead premiered on the Prince's nameday. It continues the trend towards greater production resources at the fairyland retreat, including an expanded professional troupe of singers and more elaborate scenery and costumes. Allied to these increased modes of glorification, however, are parodic allusions to the *pastorale*, French *opéra comique*, elevated opera seria styles, reform opera, and Goldonian buffo, making *Orlando paladino* very much an opera about operatic conventions. This fixation with, and occasional illogical use of, poetic and musical conventions serves a dramatic function, making for a panoply of parodic devices, procedural disruptions, and other manifestations of musical madness that echo character and plot developments.

The *Introduzione* (Allegretto 6/8 E♭) establishes a comical tone through its staging of a peaceful pastoral scene that is disrupted by Rodomonte, the saber-rattling King of Barbary, causing Eurilla and her father, Lincone, to express their "fear" in rapid musical patter associated with comedy. Unhappy Angelica expresses her anxiety about Orlando's wrath in a tender seria-style Cavatina after which she – illogically – summons Alcina for protection. The sorceress demonstrates her powers in a grand C major aria that contrasts sharply with that of the emasculated and indecisive Medoro, who dithers helplessly in the exit aria "Parto. Ma, oh dio, non posso" ("I go. But, oh god, I cannot"), which parodies Metastasian conceits. The squire Pasquale, clad in antique armor (like Don Quixote?), wriggles out of a tricky situation with Rodomonte, only to turn around and brag to Eurilla about his many travels and brave deeds in a lightning-quick catalogue aria "Ho viaggiato in Francia" ("I've traveled in France"), through which he also conveys his hunger for food and, by extension, love. The much-anticipated arrival of Orlando occurs in a long section of *recitativo accompagnato* – its first use in the opera – during which the disheveled, disoriented, stumbling, sputtering hero searches for his beloved, but finds instead Angelica's and Medoro's love nest (as famously described in Ariosto's 23rd canto). His subsequent aria is riddled with incomplete thoughts and chromatic vocal inflections indicative of his muddled state of mind.

Midway through the Act 1 finale (at m. 322) Orlando's "furia" again manifests itself in a passage of *recitativo accompagnato* at the words "Ferma, ferma Belzebu" ("Stop, stop Beelzebub [Satan]"), enabling the deranged knight to slip out of the normal mode of melodic delivery in order to exaggerate normal patterns of speech, expression, gesture, and deportment. By employing recitative here and again in the second-act finale, Haydn breaks Lorenzo da Ponte's dictum that recitative be banned from a finale,[42] and in doing so interrupts the finale's musical continuum to signal a moment of special signification. Poor Orlando, now possessed by the devil and condemned by word, deed, and music, is certifiably mad. In the ensuing "shock tutti" the others collectively remark on his disfigurement, further isolating him from society and confining him with their gaze, after which Alcina imprisons him within an iron cage – a clear sign of insanity in the eighteenth century. The act concludes with a shipwreck *stretta*, an old Metastasian standby used here as an expressive metaphor for the inner anguish of the characters and for the larger tempest raging in their midst. Navigation and madness were linked in the European imagination, the soul understood as a vessel at the mercy of the sea's raging madness.[43] Will the ship reach safe harbor? Haydn's music catapults us onto the high seas of uncertainty with its repetitive opening melody and undulating imitative motive depicting the crest and fall of turbulent ocean waves, the concluding chromaticism further undermining closure.

Parody persists in Acts II and III. Pasquale's self-aggrandizing "Vittoria, vittoria" – with its invocation of blaring trumpets (in reality horns) – sets up yet another catalogue aria where he woos Eurilla with displays of his musical prowess. Presumably attired like a French music master (having made reference to his finery, violin, and Parisian charms), he tries to impress her with his execution of the trill, instrumental imitations, rapid arpeggios, various articulations, and even the coloratura and high register of the castrato, before continuing with further displays of virtuosity on the violin.

He also uses falsetto to comic effect – yet another way for Haydn to create vocal and registral variety among the four tenors on stage. (Rodomonte is the only baritone.) Following a brief trip to the Underworld in Act III where Orlando's senses are restored, and a show-stopping coloratura aria for Angelica (composed for the talented Matilde Bologna, wife of the librettist Porta) when she reacts to Medoro's supposed death, the opera concludes with a French-style vaudeville featuring alternating sections for soloists and chorus.

Armida, the *dramma eroico* that opened the operatic season on February 26, 1784, thematizes magic, making it an excellent vehicle to celebrate the completion of the fairyland estate "le petit Versailles de l'Hongrie."[44] Preparations for the lavish production were already underway in June 1783, when, in correspondence with Artaria, Haydn begs the patience of his publisher for some requested piano trios since "I am now composing a new opera seria."[45] In August 1783 Pietro Travaglia, who was responsible for designing the stage sets and costumes, outlined the expenses anticipated in their creation and suggested cutting costs by reusing sets and props from earlier productions, including *La fedeltà premiata*, *Orlando paladino*, and Sarti's *Giulio Sabino*.[46] Singers performing the roles of the enchantress Armida (Matilde Bologna again), her confidante Zelmira, daughter of the Egyptian Sultan, and the Christian knight Rinaldo required two costumes each, while the remaining three characters – Armida's uncle, Idreno, King of Damascus, Ubaldo, Captain of the Christian soldiers, and the Danish knight Clotarco – had only one each.[47] In addition to these six soloists the production required a considerable number of extras, including soldiers, nymphs, furies, and on-stage musicians. In short, *Armida* was the most lavishly produced work by Haydn mounted on the Esterházy stage, and was one of the most frequently performed operas at court.[48]

The libretto, which Porta compiled from various sources, derives from several episodes in Torquato Tasso's sixteenth-century epic poem *Gerusalemme liberata*.[49] The three-act drama revolves around the complicated relationship between the Saracen enchantress, Armida, who has lured the Frankish crusaders into her magical realm and fallen in love with the noble Christian warrior, Rinaldo. As he vacillates between returning to the Christian camp or remaining with Armida, Rinaldo forces the sorceress through an emotional spiral from fear and grief to rage, sorrow, and ultimately vengeance in her final abandonment. The hero's love–duty conflict is the catalyst for the many psychologically charged moments and larger scenic complexes that give structure to the work.

The tripartite overture sets the stage for the drama to follow, foretelling Rinaldo's ultimate triumph over the powers of evil.[50] At the outset of the drama, however, the hero professes loyalty to Armida and the infidels in the brilliant C major *aria di bravura* "Vado a pugnar contento." Armida fears for his safety in an extended accompanied recitative and two-tempo aria in A major that exposes her beguiling beauty and her newly awakened passions. Ubaldo and his retinue of soldiers, in seeking to rescue Rinaldo in the next scene, experience the disorienting effects of Armida's witchcraft as they ascend the mountainside, after which Zelmira flirts with Clotarco in a short aria featuring a delicious turn to the minor mode at the repetition of the words "if you will follow me," painting her as a clever seductress in the ways of Eros, and Armida herself.

Even though Rinaldo and Armida profess their mutual love in a duet at the conclusion of Act I, the hero is already wrestling with his destiny in the next act. Addressing his divided loyalties in the accompanied recitative and aria "Armida . . . oh affanno"/ "Cara, è vero, io son tiranno," he agonizes over leaving Armida in a tender *aria d'affetto* in E♭ major cast in three progressively faster tempi – Adagio–Allegro–Presto – mirroring the escalation of his confusing emotions. This leads directly into Armida's intensely angry response, the accompanied recitative "Barbaro! E ardisci ancor" and rage aria in e minor, "Odio, furor, dispetto," in which the voice, eschewing coloratura, "spits out brief syllabic motifs and howls long high notes over a turbulent accompaniment."[51] The large scenic complex created by these contrasting back-to-back utterances for the opera's two main characters forms the emotional centerpiece of the opera. The trio for Ubaldo, Rinaldo, and Armida that concludes the act further drives a wedge between the lovers.

To finally free himself from Armida's yoke, Rinaldo must strike down the myrtle tree, source of her magical powers. This action takes place in the magic forest, an extended *scena* at the core of Act III that begins and ends in E♭ major and encompasses eight sections across 451 measures. At its outset Zelmira attempts to persuade Rinaldo to leave his company of crusaders whom he has rejoined at Ubaldo's urgings; the sorceress's dark, forbidding garden is transformed into a veritable paradise of seductive sounds and fragrant odors intended to seduce the wary hero. Rinaldo marvels at each new magical transformation in *recitativo accompagnato* as the orchestra indulges in luxurious tone-painting depicting "the murmur of gentle brooks" and "the warbling of colorful birds" (similar to effects in Haydn's late oratorios). Wood nymphs, whose appearance is prefaced by an eight-measure orchestral Andante passage adumbrated in the middle section of the overture, encircle the hero in an effort to protect the precious myrtle from his advancing sword (m. 53), their feminine charms preparing Zelmira's sweet pastoral song (*JHW* 26b; m. 93). A persistent Rinaldo frees himself from their clutches, but as he reaches to strike the myrtle, Armida appears "pale and altered, her hair disheveled, dressed in black with a magic wand in her hand" and begs for pity (*JHW* 26d; m. 216). Failing to win back Rinaldo's love, she unleashes her terrible wrath with a wave of her magic wand; gloomy darkness engulfs the forest as hideous monsters engage Rinaldo in combat – a battle between the forces of good and evil vividly portrayed in Haydn's score. A furious Presto in d minor (m. 307) featuring pulsating syncopated rhythms and rapidly ascending fortissimo scale passages signals the arrival of the diabolical furies. Faltering at first, Rinaldo confronts his fears and summons his courage in a prayerful two-tempo aria in which a reflective opening Largo gives way to a Presto full of resolve (*JHW* 26f; m. 378/m. 401). Triple-stop chords in the violins, sweeping sixteenth-note flourishes, and a unison arpeggio descent signal his renewed conviction. After a short struggle, Rinaldo strikes down the myrtle; the furies and "orrido bosco" disappear, and the whole scene magically transforms into the European encampment for the closing scene where, in a triumphant march, Christendom overcomes the Orient. Armida's undoing is attributable as much to her orientalized character as to her excessive female sexuality, making her an early operatic incarnation of the *femme fatale.*

Haydn wrote no more operas for Eszterháza, although some new material may have crept into *La vera costanza* when the score was reconstructed for the 1785 revival. Haydn continued revising arias and composing new material for operas staged at court, adding eight new works to the repertory in 1786, including three by Cimarosa, and reviving another nine, for a total of 125 performances – his busiest opera season ever. Plans were underway to stage Mozart's *Le nozze di Figaro* at Eszterháza in September 1790 when Prince Nicolaus died.

The London opera – Haydn's ill-fated philosopher

Following the disbanding of the opera troupe after the Prince's death, it was but a small step for Haydn to enter into a contractual agreement with the sponsors of his first trip to England in 1791 to compose an Italian opera for London. But writing an opera on the Orpheus theme in the late eighteenth century was no innocent undertaking, given the history of this myth as the birthplace of opera (*c.*1600) and the reforms of Calzabigi and Gluck in their landmark creation of 1762 (performed at Eszterháza in 1776). How unfortunate then that *L'anima del filosofo, ossia Orfeo ed Euridice* (The Soul of the Philosopher), Haydn's *dramma per musica* on the Orpheus myth to a libretto by the satirist Carlo Francesco Badini (of *Le pazzie d'Orlando* fame), was never performed during Haydn's lifetime. During rehearsal it was pulled from the stage of the newly reconstructed King's Theatre when the management failed to qualify for a license to perform opera.[52] Scholars have long believed that the work is incomplete since, in correspondence between January and March 1791, Haydn speaks of a five-act opera, whereas surviving materials indicate a work in four acts (and no libretto was ever printed).[53] Since the opera ends with a cataclysmic storm following the hero's death, however, it is difficult to imagine what might follow. Despite its problematic history, the opera is central to understanding Haydn's maturity.

Following the two-part overture (Largo, c minor; Presto, C major) the curtain rises on a distraught Eurydice, whose father, King Creonte, has promised her to Aristeaus (introduced in Virgil) despite her love for Orpheus. Surrounded by Aristeaus's henchmen, she sings a two-tempo aria, "Filomena abbandonata," in which she laments being abandoned by her lover, likening her fate to that of the mythological Philomela whose tongue was cruelly cut out by her enemy (but who eventually turned into a nightingale, enabling her to sing forever of her passion and pain.) Orpheus arrives just in time to save Eurydice; his pleading song with "lyre" accompaniment – i.e., rippling triplets for the harp and pizzicato strings – prepares the slow-moving aria through which he introduces his famed powers of musical persuasion, calming the savages. "Cara speme" opens with a classic example of a *messa di voce* – a long-held high note frequently employed by castratos to showcase the color and volume-control of their voices; Haydn, however, conceived the role of Orpheus for tenor (a progressive move, especially given the Orpheus myth). A chorus of male Coristi praises the power of music after which Creonte consents to the couple's marriage in an aria whose prominent flute part may refer to the unfortunate tethered bird mentioned in the text. The first act closes with a rapturous duet for the ecstatic couple featuring daring coloratura in thirds and sixths.

The trajectory of Act II moves from celebration to despair. The opening female chorus, a bouncy Allegretto in 2/4 based on the vaudeville finale from *Orlando paladino*, anticipates the wedding celebration but also warns of the drama's chilling conclusion. This is one of ten choruses in the opera, five of which are repeated in whole or in part, sometimes with new scoring and different text, creating large scenic tableaux. When Orpheus leaves his beloved to investigate a loud noise, Aristeaus's followers rush in to kidnap the bride. During the kerfuffle Eurydice is bitten by a poisonous snake, and as she dies sings the touching cavatina "Del mio core," whose slow tempo, reduced scoring, and rest-punctuated melody depict her ghostly pallor and gasping last breaths. Orpheus's discovery of her lifeless body sends him into paroxysms of grief in an extended accompanied recitative followed by a fast-tempo aria in f minor that includes a pair of clarinets, a new color for

Haydn to experiment with in opera. The act concludes with a defiant Creonte seeking to avenge his daughter's death in a flashy, thunderous military-style aria in C major.

Act III opens with the mournful SATB chorus "Ah sposi infelice,"[54] after which Orpheus begins his Underworld journey. While traversing the world of dead souls, the famed Thracian singer, whose song once rivaled oratory and philosophical discourse in its powers of persuasion, all but loses his voice. It is first usurped by the Sibyl, his escort in Hades, who greets him in "Al tuo seno fortunate," a brilliant aria in C major that Haydn probably wrote for an unnamed castrato. With dazzling coloratura the Sibyl implores the hero to control his passions through philosophical reflection (not song).[55]

In Act IV the master-singer's mythical Orphic powers appear to animate the voices of others, as choral forces assume an even greater role in the drama. Aided by Haydn's pictorial music, the mysteries of the Underworld are exposed in two contrasting choruses: a haunting one in f minor featuring four-part imitative counterpoint depicting the pitiful fate of the languishing unburied souls; and a rapid one in d minor for tenors and basses in which the horrid howls of the furies are matched by sforzandi blasts in the restless orchestra, replete with trombone accompaniment – the traditional orchestral timbre associated with musical depictions of the Underworld. Pluto admits Orpheus and the Sibyl to the Elysian Fields, depicted in a jaunty orchestral intermezzo and frolicking chorus. As in the Greek chorus of classical drama, Haydn's choruses assume multiple roles; they participate in and comment on the drama and help to establish the atmosphere – their commanding presence providing a tableau-like backdrop for stage-action and pantomime, and foreshadowing Haydn's Handelian leanings in his later oratorios.

Despite the warning, Orpheus looks at his beloved and loses her forever, his passion having overtaken reason. The Sibyl too vanishes, leaving Orpheus alone to lash out at his cruel fate in an accompanied recitative followed by the agitato aria "Mi sento languire." A group of pleasure-loving Bacchantes, who try to seduce him into joining their fun, are repelled by his pronouncement never to love women again. They trick him into drinking a cup of poison after which he dies. The women celebrate his demise, but their gloating is short-lived when all are washed away in a violent storm. The destructive power of this cataclysmic *dénouement* is ably depicted in the long crescendo and pumping rhythms in d minor that engulf the Bacchantes as they plead for mercy only to be silenced as the orchestra whimpers to a close. This ending resembles Virgil and particularly Ovid's *Metamorphoses*, where Eurydice dies a second death and Orpheus, renouncing the female sex, is poisoned by frenzied Maenadic women who tear him apart limb from limb, leaving his dismembered body to float away to sea. That Haydn's and Badini's hero fails to rescue Eurydice from the Underworld is a non-consummative act that maps onto the Ovidian representation of Orpheus as the first homosexual, as mirrored in his Socrates-like death. Perhaps it was this tragic ending that prompted Haydn to remark "[the opera is] entirely different from that of Gluck."[56]

The fate of *L'anima del filosofo* was that of Haydn's other operas for a long time. They were not designed for publication, touring, or spreading the composer's fame in his own day; rather, they were conceived to celebrate special occasions at court and, later, to showcase the talents of Prince Nicolaus's opera establishment. Circulation of the operas during Haydn's lifetime either involved court performers (as in the case of *La canterina* and *Lo speziale*) or German-language performances at locations with connections to the Esterházy court (such as the Erdödy court in nearby Pressburg, or *La vera costanza* performed as *Die belohnte Treue* for the Burgtheater in Vienna in 1784). While the German-texted excerpts from *Orfeo e[d] Euridice* published by Breitkopf & Härtel in 1807 may have been intended to bolster Haydn's reputation as an opera composer, they did not permit theatrical production. Like the majority of operas composed in the second half of the eighteenth century (with the exception of those by Gluck and Mozart), Haydn's operas did not maintain an active performing tradition into the nineteenth century.

A decade after the first modern Viennese revival of an opera by Haydn in 1899, *Der Apotheker* was performed alongside *Die wüste Insel* (The Desert Island) for the Haydn commemorative celebrations of May 1909. With their choice of *Die wüste Insel*, a Metastasian opera that had received only two performances at Eszterháza in 1779, the centenary Festival Committee could not have made a more stultifying choice, further validating views of Haydn's dramatic ineptitude. The mid-twentieth-century revival of *L'anima del filosofo*, and its disastrous renderings of coloratura and unstylistic orchestral playing recorded on disc, further retarded reception of Haydn's operas. Operatic scores issued by the *JHW* beginning in 1959 and several recordings by Antal Doráti in the 1970s helped acquaint scholars and listeners with the repertory. Recent performances on compact disc by Italian soprano Cecilia Bartoli – *L'anima del filosofo* of 1997 (with Christopher Hogwood conducting the Academy of Ancient Music), and *Armida* of 2000 (with Nikolaus Harnoncourt conducting Concentus Musicus Wien) – have helped convey more about stylistically correct vocal and orchestral performance than many well-intentioned stage productions, even though it is only on the stage, as in the productions undertaken annually at the Haydn Festival in Eisenstadt, that the performative dimensions of Haydn's operas can be evaluated. Since Haydn's scores are merely *scripts* for performance – i.e., dramatic action set into motion by costumed, singing actors in a theatrical setting with live orchestra (mirroring Haydn's own practice) – further assessment of Haydn's operatic achievement will continue to unfold in the theater.

PART IV

Performance and reception

14 A composer, his dedicatee, her instrument, and I: thoughts on performing Haydn's keyboard sonatas

TOM BEGHIN

In the 1790s Haydn made two extended trips to London. It is during his second, in 1794–95, that he composed his "Grand Sonata" for Piano in C major, Hob. XVI:50. The following three narratives describe its opening measures (shown in Ex. 14.1), each from a different perspective. We first take the score off a library shelf, and read it:

Narrative 1

A naked triad, in the simplest of keys, is spelled out, matter of factly, without any trace of hurry. But gradually, as if adding spice to a bland dish, Haydn throws in dissonances.[1] First, a passing tone D between E and C. Then, on the downbeat of measure 3, an upper neighbor F, which resolves to E by the middle of the measure. (This relationship is marked as "y.") But this upper neighbor (or appoggiatura, that quintessential eighteenth-century ornament) was itself preceded by a lower one. (Marked as "x.") To understand this double tension is as essential as it is puzzling. On the one hand, a slur (which, according to mid- to late eighteenth-century German sources, marked the first tone as the more expressive one) conveys the message that E is an embellishing tone to F.[2] But the usual interval of a second (two adjacent tones imitating the inflection of a "sigh") has here been inverted to a seventh. Does this inversion allow F to emancipate itself from the preceding E? If so, does F challenge the dissonance status of E, which should actually be understood as a consonance? In other words: which should be believed, x or y? With delightful delay measure 6 answers this sophistic question: not only is the second-interval restored to a dissonance–consonance pair; the effect of a slur – strong/long first tone, soft/short resolution – is materialized by no less than three performance directives: sforzando, fermata, and diminuendo. We now skip a few pages and look at mm. 120 ff. which harmonize this passage. "Y or x" does not matter any more: E and F have both become part of a descending chain of suspensions, adjusting to the laws of voice leading and counterpoint, fluidly moving in and out of dissonance or consonance status.

Imagine now – and this is more challenging – that there is no score yet, that musical ideas have yet to be imprinted onto the page. We next find ourselves

Example 14.1 Hob. XVI: 50, first movement, mm. 1–8 and 120–24

transported to a private study and become silent witnesses of a piano and composer:

> ***Narrative 2***
> I sit down at the keyboard (an English one by Broadwood or Longman & Broderip) and think how different the whole instrument is to what I am used to (a Viennese fortepiano by Walter or Schanz).[3] Let's try a C major triad, just one note at a time, very simple. I expect to be able to play clean, short notes. But how efficient are these dampers? (My Viennese piano has wedge-shaped dampers, which nestle themselves quickly between the strings. But here I see flat little feather-dusters, hardly able, I would think, to dampen the vibrations of those thick strings.) Let's start softly: C, G, E. This is different! So much after-ring, no matter how soft and short I play! It's hardly possible to create silences! But, hmm, what great potential. Listen to those moments after the attack, the delightful memory of these single tones! Let's try some dissonances. Can I lean into them the way I can back home, where I've always been able to give distinct attacks on dissonances and connect subsequent consonances all the more softly and crisply? No! (English hammerheads are thicker than Viennese and are covered with softer leather.) Isn't this interesting . . . How then to differentiate between dissonance and consonance? I get confused. Let's try again. Gain some momentum first, perhaps. Throw in a few slurs and upbeats. Now aim for

the high appoggiatura and really go for it: *sforzando*! Amazing. How long I can hold this note before it even starts decaying! (Viennese pianos, because of their more articulate hammers, thinner soundboard, and overall lighter construction, produce a much faster decay in sound.) Let us now really explore what this piano does well – and as I have heard a colleague do, the owner in fact of this piano:[4] full chords, lots of resonance, orchestral sounds! Now I am getting the hang of it.

Change of decor again. The final scene is a public performance. Listeners return to their seats after intermission. With sympathetic applause, they welcome the pianist back on stage and wait eagerly for the concert to resume. We identify with the pianist, whose thoughts we hear as she starts to play:

Narrative 3

No need to capture their attention the same way I did at the beginning of the concert.[5] I *have* their attention. So let me open not with the grandest of chords but with the simplest of triads, which I play ever so softly. In anticipation of my first sounds, I turn my neck slightly towards my left shoulder, and, as I play the first two measures, I gradually lean my right ear further towards the strings (which I aim to brush rather than to hit).[6] With these subtle bodily gestures, which my listeners won't fail to notice,[7] I invite them into my piano, into a space defined by the soundboard and the lid. Soon, I add dissonances, accelerate the pace, and increase my sound towards a long sforzato. Increasingly, I show myself to be aware of the larger acoustical space of the concert hall. Now I take full control and play those grand chords after all;[8] my open lid projects them fully into the hall. (A few years ago, following the example of an excellent colleague, I made it a habit of mine to turn my piano sideways during public concerts and to use a prop to keep the lid open.)[9] My opening statement may have appeared timid, too slight for a "grand sonata." But I will stick to it until the very end, as a skillful musical orator. And I can't wait for b. 120, that important juncture in this sonata movement.[10] My audience will be enchanted, I am certain, when they hear me revisit the intimate space from the very beginning, when they hear me mix those soft tones of the opening statement with new ones, pianissimo, legatissimo, in the highest register and with raised dampers (or open pedal as the English call it), in evocation, as it were, of an ethereally sounding dulcimer. Thank you, Haydn, for writing me such a fine concert piece!

These narratives describe the same musical events, yet are different in tone, perspective, and circumstance. The underlying particulars are straightforward: the Austrian composer Haydn travels to London, develops a keen interest in English pianos and pianists, befriends Therese Jansen who is a rising star on the London scene, and "composes expressly" for her a "grand concert sonata,"[11] a subgenre of piano sonata that Haydn has never attempted before. But the narratives are not exclusive in time or person.

In fact, they deliberately leave the door open to modern-day analysis, (re)-creation, and performance. Similarly, the "I" of narratives 2 and 3, although inspired by, is not restricted to "Haydn" or "Therese Jansen": it is I, the modern performer of Haydn sonatas, who adopts the different *personae* of analyst, composer, and performer, engaging with score, piano, and audience.

The framework for each of the narratives is outspokenly rhetorical. They correspond with three stages of the so-called rhetorical process: writing a score (3. *elocutio*), inventing and developing ideas (1. *inventio*), delivering the piece (5. *actio*). If we include the hint in narrative 3 of a larger structure (2. *dispositio*) and if we assume that "I" played by memory (4. *memoria*), then all five rhetorical stages are represented, from the initial creation of the sonata to its eventual performance. The stages are cumulative. They lead into one another and through all of them, the orator/musician produces a "work."[12]

But what is the relation between the "invented" and the "performed" work? And who does the "speaking": is it "I," Haydn, his dedicatee, the piano, or some idealized combination? Can the *persona* be separated from the work? Does one define the other?

The keyboardist as orator

A few years ago, I played a cycle of concerts featuring the complete "Haydn keyboard sonatas," or shorter "Hoboken XVI." Two-thirds of the way through, I found myself questioning the very premise and, in a program note, wrote the following confession:

> When I embarked on this cycle of concerts, my goal was to grasp a complete and well-defined repertoire. The further I advance in the project, however, the more I find myself not caring so much about "surveying" the repertoire as a whole. Instead, I become more and more intrigued by the actual forces that created it. Whenever I learn a new sonata, I find myself trying to enter Haydn's mind: why am I playing this particular statement, what does it mean, what do I want to achieve with the sonata as a whole, how can I do so best?
>
> This is exactly what eighteenth-century sources tell me to do: the ideal of composer and performer as one *persona* is strongly present in most treatises on performance, particularly in those on playing the keyboard (where it is most easily assumed by the listener that the player also is the composer). And even if one played pieces by someone else, one still was expected to perform them *as if one had composed them oneself.*[13]

One of the pieces on the program was sonata Hob. XVI: 23, in F major, with a slow movement in f minor (see Ex. 14.2). This heart-rending Adagio

Example 14.2 Hob. XVI: 23, Adagio second movement, mm. 21–39

draws its melancholic character more from its harmonies, strung together by continuous Alberti-style pulsations in the left hand, than from melodic elaboration in the right, which, in spite of the promise of a *siciliano*-type cantilena at the outset, never commits to much beyond triadic meanderings, long trills, sketches of melodic shapes that are repeated as if in reverie, doubt, or pain. Towards the end (in m. 34) the keyboardist breaks out of this interiorized mode: with a strong octave in the bass she proactively, aggressively even, plays a diminished-seventh secondary dominant, announcing an equally assertive six–four dominant chord. The insistence on the latter (it is not hard to imagine a fermata here), the chromatically sequential melodic figurations in mm. 34–35 (more active and urgent than before), and the harmonic progressions (circling around but targeting a structural, root-position dominant) are those of a cadenza, a quite dramatic one, bringing the movement to a dark close in mm. 38–39.

The analyst in me is thrilled by this topical recognition of Haydn's own improvisation, which has transformed itself, so to speak, to become part of composition and score. The performer in me is also thankful since, in contrast to comparable slow movements of earlier sonatas (Hob. XVI: 6 in G, 19 in D, or 46 in A♭) where Haydn had used a customary fermata sign to call upon my improvisational skills, I am now presented with material that can be put to direct use, bearing Haydn's authoritative stamp. But gratefulness turns to frustration as I anticipate the delivery of the piece on stage as a musical "orator." At the outset of his comments on musical delivery (*Vortrag*), Quantz states – quite bluntly – that it "can be compared to the delivery [*Vortrag*] of an orator." Of a cadenza, he writes that its purpose is

> none other than to surprise the unsuspected listener once more at the end, and to leave a special mark in their mind. Therefore, and according to this purpose, *one cadenza should suffice in one piece.*[14] [my emphasis]

To put the problem plainly: should I in this Adagio movement play the cadenza-like passage twice because Haydn (as is to be expected in a binary movement) prescribes a repeat sign? Would this not counter the very purpose of a cadenza and eventually undermine my credibility (or ethos) as a musician? Why did I so enthusiastically absorb the teachings of Quantz, C. P. E. Bach, and others (as the young Haydn himself once did) only to now find myself unable to apply them? In my own renditions of this movement, I have decided to uphold the rhetorical axiom that ornaments should be applied "only after a simple version has been heard"[15] and play the B section first *without* Haydn's cadenza, which I save for the repeat. The advantage of such an intervention is significant: the keyboardist-orator remains in her melancholic shell longer – further imprinting this emotion on her listener – and the effect of the cadenza, heralding the end of the movement, is dramatically enhanced.[16]

My own reluctance – inability even – to offer my "performed" version here in print helps explain what I perceive as a crucial turning-point in Haydn's keyboard-sonata output. In 1774, he prepared for publication a set of six sonatas, and duly dedicated them to his employer, Prince Nicolaus Esterházy. (Our example, Hob. XVI: 23, was one of them.) This was not just Haydn's first set of keyboard sonatas to be published, but was "the very first work to appear in an edition authorized by Haydn."[17] This special event, carried out in collaboration with Joseph Edler von Kurzböck, imperial printer in Vienna (not just of music), must have carried substantial psychological weight. Haydn meticulously prepared the scores, paying careful attention to the notation of ornaments, both essential (marked by shorthand notation) and arbitrary (to be added by the performer). This focus led him to combine his performative skills with his compositional goals, which more critically than ever before were made to cohabitate a single medium, that of the printed page. With wider and more prestigious distribution in sight (previous sonatas were distributed in handwritten copies through less controlled channels) and having to prepare a whole opus of sonatas (instead of single ones as before), Haydn's reputation was at stake, not just as a composer, but as a musical orator. It was not only *inventio*, *dispositio*, and *elocutio* – traditionally the three phases involved in the making of a text – that had to coexist: now *actio* (delivery) claimed room for itself too. And so, studying the resulting score as modern-day musicians with the "advantage" of knowing the overall "repertoire," we find many instances that impress us as fingerprints of a familiar master, such as the varied repeats and transitions in the minuet finale of Hob. XVI: 22 (E), the *attacca* to the finale of Hob. XVI: 24 (D), and our "cadenza."

But how "novel" were these features? Is it possible that similar – less polished but all the more fanciful – versions would have been "improvised" in the absence of a printed script, especially at the moment of a repeat, when any master-deliverer would be challenged to engage his listener more and differently? Did Haydn, when he was revealing the best of himself on an engraved plate – customary repeat signs creating a Procrustean mold for his ever developing ideas – mix "simple" and "embellished" run-throughs of the same material into one, surpassing both? Answers to these questions aside, in no other group of Haydn sonatas do we "see" such a learned keyboardist-orator so well at ease with a formal style of delivery.[18] The title page confirms this air of formality (see Table 14.1). Printed in a solemn font, it uses differences in type-size to place the focus on the Prince and

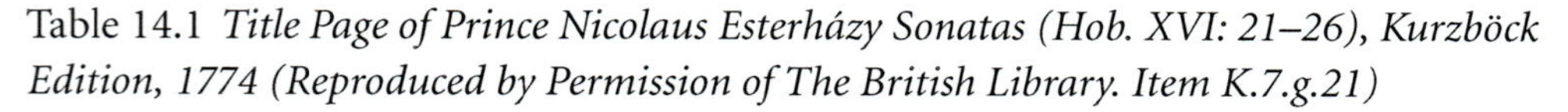

Table 14.1 *Title Page of Prince Nicolaus Esterházy Sonatas (Hob. XVI: 21–26), Kurzböck Edition, 1774 (Reproduced by Permission of The British Library. Item K.7.g.21)*

SEI
SONATE
DA
CLAVI-CEMBALO
CHE
A SUA ALTEZZA SERENISSIMA
DEL
SACRO ROMANO IMPERO
PRINCIPE
NICOLO ESTERHAZY DI GALANTHA
&c. &c.
D. D. D.
L'AUTORE
GIUSEPPE HAYDN
MAESTRO DI CAPELLA DELLA PREF. A. S. SER.

IN VIENNA, Presso Giuseppe Kurzböck Stampatore orient. di S. M. Imp. R. A. 1774.

to position the composer in a subservient role. Typographically the title reads like one of a book. In a separate preface – its very existence reinforcing this metaphor of a book – Haydn uses Italian, the international language of music, to praise the musical qualities of his Prince.[19] Clearly, the opus is directed to the music connoisseur, embodied – prestigiously – by Prince Esterházy. Haydn, the *maestro di capella*, performs for His Excellency – equally prestigiously – not in the magnificent Eszterháza Music Room, but on typeset plates.[20]

In the *Anno 776* and Auenbrugger sonata sets Haydn gradually reconnected with a context of live performance, no longer featuring himself or selected students (such as Marianne von Martínez, the Countesses Thun and Morzin) but more and more the generic keyboard player, almost exclusively female and dilettante, in Vienna and elsewhere in Europe. (Haydn's renegotiated contract with the Esterházy court of 1779 officially cleared the way for out-of-court publishing.[21]) Slowly he resolved problems like the one we examined. So it is that, in the slow movement of sonata Hob. XVI: 39 (G) of 1780 (see Ex. 14.3), Haydn prescribes a fermata – the first of its kind since pre-1773 – to indicate the need for a cadenza. Instead of pushing himself to

Example 14.3 Hob. XVI: 39, second movement, mm. 46–62

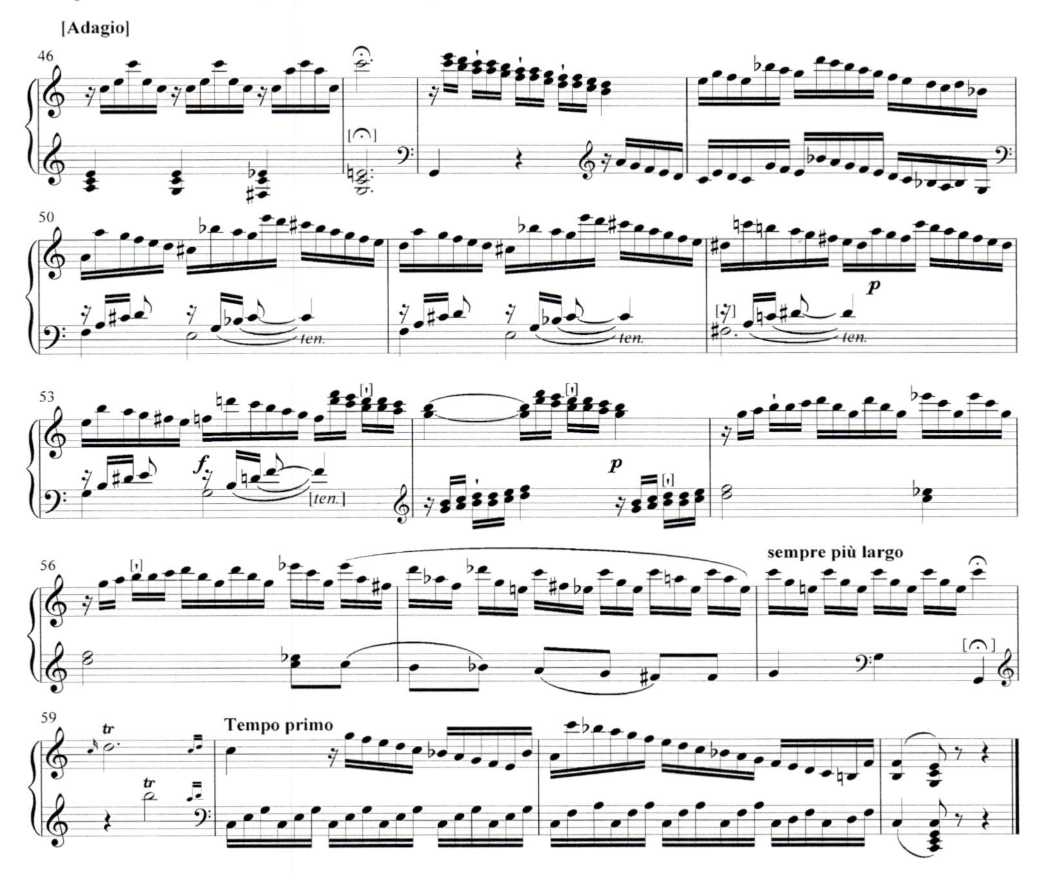

the fore, obliterating the distinction between text and performance, he now "hands" the performer a realized cadenza, to be interpolated – rather than taken for granted – into her "own" performance.[22] But what to do in the repeat? In his first collaboration with Artaria, a new and promising firm in Vienna, whose specialized music publishing targeted a growing market of players, Haydn resolves the dilemma before it ever becomes one: he simply removes the repeat sign.[23] In contrast, in the last of the Esterházy sonatas, Hob. XVI: 26 (A), he presented the buyer with a musical riddle – to play the minuet and trio "backwards" (*al rovescio*) – a true token, on the printed page, of connoisseurship, both of himself and his employer (who knew the symphony from which these palindromes were drawn).[24]

Looking at the big picture – first, the single sonatas where the distinction between text and performance, or between *elocutio* and *actio* is relatively clear; second, the 1774 Esterházy sonatas where Haydn presents himself as keyboardist-orator on engraved plates; third, a continued series of publications directed to a growing pool of (female) amateur players – I am left with a paradox. As a modern-day, professional pianist, trained in eighteenth-century musical-oratorical practices and principles, I receive most satisfaction from performing the "early" pieces, including those that the *Joseph Haydn Werke* label as "small" (*neun kleine frühe Sonaten*), where I can apply, to great effect, my skills in embellishment and variation, improvise a transition here or there, find a spot (whether explicitly invited or not) for a cadenza. The later pieces, of the 1770s and 1780s, although seemingly more tailored to my needs, come with a greater sense of wonder into the "why" or "why now" of certain ideas or statements. The two English grand sonatas (Hob. XVI: 50 and 52), finally, written for a fellow professional pianist and which I deliver almost word-by-word, also sit best with our society's modes of performances, those of the public recital and the compact disc.

Dedicatees

So far, two dedicatees have left their mark: Prince Esterházy (Hob. XVI: 21–26) and Therese Jansen (Hob. XVI: 50, but also 52). In both groups of pieces, the oratorical stance is remarkably similar: one keyboardist-orator formally addresses an audience, either private or public. In the case of the Jansen sonatas, the orating *persona* is also the dedicatee. But the dedicatee of the Esterházy sonatas, as we have suggested, was himself audience. Why is it that I have no hesitation whatsoever identifying with the dedicatee of the grand sonatas whereas in the earlier pieces I feel I must claim my rights to be composer as well, unhappy with the role of mere recipient?

In his English sonatas Haydn appears to have separated "composer" from "performer" to a degree non-existent in his earlier work. With Hob. XVI: 52, particularly, he wrote a full script that "works" perfectly well in concert performance, omitting second repeat signs in the first and last movements, making the oratorical gestures grand and fantastical, anticipating every detail of live performance on stage. Miss Jansen represents a type of pianist I know: one who is proud to publicly perform a piece not her own. She is proud, furthermore, to have studied with a famous master, Muzio Clementi, the "Father of the Piano," who almost single-handedly set the terms of piano, pianism, piano repertoire, and pedagogy for the next two centuries to come.[25] That the divorce of performer and composer – inevitable from a larger historical perspective – for Haydn occurred in London is no surprise: it was this metropolis that had inspired him to write his first real concert

Table 14.2 *Haydn's Known Dedicatees*

Prince Nicolaus Esterházy: Hob. XVI: 21–26 (publ. 1774 by Kurzböck) dedicated to by Haydn
Katharina and Marianna von Auenbrugger: Hob. XVI: 35–39, 20 (publ. 1780 by Artaria) dedicated to by Artaria but, in a letter to Artaria, Haydn regretted not having had the honor
Maria Hermenegild Esterházy, née Princess Liechtenstein: Hob. XVI: 40–42 (publ. 1784 by Bossler) composed for and dedicated to by Haydn
Marianne von Genzinger: Hob. XVI: 49 (comp. 1789–90, publ. 1791 by Artaria) composed for but, as per manuscript copy, dedicated to Maria Anna Gerlischek by Haydn published without Haydn's knowledge and without dedication
Therese Jansen: Hob. XVI: 50 (comp. 1794–95, publ. 1800) and 52 (comp. 1794; 1798 publ. by Artaria, 1799 by Longman, Clementi & Co.) composed expressly for and dedicated to by Haydn
Maria Hester Park: Hob. XVI: 51 (comp. 1794–95, publ. around 1805 by Breitkopf & Härtel) composed for and dedicated to by Haydn? published without dedication

underlined = as per published title page

sonatas in the first place. The Esterházy sonatas, on the other hand, had been idiomatically Haydn's own; his performances could not be distinguished from his compositions, and both were to be admired by the outside world.

In the spectrum of relationships between composer and performer, the Esterházy sonatas and Hob. XVI: 52 might be said to represent two extreme poles: exclusivity of performer and composer as one person in the former; separation of composer and performer in the latter. Not surprisingly, the former provoke a performer like myself to rearrange passages to my own skills and needs, whereas the latter allow me to join effortlessly in the production of the work at an advanced stage. In both cases, however, my identification with performing *persona* is one-to-one: first I identify with Haydn, then with Jansen.

The search for one performing *persona* becomes more complicated in the sonatas written and published in Vienna between 1780 and 1790, all dedicated to women. More than the sonatas for Therese Jansen (a woman but also a generic "professional pianist"), these sonatas raise questions as to the identity and gender of the dedicatee. (See Table 14.2 for a list of dedicatees.)[26] How does "dedicatee" position herself here in relation to "keyboardist-orator"? Is she "listener" or "orator"? If the former, is Haydn addressing his listener on his own terms or is he adjusting his rhetoric to his (female) addressee? If the latter, what kind of "oratory" does he expect her to demonstrate in her performances of his pieces or, for that matter, of any piece? Finally, and more pressingly, what about me? Am I simply observer of these interactions or can I actively take part in them, perhaps

Table 14.3 *Letter A: Haydn to Prince Nicolaus I Esterházy, December 5, 1766 Author's translation (with thanks to Bruce Haynes). German original: Bartha, item 6*

[December 5, 1766]

MOST SERENE HIGHNESS AND HIGH BORN / PRINCE OF THE EMPIRE!
MOST GRACIOUS AND DREAD LORD / LORD!

The most joyous Name Feast (which, YOUR HIGHNESS, with the grace of God, may spend in most complete fortune and felicity) obliged me most duly not only to deliver to HIM, in all humbleness, 6 new divertimenti but also (because, a few days ago, we were most strongly consoled by those new winter clothes) to kiss YOUR HIGHNESS' coat most obediently, [in thanks] for this special [act of] grace, [not without] adding that we, in spite of YOUR HIGHNESS' absence, much regretted by us, nevertheless venture to appear with these new clothes for the first time at YOUR HIGNESS' high Name Day during the celebratory Solemn Mass. Furthermore, I received the high order to have the divertimenti composed by me (twelve pieces in all) bound. but since YOUR HIGHNESS had returned to me some of them to be changed and I did not annotate those changes into my score, I ask you most obediently to let come to me the first 12 pieces only for the duration of three days, thereafter also the others, one by one, so that everything, including the changes, could be copied well and correctly, and bound. in this respect, I would like to inquire most respectfully in which way to have them bound? which to YOUR HIGHNESS' liking would be?

Incidentally, the two oboe players report to me (and also I myself must agree with them) that their 2 oboes are disintegrating with age, and no longer possess the proper pitch, wherefore I make the most humble suggestion that there is a Master *Rockobauer* in Vienna who in my opinion is the most skillful in such things. Because, however, this master is constantly occupied with this kind of work, but also invests a lot of precious time to build a pair of good and durable oboes with an extra joint to each set (whereby all the necessary tones can be played), as a result of which, however, the lowest price is 8 ducats. therefore, I must await YOUR HIGHNESS' high consent whether the mentioned 2 most necessary oboes may be acquired at the aforementioned price. To whom I commend myself for [YOUR] high favor and grace,

YOUR PRINCELY HIGHNESS'

Most obedient
Joseph Haydn.

even transform them into something that Haydn and his dedicatees would not have predicted?

It might be useful at this point to compare two pieces of prose by Haydn, the first directed to his Prince, his only male dedicatee, the second to his close friend Marianne von Genzinger, recipient (however not officially dedicatee) of the "Genzinger sonata" Hob. XVI: 49.[27] (See Tables 14.3 and 14.4.) Both letters (A and B) are written on the occasion of a nameday: St. Nicolas (December 6) for letter A; St. Mary (Magdalene) "today" (July 23) and St. Anne "yesterday" (July 22), together "Maria Anna" or "Marianne," for letter B.[28] Letter A strikes us as formal, written in an elevated style, respectful of the Prince, yet clear in its requests. Haydn's congratulatory wishes (cast in parentheses) are in fact part of a larger *captatio benevolentiae.* The real purpose of the letter reveals itself in two requests (*petitiones*). The trickier request (to permit the order of two new oboes) is wisely kept for last, and Haydn devotes a separate paragraph to it. After a *narratio* (sketching the miserable situation, dropping the name of a maker, only then mentioning his lowest price) he formulates the actual *petitio*, and signs the letter. The

Table 14.4 *Letter B: Haydn to Frau Marianne von Genzinger, July 23 1790 Author's translation. German original in Bartha, item 154*

[July 23, 1790]

High and Well born
Most Esteemed Frau v. Genzinger!

Already last week would it have been my obligation to reply to Your Grace's received writing, only, because this present day had already long before lain close to my heart, I, however, in anticipation, constantly made every imaginable effort [as to] how, in which way, and what exactly I should wish for Your Grace, thus those 8 days fled away, and now that my wish should express itself, my short wits come to a standstill, and know (all embarrassed) nothing at all to say: why? because? because I have not been able to fulfill those musical hopes, which Your Grace at this day would have a right to have!   o if only you would know, if only you could catch a glimpse, dearest, gracious Patroness, into my depressed heart, you would certainly feel sympathy and have forebearance with me: ever since your order, this poor, promised symphony has been floating in my fantasy, but some (unfortunately) until now pressingly urgent matters have not let this symphony come into the world!   however, the hope of gracious forebearance of this delay and the eventual arrival of a better time for its fulfillment will turn into reality this wish, which for your Grace was perhaps only one among those of today and the so many hundreds of yesterday, "perhaps" I say, because it would be bold of me to think that Your Grace should not wish herself anything better: you see thus, dearest Madam, that I cannot wish you anything for your Name Day because my wishes are too weak for you, and therefore do not bear fruit! I,   I must wish myself, and in particular [wish myself] gracious forebearance and maintenance of your continued friendship, which is so dear to me, and your affection; this is my warmest wish!   if, however, there is still room in you for one wish from me, then this wish of mine should change itself into yours, then I will be assured that nothing more remains save to wish myself privileged to eternally call myself

Your Grace's
most sincere friend and servant
Josephus Haydn

My faithful respect
to Mr. Husband and
the whole family
after tomorrow I expect an answer about the forte piano. then your Grace will receive the alteration in the Adagio.

traditional five parts of a letter – *salutatio, captatio benevolentiae, narratio, petitio, conclusio* – are represented here.[29] Haydn's style, furthermore, is appropriately grave in a letter directed to a superior: long periodic structures are syntactically clarified by punctuation marks (especially periods) and carefully chosen capitals at the beginning of sentences ("The," "Furthermore," "Incidentally," "Because," "To whom") reveal a remarkably structured grouping of his thoughts somewhere between the levels of a period and a paragraph.

By contrast, letter B resists such structuring. In fact, only two syntactical capitals are used, at the very beginning ("Already last week . . ."), and at the very end, introducing the *postscriptum* ("My faithful respect . . ."). The whole letter instead reads as a long series of shorter phrases, loosely strung together by commas, the continuous stream of words and phrases slowed down (but not interrupted) by moments of hesitation ("why? because?") and rhetorical pause ("I,   I must wish"), or on the contrary intensified by exclamations ("this is my warmest wish!") or self-citation and elaboration ("'perhaps' I say, because etc."). When reading the letter – aloud or silently – one is struck by its fine rhythm and the intense focus of composition from beginning to end, abandoned only in the *postscriptum*, which is the only informative part of the letter: it picks up on two requests from Her Grace's previous letter (dated July 11, 1790, see below). Unlike A, it is the congratulatory message that dominates here, not couched in a *captatio benevolentiae* but as the bread and butter of the letter itself. With extraordinary skill Haydn is able to transform his embarrassment in not yet having provided his friend with the symphony she has long asked for into the finest wish of all, "to call myself your friend forever," itself a standard concluding formula that is ingeniously incorporated into the contents and structure of the letter. Throughout this process of transformation, Haydn draws and exploits fine distinctions between wish, promise, hope, and gift; between "your" wish and "mine"; between the act of wishing and the object that is wished for ("symphony" and "friendship").

To compare the letters and claim that one is "more" rhetorical than the other would be to miss the point. Rather, their rhetorics differ in kind. The first is formal, more public, adopts a learned, written style, is clear in its logic, favors rehearsed structure. The other is informal, more private, adopts a conversational style, deliberately tests the limits of logic, invents its own structure. All eighteenth-century commentators would have agreed: A is more oratorical in spirit and outcome, but B is ultimately a better letter. No surprise that Haydn wrote it to a woman. Indeed, as the same male commentators would have pointed out, women were particularly good at this free, conversational style of writing, precisely because of their unlearnedness.[30] The intriguing question now becomes: if Madame von Genzinger, as a woman, drew a certain rhetoric from Haydn as a letter-writer, could the same have been true for his music?[31]

The clearest contrast, in my opinion, between a possibly male- and female-inspired rhetoric may be drawn between the sonatas for Nicolaus Esterházy (*de facto* our only male point of reference) and those for Marie Esterházy (Hob. XVI: 40–42), the new bride of the Prince's seventeen-year-old grandson Nicolaus II, herself barely fifteen years of age when they married in 1783. The two sets of sonatas have a similar ceremonial function, the former as a public testimony of a prestigious relationship between employer and court musician, the latter an equally public gesture of welcome towards an important new Esterházy family member. Whereas the princely edition had the appearance of a learned book (Table 14.1), the title page of the Marie Esterházy sonatas (Table 14.5), printed by Heinrich Philipp Bossler in Germany, entices the buyer with a framed picture, decorated with roses, leaves, and garlands, all evoking a distinct air of femininity.

Table 14.5 *Title Page of Marie Esterházy Sonatas (Hob. XVI: 40–42), Bossler Edition, 1784 (Reproduced by Permission of The British Library, Item e.440.j)*

TROIS SONATES
pour le Pianoforte
Composées & dédiées
à
Son Altesse Madame
La Princesse Marie Esterhazy
née Princesse de Lichtenstein
par Son très humble & très obeissant serviteur
Joseph Haydn.
Oeuvre 37
N° 33
A Spire chés Bossler Conseiller

The oval at the bottom, depicting an altarpiece with ceremonial fire, as a symbol of the hearth, refers to Marie's new married status.[32] The language of address is French, the language that the young Princess had mastered under the tutelage of her French governess.[33]

Imagine now the following two performances, the first from Prince Esterházy's Sonata in E major (Hob. XVI: 22), the second from Princess Esterházy's Sonata in G major (Hob. XVI: 40). (See their opening periods in Exx. 14.4 and 14.5.) Wearing his newest clothes and seated at the most magnificent harpsichord at the court (a French double, perhaps, conforming to the Prince's French taste),[34] Haydn addresses the Prince with the utmost confidence. He introduces his first thought, clear and logical, yet – conforming to the rules of oratory – in need of proof. In m. 2 he lifts his right hand as if asking his listener and himself: "Is this true?" As he switches from tonic chord (m. 1) to dominant (m. 3) he sinks into a vast chordal arpeggio, adopting an even graver tone of voice. The deep four-voice chords in m. 4, spaced out in a most correct manner, mark a

Example 14.4 Hob. XVI: 22, first movement, mm. 1–4

Example 14.5 Hob. XVI: 40, first movement, mm. 1–8

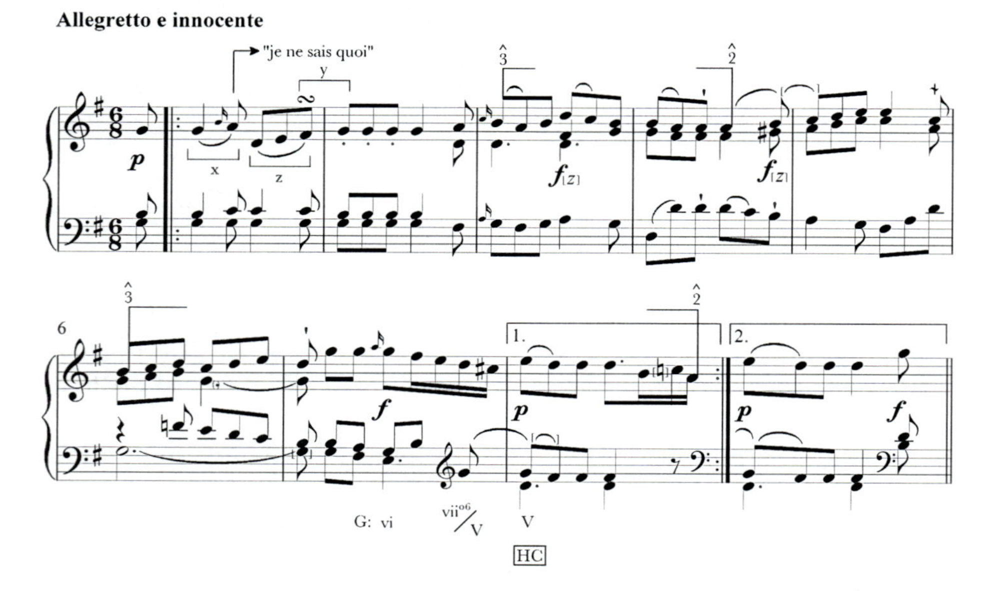

cadence equivalent to the clearest period. This is the end of an assertive opening statement, the beginning of a long, learned, three-movement oration.

Now switch to a more intimate decor. With eager anticipation, mother-in-law, governess, or music teacher by her side, the Princess puts her copy of sonatas on the desk of her delicate instrument (a Viennese one, without doubt, either a square or grand piano), and starts playing. A gentle flow of thoughts express themselves, on a tonic pedal, a touch of subdominant on a light part of the beat, a "je ne sais quoi" – is it a gentle look in the eye; a warm smile; a comforting, inviting gesture of the arm? The ideas are very simple – a three-voiced chord opens up, then closes again, giving rise to an opening motif "x" and its opposite "y." Simultaneously, not awaiting a proper introduction of the two motifs x and y, a third motif "z" emerges. These three motifs, interlocking, gently interacting with one another, but more and more submerging into the one motif "z," create an overall lilt of loosely punctuated *commata*, disarmingly innocent. Clarity is not at stake: in m. 4 a proactive left hand weakens a cadential point; in m. 7 the low E in the bass reluctantly (but then graciously) gives in to what musical etiquette prescribes: closure on a half cadence.[35]

But who is speaking? With sonata Hob. XVI: 40, is Haydn perhaps writing a letter to Marie, which she can read, imagining Haydn's voice? Or is Haydn lending his words to Marie, to be declaimed on her own terms? To find a possible answer, we must fast forward to the third sonata of the set, Hob. XVI: 42 (D), which bears striking resemblances to 40: both are cast in a mold of first-movement variations followed by a scherzo-type finale and use a similar melodic, periodic, textural, and harmonic language. Yet 42 is in so many ways more "oratorical" – in the learned, public, indeed "male" sense – than 40. With 42, is Haydn perhaps setting an example? Is he teaching his new pupil how to use to her advantage rehearsed oratorical principles and structures, skills that she might apply – however discreetly and with subtle humor – in her own public life as a Princess?

But if such master-pupil interactions exist through the course of the Marie Esterházy sonatas, how do "I" show them in my "professional" rendition of them? Clearly, by allowing dedicatees into my relationship with Haydn, I have ended up with more questions than I bargained for. These apply mostly to my performances of the Marie Esterházy sonatas (Hob. XVI: 40–42) and, to a lesser degree, the Genzinger sonata (Hob. XVI: 49).[36] Less tricky, from the perspective of the dedicatee's social status and gender, are the Auenbrugger sonatas (Hob. XVI: 35–39, 20). There the dedicatee sisters represent "a Viennese keyboardist aspiring to professionalism." Their sonatas might be described as more user-friendly versions of the Prince Esterházy sonatas. The sonata in D major Hob. XVI: 51 for Maria Hester Park presents none of the problems of the earlier Marie Esterházy sonatas. Also a two-movement sonata, it has a through-composed first movement – without repeat signs – and sits comfortably on the printed page. As such, it is a drawing-room equivalent of the English grand concert sonatas for Therese Jansen.

Keyboards

In his study of the Viennese School (1740–80) Daniel Heartz begins his section on Haydn's keyboard music as follows:

> Works for solo keyboard played a subordinate role in Haydn's oeuvre . . . Hiller in 1768 went so far as to say that "the Clavier does not suit Haydn as well as the other instruments, which he uses in the most fiery and galant symphonies." It is true that Haydn was not a keyboard virtuoso, as were Wagenseil and Steffan, with whom Hiller placed Haydn. The keyboard music of all three, being mainly for amateur performers on the harpsichord, is stylistically very similar. Amateurs evidently appreciated Haydn. Keyboard works under his name began to circulate widely in the 1760s; Breitkopf offered one as early as 1763.[37]

Several assumptions are at work here: Haydn is not a keyboard virtuoso; there is a bad fit even between Haydn the composer and keyboard instruments; nevertheless, his works, intended for amateurs, were "evidently" appreciated by them, more than those of Steffan or Wagenseil, perhaps because Haydn himself was the non-virtuoso of the three. A. Peter Brown (cited by Heartz himself "for a counterargument") would have protested loudly: the first chapter of his book seeks explicitly to revise that age-old notion that Haydn was not very interested in the keyboard. Numerous primary documents make clear that the keyboard played a consistently central role throughout Haydn's life, not only for improvisation or composition but for performance proper and everyday logistics. He "even had to tune his harpsichord in the orchestra himself."[38] Haydn was not only genuinely interested in the keyboard, the various forms this instrument had (organs, clavichords, harpsichords, pianos) and the developments it underwent during his lifetime, but he was an active and praised performer on the instrument.[39]

Unlike Brown I do not feel compelled to refute the basic premise, that "Haydn was not a keyboard virtuoso." I would argue, on the contrary, that, *because* he was not a virtuoso, his keyboard compositions are so uniquely instrumental. That is, they reflect – often more clearly than C. P. E. Bach or Mozart – his own creative responses to instrumental realities, which often become so much part of the compositional "narrative" itself. The clearest examples, so convincingly based on organological parameters, are Haydn's English sonatas, both solo and accompanied.

Imagine the following scientific paradigm. Hypothesis: "There exist two distinct schools in piano building, playing, and writing." Experiment: "Take a Viennese composer, transfer him to an English environment, and observe him: will he change his style?" The answer is a resounding yes, remarkably so for a sixty-two-year-old master, who had nothing to "prove" but, on the contrary, had been invited to London on the strengths of his existing reputation.

Haydn had made adjustments before. In a 1790 letter to Marianne von Genzinger, recipient of Hob. XVI: 49, he explains that "I know I ought to have arranged this sonata in accordance with your kind of keyboard [*Clavier*; from a few sentences before it is clear that harpsichord is meant], but I found this impossible because I am no longer accustomed to it."[40] (The actual dedicatee, as per Haydn's manuscript, was Mademoiselle Maria Anna Gerlischek, a well-to-do lady, housekeeper, and intimate of Prince Esterházy,[41] who acted as an intermediary between Madame von Genzinger in Vienna and Haydn in Eszterháza.) It is interesting that Haydn formulates this statement as an excuse: the etiquette of writing a piece for someone obviously included taking into account the type of instrument this person owned. Equally interesting are his expressions through the course of his correspondence of a desire to perform the piece for her ("Oh! how I wish that I could only play this sonata to you a few times!"), only partly satisfied by a report that he performed the new sonata "at our Mademoiselle Nanette's [von Gerlischek] in the presence of my gracious Prince." Unlike the Esterházy sonatas, it was not the Prince's approbation that Haydn now sought, but the Mademoiselle's specifically, who after all had commissioned the work. And when he writes to Her Grace that the former had expressed her approval, symbolized by the gift of a golden tobacco box, he is clearly relieved: "At first I rather doubted, because of [the sonata's] difficulty, whether I would receive any applause."

Here is a discrepancy. Haydn writes a piece for his friend, whose musicianship and instrument are known to him, yet he arranges it for his *own* instrument and furthermore takes pride in his *own* successful performance, in her absence. Haydn's solution: to convince his friend to buy a piano herself, preferably one similar to his.[42] So it is that, in his first letter of June 20, 1790, after describing the contents of the piece and famously saying about the Adagio that "it contains many things which I shall analyze for Your Grace when the time comes; it is rather difficult but full of feeling," he broaches the subject of instrument: "It is a pity that Your Grace has not one of Schanz's fortepianos, for Your Grace could then produce twice the effect." This troubling thought continues to weigh on Haydn. Still influenced by his recent successful performance of the piece – one might reasonably wonder whether Haydn had his own Schanz moved to Mademoiselle Nanette's apartment for the occasion –[43] Haydn, on June 27, picks up his old thought and elaborates:

> It's only a pity that Your Grace doesn't own a Schanz fortepiano, on which everything is better expressed. I thought that Your Grace might turn over your still tolerable harpsichord to Fräulein Peperl [her daughter], and buy a new fortepiano for yourself. Your beautiful hands and their facility of execution deserve this and much more. I know I ought to have arranged this sonata in accordance with your kind of keyboard, but I found this impossible because I am no longer accustomed to it.

Haydn more than makes up for it. Subsequent letters show that he convinced the Prince himself to buy a piano for Frau von Genzinger (whose husband Peter was Physician in Ordinary at the Esterházy court). It is now (on July 4) that Haydn goes into detail as to why she should buy a Schanz rather than a Walter, again in name of the sonata:

> Therefore I should like Your Grace to try one made by Herr Schanz, his fortepianos are particularly light in touch and the mechanism very agreeable. A good fortepiano is absolutely necessary for Your Grace, and my Sonata will gain double its effect by it.

In her reply (dated July 11, 1790), von Genzinger expresses herself "quite willing" to buy a Schanz (her rather neutral choice of words perhaps revealing a social pressure among the higher circles to buy a Walter, who, after all, enjoyed a *de facto* endorsement from the Imperial Court, which owned no less than four of his instruments).[44] Although noticeably less engaged than Haydn, she also goes on to mention the sonata (which "pleases her well") and requests one change: that Haydn alter the passage in the slow movement (mm. 57ff.) where the hands cross one another. That she singles out these rather than the seemingly much harder crossovers in the first movement (mm. 42ff.) need not necessarily surprise us: crossing left over right (rather than right over left, as before) requires a contortion of arms and body that any well-postured, right-handed noble woman would have resisted. In the same letter she makes sure the sonata does not replace Haydn's old promise of a symphony. Next is Haydn's response on July 23, letter A from above (Table 14.3).

Through the course of this fascinating correspondence, we are offered glimpses into a complex network of connections between composer, dedicatee, composition, and instrument, all stemming from Haydn's confession that he is "no longer used to writing for harpsichord." From a larger perspective (which Frau von Genzinger herself would have lacked) it is clear what he means. A good test of his statement would be to play the opening of Hob. XVI: 14 (in D major, from the early 1760s) on a piano and

Example 14.6 Hob. XVI: 47, first movement, mm. 8–12

Table 14.6 *Arrangement of Bass Keys on an Austrian Harpsichord*

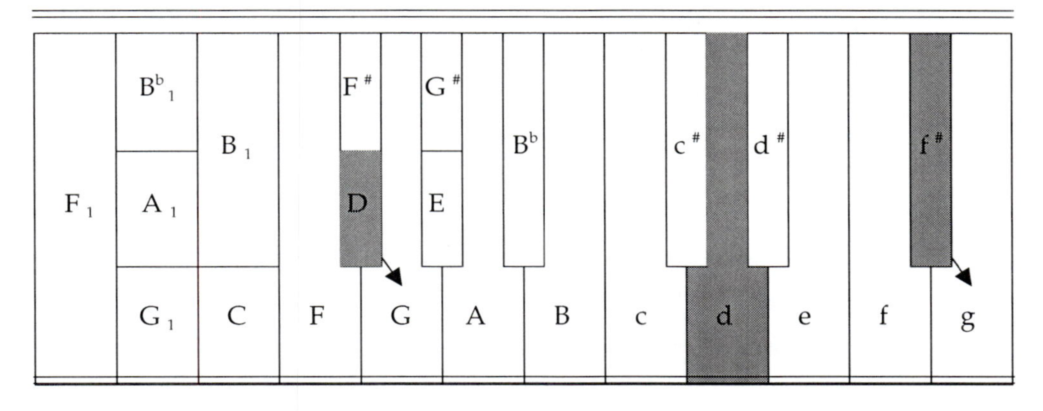

Hob. XVI: 48 (in C major, from 1789) on a harpsichord. On the other hand, to try and pin down one exact turning point in Haydn's writing style (from harpsichord to piano), as many scholars have done, would be to deny a whole group of pieces from 1776 to 1780 their capacity to embody a symbiosis of instrumental styles, of old and new together. Even speaking in terms of "old" and "new" may be a mistake: the clavichord, with its touch-sensitivity and other expressive powers, remains seriously undervalued in our reception of Haydn's keyboard music.

Recent organological research – on early German-Austrian pianos, including squares, from the 1770s and 1780s, and on the independent tradition of Austrian one-manual harpsichords – has given the modern performer of Haydn's keyboard music much to discover.[45] Haydn literature has drawn attention to a few specific passages, such as the one shown in Ex. 14.6 (from Hob. XVI: 47 in e minor), requiring a harpsichord with so-called Viennese short octave, shown in Table 14.6. But until we have such instruments under our hands again not as a *curiosum* but as a matter of course, we will have to limit ourselves to theoretical observations about "exceptional" moments in a score and will fail to reconnect with what was "normal" in performance.[46] Indeed, harpsichords with such multiple-broken octaves were the norm in Austria well up to 1780.[47] Very few *must*, but almost all of Haydn's sonatas of the 1750s and 1760s *can* be performed on them, potentially bringing alive textures and articulations in the bass hitherto unsuspected. Thus, in Ex. 14.6, what matters is not so much *that* one can play the D major chord in m. 11 as written, but *how* one can do it. The low D would be the equivalent of an F♯ on a chromatic keyboard. The tenth is grasped as an octave and the second finger on the higher D firmly locks the chord in the keyboardist's hand. (See the grey-tinted keys in Table 14.6.) The low key-dip of Austrian harpsichords, especially of the sharps (which are only a touch higher than the naturals), allows one to slide smoothly from the deep dominant chord to the light tonic ones of m.12. (See the two arrows in Table 14.6.) What we feel and hear is a ravishing resolution, that essential feature of "Viennese keyboard style."[48]

Making decisions: matching keyboard, oratory and dedicatee in space

In the form of an academic essay I have explored some of the complex problems involved in performing Haydn on keyboard. It is now time to reveal my true identity. "I" am a modern performer on historical keyboards embarking on the complete recording of Haydn's keyboard music. Transferring live performance to digital disc is no small task, as Haydn – his own 1774 experience in mind – would understand. The challenge I face is possibly greater than his. In addition to myself, I have him to account for, and, through him, all the people that surrounded him, at different points in his life. To embody all at once, to reveal all possible meanings of a sonata in one recorded performance is simply impossible.

Nonetheless, in a grant-supported project at McGill University, producer Martha de Francisco, sound engineer Wieslaw Woszczyk, and I set out to carefully match type of rhetoric, *persona* or *personae*, and instrument in acoustical space, to be reconstructed in the recording studio on the basis of samples from real historical locations.[49] Thus, playing on a grand double-manual harpsichord, "we" will address an imaginary Prince in the acoustics of the Eszterháza music room. On an earlier one-manual Austrian harpsichord, we will perform sonatas from the 1760s in the setting of a Viennese salon, as if performing for invited guests. In Haydn's study room in Eisenstadt we will "extemporize" on a clavichord along the lines of Hob. XVI: 20 (1771, in c minor). In the privacy of the night we will sit at a square piano, read aloud, and learn from Haydn's musical letters (Hob. XVI:

40–42). Addressing a London concert audience on the stage of a larger hall, we will perform two grand sonatas (Hob. XVI: 50, 52) on an English grand piano.[50] Together, conveying complementary story lines, these recorded performances will attempt to do justice to a repertoire that resists behaving like one, handed to posterity by a keyboardist-composer who displayed admirable tact when interacting with people and who adjusted to changing technologies with unmatched virtuosity.

15 Haydn and posterity: the long nineteenth century

JAMES GARRATT

Any study of Haydn's posthumous reputation must wrestle with several key problems. To start with, it may appear that Haydn's reception over the century following his death has little relevance to our engagement with the composer and his music: an essay on this topic might therefore seem to offer merely a stroll through the byways of nineteenth-century journalism and *belles lettres*, of marginal importance to our picture of Haydn. Yet many of the perspectives that emerged in the nineteenth century continue to shape popular perceptions of the composer. Indeed, Jens Peter Larsen has argued that it is an exaggeration to speak of a modern image of Haydn, as opposed to a diluted variant of earlier views.[1] If Larsen is correct, it might seem that in exploring this topic, our task is to unmask the distortions that accrued over the course of the nineteenth century, to assert our own truths against earlier fallacies. Certainly, this impulse has motivated most studies of Haydn's reputation. For Leon Botstein, the "stubborn veneer of the nineteenth century" must be "dissolved and scraped away" if a new picture of Haydn is to emerge; similarly, in 1935 Adolf Sandberger claimed that "one of the most important artistic tasks of the present" was to discard earlier images of the composer in order to "re-establish the full truth."[2] But, as is evident from Sandberger's study, such attempts to assert the unadorned truth add their own layers of ideological veneer to the picture of Haydn. It is an illusion to regard our understanding of Haydn's music as detachable from its history of dialogues with earlier musicians and critics, no matter how unappealing some nineteenth-century assessments of the composer may appear today.

At first glance, the story of Haydn's reputation over the course of the nineteenth century seems straightforward: it is a truism that his reputation suffered a clear decline, that the veneration and popularity he enjoyed during his lifetime were displaced by grudging respect and indifference. But several of the assumptions associated with this view are misleading. One misconception is that a uniform picture of Haydn was articulated throughout this period: that commentators were united in viewing Haydn as aesthetically and culturally irrelevant. Although certain tropes and ideas were extraordinarily persistent, they did not all emerge at the same time; moreover, they can be found in texts that, in other respects, present fundamentally different views of the composer. And the views of a handful of well-known figures – Berlioz, Schumann, or Wagner – do not represent those of the majority, nor do they provide a true indication of the place of Haydn's music in contemporary concert life. Many texts that, on the surface, testify to his marginal place in musical culture were intended to reshape rather than reflect reality; as a result, they present a picture that can easily be misinterpreted.

This tension between musical discourse and practice presents the most significant obstacle to a balanced appraisal of Haydn's stature. In spite of the lack of enthusiasm for Haydn on the part of many commentators, his music (or rather, a small proportion of it) was regularly performed throughout the nineteenth century: indeed, a key factor motivating lukewarm reviews of his works was their perceived ubiquity in the concert hall. It should be borne in mind, therefore, that while critical discourse provides the principal source for appraising shifting perceptions of Haydn, it does not fully convey the varied attitudes of musicians and listeners. In addition to emphasizing this diversity of standpoints, the following discussion identifies broad trends and phases in Haydn reception, highlighting the ideological and institutional factors shaping them. By acknowledging the fluidity and plurality of nineteenth-century views of Haydn, we can come closer to understanding why some ideas were so enduring.

Papa Haydn: the merry little peasant

A crucial task in studying the reception of any composer is unravelling the significance of recurrent tropes and clichés. While they can persist for decades, their meanings are by no means stable: they can remain in use long after their original aesthetic and ideological presuppositions have faded. The association of J. S. Bach's music with Gothic architecture, for example, has been perpetuated from the late eighteenth century to the present, yet has acquired and discarded a variety of very different connotations. Similarly, the numerous tropes and stock phrases applied to Haydn carried multiple meanings, and even labels that seem to be factual statements or incidental rhetoric (such as "father of the symphony," or "the lark of Rohrau") served distinct political and aesthetic agenda. Some of the most familiar of these labels did not emerge until the 1840s; others perpetuate themes already present in Haydn reception during his lifetime.

The latter is true of two of the most common nineteenth-century tropes: terms and metaphors focusing on youthful naivety, and on Haydn as a father figure (the combination of these tropes – as in the composer Alfred Julius Becher's description of him as a "lovable, eternally youthful old man" – became a biographical staple).[3] These strategies served a variety of functions. On one level, the idea of Haydn as a father figure reflects how perceptions of his character and music were shaped by his fame in the later years of his life. Yet it also served to emphasize that his significance for music history lay in his earlier achievements. Even before his death, terms normally associated with figures from the distant past were applied to Haydn. Descriptions of Haydn as an "old master" or "forefather" played a key role in the construction of the canon of modern instrumental music, and in establishing the view that the rise of the symphony was a uniquely German achievement. While, in 1790, the lexicographer Ernst Ludwig Gerber depicted Haydn as having perfected earlier developments, later German commentators represented him as the sole originator of the symphony and quartet.[4] But in addition to monumentalizing the composer, the notion of Haydn as a forefather placed him at two removes from the present. As a result of progressive conceptions of history, in particular the triadic trajectory Haydn begat Mozart begat Beethoven (a common view even during his lifetime), Haydn's later and best-known works were regarded as anomalies, the final fruits of an earlier age. As early as 1801, the theologian Johann Karl Friedrich Triest contended that Haydn's recent works, such as *The Creation*, contributed nothing new to musical development or the composer's reputation.[5] Later commentators constructed an even greater gulf between Haydn and the music of their age. In their hands, the metaphor of fatherhood was used to signify obsolescence, or as an ironic response to a quaint musical curio (of which the clearest example is the Viennese critic Eduard Hanslick's damning comment on the "sprightly, kind grandpa, so lovable you want to kiss him").[6]

Wider associations are brought into play by another key term and its cognates: *Heiterkeit.* This word is difficult to translate, since its meaning shifted significantly over the course of the nineteenth century, signifying serene optimism but also cheerfulness, gaiety, and conviviality.[7] Although eighteenth-century musicians employed a related word, *Heitere*, in order to denote a particular musical *Affekt*, later commentators used it to encompass Haydn's character, output, and place in music history: indeed, it played a defining role in shaping his posthumous reputation. The most significant aspect of the term's use is its classicizing function. For eighteenth- and early nineteenth-century critics, it was primarily associated with the art and world-view of ancient Greece, serving to contrast the youthful optimism and health of Greek culture with the pessimism and decadence of modernity. On one level, therefore, the use of this term in relation to Haydn bolstered his claim to classical status. On another, it relegated him to an age of innocence, fencing him off from the modern world. This strategy, along with the tendency to treat him as the first and least significant component of the Haydn–Mozart–Beethoven triad, received its clearest formulation from

E. T. A. Hoffmann in 1810. Hoffmann's evocation of an idyllic scene distances Haydn's childlike, unreflective mentality from the concerns of the present:

> In the main, Haydn's compositions express a childlike mood of serene well-being [*heitern Gemüts*]. His symphonies lead us through boundless green forest groves, through a jovial, bustling crowd of happy people. A swift succession of young men and girls dance past; laughing children lie in wait behind trees and rosebushes teasingly throwing flowers at each other. A life of eternal youth, abundant in love and bliss, as though before the Fall.[8]

Given the extraordinary frequency with which later authors referred to Haydn's *Heiterkeit*, it is possible to track the word's changing associations with some precision. While Hoffmann evoked the serenity of Eden, later critics focused on blander environments: for the Berlin author Ludwig Rellstab, Haydn's works call forth images of "lovely landscapes, meadows in spring and smiling skies . . . Considered as a whole, Haydn's music arouses approximately the same mood as a stroll through a beautiful park."[9] Indeed, in the writings of the critic and historian Franz Brendel, Haydn's *Heiterkeit* is more redolent of a cosy Austrian farmhouse, and amounts to a complacent, even irresponsible, cheerfulness: "The dark abysses of human anguish are almost entirely imperceptible to Haydn's contented, childlike, naive character; for him – the carefree child playing on the brink of the abyss – the negative side of life scarcely existed."[10]

Brendel's equation of *Heiterkeit* with carefree contentedness reflects not only narrowing perceptions of Haydn's expressive range, but also the shifting meaning of the word itself. The extent to which it was equated with mere cheerfulness in the second half of the nineteenth century is evident from Nietzsche's *The Birth of Tragedy* (1872). Here, Nietzsche advocated a more sophisticated conception of the ancient Greek character, arguing that it had been misunderstood as a result of a mistaken view of *Heiterkeit*: "We believe that we have correctly understood the serious and significant concept of "Greek serenity" (*Heiterkeit*), whereas wherever one looks at present one encounters the false understanding of serenity as a state of carefree cheerfulness."[11] The importance of this to perceptions of Haydn is evident from an 1856 review by the conductor and pianist Hans von Bülow. Here, Bulöw countered the views of the "priests of Haydn's cult" who proclaimed that music was, by its nature, a cheerful art: "It would surely be best to shake off the confused categories invented by schoolmasterly eunuchs, to cease misapplying to music decrees derived from the classical ideal of a Hellenic *Heiterkeit*."[12] In spite of Bülow's protests, Haydn's advocates and detractors continued to employ this concept. Thus the Catholic reformer Franz Xaver Witt sought to differentiate between the serenity of true church music and the "beery merriment" (*bierselige Heiterkeit*) of Haydn's masses; it is but a short step from Witt's remark to the title of a children's book from the 1930s: *Joseph Haydn: the Merry Little Peasant.*[13]

Many of these associations resonate in the best-known nineteenth-century gloss on Haydn: "So far as it is possible for the traits of genius to be combined with an altogether *good* man, Haydn possessed them. He goes right up to the boundaries with which morality circumscribes the intellect: he composes pure music, which has 'no past.'"[14] Nietzsche's gnomic comment illustrates how Haydn's music and character became inseparable from the critical discourse that accrued around them. By this time, it was common to equate Haydn's moral character with the serene contentment perceived in his music: Nietzsche even echoes Brendel's curious image of the child playing at the edge of the intellectual and emotional abyss, reluctant to engage in the risks and soul-searching characteristic of true genius. Like Hoffmann and Brendel, Nietzsche equated the lack of substance and depth that he perceived in Haydn's music with youthful innocence, even virginity. But the final clause of this fragment can only be understood if it is placed in its context. In this and the surrounding aphorisms, Nietzsche creates a miniature narrative of the history of music: he traces a path from Bach – on the threshold of modern music, yet looking back to the Middle Ages – to Beethoven, who epitomizes how "innocence in tones" is no longer possible for the reflective modern composer.[15] Accordingly, Haydn is seen to represent a new beginning, but also the final remnant of an innocent, earlier world: a world viewed with a mixture of nostalgia and condescension.

Patriarchs and philistines

In the decades immediately following Haydn's death, such condescension was not directed primarily at the composer but at his champions and pupils. Indeed, a key factor motivating negative assessments of Haydn was the impulse to counter the claims of his partisans: in 1858, the historian and novelist Wilhelm Heinrich Riehl blamed the decline of Haydn's reputation on the "aesthetic tyranny" of his followers – "godlike philistines" – who proclaimed his principles to be infallible and eternal.[16] This tendency was particularly prominent in Vienna. Even in the 1830s and 1840s, conservative Viennese critics – referred to by contemporaries as the "patriarchs" – represented Haydn as an unsurpassable musical paradigm. In 1834, for example, the music historian Raphael Georg Kiesewetter contended that Haydn's works remained the highest benchmark of musical beauty.[17] Similar conceptions of Haydn's stature were expressed by leading conservative figures in other Austrian and German musical centers, and also in Britain and France. Although William Crotch, a champion of Handel's oratorios, criticized Haydn's works in this genre, he feted him as "the greatest of all instrumental composers." And as late as 1839, François-Joseph Fétis elevated Haydn as a bulwark against more recent music, representing him as the "imperishable standard of a regular, pure and brilliant order of beauty," untainted by the "affected originality" of later composers.[18]

This perspective soon came under attack from advocates of living composers, whose response was to assert Haydn's irrelevance to current concerns. In 1824, the Heidelberg jurist Anton Friedrich Justus Thibaut observed that some musicians – applying false notions of technological progress to art – now regarded Haydn's symphonies as antiquated.[19] The likely stimulus for Thibaut's remarks was a series of articles by the critic and composer Adolf Bernhard Marx, whose new journal, the *Berliner allgemeine musikalische Zeitung*, was dedicated to countering the conservatism of contemporary music criticism. According to Marx, the dominant journal of the day, the Leipzig *Allgemeine musikalische Zeitung*, continued to adhere to a standpoint defined by the music of Mozart and his period: in contrast, Marx promoted Beethoven as the figurehead of a "still more accomplished, loftier period of music." As a result, Marx relegated Haydn to an earlier phase of musical and cultural development. The significance of Marx's approach derives not from its novelty, but from his systematic amplification of ideas present in earlier criticism. Thus, in Marx's conception of the development of instrumental music, Haydn is rigidly assigned to the phase of development preceding Mozart: Haydn's symphonies exhibit an "impurity" (*Beimischung*) that is wholly absent from those of his successor.[20]

Marx's clearest attempt to distance Haydn from the music and worldview of the present occurs in a review of a Berlin performance of *The Creation*. As so often in nineteenth-century appraisals of Haydn, the negative aspects of Marx's review were stimulated by the very popularity of his music (he noted that in this performance, *The Creation* "gave just as much pleasure to the public as it always does"). Marx's frustration at the conservatism of the Berlin public did not lead him to question the classical status of this work or of its "eternally fresh and youthful" composer. Nonetheless, he decisively consigns it to a past stage of human development: drawing extensively on the tropes associated with *Heiterkeit*, he claims that it is impossible for a more advanced age to identify with Haydn's childlike mentality.[21]

Marx's bifurcated approach to Haydn – which affirmed his canonic status while distancing him from modern concerns – was common throughout the second quarter of the nineteenth century. This compromise was threatened, however, by the increasing identification of the composer with conservative institutions, with negative appraisals of his works occurring in tandem with critiques of the stagnation of concert life. In the criticism of Robert Schumann, for example, hostility to Haydn emerges only when he serves as a symbol of the conservatism of the Leipzig public. A review of an 1840 performance of the "Military" Symphony notes its "pigtail-like quality (*Zopfiges*)," pointing out that the audience took greatest pleasure in the aspects of the work most distant from contemporary music: "the Turkish music (*Janitscharenmusik*) in it has something infantile and tasteless which we – in spite of the fondness for the master which persists in all quarters – should no longer deny. The scherzo, which in our opinion comes closest to our age, was curiously the sole movement not to be applauded."[22] Schumann's frustration at the composer's continuing popularity is most evident in a review of a later concert from the same series, where he complains of the tiring effect of an all-Haydn program: "Haydn's music has always been played here regularly; we can learn nothing more from him. He is like a regular house-guest who is always welcome and respectfully received; but he no longer holds any deeper interest for our age."[23]

Schumann's identification of Haydn with public conservatism found a more trenchant expression in the early writings of Hanslick. Indeed, he went so far as to blame the stagnation of Viennese musical culture entirely on the "narrow preference for one composer which stems from misconceived piety." Hanslick's ire was provoked by the under-rehearsed, annual performances of Haydn's oratorios by the Tonkünstler-Societät, which diminished them into mere "matters of habit" (*Gewohnheitssache*) rather than art-works.[24] But while the main focus of Hanslick's attacks was Viennese philistinism, his impulse to promote more recent music led him to criticize Haydn's works as well as their popularity. In promoting Mendelssohn's *Elijah*, for example, he sought to demonstrate that it provided a better exemplar of the oratorio style than *The Creation* or *The Seasons*. And in attacking the Viennese antipathy to recent music, Hanslick condemned *The Seven Words*, inveighing against its "empty, insignificant play of notes" and "contentless clichés."[25]

As these comments suggest, Hanslick's critique of Haydn reflects more than just hostility to Viennese conservatism. Rather, Hanslick – like Marx and Schumann – regarded Haydn as representing an earlier phase of musical culture, a stage transcended by Beethoven. In a review from 1856, in which he championed contemporary chamber music and challenged the dominance of Haydn's quartets in the current repertory, Hanslick distinguished between the "art-historical character of the Haydn era" and that of the modern age, represented by Beethoven: "The nature of composition was wholly different in their respective periods. Whoever, like Haydn, produced over 100 symphonies and almost as many quartets could not possibly give each its own rich individuality. If Beethoven wrote ten times fewer, he was able to put ten times more into them."[26]

Pigtailed lackey of the *ancien régime*

Hanslick's perspective on the relation between Haydn and Beethoven was shaped by the intense musical debates of the late 1840s. The prevalence of rigidly progressive conceptions of history, coupled with the politicization of musical discourse in the years around the 1848–49 revolutions, made Haydn's stature a matter of aggressive dispute. For the avowedly progressive musical party (chiefly, Brendel and other critics of the *Neue Zeitschrift für Musik*), Haydn's music embodied a "superseded standpoint" divorced from the needs of the present, an aristocratic mentality alien to the burgeoning democratic age – a line of thinking vehemently rebutted by other critics. Rejecting the idea of musical progress and obsolescence, the Viennese "patriarch" Ignaz Franz von Mosel contended that "there is no greater proof of defective theoretical and aesthetic knowledge than to describe works by Haydn and Mozart from the epochs of their most consummate mastery as 'antiquated.'"[27] Others countered the idea that the music of these composers embodied an aristocratic mentality; for instance, Johann Christian Lobe, editor of the Leipzig *Allgemeine musikalische Zeitung*, derided the notion that Haydn's music "merely mirrors the spirit of the age of the Seven Years War [1756–63]."[28] Such dissenting voices were stifled following the collapse of this and other conservative journals in 1848, resulting in the progressive stance having a decisive impact on perceptions of Haydn. Indeed, some of the politically charged tropes that emerged at this time remained in currency throughout the second half of the nineteenth century.

The notion that Haydn's music was aesthetically and ideologically superseded received its most strident expression from Brendel and another critic for his journal, the lawyer and aesthetician Ernst Gottschald. Together they decisively banished Haydn to the period before 1789. He, like Mozart (whose death was timely from the perspective of such deterministic historical schemes), was viewed as a musical embodiment of the age before the French Revolution, exemplifying art superseded by the "spirit of modernity." In contrasting the aristocratic world-view that he perceived in Haydn's music with Beethoven's democratic ideal, Gottschald employed a startlingly audacious metaphor, claiming that the distance between these composers was equivalent to the gulf separating Sophocles and Shakespeare.[29] While Brendel's comments are more circumspect, he too regarded Haydn as a product of Austrian authoritarianism, of the old order shattered by the French Revolution.[30]

This perspective pervaded every aspect of Haydn's treatment by the mid-nineteenth-century progressives. Not only was Haydn condemned as a compliant servant of the aristocracy, but his works were derided as mere table music (whose continuing popularity, according to Bülow, was dependent on the outmoded attitudes of an "aristocratic public").[31] Comparing Haydn's Symphony no. 51 with Beethoven's First Symphony, Berlioz equated his perception of Haydn's character with the aesthetic essence of the music: "Haydn's [Symphony] is humbler; it comes forward modestly, its look is respectful; it hardly dares raise its voice; it creeps around; it resigns itself in advance to passing unnoticed, and is full of gratitude to the honorable listeners who wish to hear it."[32] Similarly, both Marx and Richard Wagner depicted Haydn as a deferential lackey, content for his music to serve as mere entertainment, while Wagner argued that only the final years of his life yielded "truly noble masterworks."[33] For some moralistic commentators, the childlike quality of his music stemmed from irresponsibility and unmanliness, a failure to engage with the world; as the British Wagnerian Ernest Newman later argued, "the out-of-the-world repose that pervades his music is the expression of a spirit almost emasculated by undue seclusion from the active life of men – a spirit of weak complaisance and unambitious compromise."[34]

A similar argument was employed to highlight the limitations of Haydn's aesthetic stance. For Brendel and his circle, the cultural significance of music stemmed from its gradually increasing capacity for expressive determinacy, a development culminating in Liszt's symphonic poems and the Wagnerian *Gesamtkunstwerk*. Regarding Haydn as having contributed little to this process, Brendel depicts him as a mere craftsman – "a musician in the narrowest sense" – condemning his lack of interest in aesthetics and the other arts as philistinism.[35] The notion that Haydn's mentality had more in common with the craftsman than the artist was not new; earlier, Marx had compared his horizons to those of a jobbing musician (*Allerwelts-Musikant*), arguing that "the realm of ideas gave him only the level of intellectual capacity commensurate with the untroubled activity of his nature, folklike mentality, feelings, and beliefs."[36] With Brendel, Haydn's limitations are explicitly linked to his social class; he could only rise above his "petit-bourgeois timidity and stolidness" when composing.[37] In addition to faulting Haydn's aesthetic and intellectual outlook, Brendel attributed the restricted expressive range of his music to stunted psychological development: here, Haydn's naivety is equated with emotional and sexual immaturity. Brendel argued that Haydn's unhappy marriage rendered him incapable of representing human love; if Mozart was the "poet of sexual love," Haydn's emotional compass, and that of his music, remained childlike and repressed.[38] Similarly, the Magdeburg lawyer and critic Carl Kretschmann contended that the opposition between masculine pathos and feminine sentimentality, fundamental to Beethoven's music, is still undeveloped in Haydn: it is the absence of such sexual differentiation that accounts for the childlike essence of his works.[39]

It is vital to recognize that by no means all mid-nineteenth-century commentators represented Haydn as an emotionally stunted, reactionary, toadying philistine. Indeed, even Brendel did not question Haydn's place in the classical canon, insisting that "in his limited sphere, he is so healthy and original, so inexhaustible, that his recognition as a master of the first rank is secure."[40] If discussions from this period cast Haydn in an unfavorable light, it is largely as a result of their form: the essays of Brendel, Marx, and Wagner present teleological narratives, in which Haydn is placed at the very beginning of an aesthetic, social, and political trajectory culminating in the present (or hoped-for future). The notion that Haydn's music was superseded was the product of the dialectical systems employed by these authors: it would be mistaken to assume that their stances reflect a wider hostility or indifference to the composer.

Competing narratives: a Haydn "revival"?

Some musicologists have detected a revival of interest in Haydn in the second half of the nineteenth century. Clemens Höslinger, for example, notes that performances of Haydn in Vienna proliferated through the work of the conductor Johann Herbeck, while Adolf Sandberger highlights the significance of Riehl and of the aesthetician Hermann Kretzschmar in championing the composer.[41] Others like the composer Emil Naumann and the critic Leopold Schmidt also inveighed against the clichés and misconceptions that tarnished Haydn's reputation. Even so, it would be unhelpful to speak of a Haydn revival in this period. Although some of these commentators were influential, their aims and motivations were disparate. Moreover, there was no major event or publication to stimulate a resurgence of interest in Haydn. Carl Ferdinand Pohl's incomplete biography of the composer (the first two volumes of which appeared in 1875 and 1882; the third volume, by Hugo Botstiber, not until 1927) did little to shift perceptions, and no collected edition or catalogue of his works was initiated until the twentieth century.

Given that Haydn's champions in the first half of the nineteenth century were in general conservative figures, it might be expected that he later served as a figurehead for opponents of the New German School. As Leon Botstein argues, "Haydn conceivably could have provided a rallying point for mid-century proponents of so-called absolute music."[42] But while some commentators attempted to promote Haydn in this manner, the most prominent opponent of the New German School – Hanslick – did not. Although he maintained his earlier position, Hanslick did occasionally snipe at the progressive camp when reviewing performances of works by Haydn. Responding to a performance of *The Seasons* under Herbeck in 1861, Hanslick included a gibe at Liszt and his circle: "Anyone who denies the irrepressibly fresh substance of this oratorio must have sold himself body and soul to the Weimar musical inquisition." Similarly, in reviewing the third concert of Herbeck's series, he noted that "the music of the future [*Zukunftsmusik*] has made a great contribution to the reborn sense for Haydn." Even so, Hanslick's appraisals of Haydn scarcely suggest the intent to champion the composer. According to Hanslick, many of his techniques now appear primitive, and it is impossible for modern listeners to share the uncritical adulation expressed by earlier generations: modern Haydn appreciation amounts to recognizing "the weaknesses of the genius without loving him any the less."[43]

Other opponents of the New German School were more sympathetic towards Haydn. In discussing misconceptions of the composer, Naumann attributed his low critical standing to the party slogans and "wretched clichés" of the Wagnerians; he particularly condemned their tendency to treat earlier composers merely as precursors to modern developments. The principal focus for Naumann's attacks is Wagner himself, whose impulse to lionize Beethoven results in Haydn and Mozart being undervalued and disparaged. It is Wagner's description of Haydn as a princely servant [*fürstlicher Bedienter*] that Naumann – whose own career owed much to royal patronage – finds most objectionable, praising Nicolaus Esterházy for enabling Haydn's genius to unfold. In repudiating Wagner's perspective, Naumann casts Haydn in the role of a reformer and stresses his relevance to the present:

> This serves to demonstrate the point which leaders of extreme tendencies and parties finally reach, as a result of overrating themselves and being severely deficient in art-historical knowledge. Also derived from such impoverished, one-sided standpoints is the habit these partisans have of referring, with pitying condescension, to "good old papa Haydn." We urgently advise the younger of these unbridled geniuses – who will otherwise be forgotten in a decade – to go to "old papa Haydn" and borrow a little of his youth: something of the youth that still glows today in his "London" Symphonies . . . and will live on immortally.[44]

Other champions of Haydn from this period also highlighted how clichés and prejudices had obscured his true stature. Kretzschmar notes that the image of "cozy papa Haydn" stemmed from an underestimation of his power and diversity; Schmidt sought to rebrand the composer as a "youthful revolutionary," lamenting the persistence of the image of the wigged old man.[45] The difficulty of discarding such images is evident in Riehl's essay "Haydn's Sonaten" (1858), arguably the most remarkable nineteenth-century attempt to reappraise the composer. Riehl's perspective, shaped by his bitter hostility towards Wagner, is grounded in a radical critique of modern art music. In his view, music after Haydn degenerated as a result of reflection and introspection: it became increasingly distant from folksong and dance, spurning naturalism in favor of formalism.[46] In Riehl's conception of music history, Haydn is accorded an extraordinary significance: not only did he rejuvenate instrumental music through absorbing the *Grundton* of folk music, but his works provide the highest embodiment of this union.[47] Accordingly, in reappraising Haydn's keyboard sonatas, Riehl defines them in opposition to the "befuddlement and false pathos" of present-day music.[48] In revising the prevailing picture of Haydn, Riehl rejects some of the most established clichés of his day. Yet at a deeper level, Riehl reaffirms existing images of the composer, merely giving them a positive gloss. His decision to focus on Haydn's early sonatas is wholly in line with this agenda: it is these pieces that best correspond with his vision of the composer as the last entirely naive artist, whose reliance on instinct, "godlike lack of inhibition," and austere yet wholly German style represent the final consummation of an idyllic earlier age.[49] Thus, while rejecting the progressive trajectory that cast Haydn as a distant precursor to modern achievements, Riehl's picture of the composer is curiously similar. In contrasting Haydn, the harbinger of spring, with the "musical November frosts" of the present, Riehl reinforced the gulf between Haydn and contemporary musical culture, rather than bridging it.[50]

Epilogue

The centenary of Haydn's death provided an opportunity for musicians and scholars to reflect on Haydn's significance and historical position. The proceedings of the Haydn Centennial Festival, held in conjunction with the Third Congress of the International Musical Society in May 1909, perpetuated well-established viewpoints. A heavy emphasis was placed on Haydn's role as precursor: the opening concert presented his first and last symphonies; Guido Adler's festival speech (copies of which were given to twenty-one thousand Viennese schoolchildren) outlined how Haydn's achievements were amplified and taken further by Mozart and Beethoven; and Adler and the British president of the IMS, Alexander Mackenzie, eulogized Haydn's *Heiterkeit* and childlike simplicity.[51] While the centenary was commemorated through ceremonial speeches, concerts, and homage at Haydn's grave, little attention was paid to him in the academic portions of the congress; indeed, his music was discussed in only two of the sessions. These exceptions are worth mentioning, however, since they remind us of factors shaping Haydn's reputation that should not be overlooked. In a session on Catholic church music, the Bavarian and Austrian delegates fervently debated the question of whether Haydn's masses contravened the spirit of the liturgy (this controversy, which had raged for much of the previous century, alone contradicts the idea that his music was consigned to aesthetic irrelevance).[52] Other neglected aspects of reception are suggested by a paper which surveyed Haydn's place in Danish musical life: in addition to giving details of recent performances, it stressed Haydn's centrality to domestic music-making (in particular the popularity of four-hand arrangements of the symphonies), and in its own modest way highlights two imperatives for future research.[53]

Hitherto, the study of Haydn's posthumous reputation has focused primarily on Austria and Germany. It cannot be assumed that trends in German-speaking countries were mirrored elsewhere in continental Europe or Britain, let alone in North America. The 1909 Danish case reminds us that the marginalization of Haydn by some of the most prominent nineteenth-century critics represents only one side of the picture: the enduring cultivation of his music in the concert hall and its prominence in schools and domestic settings, while harder to quantify, are no less important. Acknowledging the plurality of factors shaping Haydn's reputation, however, is merely a start; a vital task for future research is to provide a detailed exploration of Haydn's reception in performance and criticism, tracing the fortunes of individual works and genres. If there is much work still to be done in exploring this field, one thing is clear: to regard Haydn's posthumous fate as a tale of decline and fall, especially in the century following his death, is an oversimplification that hampers our understanding of his cultural significance.

16 The kitten and the tiger: Tovey's Haydn

LAWRENCE KRAMER

One of the standard ways for a critic to set up an argument is to state that the popular image of an artist is misguided. The rhetorical manoeuvre cuts two ways, or would were it not so overused. It sets the critic up as a thoughtful expert and clears the ground for the construction of a contrary image that claims to be truer to life. What remains for both the straw man and the thoughtful expert is the necessity of the image, a narrative trope that tags the artist with certain identifying traits and provides a ready means of orientation for both apprehending the artist's work and communicating about it in social contexts. It would be easy to dismiss these images as packaging or window-dressing, both of which they are, but it would also be a mistake. The images are as unavoidable as they are useful, the basic coinage of the pragmatics of art. They are also symptomatic of the cultural trends that they serve or challenge. None of them should be believed, exactly, but all of them should be taken seriously.

This is perhaps especially true with respect to Haydn, whose fortunes, at least in the English-speaking world, have been tied exceptionally closely to a pair of images with remarkable staying power.

The first, still surprisingly alive, is the nineteenth-century image of the periwigged Papa Haydn, sturdy, cheerful, and unreflective, a higher-order artisan who ingeniously devised the Classical forms, especially the symphony – he is, of course, the "father" of the symphony – in which others would upstage him. The process starts with his most famous younger contemporary, the Icarus to Haydn's Daedalus. The artistic genius of Mozart regularly trumps the supreme skillfulness of Haydn. This image was influentially purveyed by both E. T. A. Hoffmann and Wagner, for whom Haydn conveys "the expression of a serene and childlike personality" (Hoffmann) or "serenity and placid, easy intimacy" (Wagner). It is Mozart, not Haydn, whose music "leads us to the heart of the spirit realm" (Hoffmann) and encompasses "the whole depth of the heart's infinite feeling" (Wagner).[1] The image of Haydn as a master artificer lacking in depth is very close to the common Romantic stereotype for the eighteenth century itself. It was consolidated with lasting authority by C. F. Pohl (also a German) in the first edition of *Grove's Dictionary of Music and Musicians* in 1879. Among the traits Pohl singles out for admiration, perhaps the most telling are Haydn's "studied moderation" and "the childlike cheerfulness and drollery which chase away trouble and care."[2] Pohl's entry remained unchanged until revised – but not seriously rethought – for the fifth edition of 1954. From there it is only a small step to Harold C. Schonberg's *The Lives of the Great Composers* of 1970, which celebrates Haydn for his "direct, clear, good-natured, unneurotic view toward life and art."[3]

The second image is what keeps the first alive by showing it up as misguided. This is the twentieth-century image of Haydn as the master as well as the innovator of the classical aesthetics of music, a figure of unrivaled originality and expressive range not to be upstaged by Mozart or anyone else, not even by Beethoven, the Leviathan himself. This is the Haydn who was the first to understand the very essence of modern musical logic, the Haydn who grasped the infinite possibilities of tonal, motivic, and contrapuntal development and found the techniques required to release them and bring them dramatically to life. To the educated ear, this Haydn can do anything and express anything. To call him emotionally limited is absurd. The work of such scholars as H. C. Robbins Landon, Charles Rosen, and James Webster has given this image considerable weight in the scholarly world, even though listeners – what's left of them – still seem inclined to give Haydn a back seat behind Mozart and Beethoven. Something about the first image, it seems, is not *that* misguided, never mind that the image itself is condescending and nowadays seems absurd.[4]

The second image was largely created by Donald Francis Tovey (1875–1940) in the program notes on the later symphonies collected in his *Essays in Musical Analysis* (1935–39; this influential compilation drew on the notes Tovey wrote for the Reid orchestra, which he founded in 1917 a few years after assuming the Reid Chair of Music at Edinburgh University). The twentieth-century Anglophone Haydn is essentially Tovey's Haydn. In what follows, I propose to explore in greater detail the image that Tovey created and to read it symptomatically as a means of coordinating musical aesthetics with social and cultural values.

The image has three leading aspects that can be taken up in turn, though each inevitably overlaps the others. In order of what I take to be increasing importance these are: (1) originality, understood in terms later made familiar by Harold Bloom as a capacity to be liberated rather than constrained by precedent, but – and this is the distinctive part – without the Bloomian elements of anxiety and struggle; (2) a creativity not bound by rules, understood as the manifestation of a wider and deeper freedom that is both artistic and social; and (3) the disposition of that freedom along a continuum of transformative play, of wit and critique, whimsy and pugnacity, summed up in the images – repeated in Tovey's writing on Haydn like a leitmotif – of the kitten and the tiger.

In all three aspects, Tovey's Haydn occupies a position that affords him the trappings of the Romantic outlaw without their transgressiveness; it is the position of a skeptical insider, capable of irritability and impatient of pretense, but rendered affirmative and creative by the vital energy of his own wit, in the large eighteenth-century sense of the term that embraces both intelligence and invention. Like many an eighteenth-century wit, this Haydn is a man with a mission. He is called on by his gifts to take up arms with good or high spirits against the forces of dullness, orthodoxy, and convention – forces that at their worst are genuinely stultifying and dark. This position is derived from certain strains in eighteenth-century British literary tradition, which is as much the context for the construction of Tovey's Haydn as is the history of music in German-speaking Europe. As Alexander Pope memorably defined it, "The life of a wit is a warfare on earth." If one is willing to stretch the chronology a little, Tovey's Haydn turns out to be a musical cross between Pope and William Blake.

And so, for that matter, does Tovey, whose mission it is to rescue Haydn from the pedantry that can see nothing but its own image and thus represents a mercurial genius as a periwigged pedant. Tovey's writing on Haydn is even more quirky, witty, and unpredictable than is normal for its author; it approximates the very traits that Tovey finds and admires in Haydn himself. The writing is also frequently satirical or sarcastic, at times to the point of disdain: "[The] differences [among the "London" Symphonies] grow upon us with their merits as we emancipate ourselves from the doctrine which regards them as pianoforte duets tempered by the inhibitions of two nice little school-girls with flaxen pigtails."[5] "The 'surprise' in this symphony [No. 94, nicknamed the "Surprise"] is the most unimportant feature in all Haydn's mature works."[6] "After all the a-priorities have been accepted as to powdered wigs and courtly formulas, will the a-priorists kindly predict what modulation Haydn is going to make at the end of the sixth measure of the following theme?"[7] Like Pope and Blake, Tovey at cultural war is inclined to show no mercy.

Tovey is hardly original himself in regarding Haydn as a great original, but the terms of his conception are pointedly unconventional. The originality of his Haydn is not to be measured by formal innovations in a progressive narrative of music history – the measure adopted by Pohl and his forbears. Tovey pooh-poohs the very idea of such a narrative, except in an epochal sense; for him, once music itself had reached a point of maturity, essentially with J. S. Bach, it could only change, not progress, at the highest level of accomplishment. From this standpoint, Pohl's summing up of Haydn's significance is vacuous, not to mention being uncomfortably close to damning with faint praise: "When we consider the poor condition in which he found certain important departments of music . . . it is impossible to over-rate [Haydn's] creative powers."[8]

In 1880 (just a year after the first edition of *Grove*), in his famous essay "The Study of Poetry," Matthew Arnold had severely chastised this historicist attitude as inconsistent with the work of building a literary canon. A half-century later, Tovey took the same line with regard to music. His attitude is consistent with the one expounded in a more recent and equally famous literary essay, T. S. Eliot's "Tradition and the individual talent" (1917). Eliot celebrates a general artistic mentality, "the mind of Europe," that constantly undergoes "a development which abandons nothing enroute, which does not superannuate either Shakespeare, or Homer, or the rock drawing of the Magdalenian [Cro-Magnon] draftsmen." Change may bring "refinement, perhaps, complication certainly," but what it does not bring is improvement.[9] Great art exists in a simultaneous cultural order that continually reconstitutes itself as new entries are enshrined in it.

Like Eliot, Tovey regards that order as both immanent and palpable in genuinely original works. He typically claims as much by reversals of chronology, coupled with a claim that Haydn is upstaging a nominally latter-day colleague. The second subject in the finale of the Symphony no. 104, we're told, contains "an impudent prophetic plagiarism of Brahms's cadence-theme" (in the finale of the latter's Symphony no. 2) that is also "an ingenious transformation, not to be outdone by Wagner or Liszt, of the features of the main theme."[10] And the slow movement of the Symphony no. 88 ends with "a coda in which Brahms's ninth symphony retires into a heaven where Brahms, accompanied by his faithful red hedgehog [*Der Rote Igel*, Brahms's favorite restaurant], can discuss it with Haydn, Beethoven, and Schubert over a dinner cooked by Maitre du Clavecin Couperin and washed down by the best Bach."[11] This dinner-party fantasy is admittedly troubling from a latter-day perspective; it's too smug, too clubby – no women or other lesser mortals admitted. But its emphasis, and no doubt its intention, is elsewhere. Its image of genius as conviviality is both a witty way to affirm the non-progressive character of artistic accomplishment and to debunk the convention of dealing with great artists in tones of wide-eyed piety. The ultimate point of reference is a much earlier compound of whimsy, conviviality, and wisdom: Plato's *Symposium.*

In one key respect, however, Tovey differs from Eliot. Where Eliot posits a thorough historical awareness as the precondition of original creation, Tovey traces originality to a sturdy independence of mind that allows the artist to free himself from history and concentrate on the demands of the artistic material. "The truth is," he says (and means it!), "that great artists always . . . invent everything, and that it does not in the least matter which of them invented anything first."[12] Thus he can say with a straight face, and so often that it turns from a leitmotif to a mannerism, that this or that recapitulation in the first movement of a Haydn symphony is one of Beethoven's best codas.

Perhaps Tovey overuses this trope because it encapsulates his understanding of Haydn's originality so well. There is a story behind it, one that can be gleaned by piecing together remarks scattered across essays on several of the symphonies.

The story begins with Johann Christian and Carl Philipp Emanuel Bach. Tovey regards them as the masters of Haydn's early style, much to its detriment. This style, he says, is "his most nearly regular," and "of a roughness that removes every vestige of interest from questions of detail."[13] Though inclined to remain cryptic on this point, as if not wanting to malign his hero, Tovey implies that the regularity and the roughness fed on each other; where music is regular, wit has little need to trouble itself. Between Haydn's "earliest" and his "mature" styles lies a "vast gap," which the "middle style" after 1771 diminished but could not bridge. Instead, Haydn abruptly jumped the gap as a result of his encounter with Mozart, the effect of which was "to set him free, so that his large movements became as capricious in their extended course of events as his minuets had always been in the cast of their phrases."[14] Mozart thus awakened the originality only latent in those quirky minuets. True originality does not belong to Tovey's Haydn in general, but only to the "mature" Haydn who sprang forth fully formed from the meeting of creative spirits – "one of the best-known wonders of musical history" – in the 1780s.

This Haydn inherits the identification of freedom with caprice that defines his sense of form, not from past precedent, but from the possibility of an unprecedented future. When Tovey says that Haydn writes Beethoven's codas, more is involved than an impish rhetoric that siphons Beethoven's large reservoir of prestige in Haydn's direction, and far more than the underlying technical claim that Haydn's so-called recapitulations, unlike Mozart's and Beethoven's, are typically irregular in the manner made familiar by Beethoven's codas. The trope locates the mature Haydn in a nonlinear mode of creative time that is always one step ahead of itself and two steps ahead of the listener: "Haydn is well aware of all [available] possibilities; and he always uses the one you did not expect."[15] He does so, moreover, with an effect that is as much ethical as it is aesthetic: "the life his themes live is one that has no room for meanness or triviality. This is great music; and nothing other than great music, whether tragic, majestic, or comic, can stand beside it."[16]

The progressive historical scheme of Pohl and others seems very remote from this account, but it has not quite vanished. Tovey has relocated it within the independent course of Haydn's career, which takes the shape of a sudden emergence from the cocoon of a younger, more conventional self. This emergence does far more than license Haydn's unconventional side; it makes him the very embodiment of constructive unconventionality. Haydn's genius seizes on a historical accident – the phenomenon of Mozart – to free itself from history. In that freedom lies his originality, and vice versa.

With freedom we come to the second leading trait of Tovey's Haydn, and also to a leading theme in the work of his most influential contemporary. Tovey never mentions Immanuel Kant in relation to Haydn (whom he likes to brush clean of dusty book-learning), but his representation of Haydn as a free imaginative agent is thoroughly Kantian. Both the terms that constitute Haydn's aesthetic freedom and the exemplary relation between that freedom and human freedom generally regarded could have come straight from the pages of Kant's *Critique of Judgment* (1790).

Briefly and (of course) inadequately: Kant regards art as the product of genius, which he understands as the faculty of combining imagination and understanding while leaving the imagination free. By finding the means to communicate the effects of this combination, the artist as genius also frees the imagination of others. Indeed, a communication between one freedom and another is the basis of art in general: the artist replicates the productive power of nature without being fettered by nature, and one artist finds in the example of another – as in the mutual influence of Mozart and Haydn – the substance of his own originality.

For Kant, as for many eighteenth-century writers, this circulatory system of freedoms expressed itself as an independence from rules:

> the product of a genius . . . is an example that is meant not to be imitated, but to be followed by another genius. (For in mere imitation the element of genius in the work – what constitutes its spirit – would be lost.) The other genius, who follows the example, is aroused by it to a feeling of his own originality, which allows him to exercise in art his freedom from the constraint of rules, and to do so in such a way that art itself acquires a new rule by this . . . [and] gives rise to a school for other good minds.[17]

This is not to say that rules are simply repudiated on behalf of a creative furor; the rules are played with, played on, skirted, outfoxed, anything but fetishized. By fostering an intelligent liberation from rules (which is close, for Kant, to saying: by fostering Enlightenment), art becomes the school of spirit.

Tovey's Haydn is proof of Kant's point: he is the very embodiment of art's liberating mentorship. His music is exemplary in its defiance of the symmetry and regularity so often ascribed to it; each of his mature works "has a form of its own which constantly upsets the orthodoxies of text-books."[18] This freedom of form "makes it necessary for us to anathematize our text-book knowledge before we can listen to Haydn with ears naively attuned to his note."[19] For Tovey to say so, of course, was itself not entirely unorthodox. Pohl, for one, had said so, remarking that Haydn "was no pedant with regard to rules, and would acknowledge no restrictions on genius" – the genius in question being, as usual, Mozart's.[20] Haydn himself had said so, in a statement quoted by Pohl: "Art is free, and should not be fettered by . . . mechanical restrictions. The educated ear is the sole authority on all these questions, and I think I have as much right to lay down the law as anyone."[21] But Tovey's Haydn does not lay down the law; he flaunts it. And he flaunts it so skillfully that the law (being, proverbially, an ass) does not even realize that it's been flaunted. This Haydn, retrospective construction though he may be, is the prototypical Kantian artist for whom not rules, but the manner in which genius plays with and against them, is the cardinal point: one freedom imitating another.[22]

For Tovey, the measure of this freedom is sonata form, which he never tires of telling us is fundamentally inapplicable to Haydn's music. At most it is present ironically or in ruins. "The orthodox theory of sonata form," he says, applies "fairly well" to Mozart and Beethoven, though only with some elaborate qualifications, but "for most of the mature works of Haydn this account simply will not do."[23] "Haydn's freedom and unconventionality will complicate the analysis of any of his mature works."[24] "This Symphony [no. 99] conforms just closely enough to the orthodox scheme of sonata form to make that scheme a guide that can only divert our attention from its most important points."[25] "When you come to look at it, you find not only that all the rules of form as observed by both Mozart and Beethoven are frequently violated by Haydn, but that they are so seldom observed that it would be quite impossible to infer them from his mature practice at all."[26] Poor Mozart and Beethoven at times come out sounding like hacks.

Unlike Kant's, Tovey's attitude toward rules is openly hostile; he writes not with the detachment of the philosopher but with the bite of the satirist. Yet as with satire at its most serious, the critical energy that he celebrates and imitates is only the inverse of an affirmative ideal. And as in Kant, this ideal is a concept of human freedom embodied by art but never confined by it. Tovey, accordingly, will sometimes abruptly doff his antic disposition and write with grave eloquence, nowhere more revealingly than in a comment on the slow movement of the Symphony no. 99: "this adagio is typical of that greatness in Haydn which moved Cherubini to tears, and of that freedom which taught Beethoven's inmost soul more than he, the uncouth pupil, could learn from Haydn the tired teacher."[27] No pedagogy, except a transcendental pedagogy; no social mannerism at all: just one freedom imitating another, in the communicative intimacy that is one of Kant's definitions of spirit.

This turn from the critical to the affirmative can serve to introduce the last leading trait of Tovey's Haydn. Since the key element in this trait is a higher-order, transformative playfulness, the turn might also be said to embrace a movement from Kant to Schiller, with the latter's concept of a "play drive" as the basis of aesthetic education and its social benefits.[28] But Tovey's concept is more neoclassical than that, linked more to the eighteenth-century contexts of Kantian aesthetics than to their nineteenth-century offshoots. The playfulness of Tovey's Haydn is the work of wit in the large eighteenth-century sense. It absorbs the elements of freedom and originality and gives them their ultimate rationale both aesthetic and cultural.

Play is the category through which the construction of Tovey's Haydn most often becomes musically explicit in an analytical sense. Although his usage is quite variable, Tovey's comments on the higher-order play in Haydn's symphonies tend to focus on the finales, which he seems generally to regard as transformative where the first movements are quirky or whimsical. The first movements tend to embody the critical energy of a heterodox, independent, anti-conventional spirit; the finales more often represent that spirit in purely affirmative, animating, pleasure-giving mode.

Tovey's favorite way of highlighting the transformative character of Haydn's playfulness is to invoke a little fable involving the two animals named in my title. The amiable, gamboling, seemingly innocent and harmless melodies with which many of the finales begin constitute Haydn's kittens. Similar feline creatures are also said to inhabit the slow introductions of Symphonies nos. 92 and 100, where they give unwary listeners the impression that nothing much is about to happen. Tovey values his kittens as little nubs of unsocialized energy that the convention-bound listener thinks of as charming because – being weak as kittens – they pose no obvious threat. But these themes only play at being weak; Haydn's kittens tend to scratch and pounce:

> The introduction [to Symphony no. 92] was undoubtedly in some former incarnation a saintly tabby cat whom Thoth or Ra (or whatever deity is in charge of cats) has elevated to the heavens of Haydn's imagination. My first [musical example] gives its transition from the fireside to the outside world. The allegro spiritoso, having thus begun as if butter would not melt in its mouth, promptly goes off with a bang, and works up the two principal figures (a) and (b) of its theme into a movement so spacious and full of surprises that it might well seem to be among the longest Haydn ever wrote. In fact it is among his shortest.[29]

As usual, Tovey's archness contains a serious implication. The historically accurate invocation of the sacralization of cats in ancient Egypt, together with the suggestion of an esoteric wisdom not available to the uninitiated (but perhaps available to Rosicrucians or Masons or members of other secret societies popular during the Enlightenment), alerts the reader to the principled deception that for Tovey forms the root of Haydn's art. Absolutely nothing is what it seems to be at first. The truth resides in the deception, from which truth eventually appears in the form of a surprise. And the same principle applies to Tovey's critical prose, which once again emulates Haydn's technique of clothing insight in motley.

On two occasions, moreover, we discover that the principle applies yet again to Haydn's kittens, which do not grow up to become housecats: "The finale [of Symphony no. 100] begins with one of those themes which we are apt to take for a kitten until Haydn shows that it is a promising young tiger";[30] "The finale [of Symphony no. 102] begins with one of Haydn's best themes of the kittenish type. Young tigers are also very charming as kittens, and this finale has powerful muscles with which to make its spring."[31] Both of these statements introduce longish analytical descriptions giving the effects of breadth, high energy, and mercurial change, the very stuff of self-delighting self-transformation, their formal underpinnings.

What shall we say of this tiger, who lurks behind Tovey's descriptions of Haydn's kittens even when it does not spring by name? The image suggests danger and adventure, of course, and perhaps empire (it's surely a Bengal); Haydn's tiger lives in the forest or jungle, not the zoo. And the image projects a fusion of grace and power that, like Haydn's originality, is unique to the creature and, like Haydn's freedom, roams unafraid and at will across uncharted spaces. Most significantly, perhaps, the tiger suggests a spirit indifferent to the presumed niceties of civilization, a spirit both untamed and untameable that will only glare inexplicably at you if it is caged. Tovey believed that the pedantic wardens of musical scholarship – he called them "noodles" (squishy when wet, brittle when dry) – had caged Haydn all too effectively. His subversive mission was to engineer a jailbreak.

Tovey's tiger is closely akin to the Tyger of Haydn's contemporary William Blake, at least on one reading of that notoriously ambiguous cat:

> Tyger, Tyger, burning bright
> In the forests of the night;
> What immortal hand or eye,
> Could frame thy fearful symmetry?
>
> In what distant deeps or skies
> Burnt the fire of thine eyes!
> On what wings dare he aspire?
> What the hand, dare seize the fire?[32]
>
> (1–8)

Like the Tyger, the tiger into which Haydn's kitten grows up is an emblem rooted in two great British literary traditions, traditions that eighteenth-century figures such as Pope and Jonathan Swift had brought together when one was old and the other still new. The old one was a genre, satire; the new one was a quality, the sublime.

On one hand, Tovey's Haydn has the moral and social force claimed for their own by the great British satirists from John Dryden to Samuel Johnson. The forests of the night in which he roams are dark with ignorance, repressiveness, officiousness, and sheer stupidity; he lights up these dark tracts by burning bright with wit, invention, and a reasoned irreverence that intimates the fundamental irreverence of reason itself. On the other hand, Tovey's Haydn has the spiritual and visionary force claimed for their own by poets of the sublime such as Blake and William Wordsworth. The forests of the night that he inhabits are those of cosmic space and time, mystery and majesty, and he lights the way through them by burning bright with the exemplary freedom of the Kantian genius.

Of course these categories overlap; that is part of the point. Like Pope, Tovey's Haydn can raise wit to the level of the sublime:

> Dulness oe'r all possess'd her ancient right,
> Daughter of Chaos and eternal Night . . .
> Laborious, heavy, busy, bold, and blind,
> She rul'd, in native Anarchy, the mind.[33]

Like Wordsworth, he can distill the mind-bending force of the sublime into the form of wit: if the poet traces what is keen, not dull, in him to the "obstinate questionings / Of sense and outward things, / Fallings from us, vanishings" of early childhood, then "The child is father of the man."[34] The tyranny of standard boundaries means nothing to Tovey's Haydn; he skips across or slides beneath them all the time.

Not bound by rule, Tovey's Haydn is no mere rulebreaker; no maker of law, he is no mere outlaw. He is, rather, what the majority of artist-heroes since the eighteenth century were deemed unable to be, some by themselves, some by others. This Haydn is a figure not bound by social constraint yet neither outside the social fabric nor hostile to it. He challenges the pieties of order without fomenting disorder. The kitten is father of the Tyger. Tovey's Haydn is the creative genius as model citizen.

17 Recorded performances: a symphonic study

MELANIE LOWE

Why study recordings of Haydn's symphonies? What can they tell us that the usual sources of music-historical data, i.e., paper documents, cannot? The most obvious answer is that recordings capture a performance, providing evidence of performance practices of the past as well as the present. Recordings are also important documents of reception history and can reveal patterns of consumption, changes in taste, variations of musical meaning, and shifts in the musical qualities essential for the definition of a particular musical work.[1] But since the recording process itself is just as much a performance as the activity of the musicians, a study of recordings is also a study of technology. In addition to preserving musical practices, recording inspires them, profoundly altering our musical values.

The ontology of recording

In studying recorded performances, the ontology of a recording is of vital importance. As a historical document, a recording offers a unique portal to a particular moment in the performance history of a musical composition. But the conceptual separation of the recording from the recorded musical object is crucial, for a recording of a Haydn symphony is not simply a recording of Haydn's music. Neither is it a recording of a single performance of a symphony by a particular conductor and orchestra. Also recorded are the acoustics of the hall or studio, the unique properties of the equipment used to make the recording, the placement of the microphones, and the sound of the storage medium itself. Once we enter the era of magnetic tape, we are likely not hearing a single performance but several spliced together – the best moments of several takes. Neither are we necessarily hearing the acoustics of the hall or studio, for the addition of electronic reverberation can easily alter the "size," "shape," and "material" of the recording space. Today, with digital sound processing, it's even possible to speed up or slow down passages, alter pitch independent of tempo, and perform myriad other effects of which a listener, when hearing the recording, might be completely unaware.

The process of recording, whether onto wax cylinders or the latest digital media, is the artistic representation, not acoustic reproduction, of a sound source. Construed as representation, recorded sound is "simultaneously capable of misrepresentation."[2] Ironically, as technological advances increasingly "silence" the recording and playback media, thereby bolstering the illusion that we hear if not an actual performance a faithful reproduction of one, the interpretive possibilities within the recording process increase. As we shall see, the most significant shift in the recorded history of Haydn's symphonies – from the capturing of a musical performance to the rendering of a musical text – rests on this sleight of sound.

A brief history of Haydn symphony recordings

Before the advent of electric recording in 1925, vocal and instrumental soloists provided the bulk of the classical repertory available on cylinders and shellac discs, for the complication of getting the sound of many instruments at once into recording horns set obvious limitations on the types of music that could be recorded with any facility. Still, there are some very early acoustical recordings of Haydn's symphonic music. In 1912, for example, the Victor Concert Orchestra, essentially a small band of string and brass instruments, recorded abridged versions of the finale and second movement of Haydn's Symphony no. 94. But it wasn't until the invention of microphones made the recording of larger ensembles more feasible that any of Haydn's symphonies were recorded intact by full symphony orchestras.

Between the late 1920s and the mid-1940s prominent conductors led major international orchestras in recordings mostly of Haydn's named symphonies (see list of recorded performances for details), a reflection of those works that enjoyed somewhat regular performance in the concert hall. Haydn's greatest champion of the time was Toscanini, whose recordings of at least ten symphonies speak to his estimation of Haydn as an equal to Mozart and Beethoven. Reviews of early Haydn symphony recordings, however, generally sustain the dominant narrative in Haydn reception – that cliché born early in the nineteenth century that Haydn, while enjoyable and pleasant enough, was a mere forerunner to Mozart and Beethoven. One reads, for example, in the July 1933 *Gramophone* that Haydn's "Military" Symphony "looks well forward to Beethoven, and shows what a big man Haydn could be when he wanted";[3] and in the January 1940 *Gramophone* that certain effects in Symphony no. 80 "bring Haydn into such close terms of intimacy, when one does not ask the world's weight of Wagner's woe or the dark demonism of Mozart's soul-in-danger."[4]

The late 1940s saw two major developments that would spark a decided increase in the recording of Haydn's symphonies. The introduction in 1948 of the $33\frac{1}{3}$ rpm long-playing record made possible the storage of a complete symphony on a single disc. This improvement generated a tremendous surge in the recording of large-scale classical works, from symphonies to operas and oratorios. As a result, many of the major conductors and orchestras of the time recorded essentially the same repertory as was available on 78 rpm discs, i.e., the most celebrated symphonies from the two "London" cycles and Symphony no. 88. While the LP offered Haydn increased visibility, the availability of these recordings did little to counter the general assessment of his music as "well-behaved" and proto-Beethovenian.

H. C. Robbins Landon's foundation of the not-for-profit Haydn Society in 1949, the second major development of the late 1940s, encouraged for the first time the recording of Haydn's earlier and lesser-known symphonies. Between 1950 and 1952 the Society issued recordings of thirty symphonies, the great majority of them obscure works. More "affordable" musicians were contracted but, despite real enthusiasm for Landon's efforts among music-lovers, critics, and scholars, the lack of commercial success precipitated the Society's end in 1952. Although the specialist Haydn Society label could not compete with the big-name conductors recording with the large record companies, there was some sense that Landon's original goal for the society – to record and publish editions and scholarly studies of Haydn's music, particularly the unknown works – had been accomplished with support from record sales revenue. Despite such complaints as the "acid" sound of the woodwinds and tuttis exaggerated by high recording levels, reviews express appreciation for both the availability of these recordings and Landon's scholarly notes. Moreover, they occasionally challenge explicitly the dominant narrative of Haydn reception. The July 1952 *Gramophone*, for example, asserts that "the true greatness of Haydn begins to dawn on the music lover, if he ceases to compare him unfavorably to Mozart."[5]

If Landon's efforts with the Haydn Society did much to advance our awareness and understanding of Haydn's music, Sir Thomas Beecham's recordings of the "London" Symphonies popularized it, particularly the complete "London" cycle he recorded systematically with the Royal Philharmonic Orchestra in 1957–59. For nearly a generation this set became the definitive recording of these works, despite the many textual inaccuracies and "Beecham accretions"[6] we find unacceptable today. But Beecham was a true Haydn enthusiast – "serenely sure that *he* knew what was best for Haydn," as John Barker puts it in the *American Record Guide*.[7] Indeed, one wonders, as Barker does, whether Beecham would have used critical editions had they been available to him.

The 1960s saw the commencement of three attempts to record the complete cycle of Haydn symphonies, enterprises inspired and made possible by Verlag Doblinger and Universal Edition's publication of the conductor's scores, orchestral parts, and critical editions between 1958 and 1965.

Max Goberman and the Vienna State Opera Orchestra issued forty-five Haydn symphonies on Goberman's own label, the Library of Recorded Masterpieces, before his untimely death at the age of fifty-one in 1962 brought the project to a sudden halt. Ernst Märzendorfer led the Vienna Chamber Orchestra to record the whole cycle, but since the series was issued exclusively by the American Musical Heritage Society, its limited availability in the United States and unavailability in Europe have unfortunately left those recordings practically unknown. Not surprisingly, it took a major record company, Decca, to launch the first commercially successful recording of the complete Haydn symphony cycle. Between 1969 and 1973 Antal Doráti, who initiated the Decca project, conducted the Philharmonia Hungarica on what would become not only a surprisingly lucrative series for Decca but also the authoritative (if not definitive) recordings of the Haydn symphonies on the market.

The drive to record the complete Haydn cycle, impossible without the publication of the complete parts, may be linked at least psychologically to World War II, for as John Butt suggests, "the burgeoning of authoritative collected editions from 1950 [came] in the wake of a war that had threatened to destroy virtually all the manuscript sources of western music."[8] The music-loving and record-buying public, however, was considerably less interested in such projects of preservation, at least in Haydn's case. Few listeners valued Haydn's early and middle symphonies as much as the later ones, with the exception of the "romantic" "Sturm und Drang" symphonies. Corresponding neatly to the familiar narrative of an artist's maturity, the May 1969 *Gramophone* complains that Symphonies nos. 1–3 have "not a great deal to offer musically": "no one would dream of playing [no. 2] if it were attributed to one of Haydn's contemporaries."[9] Likewise, the sense that later is better rings clear in the January 1971 *Gramophone* review of Dorati's recordings: the author, while clearly aware that the traditional numbering of Haydn's symphonies is not an exact chronology, nonetheless finds that Symphonies nos. 57–64 come not "so near as the previous set [nos. 65–72] to the threshold of Haydn's complete mastery."[10] Luckily for such listeners, during this era of "completist" urges the perennially popular named symphonies continued to be recorded on major labels by the world's leading orchestras. Further, in a "completist" gesture, perhaps, many conductors took on all twelve symphonies of the two "London" cycles.

The eruption of enthusiasm for "historically informed performance" on period instruments, led by musicians active in Britain's lively early-music scene, generated another wave of Haydn symphony recording projects in the 1980s and 1990s. In addition to several recordings of the "Sturm und Drang," "Paris," and "London" symphonies, four more attempts to record the complete Haydn symphony cycle were launched (by Solomons, Goodman, Hogwood, and Weil), all on period instruments. But despite tremendous critical acclaim and much interest (at the time, anyway) from consumers, all four projects were deemed commercially unviable by the record companies and eventually cancelled before completion. A consolation prize may be found, however, in the reviews of these recordings. Perhaps a result of hearing this music performed by ensembles more appropriate in size and sound, the traditional narratives that have dominated Haydn reception for nearly two centuries seem to be abating. In the 1992 *Fanfare*, for instance, we read that "the embryonic essays of the first five symphonies are evidence of Haydn's already sophisticated creative personality at the time he joined Count Morzin's household staff";[11] and, more to the point, that Haydn is not "Mozart without the tunes or Beethoven without the rhetoric" but rather "a master of musical syntax at least as great as his two more popular contemporaries."[12]

While the early-music scene generated much excitement for Haydn's symphonies – particularly the lesser-known ones – during the last decades of the twentieth century, the major international orchestras continued to record Haydn's more celebrated works. But a steady stream of recordings by chamber orchestras offered alternative performances – compromise positions, perhaps, between the period-instrument and "big orchestra" performances. Among them is the most significant commercial challenge to the four attempted period-instrument cycles: Adam Fischer's Austro-Hungarian Haydn Orchestra who, in 2001, completed a fourteen-year project to record the complete Haydn symphony cycle in the Haydnsaal of the Esterházy palace in Eisenstadt.

Performance practices

While it is not possible in the present context to undertake a comprehensive investigation of instrumental performance practices heard in nearly a century of recorded Haydn, there are some broad trends that are worth noting, for they suggest significant changes in the interpretation of Haydn's symphonies during the twentieth century. Moreover, by recognizing recording as artistic representation and not simply acoustic reproduction we can observe the tremendous influence the recording process itself has exerted on performance practice.

First, the selection of which Haydn symphony to record reveals much about what Haydn means to listeners and players alike. Before 1950 conductors recorded primarily works in the current concert repertory, and for Haydn that meant a handful of the late symphonies. Even after awareness and appreciation of Haydn's other symphonies increased later in the century, celebrated conductors and major international orchestras still continued to record basically the same late works, only more of them. This preference for Haydn's late symphonies by both the recording industry and the "mainstream" classical music culture (and, of course, one sustains the other here) aligns with and reinforces the dominant narrative of Haydn reception: the named symphonies of the two "London" cycles still remain the performed and recorded favorites, tacitly sustaining Haydn's status as Beethoven's old-fashioned but noteworthy predecessor.

Among specific performance practices heard in Haydn symphony recordings, differences in tempo are the most manifest. If we compare in order recordings of Symphony no. 94 by several conductors – say, Horenstein (1929), Scherchen (1950), Beecham (1957–58), Monteux (1959), Doráti (1972), Hogwood (1984), and Kuijken (1992) – we notice a decided decrease in flexibility of tempo from one recording to the next. In the slow introduction to the first movement, for example, nearly all of these conductors enjoy a certain degree of tempo rubato, slight accelerando with the building harmonic intensity in mm. 7–15, and stretching of the first violin line in the final two measures. But where Horenstein's rhythmic interpretation is quite elastic, Beecham's, Scherchen's, and Monteux's are less so. Doráti and Hogwood keep the rhythmic values relatively precise but still raise the pulse slightly in the second period. Kuijken's beat is metronomic, however, his only deviation a slight ritardando in the final two measures.

The variability of tempo in the exposition likewise supports a general trend toward an increasingly steady pulse. Horenstein's tempo varies from ♩. = 76 to ♩. = 96, often fluctuating widely in the space of only a few measures, while Kuijken's exposition holds steady at ♩. = 86 throughout. And yet, in casting a slightly wider net we also find that the tempo in Koussevitzky's recording from 1929, the same year as Horenstein's, is hardly more volatile than in Toscanini's breakneck performance from 1953, a surprising detail since Toscanini actively resisted the post-Romantic tradition of flexible tempo.[13] Similarly, Hogwood's tempo, while admittedly more steady throughout, drops at the second theme just as much as Monteux's (from ♩. = 96 to ♩. = 92). But despite these exceptions, seven decades of recorded performances of Haydn's Symphony no. 94 reveal an increasing preference for a fairly steady tempo, suggesting control, clarity, and evenness of expression as musical values that rise in importance as the twentieth century progresses.

The waning use of portamento neatly aligns with an increasing sensitivity to rhythmic precision. Of course, we must take into consideration that on earlier recordings, because orchestras generally lacked the rehearsal time to secure the unanimity of bowing, phrasing, and overall style of playing we have come to expect from today's orchestras, we are hearing only what enough players in a section do to make the effect audible. But in certain conspicuous spots in recordings of Haydn's symphonies the portamento is pronounced enough to suggest, if not necessarily coordinated practice, a certain tacit agreement of desired style and effect. The slur over the first violin line in m. 81 of the first movement of Symphony no. 94 and the parallel point lacking a slur in m. 88 provide two such choice moments. As might be expected, our two earliest recordings, Horenstein's and Koussevitzky's from 1929, enjoy huge slides at m. 81 and pronounced if somewhat smaller ones at m. 88. On Beecham's, Toscanini's, Scherchen's, and Monteux's recordings from the 1950s, the violins likewise play with portamento at both places – Toscanini's and Monteux's sounding the heaviest among the four, Scherchen's the least emphatic. Excepting the slight portamento heard on Jochum's recording from 1972, Bernstein's from 1985, and Hogwood's from 1984, none of the recordings from the 1960s onwards use any noticeable portamento in either measure. In postwar performance practice rhythmic precision becomes imperative.

Along with diminished flexibility of tempo and less frequent use of portamento, it has been suggested that the fast maximum tempos[14] heard on early recordings were acceptable precisely because musicians and audiences of the time did not expect the degree of meticulousness in rhythm and articulation that later musicians and audiences came to demand; likewise, the slower maximum tempos heard in post-war and later recordings suggest a modern preference for exact rhythms and careful articulation.[15] But a comparison of maximum tempos heard on the recordings of Haydn's Symphony no. 94 listed above in fact reveals no clear trend from faster to slower. To be sure, Koussevitzky's 1929 recording just flies – the tempo in the Vivace assai varies between ♩. = 100–112 – and the tempo in most recordings from the last quarter of the twentieth century sits between ♩. = 88–92. But then Scherchen's post-war recording from 1950, with a maximum tempo of ♩. = 76, is the slowest of the bunch, while Hogwood's maximum tempo of ♩. = 96 matches Horenstein's top speed recorded fifty-five years earlier. And Toscanini's controversial late recording provides a certain spoiler, for in this case he maintained his reputed predilection for high velocity. While precision and accuracy undoubtedly became key ingredients in modern musical taste, conductors' preferences for faster or slower tempos, at least in the recorded history of Haydn's music, seem less indicative of such a shift in musical values than do other factors in the recording process to be discussed presently.

But before turning our focus to relationships between the recording process and musical values we must briefly address three of the most contentious issues in the performance practice of Haydn's symphonies, for the points are argued as much in recordings as in the scholarly discourse. The first, whether or not to use keyboard continuo, is easily the most hotly debated question.

While we have solid evidence not only that keyboard continuo was used in orchestral performances in England in the late eighteenth century but that Haydn himself shared direction of the twelve "London" Symphonies from the fortepiano with Salomon who led on the violin, nothing so conclusive survives for the earlier symphonies or for other performances over which Haydn would have presided. The case for performance without keyboard continuo, argued most forcefully by James Webster, rests largely on the following points: (1) the Viennese custom was to lead chamber music, as Haydn's symphonies would have been understood at the time, from the violin; (2) anecdotal evidence suggests that Haydn led the Esterházy orchestra from the violin and there is no evidence of a keyboardist employed at the court other than Haydn himself; (3) the sources transmit neither figures in the autographs nor verbal instructions to use a keyboard instrument; in addition, no authentic separate keyboard or continuo parts survive; and (4) stylistic evidence in the music itself, much of which centers on the concertante writing in Symphonies nos. 6, 7, 8 and 45, does not indicate a keyboard obbligato.[16] But counter-arguments exist for each of these points, and have been used to justify the performance of Haydn's symphonies with keyboard continuo: (1) various reports indicate that orchestral music was performed with a keyboard in Vienna, for example the performance of two Haydn symphonies at a Tonkünstler Societät concert directed from the keyboard by Ignaz Umlauf;[17] (2) Haydn's direction from the violin would encroach on virtuoso violinist Luigi Tomasini's position as concertmaster of the Esterházy orchestra; (3) there are no figures in the "London" autographs, symphonies that we know were performed with keyboard, and Haydn, a fine keyboardist, would have been able instantly to realize the continuo part from the autograph scores of his own music; and (4) stylistic evidence suggests that Haydn's early symphonies require keyboard continuo to fill in missing harmonies and to secure orchestral coherence.[18]

While the major international orchestras do not, as a rule, include keyboard continuo when recording Haydn's symphonies, the decision is more or less split among period-instrument conductors. Those on the no-continuo side are Harnoncourt, Brüggen, Hogwood, and Weil; on the continuo side are Solomons, Goodman, Pinnock, and Kuijken. The two positions are argued most emphatically in performance by Hogwood's and Goodman's recorded cycles. Hogwood, following the advice of Webster, musicological consultant for the recording project, omits the continuo from all of the symphonies in the series. Despite the lean scoring, often limited to two- and three-part counterpoint, and the fact that we know nothing about the composition of Haydn's orchestra at the Morzin court, Hogwood dispenses with continuo even in Haydn's earliest symphonies. Goodman, on the other hand, goes to the opposite extreme; his recordings not only include but at times nearly feature the keyboard instrument. His recording of the "Farewell" Symphony asserts the pro-continuo position most strenuously: Goodman leaves the harpsichord at m. 205 of the finale to play the solo first violin part in duet with the bandleader. Where others have found the famous exodus in the "Farewell" confirmation of the keyboard's absence, Goodman argues that his practice of switching instruments some four dozen measures before the end "is yet further evidence that the required presence of Haydn on stage at the end of this symphony did not preclude him from directing at the harpsichord."[19] Hogwood's recordings reveal Haydn's early symphonies as intimate chamber works; Goodman's, on the other hand, assert their orchestral nature with a vengeance. With evidence on both sides of the debate primarily circumstantial, individual taste is perhaps more marked in this performance practice than in any other.

The second hot issue is the size of the orchestra. While we can only surmise that the band of players at the Morzin court was quite small, court records indicate the standard ensemble size and disposition during Haydn's tenure at the Esterházy court. Between 1761 and 1774 the Esterházy orchestra was small but perfectly suited to the private chambers in which Haydn performed his symphonies: strings 3/3/1/1/1, one bassoon, two oboes, and two horns. On occasion, when the music required it, a flute player or an additional pair of horns joined the ensemble. Haydn's orchestra increased after 1774, and by 1781 the standard ensemble included nine or ten violins or violas distributed variously, two cellos, one double bass, one flute, three oboes, three bassoons, and five horns. In performances outside Eszterháza, however, the orchestra was considerably larger. During the seasons that Haydn's "London" Symphonies were premiered, Salomon's orchestra in London numbered about forty players: strings 9/8/4/4/4, a pair each of flutes, oboes, bassoons, horns, and trumpets, and timpani; larger still, the orchestra that performed Haydn's "Paris" Symphonies for the Concert de la Loge Olympique numbered over sixty players; and orchestras performing for the Tonkünstler-Societät in Vienna, on whose concerts Haydn's symphonies were occasionally programmed, topped a hundred players.[20]

Context and venue were the key factors determining the size of the orchestra in Haydn's time. As a general rule, the size of the orchestra matched the size of the performance space; and the same basic principle can be extended to recordings of Haydn's symphonies. The top international orchestras that record Haydn's symphonies on major record labels, aiming for the broadest audience possible, typically retain their full forces. Period-instrument ensembles and chamber orchestras, which tend to court more of a specialist audience and often record on specialty labels (though that label is usually owned by a major label), use fewer players, more like the ensemble for which Haydn would have composed at Eszterháza. Ormandy, for example, conducts the full Philadelphia Orchestra on his Columbia recording of Haydn's "Farewell" Symphony, a work for which Haydn's Esterházy orchestra would have comprised twenty-one players, while Hogwood's Academy of Ancient Music uses Haydn's exact instrumentation for L'Oiseau Lyre. The Academy of St. Martin-in-the-Fields, on the other hand, retains the smaller forces of the chamber orchestra even on their recording of the "Paris" Symphonies for Philips. As in the eighteenth century, the recorded performances of Haydn's symphonies suggest a different mode of reception for ensembles of different sizes: we may luxuriate in the splendor and magnificence of the full Philadelphia sound while we embrace the intimacy and transparency of Hogwood's elegant yet invigorating chamber orchestra.

The third contentious issue is whether to perform Haydn's symphonies on modern or period instruments. For the most part, the orchestras that record Haydn are firmly in one camp or the other: the large, major international orchestras perform on modern instruments while the smaller, specialist chamber orchestras striving for historically informed Haydn perform on period instruments. But certain chamber orchestras – the Academy of St. Martin-in-the-Fields, the Orchestra of St. Luke's, and the Austro-Hungarian Haydn Orchestra among them – perform Haydn's symphonies on modern instruments and, it seems, occasionally feel the need to defend the decision not to use period instruments. Adam Fischer, for one, in the liner notes accompanying his recording of the complete Haydn symphony cycle, explains that "it is an important intention of the Austro-Hungarian Haydn Orchestra to offer an alternative to historic ensembles for eighteenth-century music. Our style is based on this living tradition of Austro-Hungarian music making . . . Some elements of that tradition have already been developed on new instruments, and can be realized better on them."[21] The criticism Fischer attempts to head off is that the performances heard on his recordings, because they do not employ period instruments, are not historically correct – or, to use the loaded term, "authentic." (Hogwood's Haydn cycle, for instance, bills itself as performed "on authentic instruments" rather than the more appropriate "on period instruments." One could infer from such wording that performing Haydn's symphonies on anything but the instruments Haydn himself would have known is somehow bogus.)

Underlying the choice of instrument, like many choices in the performance practice of Haydn's music, is the question of whether one should strive to match an ideal historical model or perform in the manner most appealing to contemporary listeners. To be sure, these two positions are not necessarily at odds – one need look only to the commercial success of many period-instrument ensembles. But they have become polarized in both the journalistic and scholarly press, as the choice of instrument is often pivotal in debates about the nature and limits of musical "authenticity."

"Authenticity," technology, and Haydn's modern listener

There is perhaps no more contentious notion in the performance of "early music" (a category which, in current parlance, has come to include all music composed before the nineteenth century) than "authenticity." In regards to recordings of Haydn's symphonies the term has been used in many ways. Record reviewers in the 1950s and 1960s generally understood "authentic" to refer to a score free of textual corruptions. Of Goberman's recordings that use Landon's critical edition, for example, the May 1962 *American Record Guide* notes that "the aim is to make available the complete 104 Symphonies of Haydn, using authentic texts."[22] This specific use of the term is a response not only to widespread performance from unreliable scores but also to the practice of adding instruments and even special effects to enhance expression. By the 1970s and 1980s, however, "authentic" became associated more with historically informed performance than textual accuracy. The January/February 1982 *Fanfare* review, for instance, reports that Solomons' recordings of the "Morzin" symphonies try to be "as authentic as possible." Comparing Doráti's and Solomons' recordings, the reviewer finds Solomons to have an "advantage in that his ensemble uses eighteenth-century instruments or exact copies and conforms to the performance practices of that time, so that we come as close as is possible to hearing these works as Haydn himself may have heard them."[23] But this is clearly not Adam Fischer's meaning of "authentic" when he writes in 2001 that "a boring performance remains a crime, even if it is historically 'correct' . . . we only play authentically if we reach the same feelings in the listener as the music did two hundred years ago. Since our sense of perception has changed much more than the instruments have, it is really not enough to recreate the sound in order to recreate the emotional effect."[24] Beyond the naive assumption that it is possible even to know, not to mention recreate, the emotional effect eighteenth-century listeners would have experienced when listening to Haydn's music, Fischer's use of the term "authentic" here clearly corroborates Richard Taruskin's estimation of the late twentieth-century usage of the word: it "simply cannot be rid of its moral and ethical overtones (and which always carries its invidious antonym in tow), being used to privilege one philosophy of performance over all others."[25]

The concurrence of "authentic" performance and certain advances in recording technology suggests a paradigm shift in our conception of just what a recording of a Haydn symphony should be. As Taruskin, Laurence Dreyfus, and others have argued, historical performance is a thoroughly *modern* invention. Its various styles align with modern taste and embrace such modern values as objectivity and authority while "shocking," at least in the early years of the movement, audiences expecting a "traditional" (i.e., big orchestra, modern instruments) performance.[26] Further, the ambition of an "authentic," historically informed recording is to present untainted the composer's "true" text – a Haydn symphony exactly as Haydn would have known it. Hogwood, for one, while asserting that "a recording should not be a mere imitation of one performance at a particular moment in the past," nonetheless admits that "it's fascinating to work out what would have been the precise sound of Haydn's orchestra."[27] Indeed, by taking Haydn's articulations at face value, respecting evidence from mechanical clocks and metronome marks, and following scholarly advice on other matters of performance practice including ensemble size, composition, and positioning, the precise sound of Haydn's orchestra is just the sound he attempts to recreate. But without innovations in recording technology, a "precise" rendition of Haydn's text (however spurious the notion in and of itself) would be nearly impossible to achieve. Beyond assuring the audibility of divided instrumental sections or manufacturing a historical (or hypothetical) room's acoustics etc., the ability to combine the best moments of various takes into a single whole recording is essential when rendering a true and accurate text is the first priority.

But the historical performance movement is in fact only the most recent manifestation of this modern concern for the authority of the text within the realm of recorded classical music. The conception of a recording as a musical text was enabled, if not inspired by, arguably the most significant technological innovation in the art of recording: magnetic tape. While the medium of magnetic tape had been developed decades earlier, it wasn't until the 1950s that recording studios adopted editable tape for making master recordings, thereby allowing for easy editing and manipulation of the recorded object. Prior to the widespread use of tape for masters, musical works were recorded either uninterrupted or in four- to five-minute segments; a single take was then selected for the record. Recording sessions thus had much in common with live performance. As Robert Philip notes, early recordings "have a sense of being 'put across,' so that the precision and clarity of each note is less important than the shape and progress of the music as a whole. They are intended to convey what *happens* in the music, to characterize it. The accurate reproduction of the musical text is merely a means to this end."[28] But once masters became compiled from numerous takes of varying duration, and especially once digital technology facilitated editing in or out of even a single note, the activity and psychology of the recording studio changed dramatically. The lack of an audience and the reliance on editing relieves performers from ever having to execute a complete performance. As Philip puts it, "the overwhelming priority is to get each section *right* at least once."[29] The result, then, is not a performance of a piece of music but the rendering of a musical text.

A crucial shift in listener reception follows, one that situates the listener of a recording even further from a performance of the work recorded. As Walter Benjamin observed regarding film,

> the camera that presents the performance of the film actor to the public need not respect the performance as an integral whole. Guided by the cameraman, the camera continually changes its position with respect to the performance. The sequence of positional views which the editor composes from the material supplied him constitutes the completed film. It comprises certain factors of movement which are in reality those of the camera . . . The audience's identification with the actor is really an identification with the camera.[30]

Substitute microphones for cameras, and so it is with a musical recording. Instead of hearing an intact performance from a single listener's orientation, we hear a compilation of numerous takes, the placement of the microphones, subsequent rebalancing, additional reverberation, etc. – in short, what the technology *allows* us to hear and, more importantly, what the engineers, producers, and editors guiding that technology *want* us to hear. To listen to a recording of a Haydn symphony is to experience a collaborative artistic representation of the musical work: the musical performance is both practically and conceptually displaced by technological performance.

Selected recorded performances

Conductor, orchestra, and year of recording

Complete Haydn symphony cycle

Ernst Märzendorfer	Vienna Chamber Orchestra	1960s
Antal Doráti	Philharmonia Hungarica	1960s–70s
Adam Fischer	Austro-Hungarian Orchestra	1980s–2000s

Complete Haydn symphony cycle attempts

Max Goberman	Vienna State Opera Orchestra	1960s
Derek Solomons	L'Estro Armonico	1980s
Bruno Weil	Tafelmusik	1990s
Christopher Hogwood	Academy of Ancient Music	1980s–90s
Roy Goodman	Hanover Band	1990s

Complete "London" cycles

Sir Thomas Beecham	Royal Philharmonic Orchestra	1957–59
Hermann Scherchen	Vienna Symphony Orcheestra	1950s
Leonard Bernstein	New York Philharmonic	1958, 62, 70–75
Leslie Jones	Little Orchestra of London	1960s
Eugene Jochum	London Philharmonic Orchestra	1971–73
Sir Colin Davis	Concertgebouw Orchestra	1970s–81
Sir Georg Solti	London Philharmonic Orchestra	1980s–1991
Herbert von Karajan	Berlin Philharmonic	1970s–80s
Jeffrey Tate	English Chamber Orchestra	1980s
Nikolaus Harnoncourt	Concertgebouw Orchestra	1980s–90s
Leonard Slatkin	Philharmonia Orchestra	1993–94
Frans Brüggen	Orchestra of the 18th Century	1987–91

First "London" cycle

George Szell	Cleveland Orchestra	1950s–60s
Antonio de Almeida	Symphony Orchestra of Rome	1970s
Sigiswald Kuijken	La Petite Bande	1992–93

Complete "Paris" cycle

Leslie Jones	Little Orchestra of London	1960s
Denis Vaughan	Naples Orchestra	1967
Yehudi Menuhin	Menuhin Festival Orchestra	1970s
Sir Neville Marriner	Academy of St. Martin-in-the-Fields	1975, 77, 81
Herbert von Karajan	Berlin Philharmonic	1980s
Sigiswald Kuijken	Orchestra of the Age of Enlightenment	1980s
Sir Colin Davis	Concertgebouw Orchestra	1980s
Frans Brüggen	Orchestra of the 18th Century	1980s
Daniel Barenboim	English Chamber Orchestra	1974
Hugh Wolff	St. Paul Chamber Orchestra	1990–91

Symphony no. 45

Erich Leinsdorf	Metropolitan Symphony Orchestra	1940s
Hermann Scherchen	Vienna State Opera Orchestra	1950s
Pablo Casals	Orchestra of Festival Casals de Puerto Rico	1959
Leslie Jones	Little Orchestra of London	1960s
Antal Doráti	London Symphony Orchestra	1960s
Antonio Janigro	Symphony Orchestra of Radio Zagreb	1960s
Jerzy Maksymiuk	Polish Chamber Orchestra	1977–79
Sir Charles Mackerras	Orchestra of St. Luke's	1988
Trevor Pinnock	English Concert	1989
Nikolaus Harnoncourt	Concentus Musikus Wien	1988

Symphony no. 94

	Victor Concert Orchestra	1912
Jascha Horenstein	Berlin Philharmonic Orchestra	1929
Serge Koussevitzky	Boston Symphony Orchestra	1929–40
Eduard van Beinum	Concertgebouw Orchestra	1940s
Henry Swoboda	Netherlands Philharmonic Orchestra	1940s?
F. Lehmann	Berlin Philharmonic Orchestra	1940s?
Sir Malcolm Sargent	Liverpool Philharmonic Orchestra	1948
Hermann Scherchen	Vienna Oper Orchestra	<1950
Wilhelm Furtwängler	Vienna Philharmonic Orchestra	1951?
Arturo Toscanini	NBC Orchestra	1953
Erich Leinsdorf	Rochester Philharmonic Orchestra	<1955
Hans Schmidt-Isserstedt	Northwest German Radio Orchestra	<1956
Kurt Graunke	Bayerische Staatsorchester	1957
Josef Krips	Vienna Philharmonic Orchestra	1959
Willliam Steinberg	Pittsburg Symphony Orchestra	1959
Pierre Monteux	Vienna Philharmonic Orchestra	<1960
Karl Richter	Berlin Philharmonic Orchestra	1962
Leopold Ludwig	North German Radio Orchestra	1964
Alfred Scholz	Bamberg Symphony Orchestra	1976
Sir Neville Marriner	Academy of St. Martin-in-the-Fields	1976
Christopher Hogwood	Academy of Ancient Music	1980
Leonard Bernstein	Vienna Philharmonic Orchestra	1984

Notes

1 Haydn's career and the idea of the multiple audience

1 Letter of March 29, 1789; *Briefe*, 202: "Übersende die 3te Sonate [*recte* Trio, Hob. XV: 13], welche ich also nach Ihrem Geschmack mit Variazionen ganz neu verfertigt." H. C. Robbins Landon translates this as "newly rewritten with variations," but this seems implausible (*CCLN*, 82).

2 *Briefe*, 202; the terms Capriccio and Fantasia were sometimes used interchangeably, though possibly Haydn used the former to remind Artaria of his previous publication. Presumably by "besonderer Ausarbeitung" Haydn meant the unusual structure of the work, "Ausarbeitung" being a rhetorical term sometimes meaning working-out, sometimes meaning the figural details once the structure is set; see the diagram of the piece in Elaine R. Sisman, "Haydn's solo keyboard music," in Robert L. Marshall (ed.), *Eighteenth-Century Keyboard Music* (New York: Schirmer, 1994; 2nd ed., 2003), 294.

3 Johann Ferdinand von Schönfeld, *Jahrbuch der Tonkunst von Wien und Prag* (1796), facs. ed. Otto Biba (Munich and Salzburg, 1976); portions trans. Kathrine Talbot in Elaine Sisman (ed.), *Haydn and His World* (Princeton: Princeton University Press, 1997), 289–320.

4 See the extensive mapping of these and other related terms in Erich Reimer's article "Kenner – Liebhaber – Dilettant," in Hans Heinrich Eggebrecht (ed.), *Handwörterbuch der musikalischen Terminologie* (Wiesbaden: F. Steiner, 1974), as well as Katalin Komlós, *Fortepianos and Their Music* (Oxford: Oxford University Press, 1995), chap. 9.

5 When Triest uses "half-connoisseurs," he intends a put-down of those who slavishly look to the true connoisseurs in order to follow their judgments. Johann Karl Friedrich Triest, "Remarks on the development of the art of music in Germany in the eighteenth century," trans. Susan Gillespie, in Sisman (ed.), *Haydn and His World*, 321–94, at 345–46 (especially: "The half-connoisseurs, as usual, followed the opinion of the connoisseurs. They secretly disliked [C. P. E.] Bach's works, which they found dark and difficult."). The essay was originally serialized in the *Allgemeine musikalische Zeitung* 3 (Jan 1–March 25, 1801), nos. 14–19 and 22–26.

6 Griesinger, 14; trans. modified from Gotwals, 12.

7 The flap over Artaria's "premature" announcement of the reasonably priced publication of Op. 33 while Haydn was still trying to fulfill his expensive subscription orders (Haydn's solicitation letters to Lavater and others were dated December 3, 1781, and Artaria's advertisement was placed in the *Wiener Zeitung* on December 29) caused Haydn deep embarrassment, and it was in that context that Swieten gave Haydn "distinctly to understand that in future I should dedicate my compositions directly to the public," as Haydn told Artaria in a letter the publisher received on July 27, 1782 (Landon II, 464).

8 Johann Georg Sulzer, *Allgemeine Theorie der schönen Künste* (Leipzig, 1771–74), s.v. "Kammermusik": "Da die Kammermusik für Kenner und Liebhaber ist, so können die Stücke gelehrter und künstlicher gesetzt sein als die zum öffentlichen Gebrauch bestimmt sind, wo alles mehr einfache und cantabel sein muss, damit jedermann es fasse."

9 To Griesinger, Haydn deplored the tendency of new composers not to explore a single idea, but rather to "string out one little idea after another, . . . break off when they have hardly begun, and nothing remains in the heart when one has listened to it." Griesinger, 114; Gotwals, 61.

10 Griesinger, 24; trans. modified from Gotwals, 17.

11 See the listing in the Esterházy invertory *c.*1740 in János Hárich, "Inventare der Esterházy-Hofkapelle in Eisenstadt," *HYB* 9 (1975), 5–125, at 46: item B.20, listing the parts (Violino Princ: with 2 vns, va, basso and organo) for twelve concertos.

12 I refer to the Auenbrugger sonatas; the Lieder responding to those of Hofmann; and the premature publication of the Op. 33 string quartets when they were still in subscription. These incidents will be discussed below.

13 *Briefe*, 60; *CCLN*, 11.

14 Griesinger, 62; Gotwals, 36.

15 The numbering follows that in *JHW* XXVII/2.

16 William Kumbier, in a cogent rhetorical analysis of *Applausus*, discusses the details of text-setting that make this style especially

appropriate, noting its return in the B section of the final aria; "Rhetoric and expression in Haydn's *Applausus* cantata," *HYB* 18 (1993), 213–65, at 234–38.

17 Letter of 22 September 1802; *Briefe*, 410; *CCLN*, 209.

18 *Briefe*, 76–82; *CCLN*, 18–21, reproduced in Landon II, 397–99.

19 I explore the nature and implications of this construction for Haydn's knowledge of rhetoric in *Haydn and the Classical Variation* (Cambridge, MA: Harvard University Press, 1993), chap. 2, "The rhetoric of variation."

20 Ernst Kris and Otto Kurz, *Legend, Myth, and Magic in the Image of the Artist: A Historical Experiment*, preface by E. H. Gombrich (New Haven and London: Yale University Press, 1979), cited in Leon Botstein, "Haydn and the demise of philosophical listening," in Sisman (ed.), *Haydn and His World*, 255–85 (270).

21 Thomas Tolley, *Painting the Cannon's Roar: Music, the Visual Arts and the Rise of an Attentive Public in the Age of Haydn, c.1750 to c.1810* (Aldershot: Ashgate, 2001), 50–51.

22 Letter of July 20, 1781; *CCLN*, 31; *Briefe*, 101.

23 A. Peter Brown, "Joseph Haydn and Leopold Hofmann's 'Street Songs,'" *JAMS* 33 (1980), 356–83.

24 *Briefe*, 77–78; *CCLN*, 20; Landon II, 399.

25 Mozart, *The Letters of Mozart and His Family* [hereinafter *Letters*], 3rd rev. ed., trans. Emily Anderson (London: Macmillan, 1985), 833; Mozart, *Briefe und Aufzeichnungen* [hereinafter *MBA*, ed. Wilhelm A. Bauer and Otto Erich Deutsch, iii (Kassel: Bärenreiter, 1963), 245–46. I offer a new understanding of this letter in "Observations on the first phase of Mozart's 'Haydn' quartets," in Dorothea Link (ed.), *Words about Mozart in Honour of Stanley Sadie* (Woodbridge, Suffolk: Boydell and Brewer, 2005), 33–58, at 36–41.

26 See Theresa M. Neff, "Baron van Swieten and late eighteenth-century musical culture" (Ph.D. diss., Boston University, 1998), 61–62.

27 On this topic, see Elaine Sisman, "Haydn, Shakespeare, and the rules of originality," in Sisman (ed.), *Haydn and His World*, 3–56. On the controversy in general, see Hubert Unverricht, *Geschichte des Streichtrios* (Tutzing: H. Schneider, 1969); Klaus Winkler, "Alter und Neuer Musikstil im Streit zwischen den Berlinern und Wienern zur Zeit der Frühklassik," *Die Musikforschung* 33 (1980), 37–45; Landon II, 128–32; Daniel Heartz, *Haydn, Mozart, and the Viennese School, 1740–1780* (New York: Norton, 1995), 256–61; on his deducing that it was Dittersdorf who wrote the *Wiener Diarium* piece, see 443–46.

28 Griesinger, 18–19; Gotwals, 14.

29 Johann Adam Hiller, *Wochentliche Nachrichten* (Leipzig, 1767), 14, quoted by Mark Evan Bonds, "Haydn, Laurence Sterne, and the origins of musical irony," *JAMS* 44 (1991), 83.

30 *Briefe*, 89; *CCLN*, 24. The phrase "einsichtsvollen Welt" is translated by Landon as "judicious public."

31 Letter of February 25, 1780; translation somewhat altered from Landon, *CCLN*, 25. The extensive literature on this letter includes Elaine Sisman, "Haydn's hybrid variations," in Jens Peter Larsen, Howard Serwer, and James Webster (eds.), *Haydn Studies* (New York: Norton, 1981), 509–15; Jürgen Neubacher, "'Idee' und 'Ausführung.' Zum Kompositionsprozess bei Joseph Haydn," *Archiv für Musikwissenschaft* 41 (1984), 187–207; A. Peter Brown, *Joseph Haydn's Keyboard Music: Sources and Style* (Bloomington: Indiana University Press, 1986), 23–25; Sisman, *Haydn and the Classical Variation*, 120–21.

32 Christian Gottlob Neefe, "Ueber die musikalische Wiederholung," *Deutsches Museum* 1 (August, 1776), 745–51. I discuss this article in *Haydn and the Classical Variation*, 16–18. Neefe, an organist and composer, is known to music history primarily as Beethoven's first teacher in Bonn, sponsor of his first publication in 1783.

33 I consider the rhetorical perspectives of this issue in more detail in "Rhetorical truth in Haydn's chamber music: genre, tertiary rhetoric, and the Op. 76 quartets," in Tom Beghin, Elisabeth LeGuin, and Sander Goldberg (eds.), *Engaging Rhetoric: Essays on Haydn and Performance* (Chicago: University of Chicago Press, in press).

34 I describe the structural principles of these "hybrid" forms of variation in *Haydn and the Classical Variation*, 150–63.

35 Leopold Mozart said in 1773 that "both of them, in particular the elder, play extraordinarily well." Letter of August 12, 1773; Mozart, *Letters*, 236. See also A. Peter Brown, *Haydn's Keyboard Music*, 25. The dedication, as it appears on the title page, comes from Artaria, the publisher, as was not uncommon, but Haydn expressed disappointment about this in a letter of March 20, 1780. It is possible that he had the dedication in mind and saw Artaria take it away from him, not that it was never his own idea. A reproduction of the title page appears in Brown, *Keyboard Music*, 24.

36 Letter of 11 December 1801; *Briefe*, 389; in *CCLN*, 197, Landon famously translates the expletive as "Frenchified trash," which I have altered to get more at the sense of both food

matter and detritus included in the meaning of Quark, which means both curds and something much more distasteful; Johann Christoph Adelung's *Grammatisch-kritisches Wörterbuch der hochdeutschen Mundart* (Leipzig, 1801) says it is a respectable word to use when one means the vulgar "Dreck."

37 Gotwals, 39–40, 186–88. The relevant documents are reproduced in Landon V, 118–20.

38 See Elaine Sisman, "The voice of God in Haydn's *Creation*," in Vera Lampert and László Vikárius (eds.), *Essays in Honor of László Somfai: Studies in the Sources and the Interpretation of Music* (Lanham, MD: Scarecrow Press, 2004), 139–53. Many other writers have discussed the text and organization of Haydn's *Creation*, among them Nicholas Temperley, *Haydn:* The Creation (Cambridge: Cambridge University Presss, 1991); Bruce C. MacIntyre, *Haydn:* The Creation (New York: Schirmer, 1998); Georg Feder, *Joseph Haydn:* Die Schöpfung (Kassel: Bärenreiter, 1999); Landon IV, 342–426; William A. Kumbier, "A 'new quickening': Haydn's *The Creation*, Wordsworth, and the pictorialist imagination," *Studies in Romanticism* 30 (1991), 535–63; Noam Flinker, "Miltonic voices in Haydn's *Creation*," in James D. Simmonds (ed.), *Milton Studies* 27 (Pittsburgh: University of Pittsburgh Press, 1992), 139–64.

39 Gotwals, 63 on the former; 62 and 155 on the latter.

40 The literature on this comment and on meaning in the instrumental works is extensive. See especially Richard Will, "When God met the sinner and other dramatic confrontations in eighteenth-century instrumental music," *ML* 78 (1997), 175–209; James Webster, *Haydn's "Farewell" Symphony and the Idea of Classical Style: Through-Composition and Cyclic Integration in the Instrumental Music* (Cambridge: Cambridge University Press, 1991), chap. 7, "Extramusical associations"; Horst Walter, "Über Haydns 'charakteristische' Sinfonien," in Gerhard J. Winkler, ed., *Das symphonische Werk Joseph Haydns* (Eisenstadt, 2000), 65–78; and Elaine Sisman, "Haydn's theater symphonies," *JAMS* 43 (1990), 292–352, where I suggest Symphony no. 26, "Lamentation," as the Adagio in question.

41 Charles Neete quoted Beethoven as saying this in 1815; see Elaine Sisman, "After the heroic style: fantasia and the 'characteristic' sonatas of 1809," *Beethoven Forum* 6 (1998), 68–96, at 78–82.

42 Griesinger, 117–18; Gotwals, 62–63. Griesinger mistakenly placed this passage in the Agnus Dei; see Gotwals, 236, n. 91.

2 A letter from the wilderness: revisiting Haydn's Esterházy environments

1 This and subsequent quotations from Haydn's letters are taken from *CCLN*. For the original texts, see *Briefe*.

2 Elizabeth Heckendorn Cook, *Epistolary Bodies: Gender and Genre in the 18th-Century Republic of Letters* (Stanford: Stanford University Press, 1996). See also Bruce Redford, *The Converse of the Pen: Acts of Intimacy in the Eighteenth-Century Familiar Letter* (Chicago: University of Chicago Press, 1986) and Mary A. Favret, *Romantic Correspondence: Women, Politics and the Fiction of Letters* (Cambridge: Cambridge University Press, 1993). For an illuminating reading of Mozart's letters, see David Schroeder, *Mozart in Revolt: Strategies of Resistance, Mischief and Deception* (New Haven: Yale University Press, 1999).

3 Elaine Sisman, *Haydn and the Classical Variation* (Cambridge, MA: Harvard University Press, 1993), 24. On Haydn's literary reputation, see David Schroeder, *Haydn and the Enlightenment: The Late Symphonies and their Audience* (Oxford: Clarendon Press, 1990), 21.

4 Favret, *Romantic Correspondence*, 56.

5 Rebecca Gates-Coon, *The Landed Estates of the Esterházy Princes: Hungary during the Reforms of Maria Theresia and Joseph II* (Baltimore: The Johns Hopkins University Press, 1994), 2.

6 Richard Perger, *Das Palais Esterházy in der Wallnerstrasse zu Wien* (Vienna: Franz Deuticke, 1994). As well as the Wallnerstrasse palace, the Esterházys owned several properties in the suburbs in addition to their twenty-nine estates scattered across Hungary. See also Gates-Coon, *Landed Estates*, chap. 1; János Hárich, "Das fürstlich Esterházy'sche Fideikommiß," *HYB* 4 (1968), 5–35.

7 Gates-Coon, *Landed Estates*, 11; for example, Prince Esterházy was Captain of the Hungarian Guard from 1760 until 1787.

8 On Eisenstadt, see Harald Prickler, "Eisenstadt," in *Osterreichischer Städteatlasse*, 3. Lieferung (Vienna: Franz Deuticke, 1988); Harald Prickler and Johann Seedock (eds.), *Eisenstadt: Bausteine zur Geschichte anläßich der 350-Jahrfeier der Freistadterhebung* (Eisenstadt: Nentwich-Lattner, 1998); Johann Mathias Korabinsky, *Geographisch-historisches und Produkten Lexikon von Ungarn* (Pressburg: Weber and Korabinsky, 1786); and "An Englishman in Vienna and Eisenstadt Castle in 1748 and 1749," transcribed and edited by H. C. Robbins Landon in *HYB* 18 (1993), 197–212.

9 Abraham Rees, s.v. "Eisenstadt," in *Cyclopaedia* (Philadelphia: Bradford, 1810–24); on economic conditions, see Felix Tobler,

"Wirtschaft und Gesellschaft in Eisenstadt um 1770/80," in Prickler and Seedock (eds.), *Eisenstadt: Bausteine zur Geschichte*, 466–90.
10 Cited in Landon II, 99–100.
11 Andrew F. Burghardt, *Borderland: A Historical and Geographical Study of Burgenland, Austria* (Madison: University of Wisconsin Press, 1962), 15.
12 Sarti's visit is discussed in John A. Rice, "Sarti's *Giulio Sabino*, Haydn's *Armida*, and the arrival of opera seria at Eszterháza," *HYB* 15 (1984), 181–98.
13 Amanda Gilroy and W. M. Verhoeven (eds.), *Epistolary Histories: Letters, Fiction, Culture* (Charlottesville: University Press of Virginia: 2000), 1.
14 This section is informed by the essays in Bernhard Siegert, *Relays: Literature as an Epoch of the Postal System*, trans. Kevin Repp (Stanford: Stanford University Press, 1999).
15 Alvin F. Harlow, *Old Post Bags* (New York and London: D. Appleton, 1928), 153. On the history of the postal service in Austria, see Eduard Effenberger, *Geschichte der österreichischen Post nach amtlichen Quellen* (Vienna: R. Spies, 1913); see also Horst Walter "Das Posthornsignal bei Haydn und anderen Komponisten des 18. Jahrhunderts," *HS* 4 (1976), 21–34.
16 *Geographische- und topographisches Reisebuch durch alle Staaten der österreichischen Monarchie, nebst der Reiseroute nach Petersburg durch Polen* (Vienna: Rudolph Gräffer, 1789); hereafter, *Reisebuch.*
17 See the *Wiener Diarium* report in Landon I, 382–83.
18 Landon II, 197. Archduke Ferdinand and Beatrice d'Este also supposedly reached "Eszterháza" from Vienna in five hours but it appears that the Esterházy palace in Oedenburg was meant. Landon II, 218.
19 To Nanette Peyer, May 5, 1786, *CCLN*, 52.
20 *CCLN*, 56, 81.
21 *CCLN*, 101–2.
22 Subsequent letters of 1790 indicate that Genzinger sent food to Haydn, though it was forbidden to send "*Viktualien*" through the post; Effenberger, *Geschichte*, 97.
23 *Beschreibung des hochfürstlichen Schlosses Esterhass im Königreiche Ungern* (Pressburg, 1784); *Excursion à Esterhaz en Hongrie en Mai 1784* (Vienna, 1784), both available in Landon II; Korabinsky, *Lexikon*, s.v. "Eszterháza"; see also Mátyás Horányi, *The Magnificence of Eszterháza*, trans. András Deák (London: Barrie and Rockliff, 1962); Rebecca Green, "Representing the aristocracy: the operatic Haydn and *Le pescatrici*," in Elaine Sisman (ed.), *Haydn and His World* (Princeton: Princeton University Press, 1997), 155–69; and Thomas Tolley, *Painting the Cannon's Roar* (Aldershot: Ashgate, 2001), 79–95.
24 July 20, 1781, *CCLN*, 31.
25 Henrik Marczali, *Hungary in the Eighteenth Century*, trans. Arthur B. Yolland (Cambridge: Cambridge University Press, 1910; rpt: New York: Arno Press, 1971); Miklós Molnár, *A Concise History of Hungary*, trans. Anna Magyar (Cambridge: Cambridge University Press, 2001).
26 On preserved meat, see Marczali, *Hungary*, 45. John Bland, publisher of the so-called "Razor" Quartet, visited Eszterháza in 1789. See "'Razor' Quartet," in David Wyn Jones (ed.), *Haydn* (Oxford: Oxford University Press, 2002).
27 See Landon II, 672, 496.
28 *CCLN*, 23.
29 Marczali, *Hungary*, chap. 2; Gates-Coon, *Landed Estates*, 37; Molnár, *Concise History*, 151; Tobler "Wirtschaft und Gesellschaft"; Domokos Kosáry, *Culture and Society in Eighteenth-Century Hungary*, trans. Zsuzsa Béres (Budapest: Corvina, 1987), 22–37.
30 The impact of this community on Haydn is ripe for consideration. A good start has been made in Gates-Coon, *Landed Estates*, chap. 5; Roland Widder, "Die Esterházyschen 'Siebengemeinden'," in *Die Fürsten Esterházy: Magnaten, Diplomaten & Mäzene* (Eisenstadt: Burgenländische Landesregierung, 1995), 156–71; Josef Klampfer, "Das Eisenstädter Ghetto," *Burgenländische Forschungen* 51 (1966).
31 Gerhard J. Winkler, "Das Haydn-Haus: Ein historischer Abriß," in Prickler and Seedoch (eds.), *Eisenstadt: Bausteine zur Geschichte*, 517–29; Korabinsky, *Lexikon*, s.v. "Eisenstadt."
32 "Documents from the archives of János Hárich," *HYB* 18 (1993), 9, 12.
33 Steavens recounts that "All the People here speak Latin & yesterday at Dinner I held a Discourse with an Officer of Hussars in Contempt of Cicero, & Sallust, of all Case, Number & Gender"; Landon, "Englishman," 208.
34 See for example Map 20d in *Historical Atlas of Central Europe*, ed. Paul Robert Magocsi (Seattle: University of Washington Press, 2002); Burghardt, *Borderland*, 11.
35 Quoted in Landon II, 99; Korabinsky, *Lexikon*, also describes surrounding villages as Hungarian.
36 *Reisebuch*, 4.
37 Johann Pezzl, "Sketch of Vienna," trans. H. C. Robbins Landon, in *Mozart and Vienna* (New York: Schirmer, 1991), 87–88.

38 See a similar contemporary description in Robin Okey, *The Habsburg Monarchy: From Enlightenment to Eclipse* (London: St. Martin's Press, 2001), 19.
39 Gates-Coon, *Landed Estates*, 74; descriptions of the peasant revels in Landon II, 165, 197.
40 "The Acta Musicalia of the Esterházy Archives (Nos. 175–200)," *HYB* 17 (1992), 37.
41 June 27, 1790, *CCLN*, 106; contract is translated in Landon I, 350–52.
42 See Joachim Hurwitz, "Haydn and the Freemasons," *HYB* 16 (1985), 5–98; R. William Weisberger, *Speculative Freemasonry and the Enlightenment: A Study of the Craft in London, Paris, Prague, and Vienna* (New York: East European Monographs, 1993), 109–68. Nicolaus Esterházy was master of ceremonies of the lodge "Crowned Hope" in 1790, though precisely when he became a member or where he attended meetings before this time is unclear. See H. C. Robbins Landon, *Mozart and the Masons: New Light on the Lodge "Crowned Hope"* (London: Thames and Hudson, 1982).
43 On Haydn's literary environment, see Schroeder, *Enlightenment*, 21–32; Maria Hörwarthner, "Joseph Haydn's library: an attempt at a literary-historical reconstruction," trans. Kathrine Talbot, in Sisman (ed.), *Haydn and His World*, 395–462.
44 July 20, 1781, *CCLN*, 31.
45 Landon II, 456.
46 *Reisebuch*, 50, my translation; see also Johann Pezzl, "Sketch of Vienna," s.v. section 147, "Parties."
47 Landon II, 748, n. 1. Pezzl's "Sketch" gives a vivid sense of the emerging commodity culture of Vienna in this period; see sections 99, 100, 108, 120 and 152 on Tailors, Coffee-houses, Fashions, Wines, Lemonade, respectively.

3 Haydn's aesthetics

1 Griesinger, 113.
2 This section is based on Georg Feder, "Joseph Haydn als Mensch und Musiker," in Gerda Mraz (ed.), *Joseph Haydn und seine Zeit* (Eisenstadt: Institut für österreichische Kulturgeschichte, 1972); *NG Haydn*, chap. 6.
3 Both volumes are translated with commentary in Gotwals. For the convenience of readers I cite accessible English translations of German-language sources; however, these are often inaccurate, and all translations are my own except where indicated.
4 Feder, "Joseph Haydn," 45–46; trans. Landon IV, 267.
5 Feder, "Joseph Haydn," 51.
6 Thomas Tolley, *Painting the Cannon's Roar: Music, the Visual Arts and the Rise of an Attentive Public in the Age of Haydn, c.1750 to c.1810* (Aldershot: Ashgate, 2001), chap. 2.
7 Webster, "Haydn's sacred vocal music and the aesthetics of salvation," in W. Dean Sutcliffe (ed.), *Haydn Studies* (Cambridge: Cambridge University Press, 1998), esp. 35–39.
8 Griesinger, 55–56 (Gotwals, 33).
9 Feder, "Joseph Haydn," 48–49.
10 Maria Hörwarthner, "Joseph Haydn's library: an attempt at a literary-historical reconstruction," in Elaine Sisman (ed.), *Haydn and his World* (Princeton: Princeton University Press, 1997), 395–462.
11 Bellamy Hosler, *Changing Aesthetic Views of Instrumental Music in 18th-Century Germany* (Ann Arbor: UMI, 1981); John Neubauer, *The Emancipation of Music from Language* (New Haven: Yale University Press, 1986).
12 Dies, 87 (Gotwals, 125).
13 David Schroeder, *Haydn and the Enlightenment: The Late Symphonies and their Audience* (Oxford: Oxford University Press, 1990); Mark Evan Bonds, *Wordless Rhetoric: Musical Form and the Metaphor of the Oration* (Cambridge, MA: Harvard University Press, 1991).
14 *Briefe*, 494 (Landon, III, 173–74). Such performances occurred every year on the first Thursday in June; Haydn apparently attended in 1792 (Landon III, 173n). The comparable performance in 1791, involving "about 6,000" children, is described in *The John Marsh Journals: The Life and Times of a Gentleman Composer*, ed. Brian Robins (Stuyvesant, NY: Pendragon, 1998), 495–96.
15 Dies, 130 (Gotwals, 154).
16 C.-G. Stellan Mörner, "Haydniana aus Schweden um 1800," *Haydn-Studien*, 2 (1969–70), 26 (hereafter cited as "Mörner"). Silverstolpe saw much of Haydn in 1797; although his informative memoirs were written down long afterwards, they are based on notes made at the time and, factually at least, are reliable (ibid., 30–31, note [g]).
17 Neubauer, *Emancipation*, 157–67; Wye J. Allanbrook, "'Ear-tickling nonsense': a new context for musical expression in Mozart's 'Haydn' Quartets," *The St. John's Review* 38 (1988), 6–8.
18 Horst Walter, "Gottfried van Swietens handschriftliche Textbücher zu 'Schöpfung' und 'Jahreszeiten,'" *HS* 1 (1965–67), 250–51 (Landon IV, 351).
19 Mörner, 25.
20 *Briefe*, 240; Landon II, 744.
21 Griesinger, 117 (Gotwals, 62).
22 Dies, 131 (Gotwals, 155).
23 Richard Will, "When God met the sinner, and other dramatic confrontations in

eighteenth-century instrumental music," *ML* 78 (1997), 175–209.

24 James Webster, *Haydn's "Farewell" Symphony and the Idea of Classical Style: Through-Composition and Cyclic Integration in his Instrumental Music* (Cambridge: Cambridge University Press, 1991), chap. 7; Walter, "Über Haydns 'charakteristische' Sinfonien," in Gerhard J. Winkler (ed.), *Das symphonische Werk Joseph Haydns* (Eisenstadt: Burgenländisches Landesmuseum, 2002), 65–78; on such works in general, Will, *The Characteristic Symphony in the Age of Haydn and Beethoven* (Cambridge: Cambridge University Press, 2002).

25 Bence Szabolcsi, "Joseph Haydn und die ungarische Musik," *Beiträge zur Musikwissenschaft* 1 (1959), 62–73.

26 Helmut Rösing, "Gedanken zum 'Musikalischen Hören,'" *Die Musikforschung* 27 (1974), 213–16.

27 Schroeder, *Haydn and the Enlightenment*, chap. 11.

28 Mary Hunter, "The *alla turca* style in the late eighteenth century: race and gender in the symphony and the seraglio," in Jonathan Bellman (ed.), *The Exotic in Western Music* (Boston: Northeastern University Press, 1998), 43–73.

29 Anke Riedel-Martiny, "Das Verhältnis von Text und Musik in Haydns Oratorien," *HS* 1 (1965–67), 205–40, esp. 224 ff.

30 *bonum Cantabile* (emphasis original); facs. in Robert Freeman, "Robert Kimmerling: a little-known Haydn pupil," *HYB* 13 (1982), 147; Landon I, 98.

31 Griesinger, 114–15 (Gotwals, 61).

32 *Briefe*, 436; Landon V, 284.

33 Haydn's instrumental music also often exhibits what may be called "vocality." Nancy R. November, "Haydn's vocality and the idea of 'true' string quartets," (Ph.D. diss., Cornell University, 2003).

34 *Briefe*, 101 (Landon II, 449); see A. Peter Brown, "Joseph Haydn and Leopold Hofmann's 'Street Songs,'" *JAMS* 33 (1980), 356–83.

35 *Briefe*, 536.

36 Feder, "Haydns Korrekturen zum Klavierauszug der 'Jahreszeiten,'" in Thomas Kohlhase and Volker Scherliess (eds.), *Festschrift Georg von Dadelsen zum 60. Geburtstag* (Neuhausen-Stuttgart: Hänssler, 1978), esp. 107–8, 112.

37 *Briefe*, 388–89 (Landon V, 89).

38 See Sisman, "Haydn, Shakespeare, and the rules of originality," in Sisman (ed.), *Haydn and His World*, 3–56.

39 Griesinger, 113 (Gotwals, 61). Hollace Ann Schafer made Haydn's famous utterance the foundation for her important study of Haydn's compositional process, "'A wisely ordered *Phantasie*': Joseph Haydn's creative process from the sketches and drafts for instrumental music" (Ph.D. diss., Brandeis University, 1987).

40 C. P. E. Bach, *Essay on the True Art of Playing Keyboard Instruments*, trans. William J. Mitchell (London: Norton, 1949), part 2, chap. 7; Annette Richards, *The Free Fantasia and the Musical Picturesque* (Cambridge: Cambridge University Press, 2001), 40–45, 66, 72.

41 Heinrich Schenker, "On organicism in sonata form," in Schenker, *The Masterwork in Musik*, trans. William Drabkin et al., vol. II (Cambridge: Cambridge University Press, 1996), 23.

42 Mörner, 28 (emphasis original). Given the year 1797, the work must have been from Op. 76.

43 Griesinger, 114 (emphasis original); Gotwals, 61.

44 *Briefe*, 23, 86 (Landon II, 419). Haydn's phrase "serve the widows" relates to the primary purpose of the Tonkünstler-Sozietät: to assist poor musicians and their widows and children by charity performances, to which Haydn regularly contributed especially after 1795.

45 David Gramit, *Cultivating Music: The Aspirations, Interests, and Limits of German Musical Culture, 1770–1848* (Berkeley: University of California Press, 2002), 77–79.

46 Griesinger, 24–25 (Gotwals, 17, with a serious mistranslation: "*be* an original").

47 This is not the only case of its kind; see the analysis of his autobiographical letter of 1776 in Sisman, *Haydn and the Classical Variation* (Cambridge, MA.: Harvard University Press, 1993), 24.

48 E.g., to Mme Genzinger on February 9, 1790: *Briefe*, 228 (Landon II, 737).

49 Griesinger, 114 (Gotwals, 61).

50 Mörner, 27.

51 *Briefe*, 279–80; Landon III, 521.

52 Griesinger, 116 (Gotwals, 61–62).

53 Griesinger, 104–5 (Gotwals, 56).

54 See again Sisman, "Haydn and Originality."

55 *Briefe*, 320 (Landon IV, 469).

56 *Briefe*, 104 (Landon II, 453).

57 See my other chapter in this volume, chap. 11.

58 Gretchen Wheelock, *Haydn's Ingenious Jesting with Art: Contexts of Musical Wit and Humor* (New York: Schirmer, 1992).

59 Griesinger, 117–18 (Gotwals, 62–63).

60 John A. Rice, *Empress Marie Therese and Music at the Viennese Court, 1792–1807*

(Cambridge: Cambridge University Press, 2003).
61 Wheelock, *Haydn's Ingenious Jesting*, chap. 2.
62 Charles Rosen complained about the "triviality" of a passage in the *Mass in Time of War* in *The Classical Style: Haydn, Mozart, Beethoven* (New York: Viking, 1971), 368.
63 *Briefe*, 404 (Landon V, 227).
64 *Briefe*, 265 (Landon III, 107).
65 *Briefe*, 531 (Landon III, 299).
66 Feder, 53 (Landon IV, 567–68).
67 For example, Leopold Mozart wrote his wife from Milan in November 1770, "Wolfgang . . . has so far done only a single aria for the *primo uomo*, because the latter hasn't arrived yet; he doesn't want to have to work double, and so prefers to await his presence, so as to be able to measure the garment correctly to the body." *Mozart: Briefe und Aufzeichnungen*, 7 vols. (Kassel: Bärenreiter, 1962–75), II, 304 (*The Letters of Mozart and His Family*, trans. Emily Anderson, 2nd ed., 3 vols. [London: Macmillan, 1966], I, 497).
68 *Briefe*, 60 (Landon II, 148).
69 *Briefe*, 202 (Landon II, 718).
70 For a general survey of such distinctions see László Somfai, *The Keyboard Sonatas of Joseph Haydn: Instruments and Performance Practice, Genres, and Styles*, trans. Charlotte Greenspan and the author (Chicago: University of Chicago Press, 1995), 166–70, 173–80.
71 In the *Allgemeine musikalische Zeitung*, 3/24 (11 March 1801), 407 (trans. "Remarks on the development of the art of music in the eighteenth century," in Sisman (ed.), *Haydn and His World*, 373).
72 Bonds, "Haydn, Laurence Sterne, and the origins of musical irony," *JAMS* 44 (1991), 57–91.
73 Ibid.; Webster, *"Farewell" Symphony*, 37–45 *passim*, 125, 127–30, 267–87 *passim*, 307–8.
74 Webster, "*The Creation*, Haydn's late vocal music, and the musical sublime," in Sisman (ed.), *Haydn and His World*, 57–102.
75 Webster, *"Farewell" Symphony*, 2, 114–5; Griesinger, 55–6 (Gotwals, 33).
76 Webster, "Freedom of form in Haydn's early string quartets," in Jens Peter Larsen et al. (ed.), *Haydn Studies: Proceedings of the International Haydn Conference, Washington, D.C.*, 1975 (New York: Norton, 1981), 522–30; Sisman, "Haydn's baryton pieces and his serious genres," in Eva Badura-Skoda (ed.), *Internationaler Joseph Haydn Kongress, Wien 1982* (Munich: Henle, 1986), 426–35.
77 Triest, "Remarks," 373.
78 *Historisch-biographisches Lexikon der Tonkünstler*, 2 vols. (Leipzig: Breitkopf, 1790–92), I, col. 610.
79 Landon III, 507–600, 614–15.
80 Griesinger, 113–14 (Gotwals, 60).
81 *Kritik der Urteilskraft* (1790), § 46, final paragraph (emphases original).
82 Bernard Harrison, *Haydn: The "Paris" Symphonies* (Cambridge: Cambridge University Press, 1998), 16–25; Sisman, "Haydn and originality," 9–11.
83 Ibid., 3–5.

4 First among equals: Haydn and his fellow composers

1 Griesinger, 7.
2 Griesinger, 17.
3 Haydn's autobiographical sketch prepared in 1776. Landon II, 398.
4 For instance, Wagenseil's Symphony in C (Kucaba C3, no later than 1756) shares these features and others with Haydn's Symphony no. 2 (no later than 1764). Score of the Wagenseil symphony in B. S. Brook (editor-in-chief), *The Symphony 1720–1840. Series B, Vol. 3, Georg Christoph Wagenseil 1715–1777. Fifteen Symphonies*, ed. J. Kucaba (New York: Garland, 1981), 63–101.
5 Griesinger, 12.
6 B. Harrison, *Haydn's Keyboard Music. Studies in Performance Practice* (Oxford: Clarendon, 1997), 167–95.
7 See John A. Rice, *Empress Marie Therese and Music at the Viennese Court, 1792–1807* (Cambridge: Cambridge University Press, 2003).
8 In his early twenties Haydn was occasionally employed as an extra singer at the Hofkapelle; D. Edge, "New sources for Haydn's early biography" (unpublished paper read at the American Musicological Society in 1993). For further information on Haydn's relationship with churches and with private chapels in the 1750s see O. Biba, "Haydns Kirchenmusikdienste für Graf Haugwitz," *HS* 6 (1994), 278–87; and R. Steblin, "Haydns Orgeldienst 'in der damaligen Gräfl. Haugwitzischen Kapelle,'" *Wiener Geschichtsblätter* 55/2 (2000), 124–34.
9 For Framery's 1810 description of Sarti's ecstatic reception of Haydn's *Armida* during a performance at Eszterháza in 1784, see John A. Rice, "Sarti's *Giulio Sabino*, Haydn's *Armida*, and the arrival of opera seria at Eszterháza," *HYB* 15 (1984), 197–98.
10 The particular circumstance of the opera house at the Esterházy court and Mozart's reputation were the two reasons given by Haydn for turning down a commission from Prague to compose an opera. See letter of December 1787; Landon II, 702.
11 Landon I, 351.

12 A. D. Coleridge, *The Autobiography of Karl von Dittersdorf Dictated to His Son*, [translation of *Karl Ditters von Dittersdorf. Lebenbeschreibung. Seinem Sohne in die Feder diktirt* (1801)] (London, 1896), 251–53.
13 Cliff Eisen, "The Mozarts' Salzburg music library," in Cliff Eisen (ed.), *Mozart Studies 2* (Oxford: Clarendon, 1997), 94–95, 133.
14 Reported by Leopold Mozart to his daughter, Nannerl. E. Anderson (trans. and ed.), *The Letters of Mozart and His Family*, 2nd ed. (London: Macmillan, 1966), vol. II, 886.
15 For an account of the complex network of musical patronage in London that might have led to Mozart traveling to the city see I. Woodfield, "John Bland: London retailer of the music of Haydn and Mozart," *ML* 81 (2000), 210–44.
16 H. Mautner (trans.), *Life of Mozart*, [translation of F. Niemetschek, *Leben des K. K. Kapellmeisters Wolfgang Gottlieb Mozart* (1798) with an introduction by A. Hyatt King] (London: L. Hyman, 1956), 60–61.
17 For instance, M. E. Bonds, "The sincerest form of flattery? Mozart's 'Haydn' quartets and the question of influence," *Studi Musicali* 22 (1993), 365–409.
18 E. L. Gerber, *Neues historisch-biographisches Lexikon der Tonkünstler* (Leipzig, 1812–14), vol. II, col. 569. The symphony is D7 in J. A. Rice's catalogue in B. S. Brook (ed. in chief), *The Symphony 1720–1840. Reference Volume: Contents of the Set and Collected Thematic Indexes* (New York: Garland, 1986), 286.
19 C. Burney, *A General History of Music: From the Earliest Ages to the Present Period (1789)*, with critical and historical notes by F. Mercer (New York: Dover, 1957), vol. II, 951–52.
20 Quoted in Landon III, 241.
21 H. Walter, "Haydn Gewidmete Streichquartette," in Georg Feder, Heinrich Hüschen, and Ulrich Tank (eds.), *Joseph Haydn, Tradition und Rezeption* (Regensburg: G. Bosse, 1985), 17–53.
22 J. Riepe, "Eine neue Quelle zum Repertoire der Bonner Hofkapelle im späten 18. Jahrhundert," *Archiv für Musikwissenschaft* 60 (2003), 97–114.
23 See J. Webster, "The falling-out between Haydn and Beethoven: the evidence of the sources," in L. Lockwood and P. Benjamin (eds.), *Beethoven Essays: Studies in Honor of Elliot Forbes* (Cambridge, MA: Harvard University Press, 1984), 3–45.
24 Griesinger reported this remark to Breitkopf & Härtel. O. Biba (ed.), *"Eben komme ich von Haydn." Georg August Griesingers Korrespondenz mit Joseph Haydns Verleger Breitkopf & Härtel* (Zurich: Atlantis Musik-Verlag, 1987), 178.
25 E. Anderson (trans. and ed.), *The Letters of Beethoven* (London: Macmillan, 1961), vol. I, 174.
26 See, especially, Beethoven's letter of February 1809 concerning the offer of the position of Kapellmeister at Kassel; ibid., vol. I, 214–15. For a broader consideration of this underplayed aspect of Beethoven's ambition see D. W. Jones, *The Life of Beethoven* (Cambridge: Cambridge University Press, 1998), *passim.*
27 See J. Webster, *Haydn's "Farewell" Symphony and the Idea of Classical Style: Through-Composition and Cyclic Integration in His Instrumental Works* (Cambridge: Cambridge University Press, 1991), 366–73.
28 O. Biba, "Beethoven und die 'Liebhaber Concerte' in Wien im Winter 1807/08," in R. Klein (ed.), *Beiträge '76–78: Beethoven Kolloquium 1977: Dokumentation und Aufführungspraxis* (Kassel: Bärenreiter, 1978), 82–93.
29 For a full account see Landon V, pp. 358–65; and G. Feder, *Joseph Haydn.* Die Schöpfung (Kassel: Bärenreiter, 1999), 170–73.

5 Haydn and humor

1 For a sustained practical joke that unfolds in several stages, see the trio section of Symphony no. 92 as discussed by Charles Rosen, in *The Classical Style: Haydn, Mozart, Beethoven*, rev. ed. (New York: Norton, 1997), 159–60.
2 Gretchen Wheelock, *Haydn's Ingenious Jesting with Art: Contexts of Musical Wit and Humor* (New York: Schirmer, 1992), 183.
3 See Melanie Lowe, "Expressive paradigms in the symphonies of Joseph Haydn" (Ph.D. diss., Princeton University, 1998), *passim.* For a convenient tabulation of the dance origins of each of Haydn's symphonic finale themes, see Lowe, 326–27.
4 Any view of Haydn's multi-movement symphonies and sonatas that tries to say something about the logic of all four movements must recognize the minuet as a crucial turning point. For sophisticated views of the expressive complexity of Haydn's minuets, see Wheelock, *Haydn's Ingenious Jesting*, 55–89 (her chapter entitled "Humorous manners and the 'really *new* minuet'") and also Melanie Lowe, "Falling from grace: irony and expressive enrichment in Haydn's symphonic minuets," *JM* 19 (2002), 171–221.
5 Following a notion about comedy put forth by philosopher Henri Bergson, Janet Levy has written engagingly about such mechanical effects "encrusted" onto living phrases in the music of Haydn and others. See Levy,

"'Something mechanical encrusted on the living': a source of musical wit and humor," in W. J. Allanbrook, J. M. Levy, and W. P. Mahrt (eds.), *Convention in Eighteenth- and Nineteenth-Century Music* (New York: Pendragon, 1992), 225–56. On comic distraction in Haydn's music, see Wheelock, *Haydn's Ingenious Jesting*, 154–92 (chapter entitled "The paradox of distraction").

6 There is also a subliminal taunting effect in this reiterated minor third (to profile this effect, try singing the theme on E and C instead of G and E).

7 The viola's G as a non-tonic bass note of the texture subtly increases the frantic aspect.

8 Wheelock's view of this coda as a stalled conversation is delightfully confirmed by Haydn's later part-song on the text "Die Beredsamkeit," in which chattering parties talk at each other with similar musical techniques. My thanks to James Webster for urging the importance of these part-songs as genial examples of Haydn's humor.

9 Poundie Burstein focuses on the comic incongruity of "lofty" and "lowly" in his engaging analytical essay, "Comedy and structure in Haydn's symphonies," in Carl Schachter and Hedi Siegel (eds.), *Schenker Studies 2* (Cambridge: Cambridge University Press, 1999), 67–81. Elaine Sisman adds this aspect of Haydn's art to her compelling sense of him as an artist of Shakespearean range; drawing on tropes of Haydn reception and on her own astute analyses, she seeks to "recover some part of the 'Shakespearean' Haydn: the capricious juxtapositions of high and low, serious and comic, that reflect his deepest proclivities, the theatrical effects of 'character' and 'scene' that reveal his extensive experience in the playhouse, the casting aside of rules in original ways." Sisman, "Haydn, Shakespeare, and the rules of originality," in Sisman (ed.), *Haydn and His World* (Princeton: Princeton University Press, 1997), 29.

10 Of particular bite in this bit of mockery is the cross relation between the high Fs of the fanfare and the low F♯ of the reply.

11 Momigny suggested a text for the allegro theme: "Ah mon dieu! Ah mon dieu! Que vous avez eu peur!" For an annotated translation of Momigny's essay see Ian Bent (ed.), *Music Analysis in the Nineteenth Century, Vol. 2: Hermeneutic Approaches* (Cambridge: Cambridge University Press, 1994), 127–40.

12 See James Hepokoski and Warren Darcy, "The medial caesura and its role in the eighteenth-century sonata exposition," *Music Theory Spectrum* 19 (1997), 115–54.

13 Wheelock, *Haydn's Ingenious Jesting*, 186.

14 The image of the music falling asleep in this passage is suggested in Burstein, "Comedy and structure," 67.

15 See also Levy, "Something mechanical," especially 233–38, for some wonderful examples of musical mimicry in Haydn that involve the isolation and repetition of "gestural characters."

16 Wheelock reports that this extended comedy of upbeats was a late addition to the movement. In the autograph score, Haydn rejected a much simpler version of this retransition that presented three isolated upbeats in the manner of mm. 39–44. See Wheelock, *Haydn's Ingenious Jesting*, 188.

17 On the interaction of Salomon and Haydn in this context see Landon III, 534.

18 A sustained and brilliant discussion of the recall of the minuet in Symphony no. 46 can be found in Webster, *Haydn's "Farewell" Symphony and the Idea of Classical Style* (Cambridge: Cambridge University Press, 1991), 267–87.

19 Leon Botstein, "The demise of philosophical listening: Haydn in the 19th century," in Sisman (ed.), *Haydn and His World*, 275.

20 See Mark Evan Bonds, "Haydn, Laurence Sterne, and the origins of musical irony," *JAMS* 44 (1991), 57–91.

21 Daniel K. L. Chua, "Haydn as Romantic: a chemical experiment with instrumental music," in W. Dean Sutcliffe (ed.), *Haydn Studies* (Cambridge: Cambridge University Press, 1998), 120–51.

22 Marshall Brown, "Haydn's whimsy: poetry, sexuality, repetition," in *"The Tooth that Nibbles at the Soul": Essays on Poetry and Music* (Seattle: University of Washington Press, forthcoming.)

23 Daniel Chua finds another, more forceful, way to make a similar point: "This is perhaps the greatest achievement of Haydn: he was the first to glory in the sheer artificiality of instrumental music." See Chua, "Haydn as Romantic," 146.

24 Wheelock, *Haydn's Ingenious Jesting*, 206.

6 Haydn's exoticisms: "difference" and the Enlightenment

1 Carlo Goldoni, *Lo speziale, drama giocoso in tre atti* (1768), anon. trans. in liner notes to *Franz Joseph Haydn: Lo speziale*, Il canto, dir. Fabio Maestri (Bongiovanni, 1993), GB2171/72–2, 22–71 (at 23–26).

2 Ralph Locke, "Exoticism", in *The New Grove Dictionary of Music and Musicians*, 2nd ed., ed. Stanley Sadie (London: Macmillan, 2001), 459–62 (at 459).

3 See Jonathan Bellman, *The* Style Hongrois *in the Music of Western Europe* (Boston: Northeastern University Press, 1995), 47–68 and *passim.*

4 See Karl Geiringer, "Haydn and the folksong of the British Isles," *MQ* 35 (1949), 179–208.
5 This view is stressed in Carl Dahlhaus, *Nineteenth-Century Music*, trans. J. Bradford Robinson (Berkeley: University of California Press, 1989), 302–11.
6 Matthew Head, *Orientalism, Masquerade and Mozart's Turkish Music*, Royal Musical Association Monographs 9 (London: RMA, 2000), chap. 3.
7 For further commentary see ibid., 67–70. Ex. 6.1a is reproduced from Dénes Bartha, "Mozart et le folklore musical de l'Europe centrale," in André Verchaly (ed.), *Les influences étrangères dans l'oeuvre de W. A. Mozart, Paris, 10–13 Octobre 1956* (Paris: Centre National de la recherche scientifique, 1958), 157–81, at 174–75.
8 Geoffrey Chew, "The night-watchman's song quoted by Haydn and its implications," *HS* 3 (1973–74), 106–24.
9 Triest's essay appeared serially in *Allgemeine musikalische Zeitung* 3 (1801); trans. by Susan Gillespie in Elaine Sisman (ed.), *Haydn and His World* (Princeton: Princeton University Press, 1997), 321–94, at 327.
10 Gotwals, 7–8 (Griesinger).
11 Cited in Friedrich Blume, *Classic and Romantic Music*, trans. Herter Norton (London: Faber, 1972), 28.
12 Dorinda Outram, *The Enlightenment* (Cambridge: Cambridge University Press, 1995), chap. 5 "Europe's mirror? The Enlightenment and the Exotic," 63–79, at 77.
13 For a classic statement of this view see Edward W. Said, *Orientalism: Western Conceptions of the Orient* (1978; repr. London: Penguin, 1995). For Said, orientalism is not a neutral scholarly representation of "the Orient" but a regime of power and knowledge that seeks to master and define that (geographically nebulous) territory. The presence of negative stereotypes of "the Orient" in orientalist discourse is noted by Said but such stereotypes are not the basis of his critique.
14 See Judith L. Schwartz, "Cultural stereotypes and music in the 18th century," *Studies on Voltaire and the Eighteenth Century* 151–55 (1976), 1989–2013; Head, *Orientalism, Masquerade and Mozart's Turkish Music*, 1–8.
15 Cited from Bruce Alan Brown, "Gluck and *opéra-comique*," liner notes to C. W. Gluck, *La rencontre imprévue ou les pèlerins de la mecque*, dir. John Eliot Gardiner (Erato, 1991; 1991-09-03), 34.
16 Andrew Varney, *Eighteenth-Century Writers in Their World* (London: Macmillan, 1999), 4.
17 See David Wyn Jones, "Minuets and trios in Haydn's quartets," in David Young (ed.), *Haydn the Innovator: A New Approach to the String Quartets* (Todmorden, Lancs: Arc Music, 2000), 90.
18 Roy Porter, *The Enlightenment* (London: Macmillan, 1990), 51.
19 See Outram, *The Enlightenment*, 77–79.
20 Matthew Craske, *Art in Europe 1700–1830* (Oxford: Oxford University Press, 1997), 92–96, at 92.
21 Thomas Tolley, *Painting the Cannon's Roar: Music, the Visual Arts and the Rise of an Attentive Public in the Age of Haydn, c.1750 to c.1810* (Aldershot: Ashgate, 2001), 74.
22 Roger Fiske, *Scotland in Music: A European Enthusiasm* (Cambridge: Cambridge University Press, 1983), 45, from which derives the information in this paragraph.
23 [William Napier, compiler], *A Selection of the most Favourite Scots-Songs, Chiefly Pastoral. Adapted for the Harpsichord with an Accompaniment for a Violin by Eminent Masters. Respectfully Inscribed to Her Grace The Duchess of Gordon. Price One Pound Six Schillings* [vol. I] (London: W. Napier, [1790]), prefaced by [William Tytler] "A Dissertation on the Scottish Music." Quotations in this paragraph are from 1, 15 and 2 respectively. The reference to Gesualdo appears on 4–6. On the source of this dissertation see Karl Geiringer, preface to *JHW* 33: 2,1, ix–x who observes that it was taken unacknowledged from Hugo Arnot, *The History of Edinburgh* (1770), where it was an appendix by Tytler (1711–92).
24 Advertisement, *The Morning Chronicle* (November 3, 1791) for *A Selection of original Scots songs in three parts. The harmony by Haydn, dedicated by permission to Her Royal Highness the Duchess of York*, vol. II (London: Napier, [1792]), cited Geiringer, preface to *JHW* 32: 1, x.
25 For the political context of English imperialism in Scotland see Fiske, *Scotland in Music*, 10.
26 Griesinger's letter to Breitkopf & Härtel (January 20, 1802), cited in Marjorie Rycroft, Kirsten McCue, and Warwick Edwards (eds.), *JHW* 32: 3, preface, xii col. 2 (my translation).
27 *Fifty Scottish songs with symphonies and accompaniments wholly by Haydn*, vol. III (London: For George Thomson, 1802), preface, 2, n. The preface is reproduced in *JHW* 32: 3, 379–80.
28 Elaine Sisman, "Haydn, Shakespeare, and the rules of originality," in Sisman (ed.), *Haydn and His World*, 3–56.
29 Evident from a comparison with the incipits of the *Verbunkos* repertory in Géza Papp, "Die Quellen der 'Verbunkos-Musik': Ein bibliographischer Versuch," *Studia Musicologica* 21 (1979), 151–217.

30 The death of Joseph II in 1790 and his hated "Germanizing policies" was met with a strong nationalist movement styled "The Reform Period" that led to the war of independence against Austria in 1848–49. See László Dobszay, *A History of Hungarian Music*, trans. Mária Steiner and Paul Merrick (Budapest: Corvina, 1993), 131. R. J. W. Evans summarises these policies as: 1) use of German in public life (from 1784), and 2) abolition of the Hungarian constitution "based on a regularly convoked diet, a distinct and native administrative structure, and a separate legal system." See the entry on "Hungary" in *A Dictionary of Eighteenth-Century History*, ed. Jeremy Black and Roy Porter (London: Penguin, 1996), 339–40, at 339. Maria Szlatky notes that a Republican plot was suppressed in 1795 in s.v. "Hungary" John W. Yolton et al., *The Blackwell Companion to the Enlightenment* (Oxford: Blackwell, 1995), 235. Of significance for Haydn's works in the *style hongrois* in the 1780s and 1790s was the literary movement that "fought for the right to use the Hungarian language" (ibid.), leading to the first periodical in Hungarian, *Magyar Hirmondó*, in 1780.
31 See *JHW* 5, preface by Günther Thomas, xxi–xxii.

7 Orchestral music: symphonies and concertos

1 Bellamy Hosler, *Changing Aesthetic Views of Instrumental Music in 18th-Century Germany* (Ann Arbor: UMI Research Press, 1981), 5, 10–11.
2 Landon II, 399.
3 Contemporary writers such as J. J. Momigny interpreted the symphonies of Haydn and Mozart programmatically. See Malcolm Cole, "Momigny's analysis of Haydn's Symphony 103," *MR* 30 (1969), 261–84.
4 Griesinger, 62.
5 Richard Will, "When God met the sinner, and other dramatic confrontations in eighteenth-century instrumental music," *ML* 78 (1997), 194.
6 Dies, 155.
7 H. C. Robbins Landon and Gretchen Wheelock have opted for the slow movement of Symphony no. 28, while Elaine Sisman points to the second movement of no. 26. See Will, "When God met the sinner," 195.
8 These principles of rhetoric have been examined by Mark Evan Bonds in "The symphony as Pindaric ode," in Elaine Sisman (ed.), *Haydn and His World* (Princeton: Princeton University Press, 1997), 131–53.
9 Griesinger, 56.
10 A. Peter Brown, *The Symphonic Repertoire*, vol. II: *The First Golden Age of the Viennese Symphony: Haydn, Mozart, Beethoven, and Schubert* (Bloomington: Indiana University Press, 2002), 35.
11 Griesinger, 13. For an examination of the issues, see Gretchen A. Wheelock, *Haydn's Ingenious Jesting with Art: Contexts of Musical Wit and Humor* (New York: Schirmer, 1992).
12 Maria Hörwarthner, "Joseph Haydn's library: an attempt at a literary-historical reconstruction," trans. Kathrine Talbot, in Sisman (ed.), *Haydn and His World*, 420.
13 Shaftesbury, Anthony Ashley Cooper, *Characteristics of Men, Manners, Opinions, Times*, 4th ed., vol. I (London, 1727), 266.
14 James Webster, *Haydn's "Farewell" Symphony and the Idea of Classical Style* (Cambridge: Cambridge University Press, 1991). Daniel Heartz had written about the same issue in 1983. See his *Haydn, Mozart and the Viennese School 1740–1780* (New York: Norton, 1995), 355.
15 Melanie Lowe, "Falling from grace: irony and expressive enrichment in Haydn's symphonic minuets," *JM* 19 (2002), 171–221.
16 Some symphonies, such as nos. 37 and 72, are out of place in Mandyczewski's list, coming much earlier than the numbers suggest. Two have been added to his 104 symphonies, both early symphonies (Hob. I: 107 and 108; Hob. I: 106 is thought to be the overture to *Le pescatrici*). Four catalogues, prepared or inspected by Haydn, have allowed the symphonies to be authenticated: the *Entwurf Katalog*, the *Kees Catalogue*, the *Quartbuch*, and the *Haydn-Verzeichnis*. For descriptions of them, see Brown, *The Symphonic Repertoire*, vol. II, 25–26.
17 For more details on chronology, authenticity and editions, see Brown, *The Symphonic Repertoire*, vol. II, 23–37.
18 For a good survey of the concertos see Jones, 41–51.
19 Landon IV, 227–28. A reviewer at the time agreed that a trumpet with chromatic notes represented an important step forward, but lamented the disappearance of the distinctive tone.
20 Griesinger, 15–16.
21 Ibid., 13.
22 Landon I, 351.
23 *NG Haydn*, 13–14.
24 Dies, 100.
25 Daniel Heartz, "Haydn und Gluck im Burgtheater um 1760: *Der neue krumme Teufel, Le Diable à quatre* und die Sinfonie 'Le Soir,'" in Christoph-Hellmut Mahling and Sigrid Wiesmann (eds.), *Bericht über den*

Internationalen Musikwissenschaflichen Kongreß Bayreuth 1981 (Kassel: Bärenreiter, 1984), 120–35.
26 Will, "When God met the sinner," 196–208.
27 Heartz, *Haydn, Mozart and the Viennese School*, 281.
28 Landon I, 569. Neal Zaslaw, "Mozart, Haydn, and the *sinfonia da chiesa*," *JM* 1 (1982), 113.
29 Heartz, *Haydn, Mozart*, 285–94; Elaine Sisman, "Haydn's theater symphonies," *JAMS* 43 (1990), 294; Webster, "Haydn's symphonies between 'Sturm und Drang' and 'Classical style': art and entertainment," in W. Dean Sutcliffe (ed.), *Haydn Studies* (Cambridge: Cambridge University Press, 1998), 218–45; and Bonds, "Haydn's 'Cours complet de la composition' and the 'Sturm und Drang,'" in ibid., 152–76.
30 Landon II, 291–94.
31 This may have prompted Mendelssohn's similar instrumentation in the second movement of the "Italian" Symphony.
32 Dies, 100–2.
33 For a detailed analysis of this movement, see Webster, *Haydn's "Farewell" Symphony*, 30–57. For differing views, especially of the "episode" in the development, see Landon II, 302, and Charles Rosen, *Sonata Forms* (New York: Norton, 1980), 156, 160.
34 Sisman, "Haydn's theater symphonies," 311ff.
35 Ibid., 339–40.
36 Ibid., 311–12.
37 See Landon II, 564 and *The Symphonies of Joseph Haydn* (London: Universal Edition and Rockliff, 1955), 389.
38 The Paris audience, familiar with his symphonies for as much as a decade prior to this, has been examined by Bernard Harrison in *Haydn: The "Paris" Symphonies* (Cambridge: Cambridge University Press, 1998), 5–44.
39 See my *Haydn and the Enlightenment: The Late Symphonies and their Audience* (Oxford: Oxford University Press, 1990), 84.
40 For a closer examination of this movement, see ibid., 85–88.
41 *CCLN*, 60.
42 For a thorough analysis, see Richard Will, *The Characteristic Symphony in the Age of Haydn and Beethoven* (Cambridge: Cambridge University Press, 2002), 83–128.
43 Griesinger, 21.
44 *CCLN*, 131. In fact, the claim was inflated, as there is little evidence of change.
45 Ibid., 131.
46 Landon III, 241.
47 Schroeder, *Haydn and the Enlightenment*, 151–57.
48 Other writers have noted this passage, such as Eugene K. Wolf in "The recapitulations in Haydn's London symphonies," *MQ* 52 (1966), 78.
49 The character of the dance is similar to a *Passepied*, noted in Schroeder, *Haydn and the Enlightenment*, 150.

8 The quartets

1 Early complete editions of Haydn's quartets include eighty-three works. The extra fifteen include the string quartet adaptation of Haydn's *Seven Last Words*, published as Op. 51; the six "Op. 3" quartets, which are in fact by Roman Hofstetter; Op. 1 no. 5, which is a symphony; and Op. 2 nos. 3 and 5, which are sextets with horns. To the sixty-seven thus left after removing the arrangements and spuriosities is added "Opus 0," an early work discovered after the nineteenth-century editions were made.
2 James Webster, "Towards a history of Viennese chamber music in the early classical period," *JAMS* 27 (1974), 212–47.
3 Roger Hickman, s.v. "String Quartet," in *The New Grove Dictionary of Music and Musicians*, ed. Stanley Sadie (London: Macmillan, 2001).
4 Ibid. See also Janet M. Levy, "The Quatuor Concertant in Paris in the latter half of the eighteenth century," (Ph.D. diss., Stanford University, 1971).
5 Griesinger, 13.
6 Landon IV, 502.
7 Or occasionally to confuse potential publishers. For example, Haydn offered Opp. 54/55 more or less simultaneously to two different publishers, with the works differently ordered. See Landon IV for the presumed order of composition for each opus.
8 Landon III, 460. See also Simon McVeigh, s.v. "Quartet," in Jones.
9 *NG Haydn*, 22–23.
10 Landon III, 24n.1, 60ff, 65ff.
11 Fredrik Silverstolpe, letter of June 14, 1797, quoted in Landon IV, 255.
12 See W. Dean Sutcliffe, *Haydn: String Quartets, Op. 50* (Cambridge: Cambridge University Press, 1992), 7: "Haydn was too busy pursuing his own musical ideals to be able to absorb many external models or adverse judgments."
13 Roger Hickman, "The flowering of the Viennese string quartet in the late eighteenth century," *MR* 50 (1989), 157.
14 This information is chiefly taken from Mary Sue Morrow, *Concert Life in Haydn's Vienna: Aspects of a Developing Musical and Social Institution*, vol. VII, *Sociology of Music* (New York: Pendragon, 1989).
15 The Italian violinist Regina Strinasacchi, who spent time in Vienna, was evidently renowned as a chamber player. See s.v.

"Strinasacchi" in the *New Grove Dictionary*, and Morrow, *Concert Life*, 170.

16 Ludwig Finscher, *Studien zur Geschichte des Streichquartetts*, Walter Wiora (ed.), *Saarbrücker Studien zur Musikwissenschaft* (Kassel: Bärenreiter, 1974), 298–99.

17 See Momigny's comment: "A work in four parts in which two or three parts are only filler is not a true quartet, but simply a piece in four parts. Ignorant composers [i.e. not Mozart and Haydn] are incapable of writing true quartets," in A. L. Millin, *Dictionnaire des Beaux-Arts*, s.v. "Quatuor," from ibid., 294. See also Morrow, *Concert Life*, 9; a citation from the *Zeitung für die elegante Welt* of 1805 describing chamber music gatherings: "Sunday mornings, and perhaps also Fridays, are usually devoted to true music, which one never loses sight of here."

18 McVeigh, s.v. "Quartet."

19 See n. 7 above.

20 Griesinger, 7.

21 Dies, 98.

22 Johann Georg Sulzer, *Allgemeine Theorie der schönen Künste in Einzeln, nach Alphabetischer Ordnung der Kunstwörter auf einander folgenden Artikeln abgehandelt*, 4th ed., 4 vols. (Leipzig: 1792–99; reprint, Facsimile, Hildesheim: Georg Olms, 1967), s.v. "Quartet; Quatuor." Cf. also Finscher, *Studien zur Geschichte*, 279–83 for a discussion of the special primacy of four-part writing from the Renaissance on.

23 Charles Rosen, *The Classical Style* (New York: Norton, 1972), 140, makes a similar observation about this movement.

24 For a related but different reading of this movement see McVeigh, s.v. "Quartet," 313.

25 Gretchen Wheelock, *Hayden's Ingenious Jesting with Art* (New York: Schirmer, 1992), chap. 4.

26 Letter to Zelter, November 9, 1829. Cited in Finscher, *Studien Zur Geschichte*, 288.

27 Ibid., 285–89.

28 See Mara Parker, *The String Quartet, 1750–1797: Four Types of Musical Conversation* (Aldershot: Ashgate, 2002) for an extended examination of how different textures adumbrate different kinds of discourse.

29 Carpani, *Le Haydine* (1812), cited in Finscher, *Studien Zur Geschichte*, 288.

30 Koch, *Musikalisches Lexikon*, (1802), cited in Parker, *The String Quartet*, 21.

31 Wheelock, *Haydn's Ingenious Jesting*, 94.

32 Gretchen Wheelock comments on Haydn's deployment of the fermata as a moment when the conversation extends to the audience in "The 'rhetorical pause' and metaphors of musical conversation in Haydn's quartets," in Georg Feder and Walter Reicher (eds.), *Internationales musikwissenschaftliches Symposium "Haydn und das Streichquartett," Eisenstadt 2002* (Tutzing: Schneider, 2003), 67–85.

33 Haydn would not have distinguished between Magyar and Romani, but rather thought of the music of professional Gypsy musicians as part of Hungary's musical heritage. See Jonathan Bellman, *The Style Hongrois in the Music of Western Europe* (Boston: Northeastern University Press, 1993), 11–12.

34 Reginald Barret-Ayres, *Joseph Haydn and the String Quartet* (New York: Schirmer, 1974), 300.

35 William Drabkin, *A Reader's Guide to Haydn's Early String Quartets* (Westport CT: Greenwood, 2000), 139–42.

9 Intimate expression for a widening public: the keyboard sonatas and trios

1 As recounted to A. C. Dies, in Gotwals, 141.

2 As recounted to G. A. Griesinger, in Gotwals, 63.

3 The revised inventory of Haydn's keyboard compositions rests on Georg Feder's research for the *JHW* edition (see his "Probleme einer Neuordnung der Klaviersonaten Haydns," *Festschrift Friedrich Blume zum 70. Geburtstag* [Kassel: Bärenreiter, 1963], 92–103). For a current listing of the keyboard music, see Feder, work-list to s. v. "Joseph Haydn," in *The New Grove Dictionary of Music and Musicians*, ed. Stanley Sadie (London: Macmillan, 2001), vol. XI, 242–7. A. Peter Brown, *Joseph Haydn's Keyboard Music: Sources and Style* (Bloomington: Indiana University Press, 1986), xvi–xix, provides a concordance of the competing editorial numberings of the solo sonatas and keyboard trios.

4 Brown, *Keyboard Music*; László Somfai, *The Keyboard Sonatas of Joseph Haydn: Instruments and Performance Practice, Genres and Styles* (Chicago: University of Chicago Press, 1995); Bernard Harrison, *Haydn's Keyboard Music: Studies in Performance Practice* (Oxford: Clarendon, 1997); Elaine Sisman, "Haydn's solo keyboard music," in Robert Marshall (ed.), *Eighteenth-Century Keyboard Music* (New York: Schirmer, 1994), 270–307; Charles Rosen, *The Classical Style* (New York: Norton, 1997), 351–65; W. Dean Sutcliffe, "The Haydn piano trio: textual facts and textural principles," in W. Dean Sutcliffe (ed.), *Haydn Studies* (Cambridge: Cambridge University Press, 1998), 246–90.

5 On the latter, see Gretchen Wheelock, "The classical repertory revisited: instruments, players, and styles," in James Parakilas (ed.), *Piano Roles* (New Haven: Yale University Press, 1999), 109–20.

6 Brown, *Keyboard Music*, 172–97; Michelle Fillion, Prefaces to *Early Viennese Chamber Music with Obbligato Keyboard:* vol. I: *Six Keyboard Trios;* vol. II: *Six Ensemble Works for Two to Five Performers* (Madison, Wisconsin: A-R Editions, 1989).
7 As recounted to Griesinger, in Gotwals, 15.
8 Recorded in 1986: Decca 436 455–2.
9 Brown, *Keyboard Music*, 11–13.
10 Both survive in copies in the hand of a Fürnberg copyist known from manuscripts of Haydn's early string quartets and symphonies; see Georg Feder, "Haydns frühe Klaviertrios: Eine Untersuchung zur Echtheit und Chronologie," *HS* II/4 (1970), 294–95 and 305.
11 The manuscript collection *A* Wn S.m. 11084, with Haydn's Concertino Hob. XIV: 11.
12 Its main source, now in the National Széchényi Library, Budapest, was preserved in Haydn's estate; see Feder, "Frühe Klaviertrios," 296; on its dating, see Feder, *New Grove*, 243.
13 Brown, *Keyboard Music*, 203–29; Harrison, *Performance Practice*, 167–95.
14 Brown, 219–25; the *Versuch* was first advertised in 1763 in the *Wienerisches Diarium*.
15 Harrison, *Performance Practice*, 183–84.
16 Feder, "Probleme," 102.
17 Harrison, *Performance Practice*, 16–17.
18 Landon II, 42–43.
19 Haydn's letter to Artaria (February 25, 1780), in *CCLN*, 25.
20 Harrison, *Performance Practice*, 22–23.
21 Somfai, *Keyboard Sonatas*, 178–79. Brown, *Keyboard Music*, 26, downplays this collection as evidence of Haydn's distraction with opera production.
22 Tom Beghin, "Haydn as orator: a rhetorical analysis of his keyboard sonata in D major, XVI: 42," in Elaine Sisman (ed.), *Haydn and His World* (Princeton: Princeton University Press, 1997), 201–54.
23 Cramer's *Magazin der Musik* (1785), 535, cited by Brown, *Keyboard Music*, 27.
24 Haydn's letters to Artaria of *c.* July 22, 1782 and June 18, 1783, in *CCLN*, 37 and 42; on the appeal from Cramer's *Magazin* (April 1783), see Brown, *Keyboard Music*, 26.
25 Alan Tyson, "Haydn and two stolen trios," *MR* 22 (1961), 21–27.
26 Katalin Komlós, "The Viennese keyboard trio in the 1780s: sociological background and contemporary reception," *ML* 68 (1987), 224–26; Michelle Fillion, s.v. "Accompanied keyboard music," *New Grove*, vol. I, 53–55.
27 Reproduced in Brown, *Keyboard Music*, 236.
28 Hob. I: 717, classified Hob. XV: 32 as a trio on the basis of the Preston edition of 1794; on the likely precedence of the duo scoring, see Irmgard Becker-Glauch's Vorwort to *JHW* 17/3 (1986), ix.
29 Letter of September 23, 1785, in Ernst Suchalla, *Briefe von Carl Philipp Emanuel Bach an Johann Gottlob Immanuel Breitkopf und Johann Nikolaus Forkel* (Tutzing: Schneider, 1985), 510.
30 Reproduced in Brown, *Keyboard Music*, 31.
31 Letters to Artaria of August 10, and October 26, 1788 (*CCLN*, 77, 79). On Haydn's keyboard instruments, see Horst Walter, "Haydns Klaviere," *HS* 2/4 (1970), 256–88; Harrison, *Performance Practice*, 1–32.
32 Walter, "Klaviere," 266, proposes with little evidence that Haydn's Wenzel Schanz was in the form of a grand; this view is contested by Richard Maunder, *Keyboard Instruments in Eighteenth-Century Vienna* (New York: Oxford University Press, 1998), 129, who argues that it was "almost certainly" a square.
33 Letter of July 4, 1790, to Frau Genzinger regarding the purchase of her Schanz instrument, in *CCLN*, 107.
34 *CCLN*, 106.
35 Letter to Artaria of March 29, 1789, in *CCLN*, 82–83.
36 Quoted in Brown, *Keyboard Music*, 36.
37 Further elaborated in Katalin Komlós, *Fortepianos and Their Music: Germany, Austria, and England, 1760–1800* (Oxford: Clarendon Press, 1995), 69–71.
38 *CCLN*, 107–8.
39 The sources for Hob. XV: 17 specify flute *or* violin.
40 Landon III, 157.
41 In the manner of the Symphonies nos. 45–46, as observed by James Webster, *Haydn's "Farewell" Symphony and the Idea of Classical Style* (Cambridge: Cambridge University Press, 1991). Other examples of cyclic integration are found in Hob. XV: 26, 31, and the celebrated Sonata no. 52.
42 The composition date of Hob. XV: 27–29 is disputed, but the consensus is that they were likely completed by August 1795; see Feder, *New Grove*, 242.
43 According to Dies, Nicolaus II reappointed Haydn in summer 1794.
44 Brown, *Keyboard Music*, 54–55. Thomas Tolley believes Hob. XVI: 51 May have been written for Maria Hester Park. See his "Haydn, the engraver Thomas Park, and Maria Hester Park's 'little Sonat,'" *ML* 82 (2001), 421–31.
45 It shared the fate of another Bartolozzi Sonata, the famous Hob. XVI: 52, which was withheld until the Artaria first edition of December 1798, likewise with dedication to Kurzböck.

46 *Allgemeine musikalische Zeitung* I, no. 38 (June 19, 1799), cols. 599–602, cited in Brown, *Keyboard Music*, 56.
47 Bart van Oort, "Haydn and the English classical piano style," *Early Music* 28 (2000), 73–89.
48 Becker-Glauch, Vorwort, vii.
49 The inventory of this collection is listed in: Laurie Shulman, "The Breitkopf & Härtel *Oeuvres complettes de J. Haydn*," in Jens Peter Larsen, Howard Serwer, and James Webster (eds.), *Haydn Studies* (New York: Norton, 1981), 139.
50 Robert Schumann, *Gesammelte Schiften*, ed. Martin Kreisig (Leipzig: Breitkopf & Härtel, 1914), vol. I, 450, quoted in Leon Botstein, "The consequences of presumed innocence: the nineteenth-century reception of Joseph Haydn," in Sutcliffe (ed.), *Haydn Studies*, 10–11.
51 Especially in the Bartolozzi set Hob. XV: 27–29; see Sutcliffe, "The Haydn piano trio," 246–90.
52 *Allgemeine deutsche Bibliothek*, 117/1 (1789), cited in Brown, *Keyboard Music*, 36.

10 Sacred music

1 John Harper, *The Forms and Orders of Western Liturgy from the Tenth to the Eighteenth Century: A Historical Introduction and Guide for Students and Musicians* (Oxford: Oxford University Press, 1991), 12, 155–65.
2 Jones, "Catholicism," 37–39, "Liturgy," 215–16. Bruce C. MacIntyre, *The Viennese Concerted Mass of the Early Classic Period* (Ann Arbor: UMI Research Press, 1986), 13–26. Reinhard Pauly, "The reforms of church music under Joseph II," *MQ* 43 (1957), 372–82.
3 *NG Haydn*, worklist.
4 Harper, *The Forms and Orders of Western Liturgy*, 163–64. Jones, "Catholicism," 39, "Liturgy," 215. MacIntyre, *The Viennese Concerted Mass*, 15.
5 James Dack and Marianne Helms (eds.), *JHW* XXIII/1b, *Messen Nr. 3–4* (Munich: Henle, 1999), Kritischer Bericht, 180.
6 Marianne Helms, and Fred Stoltzfus (eds.), *JHW* XXII/1, *Stabat mater* (Munich: Henle, 1993), Vorwort, vii–viii.
7 Harper, *The Forms and Orders of Western Liturgy*, 131–33.
8 Geoffrey Chew, "Haydn's pastorellas: genre, dating and transmission in the early church music," in Otto Biba and David Wyn Jones (eds.), *Studies in Music History Presented to H. C. Robbins Landon on his Seventieth Birthday* (London: Thames and Hudson, 1996), 21–43.
9 Gotwals, 10 (Griesinger), 87 (Dies).
10 James Dack and Georg Feder (eds.), *JHW* XXIII/1a, *Messen Nr. 1–2* (Munich: Henle, 1992), Vorwort, x–xi.
11 Landon II, 398.
12 Gotwals, 117 (Dies).
13 Landon II, 398.
14 Dack and Helms (eds.), *JHW* XXIII/1b, Vorwort, x.
15 Landon I, 350–52.
16 Landon II, 168.
17 Dack and Feder (eds.), *JHW* XXIII/1a, Vorwort, viii–ix.
18 James Webster, "Haydn's sacred vocal music and the aesthetics of salvation," in W. Dean Sutcliffe (ed.), *Haydn Studies* (Cambridge: Cambridge University Press, 1998), 35–69.
19 Landon II, 144.
20 Dack and Helms (eds.), *JHW*, XXIII/1b, Vorwort, viii–ix. Denis McCaldin, "The *Missa Sancti Nicolai*: Haydn's long 'Missa brevis,'" *Soundings* 3 (1973), 3–17.
21 Jeremiah W. McGrann, "Of saints, namedays, and Turks: some background on Haydn's masses written for Prince Nicolaus II Esterházy," *JMR* 17 (1998), 195–210.
22 Martin Chusid, "Some observations on liturgy, text and structure in Haydn's late masses," in H. C. Robbins Landon and Roger E. Chapman (eds.), *Studies in Eighteenth-Century Music: A Tribute to Karl Geiringer on his Seventieth Birthday* (New York: Oxford University Press, 1970), 125–35.
23 Edward Olleson, "Georg August Griesinger's correspondence with Breitkopf & Härtel," *HYB* 3 (1965), 12.
24 No. 1 [*Heiligmesse*] (1802), no. 2 [*Paukenmesse*] (1802), no. 3 [*Nelsonmesse*] (1803), no. 4 [*Schöpfungsmesse*] (1804), no. 5 [*Missa Cellensis*] (1807), no. 6 [*Harmoniemesse*] (1808), no. 7 [*Mariazellermesse*] (1823).
25 C. I. Latrobe (ed.), *A Selection of Sacred Music* . . . (London: Birchall, 1806–26), 6 vols. V. Novello (ed.), *A Collection of Sacred Music* (London, 1811), 2 vols.; *A Collection of Motetts* . . .(London: H. Falkner, 1818–24); *Haydn's Masses, with an Accompaniment for the Organ* . . . (London: W. Galloway, 1822–25), nos. 1–6 = Breitkopf & Härtel nos. 1–6, no. 7 *Nikolaimesse*, no. 8 *Kleine Orgelsolomesse*, no. 11 *Missa brevis* in F, no. 12 *Große Orgelsolomesse*, no. 15 *Mariazellermesse*, no. 16 *Theresienmesse*. (Nos. 9, 10, 13, and 14 are not by Haydn.) Further: "Novello's Cheap Musical Classics," "Novello's Original Octavo Editions" etc. (J. Alfred Novello).
26 Dack and Feder (eds.), *JHW*, XXIII/1a, Vorwort, x.

27 J. D. Brown, *Biographical Dictionary of Musicians* (London, 1886). See Ulrich Tank, "Joseph Haydns geistliche Musik in der Anschauung des 19. Jahrhunderts," in Georg Feder, Heinrich Hüschen and Ulrich Tank (eds.), *Joseph Haydn. Tradition und Rezeption. Bericht über die Jahrestagung der Gesellschaft für Musikforschung. Köln 1982, Kölner Beiträge zur Musikforschung*, Bd. 144 (Regensburg: Gustav Bosse, 1985), 231–32.
28 Tank, "Joseph Haydns geistliche Musik," in *Joseph Haydn. Tradition und Rezeption*, 229–31.
29 Respectively, C. A. von Mastiaux, *Über Choral- und Kirchengesänge* (Munich, 1813); Ludwig Nohl, *Der Geist der Tonkunst* (Frankfurt, 1860). See Tank, "Joseph Haydns geistliche Musik," 234.
30 G. Weber, "Über das Wesen des Kirchenstyls," *Cäcilia, eine Zeitschrift für die musikalische Welt*, III (Mainz, 1825). See Tank, "Joseph Haydns geistliche Musik," 239–40.
31 Peter le Huray and James Day (eds.), *Music and Aesthetics in the Eighteenth and Early-Nineteenth Centuries* (Cambridge: Cambridge University Press, 1981), 5, 69–74.
32 *Morning Chronicle*, London, April 9, 1794 (of the "Military" Symphony). See Landon III, 247.
33 Landon II, 398. Olleson, "Georg August Griesinger's correspondence," 12.
34 Ernst Ludwig Gerber, *Historisch-biographisches Lexicon der Tonkünstler* (Leipzig, 1790). See Tank, "Joseph Haydns geistliche Musik," 224.
35 Webster, "Haydn's sacred vocal music."

11 The sublime and the pastoral in *The Creation* and *The Seasons*

1 On *The Creation* generally see Nicholas Temperley, *Haydn:* The Creation (Cambridge: Cambridge University Press, 1991); Bruce C. MacIntyre, *Haydn:* The Creation (New York: Schirmer, 1998); Georg Feder, *Joseph Haydn:* Die Schöpfung (Kassel: Bärenreiter, 1999). Temperley's Appendix 2 gives a concordance of the varying numberings of the individual numbers in accessible editions; I follow his scheme.
2 Letter published in the *Allgemeine musikalische Zeitung*, January 9, 1799, 1, col. 254 (Landon IV, 116).
3 Temperley, *The Creation*, chap. 3.
4 Landon IV, 350–2; V, 115–8.
5 A. Peter Brown, *Performing Haydn's* The Creation (Bloomington: Indiana University Press, 1986), 20–21.
6 Webster, "*The Creation*, Haydn's late vocal music, and the musical sublime," in Elaine Sisman (ed.), *Haydn and His World* (Princeton: Princeton University Press, 1997), 57–102, at 96–97; Matthew Head, "Music with 'no past'? Archaeologies of Joseph Haydn and *The Creation*," *19th-Century Music* 23 (1999–2000), 191–217.
7 Landon IV, 572–601; Feder, *Die Schöpfung*, 161–65, 175–90.
8 Webster, "Between Enlightenment and Romanticism in music history: 'first Viennese modernism' and the delayed nineteenth century," *19th-Century Music*, 25 (2001–02), 108–26, at 123–26.
9 *Briefe*, 362, 363 (Landon V, 47, 48); Griesinger, 104–5 (Gotwals, 56).
10 Pohl-Botstiber, 177 (Thomas, 73; Landon V, 41); compare Griesinger's unreservedly enthusiastic review in the *Allgemeine musikalische Zeitung*, May 20, 1801, 3, cols. 575–79 (Landon V, 43–5).
11 Surveyed in Landon V, 41–47, 58–59, 182–99.
12 Dies, 182 (Gotwals, 188).
13 See the facsimiles in Landon, *Haydn: A Documentary Study* (New York: Rizzoli, 1981), plates 153, 156, 173.
14 *Briefe*, 389 (Landon V, 89); Griesinger, 72 (Gotwals, 41).
15 Griesinger, 70 (Gotwals, 40); Thomas, 73.
16 Temperley, The Creation 42–45.
17 On the latter type, common in late eighteenth-century Germany, see Howard E. Smither, *A History of the Oratorio*, vol. VIII, *The Oratorio in the Classical Era* (Chapel Hill: University of North Carolina Press, 1987), 331–39.
18 Griesinger to Härtel in early 1804; Thomas, 100 (Landon V, 281). On Swieten's attitude see Herbert Zeman, "Von der irdischen Glückseligkeit: Gottfried van Swietens *Jahreszeiten*-Libretto: eine Utopie vom natürlichen Leben des Menschen," in *Die vier Jahreszeiten im 18. Jahrhundert: Colloquium der Arbeitsstelle 18. Jahrhundert, Schloss Langenburg 1983* (Heidelberg: Winter, 1986), 108–20.
19 Table 11.1 is adapted from Temperley, *The Creation*, 48; cf. 21–23.
20 Webster, "*The Creation.*"
21 Donald Francis Tovey, "Haydn: 'The Creation,'" in *Essays in Musical Analysis*, vol. V, *Vocal Music* (Oxford: Oxford University Press, 1937), 114–18; Heinrich Schenker, "The Representation of Chaos from Haydn's *Creation*," trans. William Drabkin, in Schenker, *The Masterwork in Music*, vol. II (Cambridge: Cambridge University Press, 1996), 97–105; Brown, "Haydn's Chaos: genesis and genre," *MQ* 73 (1989), 18–59; Lawrence Kramer, "Music and representation: the instance of

Haydn's *Creation*," in Steven Paul Scher (ed.), *Music and Text: Critical Inquiries* (Cambridge: Cambridge University Press, 1992), 139–62.
22 Tovey, "Haydn: 'The Creation,'" 132–33.
23 Webster, "The *Creation*," 83–88.
24 On the pastoral in eighteenth-century music, see Ellen Harris, *Handel and the Pastoral Tradition* (Oxford: Oxford University Press, 1980); Richard Will, *The Characteristic Symphony in the Age of Haydn and Beethoven* (Cambridge: Cambridge University Press, 2002), introduction and *passim*.
25 Rosen, *The Classical Style: Haydn, Mozart, Beethoven* (New York: Viking, 1971), 162–63.
26 William Empson, *Some Versions of Pastoral* (London: Chatto & Windus, 1935), chap. 2, "Double plots."
27 William A. Kumbier, "A 'new quickening': Haydn's *The Creation*, Wordsworth, and the pictorialist imagination," *Studies in Romanticism*, 30 (1991), 535–63; 535–45. Will, *Characteristic Symphony*, 143–48.
28 *Allgemeine musikalische Zeitung*, March 10, 1802, 4, col. 389 (Landon IV, 594); cf. Kumbier, "A 'new quickening,'" 545–55.
29 Tovey, "Haydn: 'The Creation,'" 124.
30 Critiqued by Temperley, 49–51.
31 "The closing numbers of *Die Schöpfung*," in Landon and Roger E. Chapman (eds.), *Studies in Eighteenth-Century Music: A Tribute to Karl Geiringer on his Seventieth Birthday* (Oxford: Oxford University Press, 1970), 315–22; compare Landon IV, 425–26.
32 Ibid., 316, 320.
33 *Paradise Lost*, IV, 750–52, 758–61.
34 David Wyn Jones, *Beethoven: "Pastoral" Symphony* (Cambridge: Cambridge University Press, 1995), 11–16; Will, *Characteristic Symphony*, 143–55. Admittedly Zeman, "Glückseligkeit," had treated it as such in all but name.
35 Brian Loughrey (ed.), *The Pastoral Mode: A Casebook* (London: Macmillan, 1984); Paul Alpers, *What is Pastoral?* (Chicago: University of Chicago Press, 1996). On eighteenth-century literary thought, J. E. Congleton, *Theories of Pastoral Poetry in England 1684–1798* (Gainsville: University of Florida Press, 1952); Helmut J. Schneider (ed.), *Deutsche Idyllentheorien im 18. Jahrhundert* (Tübingen: Narr, 1988).
36 James Carson Webster, *The Labors of the Months in Antique and Mediaeval Art* (Princeton: Princeton University Press, 1938); Bridget Ann Henisch, *The Medieval Calendar Year* (University Park: Pennsylvania State University Press, 1999).
37 On the orientation of the libretto towards the values of the rulers rather than the ruled, see David Gramit, *Cultivating Music: The Aspirations, Interests, and Limits of German Musical Culture, 1770–1848* (Berkeley: University of California Press, 2002), 79–82; of course, most pastorals portray country life sympathetically, notwithstanding its actual harshness (see Henisch, *Calendar Year*, chap. 8).
38 Winfried Kirsch, "Vergangenes und Gegenwärtiges in Haydns Oratorien: Zur Dramaturgie der *Schöpfung* und der *Jahreszeiten*," in Christoph-Hellmut Mahling (ed.), *Florilegium Musicologicum: Festschrift Hellmut Federhofer zum 75. Geburtstag* (Tutzing: Schneider, 1988), 169–87; 183.
39 On this technique see Webster, "*The Creation*," 81–89.
40 Jones, *Pastoral Symphony*, 11–14; Will, *Characteristic Symphony*, 177–87.
41 Webster, "*The Creation*," 89–92.
42 This interpretation is adumbrated in Zeman, "Glückseligkeit," 120.

12 Miscellaneous vocal genres

1 A. Peter Brown, "Notes on Haydn's Lieder and canzonettas," in Darwin F. Scott (ed.), *For the Love of Music: Festschrift in Honor of Theodore Front on His 90th Birthday* (Lucca, Italy: Lim Antiqua, 2002), 77–103.
2 For a comprehensive account of the repertory, see Max Friedlaender, *Das deutsche Lied im 18. Jahrhundert*, i–ii (Stuttgart: Cotta, 1902).
3 See Roswitha Strommer, "Wiener literarische Salons zur Zeit J. Haydns," in Herbert Zeman (ed.), *Joseph Haydn und die Literatur seiner Zeit, Jahrbuch für österreichische Kulturgeschichte* 6 (1976), 97–121.
4 For a good cross-section of the contemporary Viennese Lieder repertory, complete with informative Preface, see Margarete Ansion and Irene Schlaffenberg (eds.), *Das Wiener Lied von 1778 bis Mozarts Tod, DTÖ* XXVII/2, Bd. 54 (Vienna, 1920).
5 *CCLN*, 28.
6 See his letter of July 20, 1781 in *CCLN*, 31. The subject is discussed in detail in A. Peter Brown, "Joseph Haydn and Leopold Hofmann's 'Street Songs,'" *JAMS* 33 (1980), 356–83.
7 For a brief summary of this repertory, see the Introduction to the anthology edited by Timothy Roberts, *O Tuneful Voice: 25 Classical English Songs* (Oxford, 1992), iv–vi.
8 On the musical conception of Hunter's lyrics, see A. Peter Brown, "Musical settings of Anne Hunter's poetry: from national song to canzonetta," *JAMS* 47 (1994), 39–89.
9 See Marianne Helms, *Kritischer Bericht* to *JHW* XXIX/1, 76–77.

10 For a historical survey of the six-note motif, see Peter Williams, *The Chromatic Fourth During Four Centuries of Music* (Oxford: Oxford University Press, 1997).
11 William Kumbier, "Haydn's English canzonettas: transformations in the rhetoric of the musical sublime," in P. Barker, S. W. Goodwin, and G. Handwerk (eds.), *The Scope of Words: In Honor of Albert S. Cook* (New York: P. Land, 1991), 73–93.
12 On the dual rhetoric of the song see Katalin Komlós, "Viola's willow song: 'She never told her love,'" *MT* 140 (1999), 36–41.
13 On the "English" character of Haydn's songs, see Marion Scott, "Some English affinities and associations of Haydn's songs," *ML* 25 (1944), 1–12.
14 See also Katalin Komlós, *Fortepianos and Their Music: Germany, Austria, and England, 1760–1800* (Oxford: Oxford University Press, 1995), 80–81. A. Peter Brown suggests that the melancholy "Spirit's Song" provided Beethoven with "an effective model for the dungeon scene that opens Act 2 of *Fidelio*," and draws a convincing parallel between "O Tuneful Voice" and that composer's "Adelaide"; see his "Notes on Haydn's Lieder and canzonettas," 98–103.
15 *CCLN*, 31 and 306, respectively; also the reminiscence of William Thomas Parke, in his *Musical Memoirs* (London, 1830), 198.
16 The most thorough treatment of the subject is László Somfai, "Opus-Planung und Neuerung bei Haydn," *Studia Musicologica* 22 (1980), 87–110.
17 *CCLN*, 32.
18 See Marianne Helms, "Zur Entstehung des zweiten Teils der 24 deutschen Lieder," in Eva Badura-Skoda (ed.), *Internationaler Joseph Haydn Kongress, Wien 1982* (Munich: Henle, 1986), 116–26.
19 *CCLN*, 43.
20 See Wolfgang's letter to his father from Mannheim, Nov. 12, 1778, in Emily Anderson, ed. and trans., *The Letters of Mozart and His Family*, 3rd ed. (London: Macmillan, 1985), 631.
21 See letters of February 9 and March 14, 1790, and Sept. 17, 1791, in *CCLN*, 97, 99, 118.
22 For an exhaustive survey of through-composition in Haydn's music see James Webster, *Haydn's "Farewell" Symphony and the Idea of Classical Style: Through-Composition and Cyclic Integration in His Instrumental Music* (Cambridge: Cambridge University Press, 1991), esp. 6–9, 155–66, and 186–94.
23 "Viennese amateur or London professional? A reconsideration of Haydn's tragic cantata *Arianna a Naxos*," in David Wyn Jones (ed.), *Music in Eighteenth-Century Austria* (Cambridge: Cambridge University Press, 1996), 232–45.
24 Landon III, 47.
25 See Berthold Over, "Arianna travestita: Haydns Kantate *Arianna a Naxos* in geistlichem Gewand," *HS* VII/3–4 (1998), 384–97; Landon IV, 325; *CCLN*, 175.
26 Collections of catches and glees are represented by several volumes in the Esterházy Collection, one-time music library of Joseph Haydn, housed in the National Széchényi Library in Budapest. This material (compositions by Barthélemon, Cooke, Harrison, Callcott, Webbe, and others) was acquired by, or presented to Haydn, during his London sojourns. Haydn collaborated in the publication of one such album, preparing accompaniment to the pieces composed by the Earl of Abingdon. See *Twelve Sentimental Catches and Glees for 3 voices / Melodized by the Earl of Abingdon, the Accompaniments for the Harp or Piano Forte by the celebrated Dr. Haydn* (London: Monzani, 1795).
27 See "Joseph Haydn," *The New Grove Dictionary of Music and Musicians*, ed. Stanley Sadie (London: Macmillan, 2001), 2nd ed., vol. XI, 198.
28 See Haydn's letter of Sept. 23, 1799, to Ernst Ludwig Gerber, *CCLN*, 167.
29 Ibid.
30 See details and a comparative Table in Paul Mies, *Kritischer Bericht* to *JHW* XXX, 9.
31 For more on the lyrics see Paul Mies, "Textdichter zu J. Haydns 'Mehrstimmigen Gesängen,'" *HYB* I (1962), 201.
32 Haydn's personal library contained Ramler's *Blumenlese* and the collected works of Gellert. See Maria Hörwarthner, "Joseph Haydns Bibliothek – Versuch einer literarhistorischen Rekonstruktion," in Zeman (ed.), *Joseph Haydn und die Literatur seiner Zeit*, 157–207.
33 Certain passages as examples for "key text-phrases" are cited in James Webster, "The *Creation*, Haydn's late vocal music, and the musical sublime," in Elaine Sisman (ed.), *Haydn and His World* (Princeton: Princeton University Press, 1997), 57–102.

13 Haydn in the theater: the operas

1 The works list in *NG Haydn*, compiled by Georg Feder, gives a total of twenty-six dramatic works, including eighteen Italian and seven German, some with two versions and several with incomplete sources.
2 Gotwals, 11 (Griesinger). This story may be apocryphal.
3 He gave keyboard lessons, performed in pick-up orchestras, played the violin and organ

for various functions, and furthered his education through self-study.

4 Gotwals, 61 (Griesinger). "Now and then Haydn said that instead of so many string quartets, sonatas, and symphonies, he should have written more vocal music, for he could have become one of the leading opera composers" (63).

5 In a letter to Prague theater director Franz Roth in 1787, Haydn explained that: "all my operas are too closely connected with our personal circle (Esterház in Hungary), and moreover they would not produce the proper effect, which I calculated in accordance with the locality." Landon II, 702.

6 Bartha and Somfai catalogue surviving sources of Italian opera, including scores and parts, contained in the Esterházy collection at the National Széchényi Library in Budapest. For documentation on performances see János Hárich, "Das Repertoire des Opernkapellmeisters Joseph Haydn in Eszterháza (1780–1790)," *HYB* 1, (1962), 9–109; and Ulrich Tank, "Studien zur Esterhazyschen Hofmusik von etwa 1620 bis 1790," *Kölner Beiträge zur Musikforschung* 101 (Regensberg: Gustav Bosse, 1981).

7 Who chose the librettos Haydn set is not known. In the early years Carl Friberth, a singer at court, refashioned the texts; this role was taken over by the Italian poet Nunziato Porta in 1780.

8 For a fuller description of the opera house and its four principal parts – the auditorium (decorated in red, gold, and green), raked stage (with sets of flats, trap doors, and machinery permitting rapid scene changes), wardrobe (behind the stage), and foyer – see the entry on "Eszterháza" in Jones, 94. For images of the façade, aerial and cross-sectional views, see Somfai, 47.

9 Extrapolating from evidence about audiences for plays at Eszterháza, Thomas Tolley speculates that "in order to attract a decent [size] audience [Prince Nicolaus] apparently encouraged servants to attend, even permitting them to appear 'uncombed, drunk and disheveled,' a concession not available on other occasions." Tolley, *Painting the Cannon's Roar: Music, the Visual Arts and the Rise of an Attentive Public in the Age of Haydn* (Aldershot: Ashgate, 2001), 125 and 370 n.6.

10 Caves on either side of the auditorium were decorated with shells in the fashionable *rocaille* style; some featured frescoes, and others miniature fountains with gurgling jets and sparkling plasterwork to reflect the light of the chandeliers. Mátyás Horányi, *The Magnificence of Eszterháza*, trans. A. Deák (Budapest 1959; London 1962), 88.

11 Daniel Heartz, "Haydn's *Acide e Galatea* and the imperial wedding operas of 1760 by Hasse and Gluck," in Eva Badura-Skoda (ed.), *International Joseph Haydn Kongress, Wien 1982* (Munich: Henle, 1986), 336.

12 See entries on *Bon* and *La marchesa Nespola* by John A. Rice, in Jones, 22 and 202.

13 Jones, *Entwurf-Katalog*, 79–85, esp. 85.

14 The intermezzo was inserted in several mid-eighteenth-century stage works. See Georg Feder, "Dramatische Aspekte der *Cantarina*-Intermezzi von Sciroli (1753), Conforto (1754), Piccinni (1760) und Haydn (1766)," in Bianca Maria Antolini and Wolfgang Witzenmann (eds.), *Napoli e il teatro musicale in Europa tra sette e ottocento: studi in onore di Friedrich Lippmann* (Firenze: Leo S. Olschki, 1993), 55–67; and Gerhard Allroggen, "*La canterina* in den Vertonungen von Niccolò Piccinni und Joseph Haydn," in Georg Feder, Heinrich Hüschen, and Ulrich Tank (eds.), *Joseph Haydn: Tradition und Rezeption* (Regensburg: G. Bosse, 1985), 100–12.

15 For a textual amendment to the concluding quartet, see my "A *lieto fine* for *La canterina*," *HYB* 20 (1996), 17–23. A facsimile of the libretto is in the same issue.

16 Employment contract of May 1, 1761, clause 8. Landon I, 351.

17 An extended journal article on my research into the circumstances surrounding the preparation and reception of *Der Apotheker* at the turn of the twentieth century, including Felix Weingartner's revival for Vienna's centennial celebrations of 1909, is in preparation.

18 Rebecca Green, "Representing the aristocracy: the operatic Haydn and *Le pescatrici*," in Elaine Sisman (ed.) *Haydn and His World* (Princeton: Princeton University Press, 1997), 168.

19 Ibid., 169–73.

20 C. F. Pohl, *Joseph Haydn*, vol. II (Leipzig: Breitkopf & Härtel, 1882), 62. Since Pohl's nineteenth-century biography is the first record of this remark, it is of questionable authenticity, although he did have more sources at his disposal than we have today. Following the death of her consort in 1765, the empress renounced amusements of all kinds; this may well have been one of the few operas she had seen.

21 Horányi, *The Magnificence of Eszterháza*, 64.

22 Landon II, 197.

23 Landon II, 394 and 396. Among the new singers was Pietro Gherardi, the alto castrato who sang the role of Orfeo in Gluck's opera. His tenure from 1776–78 was the only period a castrato was available at Eszterháza.

24 Although the marriage of these older first cousins – he age thirty-six and she age thirty – apparently took place on August 3, 1777, the exact date of the opera's first performance is unknown. Landon II, 406; Günter Thomas, "Observations on *Il mondo della luna*," in Jens Peter Larsen, Howard Serwer, and James Webster (eds.), *Haydn Studies: Proceedings of the International Haydn Conference, Washington D.C., 1975* (New York: Norton, 1981), 144–47.
25 Tank, "Studien" (1981), 459. Günter Thomas (ed.), *JHW*, XXV 7/I, *Il mondo della luna* (Munich: Henle, 1979), viii.
26 Their names appear on costume receipts and in the libretto, five hundred copies of which were printed for June 28, 1777. Thomas, ed., *Il mondo della luna*, vii. Confusion arises over the various layered versions evident in the autograph, and whether the parts for Ecclitico and Ernesto were originally conceived for tenor and alto castrato respectively, or vice versa, and whether Lisetta was a soprano or an alto. Who assumed the Jermoli's roles in Gassmann's *L'amore artigiano*, which ran from April to October that year, is also not known.
27 Landon II, 403.
28 The ceiling fresco in the main concert room at Eszterháza, located in the center of the palace, depicts Apollo, god of both sun and music, driving his chariot across the sky, thereby linking light and music. Tolley, *Painting the Cannon's Roar*, 83.
29 Mary Hunter, *The Culture of Opera Buffa in Mozart's Vienna: A Poetics of Entertainment* (Princeton: Princeton University Press, 1999), 295.
30 Haydn recycled more music from this opera than from any other, as if he realized that following its troublesome gestation and short-lived reception, it would never be revived . . . despite the re-employment of the Jermolis from October 1779–March 1781.
31 For a detailed analysis of Flaminia's aria see Mary Hunter, "Text, music and drama in Haydn's Italian opera arias: four case studies," *JM* 7 (1989), 31–38.
32 Jessica Waldoff, "Sentiment and sensibility in *La vera costanza*," in W. Dean Sutcliffe (ed.), *Haydn Studies* (Cambridge: Cambridge University Press, 1998), 70–119.
33 Patricia Debly provides detailed readings of several arias and ensembles in "*La vera costanza*: a case study for musical characterization in Haydn's operas," *Studies in Voltaire and the Eighteenth Century*, vol. 305, Eighth International Congress on the Enlightenment (1992), 1509–13.
34 See my "Reading and listening: Viennese *Frauenzimmer* journals and the socio-cultural context of Mozartean opera buffa," *MQ* 87 (2004), 140–75, at 146–50.
35 Rice, "Polzelli Family," in Jones, 288–89. Although Luigia possessed only a modest talent, Haydn lovingly reworked several soubrette roles for her in numerous operas staged at Eszterháza between 1779 and 1790.
36 On the ability of the pastoral to be a refuge for contemplation and instruction as well as entertainment, see Renato Poggioli, *The Oaten Flute: Essays on Pastoral Poetry and the Pastoral Ideal* (Cambridge MA: Harvard University Press, 1975).
37 The *cor de chasse* signal "L'ancienne vue," blown when an animal is first spotted, hence the "sighting" or "viewing," was part of an elaborate system of horn calls designed by Marquis de Dampierre at Versailles in 1723 to communicate the location and progress of a hunt over long distances. J. Drew Stephen, "The motif of the hunt in romantic opera," (Ph.D. diss., University of Toronto, 2002), 38 and 74.
38 Caryl Clark, "Intertextual play and Haydn's *La fedeltà premiata*," *Current Musicology* 53 (1993), 59–81.
39 This topic is explored by Kate Galloway in an unpublished seminar paper entitled "The hunt and its extended symbolism in Haydn's *La fedeltà premiata*" (University of Toronto, Fall 2003).
40 Fillide/Celia, originally conceived for mezzo-soprano Maria Jermolli, was rewritten in 1782 for soprano Mathilde Bologna, who specialized in seria roles featuring sustained legato lines and florid vocal writing in the high register, as showcased in the upward transposition of "Deh soccorri un infelice" with bassoon solo. Bologna was one of the highest-paid singers at court, where she worked with her husband, Nunziato Porta, the court poet and costume director, from 1781–90.
41 Several articles discuss the adaptation of Haydn's opera from earlier versions; the most recent one is by Bruce Alan Brown, "*Le pazzie d'Orlando, Orlando paladino*, and the use of parody," *Italica* 64 (1987), 583–605.
42 Lorenzo Da Ponte, *Memoirs* [1823], trans. Elisabeth Abbott, ed. and annotated by Arthur Livingston (New York: Orion, 1959), 59–60.
43 Sander Gilman discusses numerous literary and artistic works linking the phenomenon of insanity to the sea (including Ruggiero's shipwreck in Canto 41 of Ariosto's *Orlando furioso*) in *Seeing the Insane* (New York: Wiley, 1982). Michel Foucault describes the Narrenschiff or "ship of fools" in *Madness and Civilization: A History of Insanity in the Age of Reason* (1961); trans. Richard Howard (New York: Vintage, 1965), 11.

44 The completion of the grand building and restoration project in 1784 was immortalized in three publications that year: a commemorative poem by Márton Dallos; "Excursion à Esterhaz en Hongrie," an entertaining description of life at "le petit Versailles de l'Hongrie" (reprinted in full in Landon II, 104–16; and the more detailed "Beschreibung des Hochfürstlichen Schlosses Esterhåss" (portions are reproduced in Somfai, 46–47, plates 72–75). The "Beschreibung" states that the theater "exceeded in magnificence and beauty anything of its kind ever viewed" and best exemplified the excellent taste of Prince Nicolaus.

45 Landon II, 476.

46 Acta Musicalia 3986, reproduced in full in Géza Staud, "Haydns *Armida,*" *Maske und Kothurn* (1982), 87–104. This original document, notorious for its illegibility, is now lost and survives only on microfilm. All three operas were in production in 1783–84, as shown in the yearly performance calendar in Tank, "Studien" (1981), 466ff. Armida's indebtedness to Sarti's opera is discussed in John A. Rice, "Sarti's *Giulio Sabino*, Haydn's *Armida*, and the arrival of opera seria at Eszterháza," *HYB* 15 (1984), 181–98.

47 Porta's requisition for costumes from October 1783 is transcribed in Georg Feder and Günter Thomas, "Dokumente zur Ausstattung von *Lo speziale, L'infedeltà delusa, La fedeltà premiata, Armida* und andere Opern Haydns," *HS* 6 (1988), 108–15. Seven watercolours depicting costumes traditionally linked to Haydn's *Armida* are traced to Salieri's 1771 opera of the same name in my "Fabricating magic: costuming Salieri's *Armida,*" *Early Music* 31/3 (August 2003), 451–61.

48 Following its premiere, it was performed another twenty times that year, and a further thirty-three times over the next four years for a total of fifty-four performances.

49 Marita McClymonds traces the sources of Haydn's libretto in two articles. "Haydn and his contemporaries: *Armida abbandonata*" in Badura-Skoda (ed.), *Internationaler Joseph Haydn Kongress*, 325–32; and "Haydn and the opera seria tradition: *Armida,*" in Antolini and Witzenmann (eds.), *Napoli e il Teatro Musicale* 191–206.

50 See b. 127 (Vivace, b♭ minor) where the fury music first appears, only to be overtaken by double statements of a military fanfare in the winds (mm. 159 and 164, first stated in the dominant in the overture's opening section at mm. 43 and 48). In the preface to *Alceste* (1767) Calzabigi and Gluck advocated overtures that would presage the opera's action and argument, advice Salieri heeded in his setting of *Armida* in 1771; his autograph annotations describe the overture as "a kind of pantomime." See John A. Rice, *Antonio Salieri and Viennese Opera* (Chicago and London: University of Chicago Press, 1998), 166–67.

51 Mary Hunter, s.v. "Armida," *The New Grove Dictionary of Opera* (London: Macmillan, 1992), I, 199.

52 The political and theatrical intrigues preventing the May 31, 1791, premiere are discussed in Curtis Price, "Italian opera and arson in late eighteenth-century London," *JAMS* 42 (1989), 55–107; Price et al., *Italian Opera in Late Eighteenth-Century London* (Oxford: Oxford University Press, 1995); and Ian Woodfield, *Opera and Drama in Eighteenth-Century London: the King's Theatre, Garrick and the Business of Performance* (Cambridge: Cambridge University Press, 2001).

53 John Rice speculates that the four-act version of the opera is probably complete, but that "it lacks revisions that Haydn, like any opera composer, would have made as the work went through rehearsals and first performances." Jones, 203–4.

54 This scene was stunningly set as a funeral procession and onstage burial of Eurydice's body in the production by the German director Jürgen Flimm for Vienna in 1995 (revived at Covent Garden in 2001). A dejected Orpheus buries his lyre with his beloved, signaling the death of his musical powers.

55 In the 1997 Decca recording (L'oiseau-lyre 452 668–2) featuring Cecilia Bartoli and Uwe Heilmann as the lovers and The Academy of Ancient Music led by Christopher Hogwood, Bartoli rises phoenix-like from the ashes to sing this commanding role following her death as Eurydice – an unrivaled performative resurrection capable of divas whose voices are versatile enough to sing both mezzo-soprano and coloratura roles. Bringing to life two characters in one and the same voice is, as Bartoli suggests, a rational choice that helps Orpheus in identifying with the Platonic bifurcation of his soul – the two sides of the same self exemplified by the Apollonion/Dionysian or mind/body split. The animus of his soul is Eurydice *and* the Sibyl, passion and reason – the internal and external worlds of his existence that map onto the conscious and unconscious, the real world and the Underworld.

56 So wrote Haydn to Prince Anton Esterházy shortly after arriving in England in January 1791. Badini's allegorical drama more closely resembles Monteverdi's and Striggio's *fine tragico* of 1607, and even quotes several poetic lines from Rinuccini's libretto *Euridice* set by both Peri and Caccini in 1600. See Silke

Leopold, "Haydn und die Tradition der Orpheus-Opern," *Musica* 36/2 (1982), 132.

14 A composer, his dedicatee, her instrument, and I: thoughts on performing Haydn's keyboard sonatas

This essay synthesizes two earlier ones: "'Delivery, delivery, delivery!': crowning the rhetorical process of Haydn's keyboard sonatas" (in Tom Beghin, Elisabeth Le Guin, Sander Goldberg (eds.), *Engaging Rhetoric: Essays on Haydn and Performance*; Chicago: University of Chicago Press, forthcoming) and "'Your humble and obedient servant': male and female rhetoric in Haydn's Sonata Hob. XVI: 40" (delivered at the 2003 Annual Meeting of the American Musicological Society in Houston). I thank my former advisor (but mentor for life) James Webster and present advisee Erin Helyard for their constructive comments.

1 A common eighteenth-century metaphor for the effect of a dissonance.

2 On slurs as indicators of accents, see Clive Brown, *Classical and Romantic Performing Practice 1750–1900* (Oxford: Oxford University Press, 1999), 30–36.

3 Inspired by Haydn's famous utterance about his compositional process: "I sat down [at the keyboard], began to fantasize depending on whether my mood was sad or happy, etcetera." See Griesinger, 61. On "to what I am used to," see *infra* in this essay.

4 Johann Ludwig Dussek, whose Broadwood piano Haydn may have used in the summer of 1791. See Horst Walter, "Haydns Klaviere," *HS* 2 (1970), 269.

5 I am inspired here by the program of a benefit concert by "Miss Parke" on May 19, 1794. She played a solo sonata in the second act, after an overture and a song. Haydn "presided at the piano-forte" during the orchestral pieces. See Landon III, 255.

6 The Viennese hammer, attached to the key, is "pulled up" by the escapement, "brushing" the string in a slightly curved motion. English hammers, on the other hand, are "pushed up" by a hopper and "hit" the string in a straighter fashion. My narrative suggests that Haydn searches for a known (Viennese) physical feeling that the new (English) mechanics do not readily produce. See Bart van Oort, The English Classical Piano Style and its Influence on Haydn and Beethoven (DMA diss., Cornell University, 1993), 20.

7 Visual clues were considered essential in eighteenth-century performance. On a musician who is able to successfully transport himself in every affect, C. P. E. Bach adds, in this order: "One sees and hears it from him" (Man sieht und hört es ihm an.) See Carl Philipp Emanuel Bach, *Versuch über die wahre Art das Clavier zu spielen*, facsimile by Bärenreiter (Kassel, 1994), 122. (The English translation by Mitchell unfortunately combines "seeing" and "hearing" into one neutral "perceiving." See C. P. E. Bach, *Essay on the True Art of Playing Keyboard Instruments*, trans. and ed. William J. Mitchell [New York: Norton, 1949], 152.)

8 Like the ones that open the big E♭ sonata, Hob. XVI: 52, or the trio in C major Hob. XV: 27, also dedicated to Therese Jansen.

9 In his *Selbstbiographie* Václav Tomaschek tells us that Dussek was the first pianist to turn the instrument sideways on the stage, "because he wanted to show his handsome profile to the audience." See Katalin Komlós, *Fortepianos and their Music* (Oxford: Clarendon Press, 1995), 65, and Arthur Loesser, *Men, Women, and Pianos: A Social History* (New York: Dover, 1990), 239. In my narrative I suggest that, beyond the realm of anecdote, this custom is inherent to the English piano school and its more developed context of public performance. In Vienna, the lid of a keyboard would either remain closed (in the chamber) or altogether removed (in the theater), the audience gathering around the instrument or sitting at the extension of its tail (where the sound of the instrument projects best). For fascinating organological evidence, see Alfons Huber, "Deckelstützen und Schalldeckel an Hammerklavieren," in Friedemann Hellwig (ed.), *Studia Organologica: Festschrift für John Henry van der Meer zu seinem fünfundsechzigsten Geburtstag* (Tutzing: Hans Schneider, 1987), 229–50.

10 The moment when the recapitulation remains in the home key instead of modulating to the dominant (as the exposition did before).

11 I am quoting the title page of the first print by Caulfield (1800). Jansen had kept the manuscript in her possession, unpublished, for at least five years. Two other distinguished pianist-composers dedicated sonatas to her: Clementi his three sonatas Op. 33 (1794) and Dussek his Op. 13 (with violin, 1790) and Op. 43 (1800).

12 For a compelling deconstruction of the concept of a "work," see Christopher Small, *Musicking: The Meanings of Performing and Listening* (Hanover, NH: Wesleyan University Press, 1998).

13 The concert, featuring among others the Marie Esterházy sonatas Hob. XVI: 40–42, took place in UCLA's Schoenberg Hall, on February 28, 2001.

14 See Johann Joachim Quantz, *Versuch einer Anweisung die Flöte traversière zu spielen* (Berlin:

Johann Friedrich Voß, 1752; facsimile by Bärenreiter [Kassel], 1997), chap. XV, §5.

15 Expressed most clearly by Quantz, chap. XIII, §9.

16 My recipe for removing the cadenza would read as follows. Continue the Alberti pulsations in the left hand and the melodic meanderings in the right for a little while longer, in analogy with the A section; replace the brutally final diminished-seventh chord by a luscious Neapolitan subdominant; connect with the closing material of mm. 37–39; do not end the right hand with a 7–8 suspension quite yet but replace it by a less final 4–3.

17 László Somfai, *The Keyboard Sonatas of Joseph Haydn: Instruments and Performance Practice, Genres, and Styles* (Chicago: University of Chicago Press, 1995), 167.

18 Somfai calls them "court-style" sonatas. *The Keyboard Sonatas of Joseph Haydn*, 175.

19 For the Italian text, see *JHW* series 18, vol. II, vii. For an English translation, see A. Peter Brown, *Joseph Haydn's Keyboard Music: Sources and Style* (Bloomington: Indiana University Press, 1986), 21.

20 The print was set in type rather than engraved on plates. In September 1773 Empress Maria Theresa had visited Eszterháza, which may have prompted the idea of a formal edition of keyboard sonatas, dedicated to the Prince. See Somfai, *The Keyboard Sonatas of Joseph Haydn*, 167.

21 See *NG Haydn*, 22.

22 The boundaries of the cadenza are drawn clearly by the fermata and the six–four chord, on the one end (m. 47), and a double trill, on the other (m. 59), the resolution of which, in the high register, is left to be imagined. These clear signs have led James Webster to state that "there is only one written-out cadenza in Haydn's authenticated keyboard sonatas" (in XVI: 39). The example of XVI: 23, as Webster would grant, is "cadenza-like," however not a cadenza. This clash of critical nomenclature, on the one hand, and effect in performance, on the other, also separates our respective approaches to improvisation in Haydn's keyboard music, at least for the time being. Whereas Webster distinguishes between "compositional," "performative," and "rhetorical improvisation," I turn to rhetoric as an umbrella and deliberately seek to blur distinctions between performance and composition. This has crucial consequences. Webster, although sensitive to its complexities, still views a Haydn score as "res facta" and refers to it as a "finished work." My stance, on the other hand, is outspokenly one of a performer, who (almost per definition, and certainly in eighteenth-century terms) must challenge the notion of a finished work, including any set definitions of internal features. See both Webster's "The rhetoric of improvisation in Haydn's keyboard music" and my "Delivery, delivery, delivery! crowning the rhetorical process of Haydn's keyboard sonatas," in Beghin, Le Guin, and Goldberg (eds.), *Engaging Rhetoric*.

23 Webster mentions two more instances of written-out cadenzas in Haydn's keyboard music: his piano trios Hob. XV: 5 (in G, 784) and 9 (in A, 1785), both published by Forster in London. Both are post-1774 and omit repeat signs as well.

24 Symphony Hob. I: 47 (in G, of 1772). Also Gerhard J. Winkler interprets "formal and technical tricks" of this kind as directly addressing the Prince. See his "Joseph Haydn's 'experimental studio' in Esterháza," *MQ* 80 (1996), 346.

25 On Clementi's revolutionizing activities as pianist, piano composer, publisher, and manufacturer, see James Parakilas and Gretchen Wheelock in James Parakilas (ed.), *Piano Roles* (New Haven and London: Yale University Press, 1999), 77–93.

26 This list excludes the "anno 1776" sonatas – published abroad without Haydn's consent – and sonatas Hob. XVI: 34 (e) and 48 (C), published without dedication. Also excluded is Haydn's re-dedication of Hob. XVI: 52, in the Viennese edition by Artaria to "Mademoiselle Madelaine de Kurzbek" in 1798, one year before Jansen herself had the piece published in London (by Longman, Clementi & Co). Madelaine, incidentally, was the daughter of Joseph von Kurzböck, Haydn's very first publisher back in 1774. Mrs. Maria Hester Park (not to be confused with the professional pianist-composer and singer "Miss Maria Parke") replaces Rebecca Schroeter as likely candidate for Hob. XVI:51. See Thomas Tolley, "Haydn, the engraver Thomas Park, and Maria Hester Park's 'little Sonat'," *ML* 82 (2001), 421–31.

27 For other rhetorical readings of Haydn letters, see Elaine Sisman in *Haydn and the Classical Variation* (Cambridge, MA: Harvard University Press, 1993), 24 (of Haydn's autobiographical letter), and Rebecca Green's chapter in this volume.

28 Haydn speaks of wishes "today" and those of "yesterday" [*gestrichen*, Haydn's version of *gestrigen*]. Through his mother Anna Maria (Koller) and his wife Maria Anna (Keller) Haydn must have been sensitized to these back-to-back namedays. This delightful fact has been

overlooked by Bartha and Landon, who date the letter August 15, Virgin Mary's Ascension Date. My corrected date also fits the other indication of time in Haydn's letter: "Thus those 8 days fled away," i.e., since the receipt of Genzinger's last letter, written on July 11. See *Breife*, 248, n. 1, and Landon II, 747, n. 4. For saints and namedays: see Catholic Online, http://www.catholic.org/saints/f_day/, accessed 12/19/02.

29 Dietmar Schmitz, "La théorie de l'art épistolaire et de la conversation dans la tradition latine et néolatine," in Bernard Bray and Christoph Strosetzki (eds.), *Art de la lettre/Art de la conversation à l'époque classique en France* (Paris: Klincksieck, 1995), 17.

30 C. F. Gellert makes this point in his "Thoughts on a good German letter" (1742). See Bern Witte (ed.), *Christian Fürchtegott Gellert: Gesammelte Schriften* vol. IV (Berlin: Walter de Gruyter, 1989), 102–3.

31 Haydn owned a letter manual. But the model provided there for a "Nameday congratulatory letter directed to a woman" is much less ingenious and spontaneous. See *Der grätzerische Secretär* (Graz: Trötscher, 1800), 114. On Haydn's library, see Maria Hörwarthner, "Joseph Haydn's library: an attempt at a literary-historical reconstruction," trans. Kathrine Talbot, in Elaine Sisman (ed.), *Haydn and His World* (Princeton: Princeton University Press, 1997), 395–462.

32 Herbert Freudenthal, *Das Feuer im deutschen Glauben und Brauch* (Berlin: Walter de Gruyter, 1931), 60–62. Thanks also to art historian Louise Rice.

33 Governesses in the highest circles of Austrian nobility were almost exclusively French. See Irene Hardach-Pinke, "Erziehung und Unterricht durch Gouvernanten," in Elke Kleinau and Claudia Opitz (eds.), *Geschichte der Mädchen- und Frauenbildung* vol.I (Frankfurt: Campus Verlag, 1996), 409–27.

34 As suggested by Brown. No hard evidence exists, however. See his *Joseph Haydn's Keyboard Music*, 135.

35 My transcription restores the value of E in m. 7 as a clear dotted quarter from the 1784 edition by Bossler. *JHW* editor Georg Feder, puzzled by the harmonic ambiguity, changed the E on the third eighth to A, the bass of a root-position dominant. In my reading, this editorial intervention destroys the subtle, natural, feminine flow of the opening period.

36 The latter case is complex for different reasons: von Genzinger, like Prince Esterházy, was a connoisseur as well as a keyboard player: she was a keen admirer of Haydn's symphonies, which she arranged for keyboard. Hob. XVI: 49 is between a concert-style and a ladies' sonata. See Somfai, *The Keyboard Sonatas of Joseph Haydn*, 179.

37 Daniel Heartz, *Haydn, Mozart and the Viennese School 1740–1780* (New York and London: Norton, 1994), 313.

38 Griesinger, *Biographische Notizen*, 16.

39 Brown, *Joseph Haydn's Keyboard Music*, chaps. 1 and 2.

40 For the correspondence discussed here, see Bartha, *Briefe*, 240–46.

41 But she would soon (in December) marry court violinist Johann Tost. See Landon II, 81.

42 Haydn had purchased a piano from Wenzel Schanz in 1788. Richard Maunder is "almost certain" that it was a square. See his *Keyboard Instruments in Eighteenth-Century Vienna* (Oxford: Clarendon Press, 1998), 129.

43 The letter clearly reads: "at our Mademoiselle Nanette's" (*bey unser Mademoiselle Nanette*).

44 As per Walter's own words, in his petition (dated December 15, 1790) for the title of Imperial Instrument Maker. See John A. Rice, "Anton Walter, instrument maker to Leopold II," in *Journal of the American Musical Instrument Society* 15 (1989), 49.

45 In particular, work by Alfons Huber, Michael Latcham, and Richard Maunder.

46 I here react to Somfai, who writes about Capriccio Hob. XVII: 1 (in G, 1765), which has two "unusual" stretches, that it "may be played without arpeggiation only on a rare instrument such as one finds occasionally in a museum as a curiosity" (*The Keyboard Sonatas*, 17). A recent symposium and a lavish publication on the Austrian harpsichord has started to rectify this misperception. See Alfons Huber (ed.), *Das Österreichische Cembalo: 600 Jahre Cembalobau in Österreich* (Tutzing: Hans Schneider, 2001).

47 The Viennese short octave (and Viennese production of harpsichords, for that matter) remained current for many years after. See Maunder, *Keyboard Instruments in Eighteenth-Century Vienna*, 47.

48 I am convinced that a revival of the Austrian harpsichord will shed new light on the emergence of an idiomatically Viennese keyboard style around 1750 and will prompt us to view the transition from (Viennese) harpsichord to (Viennese) piano as much more fluid than thus far acknowledged. My observations are based on trying out two surviving instruments: J. C. Pantzner (1747), in the Vienna Kunsthistorisches Museum, and J. Leydecker (1755), in the Steiermärkischen Landesmuseum Joanneum in Graz.

49 Using new technologies of "surround" recording and "wave field synthesis."

50 This project is funded by the Fonds Québécois de la recherche sur la société et la culture and the Social Sciences and Humanities Research Council of Canada. All instruments used are replicas, some of them built for the occasion; they include a clavichord, a Viennese harpsichord, a French double manual harpsichord, a South German square piano, an early Walter fortepiano, an English Longman, Clementi & Co. grand, and a Stodart square. Builders are Joris Potvlieghe, Martin Pühringer, Yves Beaupré, and Chris Maene.

15 Haydn and posterity: the long nineteenth century

1 Jens Peter Larsen, "Joseph Haydn – Eine Herausforderung an uns," in Eva Badura-Skoda (ed.), *Internationaler Joseph Haydn Kongress, Wien 1982* (Munich: Henle, 1986), 9–20 (9–10).

2 Adolf Sandberger, "Zur Einbürgerung der Kunst Josef Haydns in Deutschland," *Neues Beethoven Jahrbuch* (1935), 5–25 (25). Leon Botstein, "The demise of philosophical listening: Haydn in the 19th Century," in Elaine Sisman (ed.), *Haydn and His World* (Princeton: Princeton University Press, 1997), 255–85, at 281. (A later version of this thought-provoking essay appeared as "The consequences of presumed innocence: the nineteenth-century reception of Joseph Haydn," in W. Dean Sutcliffe (ed.), *Haydn Studies* [Cambridge: Cambridge University Press, 1998], 1–34.)

3 Alfred Julius Becher, Review of Haydn's *The Creation*, *Sonntagsblätter* 2 (1843), no. 47, as quoted in Clemens Höslinger, "Der überwundene Standpunkt: Joseph Haydn in der wiener Musikkritik des 19. Jahrhunderts," *Jahrbuch für österreichische Kulturgeschichte* 1/ii: *Beiträge zur Musikgeschichte des 18. Jahrhunderts* (1971), 133.

4 Ernst Ludwig Gerber, *Historisch-Biographischen Lexikons der Tonkünstler*, 2 vols. (Leipzig, 1790), vol. I, 610; compare, for example, Gottfried Wilhelm Fink, "Symphonie," in Gustav Schilling (ed.), *Encyclopädie der gesammten musikalischen Wissenschaften, oder Universal-Lexicon der Tonkunst*, 6 vols. (Stuttgart: F. H. Köhler, 1835–42), vol. VI, 541–51.

5 Johann Karl Friedrich Triest, "Remarks on the development of the art of music in Germany in the eighteenth century," trans. Susan Gillespie, in Sisman (ed.), *Haydn and His World*, 373–74. See also Matthew Head, "Music with 'no past?' Archaeologies of Joseph Haydn and *The Creation*," *19th-Century Music* 23 (2000), 191–217.

6 Eduard Hanslick, "Gesellschaftsconcerte" (1861), *Aus dem Concertsaal: Kritiken und Schilderungen aus dem letzten 20 Jahren des wiener Musiklebens* (Vienna, 1870), 232.

7 Alfred Götze, *Trübners Deutsches Wörterbuch* (Berlin, 1939), III, 395–96.

8 E. T. A. Hoffmann, Review of Beethoven's Fifth Symphony (1810), *Dichtungen und Schriften sowie Briefe und Tagebücher: Gesamtausgabe*, ed. Walter Harich, 15 vols. (Weimar, 1924), vol. XII, 130.

9 Ludwig Rellstab, "Theodor: Eine musikalische Skizze," *Berliner allgemeine musikalische Zeitung* 1 (1824), 247–49, 255–58, 263–66, 271–75, 279–81 (263).

10 Franz Brendel, *Geschichte der Musik in Italien, Deutschland und Frankreich. Von der ersten christlichen Zeiten bis auf die Gegenwart* (1852; 6th ed., Leipzig, 1878), 313.

11 Friedrich Nietzsche, *Die Geburt der Tragödie*, *Nietzsche Werke*, ed. Giorgio Colli and Mazzino Montinari (Berlin and New York, 1972), ser. III, I, 61 (§9).

12 Hans von Bülow, "Über Richard Wagners Faust-Overture" (1856), *Ausgewählte Schriften: 1850–1892*, ed. Marie von Bülow (2nd ed., Leipzig, 1911), 208, 214.

13 Franz Witt, "Eine Messe in C. von Joseph Haydn," *Musica sacra* 3 (1870), 65–69, at 65, as quoted in Christoph Lickleder, *Choral und figurierte Kirchenmusik in der Sicht Franz Xaver Witts anhand der Fliegenden Blätter und der Musica sacra* (Regensburg: Bosse, 1988), 190; Opal Wheeler and Sybil Deucher, *Joseph Haydn: the Merry Little Peasant* (London, 1939).

14 Friedrich Nietzsche, *Der Wanderer und sein Schatten* (1880) (*Menschliches, Allzumenschliches*, vol. II, pt. ii), *Nietzsche Werke*, ser. IV, III (Berlin, 1967), 253 (no. 151).

15 Ibid., 253–4 (nos. 149 and 152).

16 Wilhelm Heinrich Riehl, "Haydn's Sonaten," *Musikalische Charakterköpfe: Ein kunstgeschichtliches Skizzenbuch*, 2 vols. (2nd ed., Stuttgart, 1862), vol. II, 304; Riehl, "Die göttlichen Philister," *Musikalische Charakterköpfe*, I, 205–59.

17 Höslinger, "Der überwundene Standpunkt," 119–22; Raphael Georg Kiesewetter, *Geschichte der europaeisch-abendlaendischen oder unsrer heutigen Musik* (2nd ed., Leipzig, 1846; repr. Walluf, 1972), 96–97.

18 William Crotch, *Substance of Several Courses of Lectures on Music* (London, 1831), 144 (see also Howard Irving, "William Crotch on *The Creation*," *ML* 75 (1994), 548–60); François-Joseph Fétis, s.v. "Haydn," *Biographie universelle*

des musiciens et bibliographie générale de musique (Brussels, 1839), vol. V, 83, 94.
19 Anton Friedrich Justus Thibaut, *Über Reinheit der Tonkunst*, ed. Raimund Heuler (Paderborn, 1907), 33.
20 Adolf Bernhard Marx, "Andeutung des Standpunktes der Zeitung. (Als Epilog.)," *Berliner allgemeine musikalische Zeitung* 1 (1824), 444–48 (447); [Marx], "Etwas über die Symphonie und Beethovens Leistungen in diesem Fache," *Berliner allgemeine musikalische Zeitung* 1 (1824), 165–68, 173–76, 181–84 (168).
21 Marx, "Etwas über Joseph Haidn und seinen Standpunkt in der Kunstentwicklung," *Berliner allgemeine musikalische Zeitung* 1 (1824), 299–302, 327–29 (300, 329).
22 Robert Schumann, *Gesammelte Schriften über Musik und Musiker*, ed. Heinrich Simon, 3 vols. (Leipzig, [1888]), vol. III, 78.
23 Ibid., 87.
24 Eduard Hanslick, "Die Schöpfung. Oratorium von Jos. Haydn" (1848), *Sämtliche Schriften: Historisch-kritische Ausgabe*, Dietmar Strauß (Vienna: Böhlau, 1993), vol. I/i, 212; Hanslick, "Gesellschaftsconcerte," 231.
25 Hanslick, "An Wien's Musikfreunde vor der Aufführung des 'Elias'" (1847), *Sämtliche Schriften*, vol. I/i, 122; Hanslick, "Concert des Wiener Chorregenten-Vereines" (1849), *Sämtliche Schriften*, vol. I/ii, 48–49.
26 Hanslick, "Musikalische Briefe" (1856), *Sämtliche Schriften*, vol. I/iii, 306–7.
27 Ignaz Franz von Mosel, "Die Tonkunst in Wien während der letzten fünf Decennien. Skizze," *Allgemeine Wiener Musik-Zeitung* 3 (1843), 533–34, 601–3.
28 Johann Christian Lobe, "Fortschritt," *Allgemeine musikalische Zeitung* 50 (1848), 49–51, 65–69, 169–73, 337–41 (340).
29 Ernst Gottschald, "Ein Prophet des Stillstands und zwei Artikel der *Allgmeine musikalische Zeitung*," *Neue Zeitschrift für Musik* 29 (1848), 293–96, 298–300.
30 Franz Brendel, "Robert Schumann mit Rücksicht auf Mendelssohn-Bartholdy, und die Entwicklung der modernen Tonkunst überhaupt," *Neue Zeitschrift für Musik* 22 (1845), 63–67, 81–83, 89–92, 113–15, 121–23, 145–47, 149–50 (65).
31 Bülow, "Zweite Symphonie-Soirée der königl. Capelle" (1850), *Ausgewählte Schriften*, 9.
32 Hector Berlioz, Review of Haydn's Symphony no. 51 in G, *La Revue et Gazette musicale* 16 (1849), 35, as quoted in Katharine Ellis, *Music Criticism in Nineteenth-Century France:* La Revue et Gazette musicale de Paris, *1834–80* (Cambridge: Cambridge University Press, 1995), 86.
33 Richard Wagner, *Beethoven* (1870), *Gesammelte Schriften und Dichtungen* (3rd ed., Leipzig, 1898), vol. IX, 88; Adolf Bernhard Marx, *Ludwig van Beethoven: Leben und Schaffen*, 2 vols. (Berlin, 1859; 5th ed., 1901), vol. I, 85.
34 Ernest Newman, *Gluck and the Opera* (London, 1895), 49, as quoted in Landon V, 425.
35 Brendel, *Geschichte*, 301, 310–11, 308.
36 Adolf Bernhard Marx, s.v. "Haydn, (Joseph)," in Schilling (ed.), *Encyclopädie*, vol. III, 518–26 (523).
37 Franz Brendel, "Haydn, Mozart, und Beethoven: Eine vergleichende Characteristik," *Neue Zeitschrift für Musik* 28 (1848), 1–3, 13–15, 25–27, 37–39, 49–53 (2).
38 Brendel, *Geschichte*, 308, 314.
39 [Carl Kretschmann], "Romantik in der Musik," *Neue Zeitschrift für Musik* 29 (1848), 1–6, 9–11 (2).
40 Brendel, "Robert Schumann," 65.
41 Höslinger, "Der überwundene Standpunkt," 123–24; Sandberger, "Zur Einbürgerung," 25.
42 Botstein, "The consequences of presumed innocence," 10.
43 Hanslick, "Gesellschaftsconcerte," 231, 232, 233.
44 Emil Naumann, *Deutsche Tondichter von Sebastian Bach bis auf die Gegenwart* (2nd ed., Berlin, 1875), 398–99, 147–48.
45 Hermann Kretzschmar, *Führer durch den Concertsaal* (Leipzig, 1888), vol. I, 36; Leopold Schmidt, *Joseph Haydn* (Berlin, 1898), 116.
46 Anon. [Wilhelm Heinrich Riehl], "Das Volkslied in seinem Einfluß auf die gesammte Entwickelung der modernen Musik," *Die Gegenwart. Eine encyclopädische Darstellung der neuesten Zeitgeschichte für alle Stände* (Leipzig, 1849), vol. III, 667–86 (674).
47 Riehl, "Die göttlichen Philister," 221, 227.
48 Riehl, "Haydn's Sonaten," 334.
49 Ibid., 310, 319, 327–8.
50 Ibid., 302.
51 Guido Adler (ed.), *Haydn-Zentenarfeier. III. Kongress der Internationalen Musikgesellschaft Wien: Bericht* (Vienna and Leipzig, 1909), 36, 4, 46, 47, 41.
52 Ibid., esp. pp. 531, 548–50 (the most comprehensive survey of the reception of Haydn's church music is Ulrich Tank, "Joseph Haydns geistliche Musik in der Anschauung des 19. Jahrhunderts," in Georg Feder, Heinrich Hüschen, and Ulrich Tank (eds.), *Joseph Haydn: Tradition und Rezeption. Bericht über die Jahrestagung der Gesellschaft für Musikforschung, Köln, 1982. Kölner Beiträge zur Musikforschung* 144. Regensburg: Bosse, 1985: 215–62.
53 Ibid., 529–30 (S. Levysohn, "Die Pflege der Haydnschen Musik in Dänemark").

16 The kitten and the tiger: Tovey's Haydn

1 E. T. A. Hoffmann, "Beethoven's instrumental music" (1813), and Richard Wagner, "The music of the future" (1850), translations unattrib., rpt. in Oliver Strunk (ed.), *Source Readings in Music History: The Romantic Era* (New York: Norton, 1965), 36–37, 150–51.

2 *Grove's Dictionary of Music and Musicians*, 4 vols. (London: Macmillan, 1879), vol. I, 719. From 1863 to 1866 Pohl lived in London, working at the British Museum on his book *Mozart und Haydn in London* (note the reverse chronology of the names); in 1866 he became archivist and librarian to the Gesellschaft der Musikfreunde [Society of the Friends of Music] in Vienna.

3 Harold C. Schonberg, *The Lives of the Great Composers*, 2 vols. (1970, rpt. London: Futura, 1975), vol. I, 67.

4 Landon; Rosen, *The Classical Style: Haydn, Mozart, Beethoven* (New York: Norton, 1971);Webster, *Haydn's "Farewell" Symphony and the Idea of Classical Style: Through-Composition and Cyclic Integration in His Instrumental Music* (Cambridge: Cambridge University Press, 1991).

5 Tovey, *Essays in Musical Analysis: Symphonies and Other Orchestral Works*, new ed. (London: Oxford University Press, 1981), 369.

6 Tovey, *Symphonies*, 346.

7 Tovey, *Symphonies*, 374.

8 *Grove* (1st ed.), vol. I, 719.

9 From T. S. Eliot, "Tradition and the individual talent," in David Richter (ed.), *The Critical Tradition: Classic Texts and Contemporary Trends*, 2nd ed. (Boston: Beford Books, 1998), 500.

10 Tovey, *Symphonies*, 375.

11 Ibid., 341.

12 Ibid., 358.

13 Ibid., 338.

14 Ibid., 338.

15 Ibid., 347.

16 Ibid., 346.

17 From section 49 of *The Critique of Judgment*, "On the powers of the mind which constitute genius," quoted in the translation by Werner S. Pluhar (Indianapolis: Hackett, 1987).

18 Tovey, *Symphonies*, 363–64.

19 Ibid., 357–58.

20 *Grove* (1st ed.), vol. I, 719.

21 Ibid.

22 One freedom imitating another: see Jacques Derrida, "Economimesis," in Julian Wolfreys (ed.), *The Derrida Reader: Writing Performances* (Lincoln: University of Nebraska Press, 1998), 263–93.

23 Tovey, *Symphonies*, 338.

24 Ibid., 342.

25 Ibid., 355.

26 Ibid., 338.

27 Ibid., 357.

28 Friedrich Schiller, *On the Aesthetic Education of Man* (1795), trans. Reginald Snell (New York: Ungar, 1965).

29 Tovey, *Symphonies*, 344.

30 Ibid., 360.

31 Ibid., 368.

32 "The Tyger," from *Songs of Experience* (1794); text from *The Poetry and Prose of William Blake*, ed. David V. Erdman (Garden City, NY: Doubleday, 1965), 24.

33 From *The Dunciad: Book I*, ll.11–12, 15–16, in *The Poems of Alexander Pope*, ed. John Butt (New Haven: Yale University Press, 1963), 721.

34 From "Ode: Intimations of Immortality," ll. 145–47 and epigraph, in *Wordsworth: Poetical Works*, ed. Thomas Hutchinson, rev. Ernest de Selincourt (Oxford: Oxford University Press, 1969), 461 and 460.

17 Recorded performances: a symphonic study

1 See José Bowen, "Finding the music in musicology: performance history and musical works," in N. Cook and M. Everist (eds.), *Rethinking Music* (Oxford: Oxford University Press, 1999), 424–51.

2 Rick Altman, *Sound Theory/Sound Practice* (New York: Routledge, 1992), 40.

3 W. R. A., Review of Haydn, "Military" Symphony, Knappertsbusch conducting the Berlin Grand Symphony Orchestra, *The Gramophone* (July, 1933), 58.

4 W. R. A., Review of Haydn, Symphony no. 8, Stiedry conducting the Orchestra of New Friends of Music, *The Gramophone* (January, 1940), 290.

5 A. R., Review of Haydn, Symphonies nos. 21 and 42, Litschauer conducting the Vienna Chamber Orchestra, *The Gramophone* (July, 1952), 54.

6 For instance, on his 1950 recording of Symphony no. 93 for Columbia, Beecham instructed the strings to play pizzicato instead of arco at the end of the third-movement trio.

7 John W. Barker, Review of Haydn, The "Salomon" Symphonies, Set I (nos. 93–98); Symphony no. 40, Sir Thomas Beecham conducting the Royal Philharmonic Orchestra; *American Record Guide* (July/August, 1981), 18.

8 John Butt, *Playing With History* (Cambridge: Cambridge University Press, 2002), 166.

9 R. F., Review of Haydn, Symphonies nos. 1–2, *Lo speziale* Overture, Max Goberman conducting the Vienna State Opera Orchestra; Symphony no. 3, Goberman conducting the New York Sinfonietta, *The Gramophone* (May, 1969), 1560.

10 S. S., Review of Haydn, Symphonies nos. 57–64, Antal Doráti conducting the Philharmonia Hungarica, *The Gramophone* (January, 1971), 1150.
11 John Wiser, Review of Haydn, Symphonies nos. 1–5, 6–8, 76–78, Roy Goodman conducting The Hanover Band, *Fanfare* (March/April 1992), 211.
12 David Hurwitz, Review of Haydn, Symphonies nos. 100 and 103, Sir Charles Mackerras conducting the Orchestra of St. Luke's, *Fanfare* (March/April, 1992), 213.
13 Toscanini's recordings, however, show his reputation for fast and steady tempos to be somewhat exaggerated. See Bowen, "Can a symphony change? Establishing methodology for the historical study of performance styles," in *Musik als Text: Bericht über den Internationalen Kongress der Gesellshaft für Musikforschung, Freiburg im Breisgau 1993* (Freiburg im Breisgau, 1998), 160–72; and Bowen, "Tempo, duration, flexibility: techniques in the analysis of performance," *JMR* 16 (1996), 111–56.
14 The "maximum tempo" is the highest tempo reached during the performance of a single movement.
15 See, for example, Robert T. Philip, *Early Recordings and Musical Style* (Cambridge: Cambridge University Press, 1992), 234.
16 See Webster, "On the absence of keyboard continuo in Haydn's symphonies," *Early Music* 18 (1990), 599–608.
17 Irmgard Leux-Henschen, *Joseph Martin Kraus in seinen Briefen* (Stockholm: Edition Reimers, 1978), 105.
18 See Landon, *The Symphonies of Joseph Haydn* (London: Universal Edition and Rockliff, 1955), 118.
19 Matthew Rye, Compact disc liner notes to Roy Goodman and The Hanover Band's recording of Haydn's Symphonies nos. 45–47 (London: Hyperion Records, 1991), 4.
20 All of the players may have performed only during a program's choral centerpiece and not during the orchestral works.
21 Adam Fischer, Compact disc liner notes to Fischer and the Austro-Hungarian Orchestra's recording of Haydn's complete symphonies, (Brilliant Classics, 2001), 11.
22 J. W. B., "Yet another series by the intrepid LRM," *American Record Guide* 28/9 (May, 1962), 731.
23 J. B., Review of Haydn Symphonies nos. 1, 37, 18, 2, 15, 4, and 10, Solomons conducting L'Estro Armonico, *Fanfare* (Jan/Feb 1982), 114.
24 Fischer, Notes to complete Haydn symphonies, 11.
25 Richard Taruskin, *Text and Act* (Oxford: Oxford University Press, 1995), 90.
26 See Taruskin, *Text and Act*; Laurence Dreyfus, "Early music defended against its devotees: a theory of historical performance in the twentieth century," *MQ* 69 (1983), 297–322.
27 Antony Hodgson, "Christopher Hogwood: a new Haydn symphony AAM recording project," *Hi-Fi News and Record Review* (March 1990), 95.
28 Philip, *Early Recordings*, 230.
29 Ibid., 230.
30 Walter Benjamin, "The work of art in the age of mechanical reproduction," in *Illuminations* (1936; London: Fontana Press, 1992), 222.

Bibliography

"The Acta Musicalia of the Esterházy Archives (nos. 175–200)," *HYB* 17 (1992), 1–84.

Adler, Guido (ed.). *Haydn-Zentenarfeier. III. Kongress der Internationalen Musikgesellschaft Wien: Bericht.* Vienna and Leipzig, 1909.

Allanbrook, Wye Jamison. "'Ear-tickling nonsense': a new context for musical expression in Mozart's 'Haydn' quartets." *The St. John's Review* 38 (1988), 1–24.

Allroggen, Gerhard. "*La canterina* in den Vertonungen von Niccolò Piccinni und Joseph Haydn." In Georg Feder, Heinrich Hüschen, and Ulrich Tank (eds.). *Joseph Haydn: Tradition und Rezeption.* Regensburg: G. Bosse, 1985: 100–12.

Alpers, Paul. *What is Pastoral?* Chicago: University of Chicago Press, 1996.

Altman, Rick. *Sound Theory/Sound Practice.* New York: Routledge, 1992.

Anderson, Emily (ed. and trans.). *The Letters of Mozart and His Family*, 3rd ed. London: Macmillan, 1985.

— (ed. and trans.). *The Letters of Beethoven.* London: Macmillan, 1961.

L'anima del filosofo. 1997 Decca recording (L'oiseau-lyre 452 668–2).

Anison, Margarete and Irene Schlaffenberg (eds.). *Das Wiener Lied von 1778 bis Mozarts Tod. DTÖ* XXVII/2 Bd. 54. Vienna, 1920.

Bach, Carl Philipp Emanuel. *Essay on the True Art of Playing Keyboard Instruments*, trans. William J. Mitchell. London: Norton, 1949; facsimile by Kassel: Bärenreiter, 1994.

Barker, John W. Review of Haydn, The Salomon Symphonies, Set I (nos. 93–98), Symphony no. 40, Sir Thomas Beecham conducting the Royal Philharmonic Orchestra. *American Record Guide* (July/August, 1981), 17–19.

Barret-Ayres, Reginald. *Joseph Haydn and the String Quartet.* New York: Schirmer, 1974.

Bartha, Dénes. "Mozart et le folklore musical de l'Europe centrale." In André Verchaly (ed.), *Les influences étrangères dans l'oeuvre de W. A. Mozart, Paris, 10–16 Octobre 1956.* Paris: Centre national de la recherche scientifique, 1958: 157–81.

— (ed.). *Joseph Haydn: Gesammelte Briefe und Aufzeichnungen.* Kassel: Bärenreiter, 1965.

— and László Somfai, *Haydn als Opernkapellmeister.* Budapest: Hungarischen Akademie der Wissenschaften, 1960.

Becker-Glauch, Irmgard and Heinrich Wiens (eds.). *Applausus. JHW* XXVII/2. Munich: Henle, 1969.

Beghin, Tom. "Haydn as orator: a rhetorical analysis of his keyboard sonata in D major, XVI: 42." In Elaine Sisman (ed.). *Haydn and His World.* Princeton: Princeton University Press, 1997: 201–54.

— "'Delivery, delivery, delivery!': crowning the rhetorical process of Haydn's keyboard sonatas." In Tom Beghin, Elisabeth Le Guin, and Sander Goldberg (eds.). *Engaging Rhetoric: Essays on Haydn & Performance.* Chicago: University of Chicago Press, forthcoming.

Bellman, Jonathan. *The* Style Hongrois *in the Music of Western Europe.* Boston, MA: Northeastern University Press, 1995.

Benjamin, Walter. *Illuminations.* 1936; repr. London: Fontana Press, 1992.

Biba, Otto. "Beethoven und die 'Liebhaber Concerte' in Wien im Winter 1807/08." In R. Klein (ed.). *Beiträge '76–78: Beethoven Kolloquium 1977: Dokumentation und Aufführungspraxis.* Kassel: Bärenreiter, 1978: 82–93.

— "Haydns Kirchenmusikdienste für Graf Haugwitz." *HS* 6 (1994), 278–87.

— (ed.) *"Eben komme ich von Haydn." Georg August Griesingers Korrespondenz mit Joseph Haydns Verlager Breitkopf & Härtel.* Zurich: Atlantis Musik-Verlag, 1987.

Black, Jeremy and Roy Porter (eds.). *A Dictionary of Eighteenth-Century History.* Harmondsworth: Penguin, 1996.

Blume, Friedrich. *Classic and Romantic Music.* Herter Norton (trans.). London: Faber, 1972.

Bonds, Mark Evan. "Haydn, Laurence Sterne, and the origins of musical irony." *JAMS* 44 (1991), 57–91.

— *Wordless Rhetoric: Musical Form and the Metaphor of the Oration.* Cambridge, MA: Harvard University Press, 1991.

— "The sincerest form of flattery? Mozart's 'Haydn' quartets and the question of influence." *Studi Musicali* 22 (1993), 365–409.

— "The symphony as Pindaric ode." In Elaine Sisman (ed.). *Haydn and His World.* Princeton: Princeton University Press, 1997: 131–53.

Botstein, Leon. "The demise of philosophical listening: Haydn in the 19th century." In Elaine Sisman (ed.). *Haydn and His World.* Princeton: Princeton University Press, 1997: 255–85.

— "The consequences of presumed innocence: the nineteenth-century reception of Joseph Haydn." In W. Dean Sutcliffe (ed.). *Haydn Studies.* Cambridge: Cambridge University Press, 1998: 1–34.

Bowen, José. "Tempo, duration, flexibility: techniques in the analysis of performance." *JMR* 16 (1996), 111–56.

— "Can a symphony change? Establishing methodology for the historical study of performance styles." In *Musik als Text: Bericht über den Internationalen Kongress der Gesellshaft für Musikforschung, Freiburg im Breisgau 1993.* Freiburg im Breisgau, 1998: 160–72.

— "Finding the music in musicology: performance history and musical works." In Nicholas Cook and Mark Everist (eds.). *Rethinking Music.* Oxford: Oxford University Press, 1999: 424–51.

Brendel, Franz. "Robert Schumann mit Rücksicht auf Mendelssohn-Bartholdy, und die Entwicklung der modernen Tonkunst überhaupt." *Neue Zeitschrift für Musik* 22 (1845), 63–67, 81–83, 89–92, 113–15, 121–23, 145–47, 149–50.

— *Geschichte der Musik in Italien, Deutschland und Frankreich. Von der ersten christlichen Zeiten bis auf die Gegenwart* (1852). 6th ed. Leipzig: H. Matthes, 1878.

Brown, A. Peter. "Joseph Haydn and Leopold Hofmann's 'Street Songs.'" *JAMS* 33 (1980), 356–83.

— *Joseph Haydn's Keyboard Music: Sources and Style.* Bloomington: Indiana University Press, 1986.

— *Performing Haydn's* The Creation. Bloomington: Indiana University Press, 1986.

— "Haydn's Chaos: genesis and genre." *MQ* 73 (1989), 18–59.

— "Musical settings of Anne Hunter's poetry: from national song to canzonetta." *JAMS* 47 (1994), 39–89.

— "Notes on Haydn's Lieder and canzonettas." In Darwin F. Scott (ed.). *For the Love of Music: Festschrift in Honor of Theodore Front on His 90th Birthday.* Lucca, Italy: Lim Antiqua, 2002: 77–103.

— *The Symphonic Repertoire*, vol. II, *The First Golden Age of the Viennese Symphony: Haydn, Mozart, Beethoven and Schubert.* Bloomington: Indiana University Press, 2002.

Brown, Bruce Alan. "*Le pazzie d'Orlando, Orlando paladino*, and the use of parody." *Italica* 64 (1987), 583–605.

— "Gluck and opéra-comique." Liner notes to C. W. Gluck, *La rencontre imprévue ou les pèlerins de la mecque.* Erato 1991-09-03.

Brown, Clive. *Classical and Romantic Performing Practice 1750–1900.* Oxford: Oxford University Press, 1999.

Brown, Marshall. "Haydn's whimsy: poetry, sexuality, repetition." In *"The Tooth that Nibbles at the Soul": Essays on Poetry and Music.* Seattle: University of Washington Press, forthcoming.

Bülow, Hans von. *Ausgewählte Schriften: 1850–1892.* ed. Marie von Bülow. 2nd ed. Leipzig: Breitkopf & Härtel, 1911.

Burghardt, Andrew F. *Borderland: A Historical and Geographical Study of Burgenland, Austria.* Madison: University of Wisconsin Press, 1962.

Burney, Charles. *A General History of Music, from the Earliest Ages to the Present Period* (1789), with critical and historical notes by Frank Mercer. 2 vols. New York: Dover, 1957.

Burstein, Poundie. "Comedy and structure in Haydn's symphonies." In Carl Schachter and Hedi Siegel (eds.). *Schenker Studies 2.* Cambridge: Cambridge University Press, 1999: 67–81.

Butt, John. *Playing With History.* Cambridge: Cambridge University Press, 2002.

La canterina, facsimile of the libretto, *HYB* 20 (1996), 1–16.

Chew, Geoffrey. "The night-watchman's song quoted by Haydn and its implications." *HS* 3 (1973–74), 106–24.

— "Haydn's pastorellas: genre, dating and transmission in the early church music." In Otto Biba and David Wyn Jones (eds.). *Studies in Music History Presented to H. C. Robbins Landon on his Seventieth Birthday.* London: Thames and Hudson, 1996: 21–43.

Chua, Daniel K. L. "Haydn as Romantic: a chemical experiment with instrumental music." In W. Dean Sutcliffe (ed.). *Haydn Studies.* Cambridge: Cambridge University Press, 1998: 120–51.

Chusid, Martin. "Some observations on liturgy, text and structure in Haydn's late masses." In H. C. Robbins Landon and Roger E. Chapman (eds.). *Studies in*

Eighteenth-Century Music: A Tribute to Karl Geiringer on his Seventieth Birthday. Oxford: Oxford University Press, 1970: 125–35.

Clark, Caryl. "Intertextual play and Haydn's *La fedeltà premiata.*" *Current Musicology* 53 (1993), 59–81.

— "A *lieto fine* for *La canterina.*" *HYB* 20 (1996), 17–23.

— "Fabricating magic: costuming Salieri's *Armida.*" *Early Music* 31 (2003), 451–61.

— "Reading and listening: Viennese *Frauenzimmer* journals and the socio-cultural context of Mozartean opera buffa." *MQ* 87 (2004), 140–75.

Cole, Malcolm. "Momigny's analysis of Haydn's Symphony 103." *MR* 30 (1969), 261–84.

Congleton, James Edmund. *Theories of Pastoral Poetry in England 1684–1798.* Gainesville, FL: University of Florida Press, 1952.

Cook, Elizabeth Heckendorn. *Epistolary Bodies: Gender and Genre in the 18th-Century Republic of Letters.* Stanford: Stanford University Press, 1996.

Craske, Matthew. *Art in Europe 1700–1830.* Oxford: Oxford University Press, 1997.

Crotch, William. *Substance of Several Courses of Lectures on Music.* London: Longman, Rees, Orme, Brown, and Green, 1831.

Dack, James and Georg Feder (eds.). *JHW*, XXIII/1a, *Messen Nr. 1–2.* Munich: Henle, 1992.

— and Marianne Helms (eds.). *JHW*, XXIII/1b, *Messen Nr. 3–4.* Munich: Henle, 1999.

Dahlhaus, Carl. *Nineteenth-Century Music.* J. Bradford Robinson (trans.). Berkeley: University of California Press, 1989.

Da Ponte, Lorenzo. *Memoirs* [1823], trans. Elisabeth Abbott, ed. and annotated by Arthur Livingston. New York: Orion, 1959.

Debly, Patricia. "*La vera costanza*: a case study for musical characterization in Haydn's operas." *Studies in Voltaire and the Eighteenth Century* 305, Eighth International Congress on the Enlightenment (1992), 1509–13.

Derrida, Jacques. "Economimesis." In Julian Wolfreys (ed.). *The Derrida Reader: Writing Performances.* Lincoln: University of Nebraska Press, 1998: 263–93.

Dies, Albert Christoph. *Biographische Nachrichten von Joseph Haydn.* Vienna: Camesina, 1810.

Dittersdorf, Karl von. *Karl Ditters von Dittersdorf, Lebenbeschreibung. Seinem Sohne in die Feder diktirt*, 1801; *The Autobiography of Karl von Dittersdorf Dictated to His Son.* A. D. Coleridge (trans.). London, 1896.

Dobszay, László. *A History of Hungarian Music.* Mária Steiner and Paul Merrick (trans.). Budapest: Corvina, 1993.

Drabkin, William. *A Reader's Guide to Haydn's Early String Quartets.* Westport CT: Greenwood, 2000.

Dreyfus, Laurence. "Early music defended against its devotees: a theory of historical performance in the twentieth century." *MQ* 69 (1983), 297–322.

Edge, Dexter. "New sources for Haydn's early biography." Unpublished paper read at annual meeting of the American Musicological Society, 1993.

Effenberger, Eduard. *Geschichte der österreichischen Post nach amtlichen Quellen.* Vienna: R. Spies, 1913.

Eisen, Cliff. "The Mozarts' Salzburg music library." In Cliff Eisen (ed.). *Mozart Studies* 2. Oxford: Clarendon Press, 1997: 85–138.

Eliot, T. S. "Tradition and the individual talent." In David Richter (ed.). *The Critical Tradition: Classic Texts and Contemporary Trends*, 2nd ed. Boston: Beford Books, 1998: 500.

Ellis, Katharine. *Music Criticism in Nineteenth-Century France: La Revue et Gazette musicale de Paris, 1834–80.* Cambridge: Cambridge University Press, 1995.

Empson, William. *Some Versions of Pastoral.* London: Chatto & Windus, 1935.

Erdman, David U. (ed.). *The Poetry and Prose of William Blake.* Garden City, NY: Doubleday, 1965.

Favret, Mary A. *Romantic Correspondence: Women, Politics and the Fiction of Letters.* Cambridge: Cambridge University Press, 1993.

Feder, Georg. "Probleme einer Neuordnung der Klaviersonaten Haydns." *Festschrift Friedrich Blume zum 70. Geburtstag.* Anna Amelia Abert (ed.). Kassel: Bärenreiter, 1963: 92–103.

— "Haydns frühe Klaviertrios: Eine Untersuchung zur Echtheit und Chronologie." *HS* 2 (1970), 289–316.

— "Joseph Haydn als Mensch und Musiker." In Gerda Mraz (ed.). *Joseph Haydn und seine Zeit.* Eisenstadt: Institut für österreichische Kulturgeschichte, 1972: 43–56.

— "Haydn's Korrekturen zum Klavierauszug der 'Jahreszeiten.'" In T. Kohlhase and V. Scherliess (eds.). *Festschrift Georg von Dadelsen sum 60. Geburtstag.* Neuhausen-Stuttgart: Hännsler, 1978: 101–12.

— "Dramatische Aspekte der *Cantarina*-Intermezzi von Sciroli (1753), Conforto (1754), Piccinni (1760) und Haydn (1766)." In Bianca Maria Antolini and Wolfgang Witzenmann (eds.). *Napoli e il teatro musicale in Europa tra sette e ottocento: studi in onore di Friedrich Lippmann.* Firenze: Leo S. Olschki, 1993: 55–67.

— *Joseph Haydn: Die Schöpfung.* Kassel: Bärenreiter, 1999.

— (ed.). *Klaviersonaten, JHW* XVIII, vol. 1–3. Munich: Henle, 1966–1970.

— Heinrich Hüschen, and Ulrich Tank (eds.). *Joseph Haydn, Tradition und Rezeption.* Regensburg: G. Bosse, 1985.

— and Günter Thomas. "Dokumente zur Ausstattung von *Lo speziale, L'infedeltà delusa, La fedeltà premiata, Armida* und andere Opern Haydns." *HS* 6 (1988), 88–115.

Fétis, François-Joseph. *Biographie universelle des musiciens et bibliographie générale de musique.* Brussels: Meline, Cans et Compagnie, 1839.

Fillion, Michelle. *Early Viennese Chamber Music with Obbligato Keyboard*, Vol. I: *Six Keyboard Trios;* Vol. II: *Six Ensemble Works for Two to Five Performers.* Madison, WI: A-R Editions, 1989.

— "Accompanied keyboard music." In Stanley Sadie (ed.). *The New Grove Dictionary of Music and Musicians*, rev. ed., vol. I. London: Macmillan, 2001: 53–55.

Finscher, Ludwig. *Studien zur Geschichte des Streichquartetts.* Walter Wiora (ed.), *Saarbrücker Studien zur Musikwissenschaft.* Kassel: Bärenreiter, 1974.

Fischer, Adam. Notes to Fischer and the Austro-Hungarian Orchestra's recording of Haydn's complete symphonies. Brilliant Classics, 2001.

Fiske, Roger. *Scotland in Music: A European Enthusiasm.* Cambridge: Cambridge University Press, 1983.

Flinker, Noam. "Miltonic voices in Haydn's *Creation.*" *Milton Studies* 27, James D. Simmonds (ed.). Pittsburgh 1992: 139–64.

Foucault, Michel. *Madness and Civilization: A History of Insanity in the Age of Reason* (1961); trans. Richard Howard. New York: Vintage, 1965.

Freeman, Robert. "Robert Kimmerling: a little-known Haydn pupil." *HYB* 13 (1982), 143–79.

Freudenthal, Herbert. *Das Feuer im deutschen Glauben und Brauch.* Berlin, Leipzig: Walter de Gruyter, 1931.

Friedlaender, Max. *Das deutsche Lied im 18. Jahrhundert,* 2 vols. Stuttgart and Berlin: Cotta, 1902.

Galloway, Kate. "The hunt and its extended symbolism in Haydn's *La fedeltà premiata.*" Unpublished paper, University of Toronto (Fall 2003).

Gates-Coon, Rebecca. *The Landed Estates of the Esterházy Princes: Hungary During the Reforms of Maria Theresia and Joseph II.* Baltimore: The Johns Hopkins University Press, 1994.

Geiringer, Karl. "Haydn and the folksong of the British Isles." *MQ* 35 (1949), 179–208.

— *Haydn: A Creative Life in Music.* 3rd ed. Berkeley: University of California Press, 1968.

Geographische- und topographisches Reisebuch durch alle Staaten der österreichischen Monarchie, nebst der Reiseroute nach Petersburg durch Polen. Vienna: Rudolph Gräffer, 1789.

Gerber, Ernst Ludwig. *Historisch-biographisches Lexikon der Tonkünstler,* 2 vols. Leipzig: Breitkopf, 1790–92.

Gilman, Sander L. *Seeing the Insane.* New York: Wiley, 1982.

Gilroy, Amanda and W. M. Verhoeven (eds.). *Epistolary Histories: Letters, Fiction, Culture.* Charlottesville: University Press of Virginia, 2000.

Goehring, Edmund J. "Despina, Cupid, and the pastoral mode of *Così fan tutte.*" *Cambridge Opera Journal* 7 (1995), 107–33.

Gottschald, Ernst. "Ein Prophet des Stillstands und zwei Artikel der *Allgemeine musikalische Zeitung.*" *Neue Zeitschrift für Musik* 29 (1848), 293–96, 298–300.

Gotwals, Vernon (trans. and ed.). *Joseph Haydn: Eighteenth-Century Gentleman and Genius.* Madison: University of Wisconsin Press, 1963.

Gramit, David. *Cultivating Music: The Aspirations, Interests, and Limits of German Musical Culture, 1770–1848.* Berkeley: University of California Press, 2002.

Green, Rebecca. "Representing the aristocracy: the operatic Haydn and *Le pescatrici.*" In Elaine Sisman (ed.). *Haydn and His World.* Princeton: Princeton University Press, 1997: 154–200.

Griesinger, Georg August. *Biographische Notizen über Joseph Haydn.* Leipzig: Breitkopf & Härtel, 1810; Vienna: Paul Kaltschmid, 1954.

Hanslick, Eduard. *Aus dem Concertsaal: Kritiken und Schilderungen aus dem letzten 20 Jahren des wiener Musiklebens.* Vienna: W. Braumüller, 1870.

— *Sämtliche Schriften: Historisch-kritische Ausgabe.* vol. I/i–iii. ed. Dietmar Strauß. Vienna: Böhlau, 1993.

Hardach-Pinke, Irene. "Erziehung und Unterricht durch Gouvernanten." In Elke Kleinau and Claudia Opitz (eds.). *Geschichte der Mädchen- und Frauenbildung* vol. I. Frankfurt: Campus Verlag, 1996: 409–27.

Hárich, János. "Das Repertoire des Opernkapellmeisters Joseph Haydn in Eszterháza (1780–1790)." *HYB* 1 (1962), 9–109.

— "Das fürstlich Esterházy'sche Fideikommiß." *HYB* 4 (1968), 5–35.

— "Inventare der Esterházy-Hofkapelle in Eisenstadt." *HYB* 9 (1975), 5–125.

— "Documents from the archives of János Hárich." *HYB* 18 (1993), 1–109; (1994), 1–359.

Harlow, Alvin F. *Old Post Bags.* New York and London: D. Appleton, 1928.

Harper, John. *The Forms and Orders of Western Liturgy from the Tenth to the Eighteenth Century. A Historical Introduction and Guide for Students and Musicians.* Oxford: Oxford University Press, 1991.

Harris, Ellen. *Handel and the Pastoral Tradition.* Oxford: Oxford University Press, 1980.

Harrison, Bernard. *Haydn's Keyboard Music: Studies in Performance Practice.* Oxford: Clarendon, 1997.

— *Haydn: The "Paris" Symphonies.* Cambridge: Cambridge University Press, 1998.

Head, Matthew. "Music with 'no past'? Archaeologies and Joseph Haydn and *The Creation.*" *19th-Century Music* 23 (1999–2000), 191–217.

— *Orientalism, Masquerade and Mozart's Turkish Music.* Royal Musical Association Monographs 9. London: RMA, 2000.

Heartz, Daniel. "Haydn und Gluck im Burgtheater um 1760: *Der neue krumme Teufel, Le Diable à quatre* und die Sinfonie 'Le Soir.'" In Christoph-Hellmut Mahling and Sigrid Wiesmann (eds.). *Bericht über den Internationalen Musikwissenschaftlichen Kongress, Bayreuth 1981.* Kassel: Bärenreiter, 1984: 120–35.

— "Haydn's *Acide e Galatea* and the imperial wedding operas of 1760 by Hasse and Gluck." In Eva Badura-Skoda (ed.). *Internationaler Joseph Haydn Kongress, Wien 1982.* Munich: Henle, 1986: 332–40.

— *Haydn, Mozart, and the Viennese School, 1740–1780.* New York: Norton, 1995.

Helms, Marianne. "Zur Entstehung des zweiten Teils der 24 deutschen Lieder." In Eva Badura-Skoda (ed.). *International Joseph Haydn Kongress, Wien 1982.* Munich: Henle, 1986: 116–26.

— and Fred Stoltzfus (eds.). *JHW*, XXII/1, *Stabat mater.* Munich: Henle, 1993.

Henisch, Bridget Ann. *The Musical Calendar Year.* University Park, PA: Pennsylvania State University Press, 1999.

Hepokoski, James and Warren Darcy. "The medial caesura and its role in the eighteenth-century sonata exposition." *Music Theory Spectrum* 19 (1997), 115–54.

Hickman, Roger. "The flowering of the Viennese String Quartet in the late eighteenth century." *MR* 50 (1989), 157–80.

— s.v. "String Quartet" in Stanley Sadie (ed.), *The New Grove Dictionary of Music and Musicians*, 2nd ed. London: Macmillan, 2002.

Historical Atlas of Central Europe, Paul Robert Magocsi (ed.). Seattle: University of Washington Press, 2002.

Hodgson, Antony. "Christopher Hogwood: A new Haydn symphony AAM recording project." *Hi-Fi News and Record Review* (March 1990), 95–97.

Hoffmann, E. T. A. "Beethoven's instrumental music" (1813), trans. unattrib. in Oliver Strunk (ed.). *Source Readings in Music History: The Romantic Era.* New York: Norton, 1965: 36–37.

— *Dichtungen und Schriften sowie Briefe und Tagebücher: Gesamtausgabe*, ed. Walter Harich. 15 vols. Vol. XII. Weimar: Lichtenstein, 1924.

Horányi, Mátyás. *The Magnificence of Eszterháza*, trans. András Deák. London: Barrie and Rockliff, 1962.

Hörwarthner, Maria. "Joseph Haydns Bibliothek – Versuch einer literarhistorischen Rekonstruktion." In Herbert Zeman (ed.). *Joseph Haydn und die Literatur seiner Zeit, Jahrbuch für österreichische Kulturgeschichte* 6 (1976), 157–207. Trans. Kathrine Talbot as "Joseph Haydn's library: an attempt at a literary-historical reconstruction." In Elaine Sisman (ed.). *Haydn and His World.* Princeton: Princeton University Press, 1997: 395–462.

Hosler, Bellamy. *Changing Aesthetic Views of Instrumental Music in 18th-Century Germany.* Ann Arbor: University of Michigan, 1981.

Höslinger, Clemens. "Der überwundene Standpunkt: Joseph Haydn in der wiener Musikkritik des 19. Jahrhunderts." *Jahrbuch für österreichische Kulturgeschichte* 1/ii: *Beiträge zur Musikgeschichte des 18. Jahrhunderts* (1971), 116–42.

Huber, Alfons. "Deckelstützen und Schalldeckel an Hammerklavieren." In Friedemann Hellwig (ed.). *Studia Organologica: Festschrift für John Henry van der Meer zu seinem fünfundsechzigsten Geburtstag.* Tutzing: Hans Schneider, 1987: 229–50.

— (ed.). *Das österreichische Cembalo: 600 Jahre Cembalobau in Österreich.* Tutzing: Hans Schneider, 2001.

Hunter, Mary. "Text, music, and drama in Haydn's Italian opera arias: four case studies." *JM* 7 (1989), 29–57.

— "Armida." In Stanley Sadie (ed.), *The New Grove Dictionary of Opera.* London: Macmillan, 1992: vol. I, 198–99.

— "The *alla turca* style in the late eighteenth century: race and gender in the symphony and the seraglio." In Jonathan Bellman (ed.). *The Exotic in Western Music.* Boston: Northeastern University Press, 1998: 43–73.

— *The Culture of Opera Buffa in Mozart's Vienna: A Poetics of Entertainment.* Princeton: Princeton University Press, 1999.

Hurwitz, David. Review of Haydn, Symphonies nos. 100 and 103, Sir Charles Mackerras conducting the Orchestra of St. Luke's. *Fanfare* (March/April, 1992), 213.

Hurwitz, Joachim. "Haydn and the Freemasons." *HYB* 16 (1985), 5–98.

Irving, Howard. "William Crotch on *The Creation.*" *ML* 75 (1994), 548–60.

Jones, David Wyn. *Beethoven: "Pastoral" Symphony.* Cambridge: Cambridge University Press, 1995.

— *The Life of Beethoven.* Cambridge: Cambridge University Press, 1998.

— "Minuets and trios in Haydn's quartets." In Robert Young (ed.). *Haydn the Innovator: A New Approach to the String Quartets.* Todmorden, Lancs: Arc Music, 2000: 81–97.

— (ed.). *Oxford Composer Companion: Haydn.* Oxford: Oxford University Press, 2002.

Kant, Immanuel. *Kritik der Urteilskraft*, ed. K. Vorländer. Hamburg: Meiner, Philosophische Bibliothek, 1924. Trans. Werner S. Pluhar, *The Critique of Judgment.* Indianapolis: Hackett, 1987.

Kerman, Joseph. "Viewpoint." *19th Century Music* 2 (1978–79), 186–91.

Kiesewetter, Raphael Georg. *Geschichte der europaeisch-abendlaendischen oder unsrer heutigen Musik*, 2nd ed. Leipzig: Breitkopf & Härtel 1846; repr. Walluf, 1972.

Kirsch, Winfried. "Vergangenes und Gegenwärtiges in Haydns Oratorien: Zur Dramaturgie der *Schöpfung* und der *Jahreszeiten.*" In Christoph-Helmut Mahling (ed.). *Florilegium Musicologicum: Festschrift Hellmut Federhofer zum 75. Geburtstag.* Tutzing: Schneider, 1988: 169–87.

Klampfer, Josef. "Das Eisenstädter Ghetto," *Burgenländische Forschungen* 51 (1966).

Komlós, Katalin. "The Viennese keyboard trio in the 1780s: sociological background and contemporary reception." *ML* 68 (1987), 222–34.

— *Fortepianos and Their Music: Germany, Austria, and England, 1760–1800.* Oxford: Clarendon Press, 1995.

— "Viola's willow song: 'She never told her love.'" *MT* 140 (1999), 36–41.

Korabinsky, Johann Mathias. *Geographisch-historisches und Produkten Lexikon von Ungarn.* Pressburg: Weber and Korabinsky, 1786.

Kosáry, Domokos. *Culture and Society in Eighteenth-Century Hungary*, trans. Zsuzsa Béres. Budapest: Corvina, 1987.

Kramer, Lawrence. "Music and representation: the instance of Haydn's *Creation.*" In Steven Paul Scher (ed.). *Music and Text: Critical Inquiries.* Cambridge: Cambridge University Press, 1992: 139–62.

Kretschmann, Carl. "Romantik in der Musik." *Neue Zeitschrift für Musik* 29 (1848), 1–6, 9–11.

Kretzschmar, Hermann. *Führer durch den Concertsaal.* Vol. I. Leipzig: A. G. Liebeskind, 1888.

Kucaba, John (ed). *Georg Christoph Wagenseil 1715–1777. Fifteen Symphonies*, series B. vol. 3. *The Symphony 1720–1840.* Barry S. Brook (editor-in-chief). New York: Garland, 1981.

Kumbier, William A. "A 'new quickening': Haydn's *The Creation*, Wordsworth, and the pictorialist imagination." *Studies in Romanticism* 30 (1991), 535–63.

— "Haydn's English canzonettas: transformations in the rhetoric of the musical sublime." In P. Barker, S. W. Goodwin, and G. Handwerk (eds.). *The Scope of Words: In Honor of Albert S. Cook.* New York: P. Land, 1991: 73–93.

— "Rhetoric and expression in Haydn's *Applausus* Cantata." *HYB* 18 (1993), 213–65.

Landon, H. C. Robbins. *The Symphonies of Joseph Haydn.* London: Universal Edition and Rockliff, 1955.

— *The Collected Correspondence and London Notebooks of Joseph Haydn*. London: Barrie & Rockliff, 1959.

— *Haydn: Chronicle and Works*. 5 vols. London: Thames and Hudson; Bloomington: Indiana University Press, 1976–80.

— *Haydn: A Documentary Study*. New York: Rizzoli, 1981.

— *Mozart and the Masons: New Light on the Lodge "Crowned Hope."* London: Thames and Hudson, 1982.

— (trans. and ed.) "An Englishman in Vienna and Eisenstadt Castle in 1748 and 1749." *HYB* 18 (1993), 197–212.

Larsen, Jens Peter. "Joseph Haydn – Eine Herausforderung an uns," in Eva Badura-Skoda (ed.). *International Joseph Haydn Kongress, Wien 1982*. Munich: Henle, 1986: 9–20.

— Howard Serwer, and James Webster (eds.). *Haydn Studies*. New York: Norton, 1981.

le Huray, Peter and James Day (eds.). *Music and Aesthetics in the Eighteenth and Early-Nineteenth Centuries*. Cambridge: Cambridge University Press, 1981.

Leopold, Silke. "Haydn und die Tradition der Orpheus-Opern." *Musica* 36 (1982), 131–35.

Leux-Henschen, Irmgard. *Joseph Martin Kraus in seinen Briefen*. Stockholm: Edition Reimers, 1978.

Levarie, Siegmund. "The closing numbers of *Die Schöpfung*." In H. C. Robbins Landon and Roger E. Chapman (eds.). *Studies in Eighteenth-Century Music: A Tribute to Karl Geiringer on his Seventieth Birthday*. Oxford: Oxford University Press, 1970: 315–22.

Levy, Janet M. "The Quatuor Concertant in Paris in the latter half of the eighteenth century." Ph.D. diss., Stanford University, 1971.

— "'Something mechanical encrusted on the living': a source of musical wit and humor." In W. J. Allanbrook, J. M. Levy, and W. P. Mahrt (eds.). *Convention in Eighteenth- and Nineteenth-Century Music*. New York, Pendragon Press, 1992.

Lickleder, Christoph. *Choral und figurierte Kirchenmusik in der Sicht Franz Xaver Witts anhand der Fliegenden Blätter und der Musica sacra*. Regensburg: Feuchtinger & Gleichauf, 1988.

Link, Dorothea. "*L'arbore di Diana*: a model for *Così fan tutte*." In Stanley Sadie (ed.). *Wolfgang Amadè Mozart: Essays on his Life and his Music*. Oxford: Oxford University Press, 1995: 362–73.

Lobe, Johann Christian. "Fortschritt." *Allgemeine musikalische Zeitung* 50 (1848), 48–51, 65–69, 169–73, 337–41.

Locke, Ralph. "Exoticism," s.v. Stanley Sadie (ed.). *The New Grove Dictionary of Music and Musicians*, 2nd ed. London: Macmillan, 2001.

Loesser, Arthur. *Men, Women, and Pianos: A Social History*. New York: Dover, 1990.

Loughrey, Bryan (ed.). *The Pastoral Mode: A Casebook*. London: Macmillan, 1984.

Lowe, Melanie. "Expressive paradigms in the symphonies of Joseph Haydn." Ph.D. diss., Princeton University, 1998.

— "Falling from grace: irony and expressive enrichment in Haydn's symphonic minuets." *JM* 19 (2002), 171–221.

MacIntyre, Bruce. *The Viennese Concerted Mass of the Early Classic Period.* Ann Arbor: UMI Research Press, 1986.

— *Haydn:* The Creation. New York: Schirmer, 1998.

McCaldin, Denis. "The *Missa Sancti Nicolai*: Haydn's long 'Missa brevis.'" *Soundings* 3 (1973), 3–17.

McClymonds, Marita. "Haydn and his Contemporaries: *Armida abbandonata.*" In Eva Badura-Skoda (ed.). *International Joseph Haydn Kongress, Wien 1982.* Munich: Henle, 1986: 325–32.

— "Haydn and the opera seria tradition: *Armida.*" In Bianca Maria Antolini and Wolfgang Witzenmann (eds.). *Napoli e il Teatro Musicale in Europa tra Sette e Ottocento.* Florence, 1993: 191–206.

McGrann, Jeremiah W. "Of saints, namedays, and Turks: some background on Haydn's masses written for Prince Nikolaus II Esterházy." *JMR* 17 (1998), 195–210.

Magocsi, Paul Robert (ed.). *Historical Atlas of Central Europe.* Seattle: University of: Cambridge Washington Press, 2002.

Marczali, Henrik. *Hungary in the Eighteenth Century,* trans. Arthur B. Yolland. Cambridge: Cambridge University Press, 1910; rpt: New York: Arno Press, 1971.

Marsh, John. *The John Marsh Journals: The Life and Times of a Gentleman Composer,* Brian Robins (ed.). Stuyvesant, NY: Pendragon, 1998.

Marx, Adolf Bernhard. "Andeutung des Standpunktes der Zeitung. (Als Epilog.)" *Berliner allgemeine musikalische Zeitung* 1 (1824), 444–48.

— "Etwas über die Symphonie und Beethovens Leistungen in diesem Fache." *Berliner allgemeine musikalische Zeitung* 1 (1824), 165–68, 173–76, 181–84.

— "Etwas über Joseph Haidn und seinen Standpunkt in der Kunstentwicklung." *Berliner allgemeine musikalische Zeitung* 1 (1824), 299–302, 327–29.

— *Ludwig van Beethoven: Leben und Schaffen,* 2 vols. Berlin: O. Janke 1859; 5th ed., 1901.

Maunder, Richard. *Keyboard Instruments in Eighteenth-Century Vienna.* Oxford: Clarendon Press, 1998.

Mies, Paul. *Kritischer Bericht* to *JHW* XXX, Munich: Henle, 1958.

— "Textdichter zu J. Haydns, 'Mehrstimmigen Gesängen,'" *HYB* 1 (1962), 201.

Molnár, Miklós. *A Concise History of Hungary,* trans. Anna Magyar. Cambridge: Cambridge University Press, 2001.

Momigny, J.-J. de "Analysis of Haydn's Symphony [no. 103 in E♭ ("Drumroll")]." In Ian Bent (ed.). *Music Analysis in the Nineteenth Century.* Vol. II. Cambridge: Cambridge University Press, 1994.

Mörner, C.-G. Stellan. "Haydniania aus Schweden um 1800." *HS* 2 (1969–70), 1–33.

Morrow, Mary Sue. *Concert Life in Haydn's Vienna: Aspects of a Developing Musical and Social Institution.* New York: Pendragon, 1989.

Mosel, Ignaz Franz von. "Die Tonkunst in Wien." *Allgemeine Wiener Musik-Zeitung* 3 (1843): 533–34, 601–3.

Mozart, Wolfgang Amadeus. *Mozart: Briefe und Aufzeichnungen,* Wilhelm Bauer and Otto Erich Deutsch (eds.), 7 vols. Kassel: Bärenreiter, 1962–75; trans. E. Anderson. *The Letters of Mozart and His Family,* 2nd ed., 3 vols. London: Macmillan, 1966.

Naumann, Emil. *Deutsche Tondichter von Sebastian Bach bis auf die Gegenwart*, 2nd ed. Berlin: R. Oppenheim, 1875.

Neefe, Christian Gottlob. "Ueber die musikalische Wiederholung." *Deutsches Museum* 1 (August, 1776), 745–51.

Neff, Theresa M. "Baron van Swieten and late eighteenth-century musical culture." Ph.D. diss., Boston University, 1998.

Neubacher, Jürgen. "'Idee' and 'Ausführung.' Zum Kompositionsprozess bei Joseph Haydn." *Archiv für Musikwissenschaft* 41 (1984), 187–207.

Neubauer, John. *The Emancipation of Music from Language*. New Haven: Yale University Press, 1986.

Niemetschek, Franz Xaver. *Leben des K. K. Kapellmeisters Wolfgang Gottlieb Mozart*, 1798; *Life of Mozart*. H. Mautner (trans.). London: L. Hyman, 1956.

Nietzsche, Friedrich. *Die Geburt der Tragödie, Nietzsche Werke*, ser. III, vol. I. Giorgio Colli and Mazzino Montinari (eds.) Berlin and New York: Walter de Gruyter, 1972.

— *Der Wanderer und sein Schatten* (1880) (*Menschliches, Allzumenschliches*, vol. II, pt. ii.). *Nietzsche Werke*. Giorgio Colli and Mazzino Montinari (eds.), ser. IV, vol. III. Berlin and New York: Walter de Gruyter, 1967.

November, Nancy R. "Haydn's vocality and the idea of 'true' string quartets." Ph.D. diss., Cornell University, 2003.

Okey, Robin. *The Habsburg Monarchy: From Enlightenment to Eclipse*. London: St. Martin's Press, 2001.

Olleson, Edward. "Georg August Griesinger's correspondence with Breitkopf & Härtel." *HYB* 3 (1965), 5–53.

Oort, Bart van. "The English classical piano style and its influence on Haydn and Beethoven." DMA diss., Cornell University, 1993.

— "Haydn and the English classical piano style," *Early Music* 28 (2000), 73–89.

Outram, Dorinda. *The Enlightenment*. Cambridge: Cambridge University Press, 1995.

Over, Berthold. "Arianna travestita: Haydns Kantate *Arianna a Naxos* in geistlichem Gewand." *HS* 7 (1998), 384–97.

Papp, Géza. "Die Quellen der 'Verbunkos-Musik': Ein bibliographischer Versuch." *Studia Musicologica* 21 (1979), 151–217.

Parakilas, James (ed.). *Piano Roles*. New Haven and London: Yale University Press, 1999.

Parke, William Thomas. *Musical Memoirs*. London, 1830.

Parker, Mara. *The String Quartet, 1750–1797: Four Types of Musical Conversation*. Aldershot: Ashgate, 2002.

Pauly, Reinhard G. "The reforms of church music under Joseph II." *MQ* 43 (1957), 372–82.

Perger, Richard. *Das Palais Esterházy in der Wallnerstraße zu Wien*. Vienna: Franz Deuticke, 1994.

Pezzl, Johann. "Sketch of Vienna." trans. H. C. Robbins Landon. In *Mozart and Vienna*. New York: Schirmer, 1991.

Philip, Robert T. *Early Recordings and Musical Style*. Cambridge: Cambridge University Press, 1992.

Poggioli, Renato. *The Oaten Flute: Essays on Pastoral Poetry and the Pastoral Ideal.* Cambridge, MA: Harvard University Press, 1975.

Pohl, Carl Ferdinand. *Joseph Haydn.* Vol. I, Berlin, 1875; Vol. II, Leipzig 1882; Vol. III completed by Hugo Botstiber, Leipzig 1927.

Porter, Roy. *The Enlightenment.* London: Macmillan, 1990.

Price, Curtis. "Italian Opera and arson in late eighteenth-century London." *JAMS* 42 (1989), 55–107.

— *et al. Italian Opera in Late Eighteenth-Century London.* Oxford: Clarendon Press, 1995.

Prickler, Harald and Johann Seedoch (eds.). *Eisenstadt: Bausteine zur Geschichte.* Eisenstadt: Nentwich-Lattner, 1998.

Quantz, Johann Joachim. *Versuch einer Anweisung die Flöte traversière zu spielen.* Berlin: Johann Friedrich Voß, 1752; facsimile by Kassel: Bärenreiter, 1997.

Redford, Bruce. *The Converse of the Pen: Acts of Intimacy in the Eighteenth-Century Familiar Letter.* Chicago: University of Chicago Press, 1986.

Rees, Abraham. s.v, "Eisenstadt." In *Cyclopaedia.* Philadelphia: Bradford, 1810–24.

Reimer, Erich. "Kenner–Liebhaber–Dilettant." In *Handwörterbuch der musikalischen Terminologie,* ed. Hans Heinrich Eggebrecht. Wiesbaden: F. Steiner, 1974.

Rellstab, Ludwig. "Theodor: Eine musikalische Skizze." *Berliner allgemeine musikalische Zeitung* 1 (1824): 247–49, 255–58, 263–66, 271–75, 279–81.

Rice, John A. "Sarti's *Giulio Sabino,* Haydn's *Armida,* and the arrival of opera seria at Eszterháza." *HYB* 15 (1984), 181–98.

— "Anton Walter, instrument maker to Leopold II." *Journal of the American Musical Instrument Society* 15 (1989), 32–51.

— *Antonio Salieri and Viennese Opera.* Chicago: University of Chicago Press, 1998.

— *Empress Marie Therese and Music at the Viennese Court, 1792–1807.* Cambridge: Cambridge University Press, 2003.

Richards, Annette. *The Free Fantasia and the Musical Picturesque.* Cambridge: Cambridge University Press, 2001.

Riedel-Martiny, Anke. "Das Verhältnis von Text und Musik in Haydn's Oratorien." *HS* 1 (1965–67), 205–40.

Riehl, Wilhelm Heinrich. *Musikalische Charakterköpfe: Ein kunstgeschichtliches Skizzenbuch,* 2 vols. 2nd ed. Stuttgart: J. G. Cotta, 1862.

— "Das Volkslied in seinem Einfluß auf die gesammte Entwicklung der modernen Musik." *Die Gegenwart. Eine encyclopädische Darstellung der neuesten Zeitgeschichte für alle Stände,* vol. III. Leipzig, 1849: 667–86.

Riepe, Juliane. "Eine neue Quelle zum Repertoire der Bonner Hofkapelle im späten 18. Jahrhundert." *Archiv für Musikwissenschaft* 60 (2003): 97–114.

Roberts, Timothy (ed.). *O Tuneful Voice: 25 Classical English Songs.* Oxford: Oxford University Press, 1992.

Rosen, Charles. *The Classical Style: Haydn, Mozart, Beethoven.* New York: Norton, 1972; rev. ed., 1997.

— *Sonata Forms.* New York: Norton, 1980.

Rösing, Helmut. "Gedanken zum 'Musikalischen Hören.'" *Die Musikforschung* 27 (1974), 213–16.

Rushton, Julian. "Viennese amateur or London professional? A reconsideration of Haydn's tragic cantata *Arianna a Naxos*." In David Wyn Jones (ed.) *Music in 18th-Century Austria.* Cambridge: Cambridge University Press, 1996: 232–45.

Rye, Matthew. Notes to Roy Goodman and The Hanover Band's recording of Haydn's Symphonies nos. 45–47. London: Hyperion Records, 1991.

Said, Edward W. *Orientalism: Western Conceptions of the Orient.* (1978); rpt. Harmondsworth: Penguin, 1995.

Sandberger, Adolf. "Zur Einbürgerung der Kunst Josef Haydns in Deutschland." *Neues Beethoven Jahrbuch* (1935), 5–25.

Schafer, Hollace A. "'A wisely ordered Phantasie': Joseph Haydn's creative process from the sketches and drafts for instrumental music." Ph.D. diss., Brandeis University, 1987.

Schenker, Heinrich. "On organicism in sonata form." trans. William Drabkin. In Schenker. *The Masterwork in Musik*, vol. II. Cambridge: Cambridge University Press, 1996: 23–30.

— "The Representation of Chaos from Haydn's *Creation*," trans. William Drabkin, in Schenker. *The Masterwork in Musik*, vol. II. Cambridge: Cambridge University Press, 1996: 97–105.

Schönfeld, Johann Ferdinand von. *Jahrbuch der Tonkunst von Wien und Prag* (1796), facs. ed. Otto Biba (Munich and Salzburg, 1976); portions trans. Kathrine Talbot in Elaine Sisman (ed.), *Haydn and His World.* Princeton: Princeton University Press, 1997: 289–320.

Schiller, Friedrich. *On the Aesthetic Education of Man* (1795), trans. Reginald Snell. New York: Ungar, 1965.

Schilling, Gustav (ed.). *Encyclopädie der gesammten musikalischen Wissenschaften, oder Universal-Lexicon der Tonkunst*, 6 vols. Stuttgart: F. H. Köhler, 1835–42.

Schmidt, Leopold. *Joseph Haydn.* Berlin: Harmonie, 1898.

Schmitz, Dietmar. "La théorie de l'art épistolaire et de la conversation dans la tradition latine et néolatine." In Bernard Bray and Christoph Strosetzki (eds.). *Art de la lettre/Art de la conversation à l'époque classique en France.* Paris: Klincksieck, 1995: 11–23.

Schneider, Helmut J. (ed.). *Deutsche Idyllentheorien im 18. Jahrhundert.* Tübingen: Narr, 1988.

Schonberg, Harold C. *The Lives of the Great Composers*, 2 vols. London: Futura, 1975.

Schroeder, David P. *Haydn and the Enlightenment: the Late Symphonies and their Audience.* Oxford: Clarendon Press, 1990.

— *Mozart in Revolt: Strategies of Resistance, Mischief, and Deception.* New Haven: Yale University Press, 1999.

Schucht, Johannes. "Der überwundene Standpunkt in der Tonkunst." *Allgemeine musikalische Zeitung* 50 (1848), 536–38, 755–59.

Schwartz, Judith L. "Cultural stereotypes and music in the 18th Century." *Studies on Voltaire and the Eighteenth Century* 151–55 (1976), 1989–2013.

Schumann, Robert. *Gesammelte Schriften über Musik und Musiker*, Heinrich Simon (ed.). 3 vols. Leipzig: P. Reclam [1888].

Scott, Marion. "Some English affinities and associations of Haydn's songs." *ML* 25 (1944), 1–12.

Shulman, Laurie. "The Breitkopf & Härtel *Oeuvres complettes de J. Haydn.*" In Jens Peter Larsen, Howard Serwer, and James Webster (eds.). *Haydn Studies: Proceedings of the International Haydn Conference, Washington D.C., 1975.* New York: Norton, 1981: 137–42.

Shaftesbury, Anthony Ashley Cooper. *Characteristics of Men, Manners, Opinions, Times*, 4th ed. vol. I. London, 1727.

Siegert, Bernhard. *Relays: Literature as an Epoch of the Postal System*, trans. Kevin Repp. Stanford: Stanford University Press, 1999.

Sisman, Elaine. "Haydn's hybrid variations." In Jens Peter Larsen, Howard Serwer, and James Webster (eds.). *Haydn Studies.* New York, 1981: 509–15.

— "Haydn's baryton pieces and his serious genres." In Eva Badura-Skoda (ed.). *International Joseph Haydn Kongress, Wien 1982.* Munich: Henle, 1986: 426–35.

— "Haydn's theater symphonies." *JAMS* 43 (1990), 292–352.

— *Haydn and the Classical Variation.* Cambridge: Harvard University Press, 1993.

— "Haydn's solo keyboard music." In Robert L. Marshall (ed.). *Eighteenth-Century Keyboard Music.* New York: Schirmer, 1994: 270–307.

— "Haydn, Shakespeare, and the rules of originality," in Elaine Sisman (ed.). *Haydn and His World.* Princeton: Princeton University Press, 1997: 3–56.

— "After the heroic style: fantasia and the 'characteristic' sonatas of 1809." *Beethoven Forum* 6 (1998), 68–96.

— "The voice of God in Haydn's *Creation.*" In Vera Lampert and László Vikárius (eds.). *Essays in Honor of László Somfai: Studies in the Sources and the Interpretation of Music.* Lanham, MD: Scarecrow Press, 2004: 139–153.

— "Observations on the first phase of Mozart's 'Haydn' Quartets." In Dorothea Link (ed.). *Words about Mozart in Honour of Stanley Sadie.* Woodbridge, Suffolk: Boydell and Brewer, 2005: 33–58.

— "Rhetorical truth in Haydn's chamber music: genre, tertiary rhetoric, and the Op. 76 Quartets." In Tom Beghin, Elisabeth LeGuin, and Sander Goldberg (eds.) *Engaging Rhetoric: Essays on Haydn and Performance.* Chicago: University of Chicago Press, forthcoming.

Small, Christopher. *Musicking: The Meanings of Performing and Listening.* Hanover, NH: Wesleyan University Press, 1998.

Smither, Howard E. *A History of the Oratorio*, vol. III. *The Oratorio in the Classical Era.* Chapel Hill: University of North Carolina Press, 1987.

Somfai, László. *Joseph Haydn: Sein Leben in zeitgenössischen Bildern.* Kassel and London: Bärenreiter, 1966; trans. Mari Kuttna and Károly Ravasz as *Haydn: His Life in Contemporary Pictures.* New York: Taplinger, 1969.

— "Opus-Planung und Neuerung bei Haydn." *Studia Musicologica* 22 (1980), 87–110.

— *The Keyboard Sonatas of Joseph Haydn: Instruments and Performance Practice, Genres, and Styles*, trans. Charlotte Greenspan and the author. Chicago: University of Chicago Press, 1995.

Staud, Géza. "Haydns *Armida.*" *Maske und Kothurn* (1982), 87–104.

Steblin, Rita. "Haydns Orgeldienst in 'der damaligen Gräfl. Haugwitzischen Kapelle.'" *Wiener Geschichtsblätter* 55 (2000): 124–34.

Stephen, J. Drew. "The motif of the hunt in Romantic opera." Ph.D. diss., University of Toronto, 2002.

Strommer, Roswitha. "Wiener literarische Salons zur Zeit J. Haydns." in Herbert Zeman (ed.). *Joseph Haydn und die Literatur seiner Zeit, Jahrbuch für österreichische Kulturgeschichte* 6 (1976), 97–121.

Suchalla, Ernst. *Briefe von Carl Philipp Emanuel Bach an Johann Gottlob Immanuel Breitkopf und Johann Nikolaus Forkel.* Tutzing: Schneider, 1985.

Sulzer, Johann Georg. *Allgemeine Theorie der schönen Künste.* Leipzig, 1771–74.

Sutcliffe, W. Dean. *Haydn: String Quartets, Op. 50.* Cambridge: Cambridge University Press, 1992.

— "The Haydn piano trio: textual facts and textural principles." In W. Dean Sutcliffe (ed.). *Haydn Studies.* Cambridge: Cambridge University Press, 1998: 246–90.

Szabolcsi, Bence. "Joseph Haydn und die ungarische Musik." *Beiträge zur Musikwissenschaft* 1 (1959), 62–73.

Tank, Ulrich. "Die Dokumente der Esterházy-Archive zur fürstlichen Hofkapelle in der Zeit von 1761 bis 1770." *HS* 4 (1980), 129–333.

— "Studien zur Esterhazyschen Hofmusik von etwa 1620 bis 1790." *Kölner Beiträge zur Musikforschung* 101. Regensburg: G. Bosse, 1981.

— "Joseph Haydns geistliche Musik in der Anschauung des 19. Jahrhunderts." In Georg Feder, Heinrich Hüschen, and Ulrich Tank (eds.). *Joseph Haydn. Tradition und Rezeption. Bericht über die Jahrestagung der Gesellschaft für Musikforschung. Köln 1982. Kölner Beiträge zur Musikforschung* 144. Regensburg: G. Bosse, 1985: 215–62.

Taruskin, Richard. *Text and Act.* Oxford: Oxford University Press, 1995.

Temperley, Nicholas. *Haydn:* The Creation. Cambridge: Cambridge University Press, 1991.

Thibaut, Anton Friedrich Justus. *Über Reinheit der Tonkunst.* ed. Raimund Heuler. Paderborn: Ferdinand Schöningh, 1907.

Thomas, Günter (ed.), *JHW*, XXV 7, *Il mondo della luna*, 3 vols. Munich: Henle, 1979.

— "Observations on *Il mondo della luna.*" In Jens Peter Larsen, Howard Serwer, and James Webster (eds.). *Haydn Studies: Proceedings of the International Haydn Conference, Washington D.C., 1975.* New York: Norton, 1981: 144–47.

Tobler, Felix. "Wirtschaft und Gesellschaft in Eisenstadt um 1770/80." In Harald Prickler and Johann Seedock (eds.). *Eisenstadt: Bausteine zur Geschichte.* Eisenstadt: Nentwich-Lattner, 1998: 466–90.

Tolley, Thomas. *Painting the Cannon's Roar: Music, the Visual Arts and the Rise of an Attentive Public in the Age of Haydn, c.1750 to c.1810.* Aldershot: Ashgate, 2001.

— "Haydn, the engraver Thomas Park, and Maria Hester Park's 'little Sonat.' " *ML* 82 (2001), 421–31.

Tovey, Donald Francis. *Essays in Musical Analysis: Symphonies and Other Orchestral Works*, new ed. London: Oxford University Press, 1981.

— "Haydn: *The Creation*," *Essays in Musical Analysis*, vol. V, vocal music. Oxford: Oxford University Press, 1937: 114–18.

Triest, Johann Karl Friedrich. "Remarks on the development of the art of music in the eighteenth century," trans. Susan Gillespie. In Elaine Sisman (ed.). *Haydn and His World*. Princeton: Princeton University Press, 1997: 321–94.

Tyson, Alan. "Haydn and two stolen trios." *MR* 22 (1961), 21–27.

Unverricht, Hubert. *Geschichte des Streichtrios*. Tutzing: Schneider, 1969.

Varney, Andrew. *Eighteenth-Century Writers in Their World*. London: Macmillan, 1999.

(Die) Vier Jahreszeiten im 18. Jahrhundert: Colloquium der Arbeitsstelle 18. Jahrhundert, Schloß Langenburg 1983. Heidelberg: Winter, 1986.

Wagner, Richard. *Gesammelte Schriften und Dichtungen*. 3rd ed. Leipzig: E. W. Fritsch, 1898, vol. IX.

— "The Music of the Future" (1850), trans. unattrib. in Oliver Strunk (ed.). *Source Readings in Music History: The Romantic Era*. New York: Norton, 1965: 150–51.

Waldoff, Jessica. "Sentiment and sensibility in *La vera costanza*." in W. Dean Sutcliffe (ed.). *Haydn Studies*. Cambridge: Cambridge University Press, 1998: 70–119.

Walter, Horst. "Gottfried van Swietens handschriftliche Textbücher zu *Schöpfung* und *Jahreszeiten*." *HS* 1 (1965–67), 241–77.

— "Haydns Klaviere." *HS* 2 (1970), 256–88.

— "Das Posthornsignal bei Haydn und anderen Komponisten des 18. Jahrhunderts." *HS* 4 (1976), 21–34.

Walter, Horst. "Haydn gewidmete Streichquartette." In Georg Feder, Heinrich Hüschen and Ulrich Tank (eds.). *Joseph Haydn, Tradition und Rezeption*. Regensburg: G. Bosse, 1985: 17–53.

— "Über Haydns 'charakteristische' Sinfonien." In Gerhard J. Winkler (ed.). *Das symphonische Werk Joseph Haydns*. Eisenstadt: Burgenländisches Landesmuseum, 2002: 65–78.

Webster, James. "Towards a history of Viennese chamber music in the early Classical period." *JAMS* 27 (1974), 212–47.

— "Freedom of form in Haydn's early string quartets." In Jens Peter Larsen, Howard Serwer, and James Webster (eds.). *Haydn Studies: Proceedings of the International Haydn Conference, Washington, D.C., 1975*. New York: Norton, 1981: 522–30.

— "The falling-out between Haydn and Beethoven: the evidence of the sources." In L. Lockwood and P. Benjamin, *Beethoven Essays. Studies in Honor of Elliot Forbes*. Cambridge, MA: Harvard University Press, 1984: 3–45.

— "On the absence of keyboard continuo in Haydn's symphonies." *Early Music* 18 (1990), 599–608.

— *Haydn's "Farewell" Symphony and the Idea of Classical Style: Through-Composition and Cyclic Integration in his Instrumental Music*. Cambridge: Cambridge University Press, 1991.

— "The *Creation*, Haydn's late vocal music, and the musical sublime." In Elaine Sisman (ed.). *Haydn and His World*. Princeton: Princeton University Press, 1997: 57–102.

— "Haydn's sacred vocal music and the aesthetics of salvation." In W. Dean Sutcliffe (ed.). *Haydn Studies.* Cambridge: Cambridge University Press, 1998: 35–69.

— "Haydn's symphonies between *Sturm und Drang* and 'Classical style': art and entertainment." In W. Dean Sutcliffe (ed.). *Haydn Studies.* Cambridge: Cambridge University Press, 1998: 218–45.

— "Between Enlightenment and Romanticism in music history: 'First Viennese Modernism' and the delayed nineteenth century." *19th-Century Music* 25 (2001–2), 108–26.

— "The rhetoric of improvisation in Haydn's keyboard music." In Tom Beghin, Elisabeth Le Guin, Sander Goldberg (eds.). *Engaging Rhetoric: Essays on Haydn and Performance.* Chicago: University of Chicago Press, forthcoming.

— and Georg Feder. "Haydn, Joseph." In Stanley Sadie (ed.). *The New Grove Dictionary of Music and Musicians*, rev. ed., vol. XI. London: Macmillan, 2001: 171–204, 263–71; rpt. as *The New Grove Haydn.* London: Macmillan; New York: Palgrave, 2002.

Webster, James Carson. *The Labors of the Months in Antique and Mediaeval Art.* Princeton: Princeton University Press, 1938.

Weisberger, R. William. *Speculative Freemasonry and the Enlightenment: A Study of the Craft in London, Paris, Prague, and Vienna.* New York: East European Monographs, 1993.

Wheeler, Opal and Sybil Deucher. *Joseph Haydn: The Merry Little Peasant.* London, 1939.

Wheelock, Gretchen A. *Haydn's Ingenious Jesting with Art: Contexts of Musical Wit and Humor.* New York: Schirmer, 1992.

— "The classical repertory revisited: instruments, players, and styles." In James Parakilas (ed.). *Piano Roles.* New Haven: Yale University Press, 1999: 109–20.

— "The 'rhetorical pause' and metaphors of musical conversation in Haydn's quartets," in Georg Feder and Walter Reicher (eds.). *Internationales Musikwissenschaftliches Symposium "Haydn und das Streichquartett," Eisenstadt 2002.* Tutzing: Schneider, 2003: 67–85.

Widder, Roland. "Die Esterházyschen 'Siebengemeinden.' " In *Die Fursten Esterházy: Magnaten, Diplomaten & Mäzene.* Eisenstadt: Burgenländische Landesregierung, 1995: 156–71.

Will, Richard. "When God met the sinner, and other dramatic confrontations in eighteenth-century instrumental music." *ML* 78 (1997), 175–209.

— *The Characteristic Symphony in the Age of Haydn and Beethoven.* Cambridge: Cambridge University Press, 2002.

Williams, Peter. *The Chromatic Fourth During Four Centuries of Music.* Oxford: Oxford University Press, 1998.

Winkler, Gerhard J. "Joseph Haydn's 'experimental studio' in Eszterháza." *MQ* 80 (1996), 341–47.

— "Das Haydn-Haus: Ein historischer Abriß." In Harald Prickler and Johann Seedoch (eds.). *Eisenstadt: Bausteine zur Geschichte.* Eisenstadt: Nentwich-Lattner, 1998: 517–29.

Winkler, Klaus. "Alter und Neuer Musikstil im Streit zwischen den Berlinern und Wienern zur Zeit der Frühklassik." *Die Musikforschung* 33 (1980), 37–45.

Wiser, John. Review of Haydn, Symphonies no. 1–5, 6–8, 76–78, Roy Goodman conducting The Hanover Band, *Fanfare* (March/April 1992), 211.

Witte, Bern (ed.). *Christian Fürchtegott Gellert: Gesammelte Schriften* vol. IV. Berlin, New York: Walter de Gruyter, 1989.

Wolf, Eugene K. "The Recapitulations in Haydn's London Symphonies." *MQ* 52 (1966), 71–89.

Woodfield, Ian. "John Bland: London retailer of the music of Haydn and Mozart." *ML* 81 (2000): 210–44.

— *Opera and Drama in Eighteenth Century London: The King's Theatre, Garrick and the Business of Performance.* Cambridge: Cambridge University Press, 2001.

Yolton, John W. et al. *The Blackwell Companion to the Enlightenment.* Oxford: Blackwell, 1995.

Zaslaw, Neal. "Mozart, Haydn, and the *sinfonia da chiesa.*" *JM* 1 (1982), 95–125.

Zeman, Herbert. "Von der irdischen Glückseligkeit: Gottfried van Swietens *Jahreszeiten*-Libretto: eine Utopie vom natürlichen Leben des Menschen." In *Die Vier Jahreszeiten* in *18. Jahrhundert: Colloquium der Arbeitsstelle 18. Jahrhundert*, Schloss Langenburg 1983. Heidelberg: Winter, 1986: 108–20.

Index